WOMEN AND THE LAW

WOMEN AND THE LAW

Leaders, Cases, and Documents

Ashlyn K. Kuersten

A B C · C L I O

Santa Barbara, California   Denver, Colorado   Oxford, England

Library of Congress Cataloging-in-Publication Data

Women and the law : leaders, cases, and documents / by Ashlyn K. Kuersten.
    p. cm.
Includes bibliographical references and index.
ISBN 0-87436-878-2 (hardcover : alk. paper) ISBN 1-57607-700-4 (e-book)
   1. Women—Legal status, laws, etc.—United States—History. 2. Women lawyers—United States—History. I. Title.

  KF478.K84 2003
  342.7308'78—dc22

                        2003020339

07 06 05 04 03   10 9 8 7 6 5 4 3 2 1

ABC-CLIO, Inc.
130 Cremona Drive, P.O. Box 1911
Santa Barbara, California 93116-1911

This book is printed on acid-free paper ∞.

Manufactured in the United States of America

To Dr. Susan Matarese, my first college professor,
who taught me the true meaning of feminism,
intellectual curiosity, and how to be a strong woman

CONTENTS

Education   69

Family Law   83

Reproductive Rights   103

Violence against Women   141

Workplace Rights   157

Documents   201

PREFACE

When I prepared to teach a course on Gender and Law in the fall of 1998 for the first time, I was initially struck by how difficult it was to find information and material on many of the topics covered here. That is curious since discrimination law has become an increasingly important aspect of the American judicial system. But while discrimination law is certainly what I find most interesting about our political system, most Americans and many of my college students have a different perspective. For most college students, the term "gender discrimination" connotes a field of study about women, of women, and for women. This volume is intended to provide a solid resource for understanding gender discrimination generally and demonstrate, I hope, that this is a topic of great importance for anyone studying our system. After all, less than one-half of the cases covered here involve female litigants, and in none of the policy eras examined did women make up a majority of the politicians passing the legislation. So men are just as involved (if not more so) than are woman.

For any project of this size, there are more people than the humble author who worked to make it happen. In my case, there are several people whose assistance was positively instrumental and enormously appreciated. First, Dottie Barr, administrative assistant in the Political Science Department at Western Michigan University, used her meticulous technical skills to organize the copious amount of material I needed for this book. Her patience for dealing with my single-mindedness at times bordered on the divine. Several research assistants over the past three years were also very helpful in checking facts and finding material that was often difficult to locate: Miguel Centellas, Abby Dove, Tracy Hall, Michael Hamilton, Heather Richards, and Nenad Senic. Their interest in the subject matter and helpful suggestions made this book more readable to a wider audience. Finally, Alicia Merritt and Melanie Stafford at ABC-CLIO gave me wonderful suggestions that made my work on this project all the more enjoyable. That all being said, however, any mistakes are mine alone.

Ashlyn Kuersten
Western Michigan University

INTRODUCTION: GENDER EQUALITY IN THE UNITED STATES

When the American colonists declared their freedom from British rule, they did so partially because of their desire for a government run by the "people." They rebelled against domination by an aristocracy led by King George III. "We hold these truths to be self-evident," Thomas Jefferson penned in the Declaration of Independence, "that all men are created equal and are endowed by their Creator with certain inalienable rights, that among these are life, liberty and the pursuit of happiness." Political leaders of a government were given power only by the "consent of the governed," which the people could withdraw when they believed their interests were not adequately represented. King George was certainly not representing the interests of the colonists, and so the people withdrew their consent to be ruled by him. At the close of the Revolutionary War, the colonists devised their own government established on the principles of individual rights and popular sovereignty. Ultimate political authority came from the "people," and no government that diminished this sovereignty was legitimate. Yet popular sovereignty clearly did not include all citizens of the former colonies.

The Articles of Confederation, the first U.S. constitution, focused on government limitations and not the power of the people. That document proved inefficient, ineffective, and unwieldy; among its many problems, it provided for no uniformity of law among the states, no uniform currency, and no national defense. In an attempt to devise a more workable system of government, the Second Continental Congress met to revise the constitution and ended up creating an entirely new one. Their new constitution would not only set out the various governmental limitations that would prevent another monarchy from emerging but would also protect the freedoms of the people. Before the debates surrounding the development of this new constitutional government, Abigail Adams urged her husband, John, one of the framers of this second constitution, to "remember the Ladies, and be more generous and favorable to them than your ancestors [had been]." But no provision for gender equality found its way into the newly organized document that promised "consent of the governed." Jefferson, who later became the third president of the United States, argued vehemently against giving women the right to vote, much less legal equality with men. He said in 1816, "Were our State a pure democracy . . . there would yet be excluded from deliberations . . . women, who, to prevent depravation of morals and ambiguity of issues, should not mix promiscuously in the public meetings of men."

Even statutory law at the time (passed by state legislatures) failed to protect women's rights. In fact, the nation's largest disenfranchised group would not be able to vote until the Nineteenth Amendment was passed over 100 years later, in 1920—long after Congress gave freed slaves the right to vote in the Fifteenth Amendment. And even after the Nineteenth Amendment was passed, it would be the last mention of gender equality in the U.S. Constitution. To this day, this amendment is the only provision in the Constitution that specifically gives women "popular sovereignty."

The First Women's Movement and Reconstruction

Beginning with the Revolutionary War, women struggled to attain legal parity with men. It was an uphill battle. Judges and politicians who made the laws were men, and women urging change had to battle the honored notion of "separate spheres" for the sexes. Separate spheres was the concept that men and women had distinct spheres of influence, which left women squarely at home with children and family concerns and men in charge of all activity outside the home. This belief in women's political inferiority to men had a long tradition and even legal precedent to back it up. The colonists based their legal system on the English common law, or conventions that had been in place for centuries, including that of separate spheres. Blackstone's *Commentaries,* the standard in English law, describes the specific concept of "coverture," which drastically limited women's public role. Under coverture, a married woman lost all legal rights upon marriage to her husband and in effect came completely under her husband's control:

> By marriage the husband and wife are one person in law; that is, the very being or legal existence of the woman is suspended during marriage, or at least is incorporated into that of the husband; under whose wing, protection and cover, she performs every thing; . . . and her condition during her marriage is called her coverture.

Under this legal concept, the rights of a husband (and by extension his wife) were clear and without conflict. She could not own property, make contracts, have rights to her children, or keep any profits from employment to herself because she had no legal identity beyond her husband (or her male relative if she was unmarried). She was simply a legal extension of her husband and subsumed under his identity. He could disperse of any property she brought to the marriage without legal repercussions, as well as forcibly demand her sexual favors, since rape was a crime of property against her husband. Husbands had certain obligations to their wives, of course. They were expected to be benevolent to members of their family, though if they instead chose to be benevolent dictators within their home the law protected this right. Vestiges of this concept of coverture can be seen today in the American tradition of a wife taking her husband's last name; under coverture, the lack of her own name reflected her lack of legal identity beyond that of her husband.

But although discrimination against women was permissible as a result of statutory provisions, case precedent, and the Constitution itself, a collective effort began in 1848 to attempt to equalize women's rights. Elizabeth Cady Stanton and Lucretia Mott had been strong supporters of the abolitionist movement in the United States. In fact, they had met at the International Anti-Slavery Society meeting in London in 1840 and were both outraged that they were denied seating on the floor of the convention because of their gender. In later discussions Stanton and Mott drew parallels between the status of women in the United States and that of the slaves the abolitionist movement was trying to free. These women galvanized others into a campaign for women's rights, and in 1848 they held their first conference on the issue in Seneca Falls, New York. The convention included 300 men and women who articulated demands to relieve women from their status as second-class citizens. It would be heralded as the beginning of the first women's movement.

The Seneca Falls convention adopted

what it called a "Declaration of Sentiments," patterned after the Declaration of Independence, that urged dramatic changes in the legal and political system. Although today these first feminist activists are remembered for their efforts to secure women's suffrage, at the time their goals were much more modest yet absolutely fundamental for equal rights. The declaration sought "immediate admission to all the rights and privileges which belong to [women] as citizens of the United States." If women were to pay taxes to a government, then the government should acknowledge them as legitimate citizens, and they should receive all the rights that go along with citizenship. "Taxation without representation" had been the root cause of the Revolutionary War and the rallying cry of the colonists. In essence, the colonists sought to remove class distinctions from governmental representation and were successful. So, the conventioneers asked, why were the colonists now requiring women to pay taxes without allowing them representation? This would mean, of course, equalizing all laws to allow women legal parity with men. Listed in the declaration were calls for the rights of women to attend college, enter into careers of their choosing, and participate in political discourse (since women at the time were banned from speaking in public).

Participants at the convention were unanimous in their approval of the demands articulated in the declaration with one exception: the right to vote. Many feared that by asking for the "radical" right of suffrage, a right the activists honestly did not believe the political establishment would grant, the group would be perceived as too far-reaching, too controversial, and thus would be summarily dismissed. Shouldn't they first ask for more modest and less controversial rights, such as the right to attain an education? In the end the attendees, encouraged by the abolitionist Frederick Douglass, ultimately did demand the right to vote, but with little hope of achieving their goal in the near future.

Although few of their demands were ever enacted into law, this convention began a series of seemingly small changes to women's rights that ultimately galvanized an entire movement and forever changed contemporary mores. By the mid- to late 1800s, restrictions imposed by coverture laws slowly began to ease. One major problem with coverture laws was that inheritances could not be passed down to female children; a husband had the law on his side if he unwisely invested or disbursed his wife's family inheritance. Beginning in the 1840s and until the turn of the century, some states passed Married Women's Property Acts that allowed women to control their own property. But coverture continued to limit women's legal identity, restricting them from entering into contracts and handling their own business interests accordingly.

Other women's conventions were held following the Seneca Falls convention, but not until after the Civil War, in the debates over Reconstruction, did women leaders see a real chance to change the Constitution. When it seemed as if the newly freed slaves would receive various constitutional protections, women's groups pushed to have gender included in the Civil War amendments. Surely if freed slaves were to be promised equality via constitutional protections, women could enjoy the same privileges. But the abolitionists were reluctant to add calls for women's rights to the already tenuous political attention the freed slaves were receiving, and some women feared that by joining women's interests with the interests of the freed slaves, the issues would become too controversial and neither group would ultimately attain any legal protection. This division split women leaders, making them lose the unified voice they had created in Seneca Falls. As a result, they also lost much of their political power for decades.

Ultimately, women's inclusion in the Civil War amendments was rejected. In fact, the amendments explicitly excluded women from constitutional protection for the first time by introducing the word *male* into the Constitution. But after losing this battle, women leaders turned to the courts, hoping the judiciary would provide them with legal protections; in essence, by asking the courts to interpret the Civil War amendments, they hoped to achieve the same rights as the freed slaves without a constitutional amendment or congressional approval.

As a first step in expanding the general interpretation of the amendments, they focused their attention on the Fourteenth Amendment. Although the Fifteenth Amendment specifically allowed the freed slaves suffrage rights, the Fourteenth Amendment was broader. It gave "equal protection of the law" and equal "citizenship to all" Americans. The first vehicle in which to force the courts to broadly interpret this amendment came from an unlikely source. Myra Bradwell had completed all the requirements to become a lawyer in Illinois, but that state, like all others, denied women access to the profession. Like most lawyers-in-training, Bradwell held an apprenticeship with a practicing lawyer (in Bradwell's case, her husband). Although coverture laws prevented her from entering into contracts with her clients, her husband "gave his consent" for her contractual obligations by entering into contracts with clients for her. She believed she should be allowed to become a practicing attorney in her own right, but the state court disagreed: because she was a married woman and could not enter into legal contracts herself, she could not act as an attorney for a client, therefore the state could deny her license to practice law.

But Bradwell was convinced that the Fourteenth Amendment was on her side. In her brief to the U.S. Supreme Court, Bradwell argued that it was "neither a crime nor a disqualification [for the legal profession] to be a married woman." The citizenship protections given in the Fourteenth Amendment, she continued, gave her the same rights and privileges that men or freed slaves received. And she wanted to practice

law as a privilege of her U.S. citizenship. Further, she argued, married women often acted as legal agents for their husbands as long as they had their husbands' implied consent, as she did. Bradwell was ultimately disappointed. In 1873 the justices held: "[W]e are certainly warranted in saying that when the legislature gave to this court the power of granting licenses to practice law, it was not with the slightest expectation that this privilege would be extended to women."

But it was the concurring opinion by Justice Joseph Bradley that was probably most damaging to women hoping to gain the freedom to practice their chosen profession and enjoy the protections of the Fourteenth Amendment. In what is arguably the most quoted Court opinion pertaining to gender equality, Bradley observed a wide difference in the "destinies of man and woman." He urged that the "natural and proper timidity and delicacy which belongs to the female sex evidently unfits it for many of the occupations of civil life. [T]he paramount destiny and mission of woman are to fulfil the noble and benign offices of wife and mother . . . and is the law of the Creator."

Following this resounding defeat, women's rights activists refocused their energies. Unwilling to give up on the Civil War amendments as potential protections for women, they shifted their attention to the Fifteenth Amendment's guarantee of suffrage for freed slaves. The National Woman Suffrage Association (NWSA) had long advocated the right of women to vote. In 1872 Susan B. Anthony had persuaded the registrar in New York to permit her to vote, which culminated in her arrest as well as the arrest of several of her supporters and election supervisors. At her trial she argued that she had been "robbed of the fundamental privilege of citizenship" and denied the right of a trial by jury of her peers because the jury, judge, and her counsel were all male. She could not hire a female attorney because women were denied admittance to the bar; she was prosecuted by male judges who were chosen by male politicians because women were denied the right to vote; and she was judged by an all-male jury because women were denied the right to serve on juries. Although she received widespread newspaper coverage, public sentiment was not generally positive or sympathetic to her plight. The jury found her guilty of the crime of voting and fined her.

But women suffragists continued their quest for the vote through the courts. This time, ironically, the litigant was a man, since under coverture women could not sue in their own names. Francis Minor sued on behalf of his wife, Virginia, for being denied the right to register to vote in the state of Missouri in 1875. He argued that the right to vote was a core right of national citizenship protected by the Constitution under the Fifteenth Amendment. Certainly, Minor argued, states performed certain regulatory functions that helped determine who was qualified to vote. But the federal right of citizenship, based on the Constitution, limited states from denying suffrage solely on the basis of gender.

Like Anthony and Bradwell before him, Minor was unsuccessful. The Supreme Court ruled (in *Minor v. Happersett*) that although it was true that women had equal rights of all citizens, this did not force states to give women the right to vote. National citizenship was protected by the Constitution, but suffrage was a privilege of *state* citizenship and thus not protected. Therefore, states were free to limit (or even enlarge) citizenship rights and, by association, voting rights. It was not the role of the federal government to tell a state who did or did not have such rights to vote in their elections: "The power of the State in this particular case is certainly supreme until Congress acts." Furthermore, whereas some states allowed women to vote in certain elections (the most common of which were elections for school boards), no state in the union gave all its citizens the vote. Property quali-

fications and literacy tests were regularly used to limit the grave responsibilities of the franchise. So in this respect, the Court insisted, "men have never had an advantage over women."

What this meant was that women had fewer rights than the newly freed slaves. It would be another quarter of a century before women were given the same constitutional protection to vote, and decades until they could enjoy the privileges of equal protection of law under the Fourteenth Amendment. Many scholars compare this ruling denying women equal citizenship privileges to *Dred Scott v. Sandford* (1856), which had restricted slaves from national citizenship in the United States. That case had so enraged northern abolitionists and so damaged the Supreme Court's reputation as a nonpolitical institution of government that it served as a spark to help ignite the Civil War. Ultimately, it took a constitutional amendment (the Fourteenth) to overturn that decision.

Separate Spheres and the Right to Vote

Probably the greatest setback to the new women's rights movement was the refusal of the courts to grant women Fourteenth Amendment equal protection. Yet even some women's groups feared that expanding Fourteenth Amendment protections to women would be a detriment to the American family. "Separate spheres" assigned men and women's roles in the family; men were to support their families financially, and women were to assume responsibility for housekeeping and children. So societal interests were best served through a system of domestic and political subordination; women ran the house, and men ran the political and legal systems.

Outside of the United States, the plight of women was no better, and women around the world were demanding change. In June 1911, for example, 40,000 to 60,000 supporters of women's suffrage marched on London, presenting a remarkably unified front to the political establishment there. But part of the problem in the United States was that the women suffragists did not as a whole promote the idea of suffrage for everyone. American suffragists typically supported enfranchisement for those women who were highly literate and had upstanding "moral character." That meant that, at the least, African American women would not be afforded the same voting privileges. And even the women advocating change were not unified in their demands for equal rights. Those who called for equal rights between men and women were diametrically opposed to those who believed the sexes should be justifiably distinct in their missions and society should continue to practice the separate spheres philosophy. This friction among women's groups in the United States would further splinter the women's movement and water down its message.

Yet the traditional notion that women's peculiar and specific responsibilities were limited to the home would slowly change. Various educational institutions opened their doors to women in the first decades of the twentieth century, and many women took advantage of these opportunities. Still, this drive to educate women was less a movement for equality between the sexes than a continuation of the separate spheres. The education of women, many argued, made better mothers for educating the young and perpetuating civility and morals in the next generation. So although some undergraduate institutions allowed women entry, most professional schools stayed single sex and either explicitly forbade women from enrolling, allowed them to enroll but not gain a degree, or simply established women-only schools elsewhere. And women were still restricted in practicing professions.

Many of these issues were of concern only to educated and upper-class women who could afford a college education. Economic necessity forced increasing numbers of uneducated woman in 1900 to work outside the home to support their growing families. The conditions in which they worked were horrendous. In 1911 scores of young female workers died in the Triangle Shirtwaist Company fire in New York, prompting consumer groups to push for new laws to "protect" working women. These groups succeeded in passing maximum-hours restrictions for women, restrictions on women working night shifts, and minimum-wage laws. The reason for these laws was simple: because harsh working conditions harmed women's health and reproductive capabilities, the human race as a whole was in jeopardy. The women who disagreed with the separate spheres ideology criticized these laws as anything but "protective" of women, arguing that they succeeded only in diminishing women's ability to provide for their families.

The Supreme Court had upheld maximum-hour laws for women in 1908, and based on this decision as well as tragedies like the Triangle Shirtwaist Company fire, many states responded with restrictive labor laws for women workers. In 1878 the National Woman Suffrage Association introduced a constitutional amendment, named after Susan B. Anthony, that would allow women the right to vote. It was twelve years before Congress would even consider the amendment, which it immediately defeated.

States were also free to establish qualifications for voting, though, and women did have some success in obtaining suffrage rights at the state level. Wyoming granted women the vote in 1890; Colorado, Idaho, and Utah followed. Antisuffrage critics argued that women were incapable of making political decisions without their husbands. Unable to choose between candidates or among issues, these critics said, women would vote according to their husbands' preferences, so women's suffrage was simply giving married men two votes and leaving single men with one. Other critics feared that voting women would become more like men and this would lead to a breakdown in the American family.

Yet when women's groups succeeded in promoting the prohibition movement in the early years of the century, the leaders of the women's movement retained hope that their calls for suffrage would eventually be heard. If women banding together could get a prohibition amendment passed, maybe a suffrage amendment was also possible. The more radical wing of the women's movement, the National Woman's Party led by Alice Paul, demonstrated vehemently for a constitutional amendment granting them enfranchisement. After leaders of the movement picketed the White House, they were jailed. These radical leaders staged various successful publicity ploys, including a hunger strike, to protest their incarceration. After they generated enormous public sympathy for their plight, President Woodrow Wilson was finally forced to support the proposed suffrage amendment in 1918.

By the summer of 1920, Congress had approved the Nineteenth Amendment; the states ratified it by August. The new Nineteenth Amendment read: "The right of citizens of the United States to vote shall not be denied or abridged by the United States nor by any State on account of sex." Not only did the amendment void state laws that limited women's suffrage, but it was the first constitutional protection specific to women. It had been over a hundred years since the colonists had demanded popular sovereignty from their British king; finally, women were included in the privileges granted by national citizenship.

From Separate Spheres to Differential Treatment

The Nineteenth Amendment conferred more rights upon women than simply the right to vote, but what those rights were was unclear, and the courts did not immediately offer an interpretation. Something called "differential treatment" made legal distinctions between the sexes. Supporters of such legislation argued that this different treatment helped women; opponents held that it hurt them. Women were represented in greater numbers in the workplace than ever before in U.S. history, making up one-third of the paid labor force. But they were relegated to positions at far lower wages than their male counterparts and still could not work night shifts or certain professions (such as bartending) because of the potential injury to their "tender sensibilities." Approximately 60 percent of working women were either employed as maids in private homes or did work for hire within their own homes (e.g., doing laundry or sewing).

To further complicate the issue, once the Nineteenth Amendment was passed, the women's groups that had organized for its passage largely disbanded. The groups that had pushed for fewer restrictions on women's role outside the family were now less visible politically. As such, at the beginning of the new century the Supreme Court handed down a number of decisions that upheld "protective" legislation—or differential treatment—intended to protect women. In *Muller v. Oregon* (1908), the Court held that dangers to women's reproductive capacity was a worthy enough goal to allow states to limit women's working hours. In emphasizing the differences between the sexes, the Court held:

> That woman's physical structure and the performance of maternal functions place her at a disadvantage in the struggle for subsistence is obvious. This is especially true when the burdens of motherhood are upon her. Even when they are not, by abundant testimony of the medical fraternity, continuance for a long time on her feet at work, repeating this from day to day, tends to injurious effects upon the body, and as healthy mothers are essential to vigorous offspring, the physical well-being of woman

becomes an object of public interest and care in order to preserve the strength and vigor of the race.

The courts ignored the economic harm that such protective legislation did to women. Women were restricted from working the hours they chose or felt it necessary to work, could not earn the same money as men, were often fired from occupations that demanded longer hours, and were prohibited from working in certain occupations (specifically, jobs that involved the selling of alcohol) that paid well. The Supreme Court upheld such laws, with a few exceptions, and allowed states more leeway in shielding women from the harms of the work environment. In actuality, these protective laws ultimately hurt women workers in two distinct ways. First and most clearly, their ability to support their families was diminished as the number of hours they were allowed to work decreased. The most impoverished women were forced to take on second jobs to supplement their income, thus making the laws that limited their hours relatively moot. The laws also hurt working women by making them less useful employees than their male counterparts. If an employer was limited by the hours per week a woman could work, as well as minimum wages they could pay women, then men became more attractive employees. So women were in fact economically limited, not protected, by such laws.

World War II changed not only societal mores regarding women employees but also the protective legislation in force in most states. With the onset of the war, women entered the workforce in impressive numbers. And with male employees leaving for war, employers were all too happy to hire women to take their place, albeit at lower salaries. But once the war ended, women were encouraged to go back to their traditional family lives; birthrates soared, and women stayed at home to care for their growing families. The 1960s changed that.

The Civil Rights Movement and the Second Women's Movement

The 1960s witnessed enormous social change, and women once again organized themselves as a political force. The end of the 1950s saw various groups, predominately minority groups, demanding equal rights and individual autonomy in increasing numbers. Charismatic leaders like the Reverend Martin Luther King Jr. mobilized hundreds of thousands of Americans and urged a reevaluation of existing laws that limited African Americans from equal participation in the political and educational systems. The leaders of the civil rights movement were successful not only in changing statutory law, winning African Americans equal rights, but also in using the courts to effect this change in *Brown v. Board of Education of Topeka, Kansas* (1954). After Rosa Parks refused to give up her bus seat to a white passenger in 1955, a citywide bus boycott in Ohio lasted 381 days until the Supreme Court ruled that segregation on buses was illegal. Such use of the court system was a lesson that women activists paid close attention to and learned from. The National Association for the Advancement of Colored People (NAACP) embarked on a litigation strategy designed to seek more expansive judicial interpretation of existing constitutional rights for minorities. This was a more financially feasible alternative to expensive lobbying efforts at the congressional level to create new constitutional rights. Women's groups wished to emulate their strategy to bring about broader rights for women. But women as a group needed to unify their voice and they finally did as the decade of the 1960s began.

Improvements in contraception were introduced with the world's first birth control pill in 1960. Margaret Sanger had been instrumental in gathering funding for a synthetic combination of hormones that suppressed the release of eggs from a woman's ovaries. But in 1963 *The Feminine Mystique* by Betty Friedan was published to enormous and nearly universal popular acclaim and largely ushered in the second "wave" of the women's movement. Friedan, a journalist and a suburban, married mother of three, called the central thesis of her book "the problem that has no name":

> The problem lay buried, unspoken, for many years in the minds of American women. It was a strange stirring, a sense of dissatisfaction, a yearning that women suffered in the middle of the twentieth century in the United States. Each suburban wife struggled with it alone. As she made the beds, shopped for groceries, matched slipcover material, ate peanut butter sandwiches with her children, chauffeured Cub Scouts and Brownies, lay beside her husband at night—she was afraid to ask even of herself the silent question—"Is this all?"

Her book struck a responsive chord among white, well-educated, middle-class housewives. She had surveyed women college graduates and noted a general dissatisfaction with their lives as wives and mothers. These women seemingly "had it all"—husbands, children, nice homes, and solid incomes—yet they were not happy and yearned for "something more." Following the widespread success of her book, Friedan and others organized the National Organization for Women (NOW) to lobby for the inclusion of women in the Civil Rights Act of 1964, passage of the Equal Pay Act of 1963, repeal of criminal abortion laws, and passage of the Equal Rights Amendment. Their goal was to bring women into "full participation in the mainstream of American society now, exercising all the privileges and responsibilities thereof in truly equal partnership with men." As membership in NOW exploded, the new women's movement became a powerful political force. Because these women were active and voted, political leaders realized the folly of ignoring their pleas.

Even before Friedan's book was published, feminists fought for the formation of the President's Commission on the Status of Women in 1961, during the Kennedy administration. Although the commission brought about very little real change in women's appointments to higher positions—women made up only 2.4 percent of all appointed officials in the new administration—women's voices were heard. The Equal Pay Act of 1963 required all employers to pay the same salaries to women and men for substantially equal work, a major victory at a time when women were being paid about 63 cents to a man's dollar. The next legal success for women came in 1964 with passage of Title VII of the Civil Rights Act, which abolished protective laws that limited women from equal treatment in the workforce. Title VII was fundamentally important in allowing women equal rights in employment since it specifically prohibited employment discrimination (on account of race, creed, national origin, or sex) and provided women with a tool for challenging any employment inequalities. After its passage, protective laws that had banned night work for women and limited the number of hours women could be employed were voided.

Title VII would become the most powerful of all federal laws prohibiting gender discrimination in the workplace. But it had its opponents. Originally the act banned discrimination based on "race, color, creed, or national origin." Although women lobbied for the addition of "sex" to the list, many feared that doing so would make the bill too controversial to pass Congress and thus jeopardize the protections it would afford African Americans. An opponent, Representative Howard Smith of Virginia, agreed to introduce the sex provision into the act, thinking it would prevent the bill's passage. He was wrong.

Part of Title VII's power was a provision that created a federal agency, the Equal Employment Opportunity Commission, responsible for investigating and resolving employment discrimination claims as well as bringing suit against employers who continued to discriminate against employees. This act had an enormous impact on women's employment discrimination claims. It provides that employers cannot fail to hire, refuse to hire, discharge, or otherwise discriminate against any individual with respect to compensation, terms, conditions, or privileges of employment because of sex. The language of the act covers employment from prehiring advertising to postemployment references, including interviewing, placement, promotions, wages, benefits, working conditions, working atmosphere, seniority, transfers or reassignments, and layoffs. In essence, it defines three types of gender discrimination: disparate treatment, overt discrimination, and disparate impact. Disparate treatment occurs when an employer discriminates against an employee because of the employee's sex or race. Overt (or facial) discrimination prohibits employers from instituting a policy with any explicit sex-based classification. Discrimination under the theory of disparate impact occurs when a superficially gender-neutral rule or practice of the employer has a disproportionate effect on one sex.

Ushered in by Betty Friedan's book, the second women's movement was vastly different from the first women's movement. Whereas the first movement dealt with discrimination against women, the second was more focused on "gender" equality, and many of the strides it made involved litigation by men. Most of the cases that made their way to the courts dealt with men questioning laws that discriminated against them rather than women arguing they had been discriminated against. As in the first women's movement, however, the vast majority of judges and politicians who eventually passed laws ensuring equal rights were, of course, male. Some argue that it was a strategic move on the part of many of the

women activists to choose issues that affected men to enforce change. Nonetheless, the second women's movement can correctly be considered a movement for gender equality instead of women's rights.

One of the main goals of the second wave was, initially, to change the legal interpretation of the Equal Protection Clause of the Fourteenth Amendment. The Supreme Court had used two standards of scrutiny to evaluate potential violations of the Equal Protection Clause. If a law discriminated on the basis of race or national origin, the Court was clear that it would hold the law to the highest level of scrutiny. That is, the law was unconstitutional unless the government could show that it was necessary to achieve a "compelling" state interest. Rarely did laws that classified on the basis of race or national origin hold up under this heightened scrutiny. But if a law discriminated on the basis of any other classification (including gender), the law was presumed constitutional if it was necessary to achieve a "reasonable" state interest. That meant that laws categorizing on the basis of gender were rarely held unconstitutional. Using this standard, the Court upheld laws excluding women from juries, various positions of employment, equal schools, equal financial support for college, and equal employment benefits.

The Court typically held that a state was justified in providing differential treatment of women. Women's groups hoped change was soon to come. NOW was committed to an expansion of the Fourteenth Amendment and passage of the Equal Rights Amendment (ERA). Sex-based differential treatment of women was unconstitutional, they argued, and an ERA to the Constitution was necessary to expand (and thus equalize) the rights of women. Although many women's groups organized during this time, it was largely NOW and the American Civil Liberties Union (ACLU) that led the path through the courts. These two groups pushed to elevate gender classification to a higher level of scrutiny than the "rational basis" test that essentially upheld all gender-based classifications. One of the ACLU attorneys, Ruth Bader Ginsburg, was chosen to head up the newly formed Women's Rights Project (WRP). Over the next decade, the ACLU-WRP brought to the Court the most important gender discrimination cases in U.S. history. Ginsburg's successes in this area were so impressive that by 1993 she was nominated as a justice to the U.S. Supreme Court.

One of the more curious aspects of Ginsburg's work with the ACLU was that she did not represent women litigants exclusively; in fact, most of the plaintiff's she represented were men claiming they had been discriminated against by laws that classified on the basis of gender. Her first successful case, and arguably the most important case for gender rights, was the 1971 case *Reed v. Reed.* An Idaho statute stated that males were preferred to females as administrators of estates for those who die intestate (without a will). Ginsburg urged the Court to expand the scrutiny standard the Court had previously used in upholding gender classifications in employment; only by increasing the level of scrutiny would women enjoy full citizenship.

Reed v. Reed was a fundamentally important gender equity case because it ultimately changed constitutional interpretations for all future gender discrimination cases. In a unanimous decision, the Court held that laws that differentiated on the basis of gender must have some fair relationship to the objective of the legislation. Although the Court did not rule that sex was a suspect classification that would warrant the same level of strict scrutiny as did race-based classifications, it did prohibit unreasonable classifications based on sex. Making men the executors of estates to achieve the state objective of reducing the workload of judges was unwarranted and arbitrary, and thus in this case unconstitutional. Two years later the Court fell only one justice short of elevating gender to a suspect classification in *Frontiero v. Richardson* (1973).

Building on these successes of the early 1970s, women's groups in the next decade took to the Supreme Court several cases that changed gender discrimination laws even more. The Court held unconstitutional a federal law that required female soldiers to prove they supported their male spouses before receiving an increase in pay, and a Social Security law that granted widows but not widowers survivor benefits. Most of these cases questioned the stereotypical assumptions that husbands (and men) were the wage earners and wives the dependent caregivers. Yet the Court continually refused to make sex a suspect classification. Although it consistently ruled that "outdated misconceptions concerning the role of females in the home rather than in the marketplace" would not stand up in court, the Court urged the political process to change the law with passage of the ERA.

A New Standard of Review?

In 1976 the Court finally held that a new standard of review for gender discrimination cases was warranted. *Craig v. Boren* involved an Oklahoma law that set the drinking age at twenty-one for males and eighteen for females. A male who was under the age of twenty-one contested the law, arguing that it was simply gender discrimination. The state, for its part, argued that differences in the drinking age were necessary to prevent traffic accidents; more males than females tended to be arrested while driving under the influence of alcohol, and they were more likely to be injured or die in alcohol-related traffic accidents.

The Court, however, was not persuaded by the state's argument and held that the law constituted a denial of equal protection for males and was thus unconstitutional. But more important, although the Court did not give gender the same strict scrutiny standard for race-based claims that women's groups had hoped for, the Court did create a new "intermediate" level of scrutiny for gender discrimination claims that was a step directly below strict scrutiny. In order for a law that differentiated between men and women to prevail, now the state had to prove that the use of sex as a classifying tool was substantially related to the advancement of an "important government objective." What was different in *Craig* from the standard established in *Reed* was that the state's objective had to be more than simply "legitimate"; instead, a statutory objective had to be "important," compared to the "compelling" standard used in race-based claims.

The Court applied this intermediate standard to most claims involving gender. Three years later the Court reiterated its stance in *Orr v. Orr*, a case involving an Alabama statute that placed the obligation of alimony upon husbands but not upon wives. A husband sued, arguing the burden on husbands was imposed even if the wife had made more money during the marriage. The Court agreed:

> Legislative classifications which distribute benefits and burdens on the basis of gender carry the inherent risk of reinforcing stereotypes about the "proper place" of women and their need for special protection. Thus, even statutes purportedly designed to compensate for and ameliorate the effects of past discrimination must be carefully tailored. Where, as here, the State's compensatory and ameliorative purposes are as well served by a gender-neutral classification as one that gender-classifies and therefore carries with it the baggage of sexual stereotypes, the State cannot be permitted to classify on the basis of sex.

The holding in this case seemed to signal a radical departure from the Court's stance of earlier days regarding gender discrimination; surely protective legislation would no longer be tolerated, women's groups hoped. The Court would indeed apply the intermediate standard to most classifications involving gender. For example, it would find unconstitutional state laws that made public nursing schools single-sex, laws that considered males adults at age twenty-one but females at age eighteen, and state-supported, all-male military academies. But in contrast, the Court upheld governmental practices that required draft registration provisions for males only and statutory rape laws that applied only to female victims.

In essence, the Court used the higher, intermediate standard on traditional stereotypes regarding the "different spheres" of men and women but upheld sexual stereotypes that were less outmoded. For example, the issue of whether women should be included in draft registration requirements was held to a much lower standard—called "rational basis"—and required only that the law served a legitimate governmental interest. The level of review or scrutiny used by the Court is absolutely crucial for understanding discrimination claims. If a law excludes African Americans from draft registration or from a school because of their race, it would be clearly unconstitutional because their exclusion does not justify a "compelling" governmental objective. But because gender is not held to the same level of review, the exclusion of women from draft registration or statutory rape claims is permissible because the policy serves an "important" governmental objective.

In some ways the rulings of the 1970s were a huge success for women: at least the Court finally recognized sex discrimination inherent in protective laws. But in other ways the cases of the 1970s were a disappointment; women failed to gain the higher level of scrutiny enjoyed by race-based discrimination claimants. By 1981, when the first woman was appointed to the Supreme Court, women's groups had renewed hope that the Court would upgrade the scrutiny level in gender discrimination claims. During the presidential election campaign of

1980, Ronald Reagan promised to "diversify" the Supreme Court bench to pacify women's groups, and he carried through on his promise by nominating Sandra Day O'Connor to the Supreme Court. She had graduated top in her class at Stanford Law School (behind future chief justice William Rehnquist) in 1952 yet could only get work as a legal secretary. She became a full-time mother of three sons before sitting as majority leader in the Arizona state senate. After her confirmation to the Court, in her first opinion in *Mississippi University for Women v. Hogan* (1982), which overturned a state nursing school's policy of accepting only women, O'Connor wrote that when the purpose of a law is to exclude members of one gender "because they are presumed to . . . be innately inferior, the objective [of the law] is illegitimate." With O'Connor's appointment to the Court, four justices favored the heightened standard of review for gender discrimination cases.

But passage of a constitutional amendment protecting gender equity was still out of reach. Many women's rights activists argued that an equal rights amendment was the only way women could enjoy the same rights as men. It would automatically raise the legal level of scrutiny. The first ERA had been introduced in Congress in 1923 but never passed the House. In 1971 the House finally passed an ERA that read: "equality of rights under the law shall not be denied or abridged by the United States nor by any State on account of sex," but it had yet to be ratified by the states. Opposition to the amendment was fierce. Opponents argued that the ERA would force women to register for the draft and participate in combat, deny women their husbands' financial support and any child support they were owed, and eradicate single-sex education, sororities, heterosexual marriage, and joint filing of income tax, as well as any maternity protections women enjoyed in the workplace. These opponents were successful; by the deadline of June 1982, the states had failed

to ratify the amendment. Although many states countered with their own statewide ERAs, there is currently no federal constitutional amendment protecting the rights of citizens on the basis of sex.

There have, however, been modest gains for women on other fronts. The Equal Pay Act of 1963 guaranteed equal pay for equal work. Women who were employed by companies who violated the act could file a complaint anonymously and not fear employer retaliation. By 1973 more than $200 million in back pay had been awarded to female workers. When enforcement of the act was transferred from the Department of Labor to the EEOC, however, compliance efforts lagged. Awards dropped to less than $2 million per year during the Reagan administration and the first Bush administration. But a change in interpretation of the act occurred in 1981 when a group of female prison guards argued that they were receiving lower wages even though their jobs were comparable to those of male guards. The Court ruled that female workers could sue for discrimination even if they were not performing the same jobs as men. The issue thus became one of "comparable" rather than "equal" work.

Other successes by the women's movement included the Pregnancy Discrimination Act, passed in 1978, which required employers to treat pregnancy like any other physical condition. Under this law, part of Title VII of the Civil Rights Act of 1964, employers must provide the same disability benefits for pregnancy and childbirth as they do for any other physical disability. In 1993 Congress added to maternity benefits with the Family and Medical Leave Act (FMLA), requiring that employers with fifty or more employees provide twelve weeks of unpaid leave (within a twelve-month period) to both men and women for care for a newborn child, spouses, or parents with serious health conditions. This act is inadequate for most families, however, because it does not require that such family-care leave be paid; many lower-income families are simply unable to take advantage of it.

Women in Education

In 1972 Congress enacted Title IX of the education amendments, which specifies that "no person in the United States shall, on the basis of sex, be excluded from participation in, be denied the benefits of, or be subjected to discrimination under any education program or activity receiving federal financial assistance." Title IX was passed in part because of the importance of education for society. But Title IX would have an enormous impact on education opportunities for women and result in their entrance into many professions previously closed to them.

Although feminist authors like Mary Wollstonecraft had argued since the 1800s that educating women would allow them to better understand men, most viewed the education of women as a danger to societal peace. Still, access to education for women expanded throughout the United States beginning in the 1830s largely because it was believed that an educated mother would be able to educate her sons properly. Although the first college for women was opened in 1821 by Emma Willard, Oberlin College in Ohio admitted both men and women in 1833, and private colleges for women only such as Mount Holyoke, Vassar, and Wellesley began opening in 1837. But for most of this period, women were prevented from studying the same subject matter as their male counterparts; part of the reason was the belief that too much education would hurt women's reproductive capacity. According to Dr. Edward Clarke, a Harvard University physician who published *Sex in Education* in 1873, "Women's reproductive physiology makes it unsafe for women to undertake any intellectual activity with the same rigor as men. Excessive study diverts energy from female reproductive organs to the brain, causing a breakdown in women's health and threatening the health of future generations." The popularity of Clarke's book was profound. One bookseller in Ann Arbor, Michigan, sold over 200 copies in a single day, and immediately following its publication the presidents of Smith College and Bryn Mawr felt compelled to defend their schools to the media.

By the early 1900s women continued to get an education, even in mathematics and science, when it was realized that women would need to help their sons with their math homework. But they could not receive professional degrees; by the 1920s and 1930s, women made up less than 1 percent of law and medical school graduates. By the 1960s, women were enrolled in colleges in great numbers; but their programs of study continued to be drastically different than men's; most majored in home economics. But Title IX dramatically changed the educational environment for women. All programs within a college or university were prohibited from practicing sex discrimination in admissions, athletics, financial aid, and employment. As a result, schools were required to drop admission quotas that limited the number of women enrolled in professional degree programs like engineering, medicine, and law, and were now required to evaluate men and women candidates under the same set of admission standards. Only programs affiliated with a college that were purely social rather than academic (such as fraternities and sororities) could remain single sex.

Title IX has garnered the most attention as it relates to college athletics because it so dramatically changed college athletic departments. In 1972 fewer than 30,000 women played intercollegiate sports; some thirty years later, 160,000 did. The same number of athletic scholarships must be available for male and female students, and the same amount of money must be spent on athletic teams for both men and women. Further, the percentage of female athletes must be substantially proportionate to the percentage of women in an institution's student body. Title IX critics charge that universities are forced to dismantle their male athletic programs to comply with the law. In 2002, the Bush administration created a Commission on Opportunity in Athletics to consider changes to the law, particularly its strict proportionality standard; however, after much public pressure, the commission decided to leave Title IX as it stands.

But Title IX is most important because it opened up so many scholarship opportunities for women. Schools that had previously offered scholarships to men were now required by law to offer them to women as well. Under the law, a school can comply with Title IX requirements in three ways: make the percentage of female athletes the same as the percentage of female students, show an ongoing history of increasing opportunities for women, or show that it is accommodating the interests and abilities of women. As such, Title IX also changed admission standards for women. Beginning in 1979, women surpassed the number of men enrolled in college for the first time. Further, women now tended to perform better in college than men. This has a considerable impact on women a decade after graduating from college. A college graduate earns at least $23,000 a year more than a high school graduate; the rise in women college graduates means women are able to make more money on their own than they were before Title IX was passed. At the professional graduate level, women currently make up 50 percent of the law school graduates, nearly the same in medicine, and almost 30 percent in engineering (although they are taught by faculty that is nearly exclusively male). But the greatest impact of Title IX has been the increase in women leaders; as a result of the relatively high numbers of women graduating from professional degree programs, the pool of women leaders has grown dramatically. Women are now entering into politics in greater numbers than ever before and, unfair though it may be, having a graduate degree gives a

woman credibility with the voters that she might otherwise not have.

Another change to educational institutions in the United States during the twentieth century was the practice of affirmative action. Of course, preferential programs for military veterans had been used for over 100 years, and many such programs provided for lifetime absolute preferences for civil service positions. But since women had been largely excluded from military services, and certainly from the draft, women were unable to reap the benefits of veteran preference. That changed when President Lyndon Johnson signed an executive order in 1965 requiring companies that did business with the federal government to take "affirmative action to ensure that applicants are employed, and that employees are treated during employment without regard to their race, color, religion or national origin." Although sex was not originally included, Johnson added it in 1967.

Affirmative action is a proactive remedy for past discrimination. Yet the Court has ruled that a company cannot be required to hire an unqualified candidate, nor can it (or even a university) use quotas to expand its diversity. The effect of affirmative action policies on women's economic stability has been immense, particularly for women of color; African American women have gained not only opportunities but at least some approximations to salary equity. And all women have gained in the greater admission rates of women to professional degree programs. The increasing numbers of women professionals can be positively linked to a greater appreciation of gender diversity in the workplace.

Yet women college graduates still face daunting obstacles in the professional world. In 1996 only four women headed up Fortune 1000 companies, and women held only 1 percent of the top five jobs in the 1,000 largest corporations in the country. Men tend to be promoted more quickly than women, even when both sexes have the same education level. The income gap between male and female lawyers is growing, and the rate of women's promotion to top positions has declined dramatically. Ironically, one of the reasons given for low pay and low promotion rates for women hearkens back to the separate spheres doctrine of a century ago. Some critics of equal pay measures argue that the disparities in income between the sexes is a result of choice; that is, women choose to congregate in specialties that are congruent with gender expectations and that by virtue of market forces (and not discrimination) are low paying.

Women and Reproductive Rights

Although challenges to gender equity still exist in the workplace, women have been more successful with regard to obtaining reproductive freedom. The second wave of the women's movement was also successful in pushing for laws that increased the rights of women concerning their reproductive capacities. In 1965 in *Griswold v. Connecticut,* the Supreme Court ruled that married couples had the right to obtain information pertaining to birth control. Many states had prohibited the dispensing of such information, and the federal Comstock Act in 1873 had made it a crime to send contraceptives or information about contraceptives through the U.S. mail. In Connecticut it was a crime even to disperse information about contraceptive devices; a Planned Parenthood clinic had been charged with violating that law. Previously, the Court had given parents the right to teach their children a foreign language (1923), to send them to private schools (1925), and the right to procreate (1942). But this case was different; here the Court held that married couples enjoyed a certain zone or right to privacy. "Would we allow," Justice William Douglas asked rhetorically in his majority opinion, "the police to search the sacred precincts of marital bedrooms for telltale signs of the use of contraceptives? The very idea is repulsive

to the notions of privacy surrounding the marriage relationship." In 1972 the Court extended this same right to single people.

Finally, with *Roe v. Wade* in 1973, the Court ruled that abortion was a fundamental right based on the right to privacy established in *Griswold*. Like many states, Texas simply banned abortion except to save the pregnant woman's life. Women who could afford it could travel to states that allowed abortions. But for impoverished women this was not an option. Norma McCorvey was pregnant in Texas in 1970 and unable to obtain an abortion. A group of University of Texas graduate students, including new lawyer Sarah Weddington, took up McCorvey's case (using the name Jane Roe) and forced the Supreme Court to deal with the state law banning abortions. In a 7–2 decision, the Court held that the right to privacy was "broad enough to encompass a woman's decision whether or not to terminate her pregnancy." Further, there was no justification for limiting a woman's right to an abortion before viability of the fetus; that is, in the first trimester of a woman's pregnancy, the state had no interest in restricting her right to abortion. But as the pregnancy progressed, the state's interest in protecting the life of a woman's unborn fetus increased. In the second trimester the state could regulate the abortion in ways that were reasonably related to maternal health, and in the final trimester the state could justify regulation or outright banning of abortion.

Women's groups were elated. And the decision refocused their energies. Several right-to-life groups mobilized during the 1990s to change the less restrictive abortion laws passed in the 1970s and 1980s. The Court held that laws that required minors to notify their parents before getting an abortion must have a judicial bypass provision and that women could not be required to notify their spouses before having an abortion. But the Court also ruled that requiring a twenty-four-hour waiting period between the time a woman receives information on the procedure and the performance of an abortion is constitutional, as are restrictions on Medicaid-funded abortions for indigent women. Most recently, the debate has turned to a relatively rare procedure that goes by the technical term "intact dilation and extraction," more commonly known as "late-term abortion" or—among its opponents—"partial-birth abortion." The Court ruled that physicians could not be restricted from performing the procedure if it was to save the life of the mother; in fact, *Roe* had demanded in 1973 that state laws must have provisions that allow abortion if the woman's life is at risk. Pro-life groups have been involved in several cases regarding the rights of protestors outside abortion clinics. Members of Operation Rescue, a radical protest group, have been convicted of bombing clinics and killing doctors who perform abortions.

In 2003, Congress passed and President Bush signed into law a "partial-birth abortion ban" that many feminist groups worry will have the effect of denying the most common abortion procedures.

Gender Equality in the 1990s

The 1990s saw monumental changes in the law regarding gender equality. First, the Court continued to define Title VII's prohibitions on gender discrimination; certain gender-based classifications were allowed, the Court ruled, as long as they were bona fide occupational qualifications (BFOQs) necessary for the job. Employers could not insist upon a fetal protection policy that required women in certain hazardous positions to be sterilized; they could not refuse to hire women as prison guards, or restrict women from lifting certain weights or working long hours; nor could they hire only women for certain jobs (such as flight attendant). Employers could, however, hire only females as wet nurses and hire only females to play female roles in plays.

The 1990s also saw a second woman ascend to the U.S. Supreme Court. Ruth Bader Ginsburg, nominated by President Bill Clinton in 1993, became one of the most liberal justices to sit on the Court. Although many feared that her confirmation would be denied because of her liberal stance on gender discrimination issues during her tenure as the ACLU-WRP lead counsel, she was able to neutralize her critics. During her confirmation hearings, she was questioned extensively about her views on the subject of abortion, arguably one of the most divisive issues regarding women today. Ginsburg was able to demonstrate that although she agreed with the final holding in *Roe v. Wade*, she disagreed with the method the Court used to get there. In doing so, she showed her more moderate side to a largely conservative Senate committee. She has been on the Court for several cases involving abortion rights and consistently votes with the liberal bloc.

At the end of the twentieth century, the Court began acknowledging sexual harassment in the workplace. Surprisingly, the change in law originated largely with women's disgust over a Supreme Court nominee. In 1991 President Bush nominated Clarence Thomas to replace Thurgood Marshall, the first African American member of the Court. During the Senate confirmation hearings, allegations that Thomas had sexually harassed a former employee, Anita Hill, arose. Scenes on national television of an all-male, all-white Senate questioning Hill infuriated women; although her allegations went unreported to her superiors at the time, her story sounded familiar to women workers who had been harassed in the workplace. This fury galvanized a generation of women, much as Friedan's book had decades before. Following the Thomas-Hill confirmation battle, women's outrage over the prevalence of sexual harassment in the workplace turned into political activism; in the national election of 1992 they voted in large numbers, and they voted for Democrats and other women. As a result, more women were elected to Congress, statehouses, governor's seats, and judicial benches than ever before, calling 1992 the Year of the Woman. There was great hope that women, a group that had been relatively heterogeneous in their voting behavior in decades past, had become a powerful political force; politicians would have to deal with the gender gap and bring about an actual constitutional protection of gender equality. Congress responded by passing an expansion to Title VII that included compensatory and punitive damages to victims of sexual harassment, allowing them to recover not only their expenses involved in waging a court battle, any lost wages or back pay, but also up to $300,000 in punitive damages. Possibly as a result of the law, the number of sexual harassment lawsuits doubled between 1991 and 1998.

Yet hopes for a women's voting bloc were dashed when women failed to turn out to vote at the same levels in the following election. Experts theorized that 1992 had been an anomaly brought on largely by the Thomas-Hill confirmation hearings, which polarized the sexes on the issue of sexual harassment. The confirmation hearings did bring public attention to the issue. In the aftermath of the hearings, surveys found that most of the public believed sexual harassment was a serious problem. By 1998 several cases dealing with this relatively new issue in American law had finally worked their way through the court system. A federal study indicated that a staggering 42 percent of the government's female workers had experience an incident of sexual harassment on the job in the previous two years. The Court had previously acknowledged the existence of sexual harassment in 1986 in *Meritor Savings Bank v. Vinson,* where the justices held that sexual harassment was unlawful even if the victim experienced no economic harm. Essentially, the case specified that there were two types of sexual harassment. Quid pro quo harassment occurs when an employer or supervisor expects or demands sexual favors from an employee

and threatens the employee's job if she or he fails to submit to the demands. The second type is harassment that makes a victim's work environment hostile, even if no economic penalties are threatened or if the victim fails to acquiesce to the employer's demands. In 1998 the Court entered the fray of sexual harassment once again, resolving some of the unanswered questions pertaining to sexual harassment in the workplace.

Ironically, Justice Thomas—whose confirmation hearings galvanized women to push for changes in sexual harassment laws and mores—sat on several cases dealing with sexual harassment. In the first case, the Court ruled that employers must have anti–sexual harassment policies in place or they could be held liable for a supervisor's harassing conduct. The same year the Court ruled that same-sex harassment was actionable; it was possible for a man to be guilty of discriminating and harassing another man or a woman another woman. It was the conduct of harassment, and not the sex of those involved, that determined whether sexual harassment had occurred. Victims of harassment need only show that they were targeted because of their sex. The Court recognized, for instance, "general hostility" to the presence of people of the victim's gender or "direct comparative evidence" that the harasser treated members of both sexes differently. In a different case in 1998, the Court ruled that school districts could be held accountable for the sexual harassment of students if an individual "with authority to take corrective action" had been notified of the misconduct and had not taken steps to correct it.

The workplace was officially changed after the Court handed down its sexual harassment decisions. Leaders of the second women's movement could look back on the previous three decades with pride at how drastically the legal landscape had improved for women. Other leaders could learn from the lessons of this movement. First, in order to mobilize women at the level they sustained in the 1970s, several factors must be present. Sporadic events may energize women for a short period of time (as did the Thomas confirmation hearings), but no dramatic changes in the law will occur until men and women alike are galvanized to action. Several scholars point out that membership in interest groups is the first step; only when large numbers are mobilized for women's causes can these groups gain the financial resources to bring more women into political and judicial office and thus change the law. The largest and most successful of these groups is currently EMILY's List (the acronym standing for "Early Money Is Like Yeast" in that it "makes the dough rise"). Founded in 1985 to support pro-choice Democratic women in congressional races, it has been successful in encouraging members to back the candidates it endorses. It has become the largest financial resource for women candidates running on the Democratic Party ticket; other groups have acted similarly for Republican candidates. And having more women in political office may be the key to women's legal success in the future; issues like pay equality, child care, and health care are concerns that cross racial and economic lines for women, and women politicians support these issues more so than men. It is imperative that women continue to push for expanded legal and political rights, for there are still many limitations to gender equity in U.S. law.

Women in the United States have undergone a striking transformation since Abigail Adams's call to her husband to "remember the ladies." Today the average woman has just two children and enjoys various legal protections during both her pregnancy and her maternity leave. She has equal rights with her husband upon divorce—an issue that affects more than one-half of all current marriages—in matters involving child custody and property distribution. She is guaranteed suffrage rights and the same rights to educational facilities and financial scholarships as men. She theoretically has access to a range of birth control devices and even abortion.

Yet the courts still do not hold gender discrimination to the same level of scrutiny as race discrimination. Domestic violence and rape will impact one in seven American women, and there are few state resources to deal with this growing problem. With no policies for child care in this country, working women will continue the struggle to find affordable, quality day care for their children. Insurance companies rarely cover birth control or fertility problems yet do cover the most common medical conditions that concern men. Although the vast majority of women now work outside the home and are free to choose any profession, they earn less than 27 percent of what their male counterparts make in the same jobs, and the glass ceiling still limits women's promotions. As for political equality, women can vote, but it is unlikely that they will ever be represented by a woman president, and there is still no constitutional provision protecting against gender discrimination. And unless women organize once again to push the political establishment for changes in U.S. law, there will probably never be an equal rights amendment to the U.S. Constitution.

WOMEN AND THE LAW

Addams, Jane (1860–1935)

Born in Cedarville, Illinois, and a graduate of Rockford College (1882), Jane Addams founded Hull House in Chicago, which provided food, clothing, education, and permanent dwellings for newly arrived Europeans. She also helped found the National Association for the Advancement of Colored People (NAACP), was active in the American Civil Liberties Union (ACLU), and helped pass the Nineteenth Amendment in 1920 giving women the right to vote. Under her leadership (and that of Carrie Chapman Catt) the first feminist movement flourished.

This first women's movement sought to extend the franchise to women not because women were essentially the same as men but because they were essentially different: women were sensitive, nurturing, and spiritual, and such qualities were needed in governmental matters as much as they were needed in the home. Giving women the right to vote, then, would allow for a more democratic, nurturing element in our political system and minimize the more confrontational element men brought to the political table. Addams and her colleagues hoped that this perspective would make women's suffrage less controversial and persuade the public that the suffrage movement was a positive move for the country as a whole.

During most of her life, Addams was criticized by the press and the public for being an anarchist, a fascist, and a Communist.

Nevertheless, in 1931 she won the Nobel Peace Prize for a lifetime of work encouraging equal rights for women, African Americans, and those least advantaged in society.

> *See also* Anthony, Susan B.; Catt, Carrie Chapman; The Early Women's Movement; Feminism; Nineteenth Amendment.
> *Reference* Jean Bethke Elshtain. 2001. *Jane Addams and the Dream of American Democracy*. New York: Basic Books.

Anthony, Susan B. (1820–1906)

Born in Adams, Massachusetts, Susan B. Anthony became a staunch abolitionist during her teens. In 1837, when she would have been of an age to attend college, there was only one regular college for women (Oberlin) and one women's "seminary" (Mount Holyoke) in the United States. When her father's finances failed and she was unable to complete any type of education, she first taught school then began a campaign to get colleges around the country to admit female students. For the rest of her life, she was an adamant supporter of coeducational institutions.

Anthony was an activist for various causes; she supported the abolition of slavery, pacifism, and of course women's rights. She was incensed that she was obligated to pay taxes yet was not given a political voice. Together with Elizabeth Cady Stanton, she formed the National Woman's Loyal League and lobbied for passage of a constitutional amendment banning slavery. They were hugely successful, gaining nearly half

Susan B. Anthony, standing, and Elizabeth Cady Stanton (Library of Congress)

a million signatures on a petition in favor of the Thirteenth Amendment, which banned indentured servitude. The issue split the women's movement in half. Some activists wanted the fight to begin with women's suffrage, whereas activists like Anthony thought pushing first to give former slaves the right to vote was a strategic move, for once black men were enfranchised, women would not be far behind. As it happened, Anthony and her supporters were wrong; after former slaves won the vote, it was another fifty-five years for women to follow suit.

Anthony is the best-known protestor (and arrestee) for women's suffrage, but her case never made it to the Supreme Court. Six years after Anthony's conviction in New York State, the Supreme Court heard *Minor v. Happersett* (1875), in which the Court held that the Constitution did not give women this fundamental right. Anthony died in 1906, before the Nineteenth Amendment was passed.

Although she never married, Anthony was one of the first people in the United States to call for the legal rights of married women. Blackstone's *Commentaries*, one of the main sources of English common law used in the United States at the time, specified that "the husband and wife are one, and that one is the husband." This not only extinguished married women's existing legal rights but, more important, completely did away with any potential rights: they could not own property, earn money, make contracts, or act as guardians of their children. Anthony attempted to right injustices not only for women but also for other disadvantaged citizens, particularly freed slaves. In 1856 she organized a campaign against slavery that culminated in the passage of the Thirteenth Amendment, which outlawed slavery. When she tried to introduce women's suffrage into the Civil War amendments, the abolitionists balked. She was accused of anarchy for upsetting the "relations" between men and women and in 1872 was arrested for voting.

Despite her absence at the creation of the women's rights movement—the historic Seneca Falls convention of 1848—she forged a lasting friendship with Elizabeth Cady Stanton and Lucretia Mott, and with them later formed the National Woman Suffrage Association (NWSA). In 1878 she convinced a senator to sponsor an amendment for women's suffrage. Although it was defeated every year, Anthony did manage to get it on the Senate floor. The Nineteenth Amendment finally passed in 1920, when Anthony would have been 100 years old.

See also Addams, Jane; Catt, Carrie Chapman; Coverture; Feminism; Mott, Lucretia; National Woman Suffrage Association (NWSA); Nineteenth Amendment; Seneca Falls Convention; Stanton, Elizabeth Cady.

Reference Geoffrey C. Ward and Ken Burns. 2001. *Not for Ourselves Alone: The Story of Elizabeth Cady Stanton and Susan B. Anthony.* New York: Knopf.

Catt, Carrie Chapman (1859–1947)

Born in Ripon, Wisconsin, Carrie Chapman Catt graduated from Iowa State University in 1880 and later worked as a law clerk, teacher, principal, newspaper reporter, and superintendent of schools for a large district in Iowa. She was widowed after only a few years of marriage and went on to become probably the best-known leader of the first feminist movement. Her approach was rather radical for the times. She organized parades and protests to inform women of the importance of voting and lobbied male officeholders and members of political parties to point out the need for women's enfranchisement. She personally lobbied President Woodrow Wilson, eventually gaining his support and association with the cause of women's voting rights. Throughout her life she promoted the idea that securing the right to vote for women was the key to their political empowerment.

In 1887 she joined the Iowa Woman Suffrage Association and became a well-known lecturer for that organization. But it was not until her work with the National American Woman Suffrage Association (NAWSA) that she became a leading national suffragist. She eventually became president of NAWSA, working jointly with Susan B. Anthony. Unlike Anthony, who did not live long enough to enjoy the privileges of the Nineteenth Amendment, Catt continued as a suffragist leader long after the amendment was passed. Following its passage, she turned her energies to women's suffrage worldwide with the creation of the International Woman Suffrage Alliance (IWSA), which had branches in thirty-two nations.

Back in the United States, once women were given the right to vote, Catt began to lobby for progressive public policy changes. She founded the League of Women Voters to help inform women on issues of public policy, including world peace and child labor, the relief efforts for Jewish refugees during World War II, and the organization of the United Nations following the war.

Catt was the first woman to give a commencement address (at Iowa State University in 1921), was the first woman to be featured on the cover of *Time* (1926), which named her one of the ten greatest American women.

> *See also* Addams, Jane; Anthony, Susan B.; Feminism; League of Women Voters; National American Woman Suffrage Association (NAWSA); Nineteenth Amendment; Stanton, Elizabeth Cady.
> *Reference* Jacqueline Van Voris. 1993. *Carrie Chapman Catt: A Public Life*. New York: The Feminist Press.

Common Law

Common law, made by judges, is often contrasted with civil law, which is designed and specified by legislation. Based originally on Blackstone's *Legal Commentaries*, the cornerstone of the English legal system, and brought to this country by the colonists, it is still largely used by American courts. (Civil law systems that descend from Roman law are used in most countries of continental Europe.)

Although the United States has some civil law, it uses common law regularly where no legislative law exists. Often called "unwritten law," common law is grounded in custom, reason, natural law, and previous judicial decisions. In this system, the rulings of prior judges and courts control the rulings of judges in later cases. If the facts of a case are identical to a previous case, the new case must follow the precedent; it is the very definition of stare decisis. Law is changed when, in a new case, the facts are different than in a previous case and a judge is free to make a new ruling. Often, however, judges can change the law simply by deciding that social convention demands a fresh precedent, giving common-law judges much more power than they have in Roman-based civil law systems.

Judges have changed common law frequently in race and gender discrimination cases because of the changed views of society. For example, the Supreme Court held in

Plessy v. Ferguson (1896) that racial segregation in public facilities was not unreasonable and did not violate the Fourteenth Amendment's guarantee of equal protection of the laws. That amendment, in essence, did not require that "equal but separate accommodations for the white and colored races" were unconstitutional. Later, in *Brown v. Board of Education of Topeka, Kansas* (1954), the Court held that separate educational facilities for black and white children did indeed violate the Equal Protection Clause ideal that separate could not be "equal."

Because classification by sex was an accepted aspect of common law, laws that have discriminated against women had to be changed largely through congressional and state legislation. That is, statutory law was necessary to override the common law that had been used since colonial times. Thus the Nineteenth Amendment, passed in 1920 to give women the right to vote, directly overrode common law that had held that states did not have to allow women to vote.

> *See also* Coverture; Fourteenth Amendment; Marriage; Nineteenth Amendment.
> *Reference* Lawrence Meir Friedman. 2002. *Law in America: A Short History.* New York: Modern Library Chronicles.

Coverture (Chattel)

Throughout American history, women have faced legal inferiority, traceable to the English common law adopted by the colonists. William Blackstone produced an overview of the common law of England that the colonists relied upon for over a century (far longer than it was used in England). Women, particularly married women, were restricted from opportunities to conduct their own business and in fact did not even have their own legal identities. Blackstone's *Commentaries* viewed husband and wife legally as one person:

> By marriage the husband and wife are one person in law; that is, the very being or legal existence of the woman is suspended during marriage, or at least is incorporated into that of her husband; under whose wing, protection and cover she performs everything and is therefore called by French law femme-covert . . . under the protection and influence of her husband, her baron or lord.

Coverture provided that a woman (whether married or not) had no legal capacity; she was subsumed under the legal identity of her husband or male relative and was thus civilly dead. This meant that once a woman married, control of her property, inheritance, custody of her children, and her earnings passed to her husband. Coverture ensured that a woman had no right to contract, to sue (or be sued) in her own name, or to own property. She lost claim to her name, assets, and even her children because her husband (or another man, including her brother or father) was the sole legal guardian of his offspring (and could choose to transfer custody to someone other than his wife if he so wished). But an additional consequence was that women's participation in political affairs was also restricted; how could a woman vote, for example, if she and her husband were legally one person?

Women lobbied state legislatures for reforms beginning in the 1850s. The Married Women's Property Acts, which were passed in the mid-1800s, gave women the right to control property acquired by "inheritance, gift, bequest or devise," thus decreasing somewhat the power of coverture. Although women were still denied control over their wages and earnings, not to mention custody of their children and the right to divorce drunken or abusive husbands, they continued to accumulate some rights. By the late 1800s, other legislative acts gave women joint custody of their children, husbands were no longer able to dispose of all assets that a woman received from her family, and women were allowed to divorce their husbands (though only for cause, such as infidelity).

In 1776, when the colonists were drafting the Declaration of Independence, which would establish their right to secede from the British monarchy, Abigail Adams penned a letter to her husband, John, one of the framers of the document. In that letter she pleaded with him to include women in the declaration. She warned that women could begin a rebellion of their own, much like the colonists were doing because they had no voice in their own government. Some of the highlights of that letter:

I long to hear that you have declared an independency. And, by the way, in the new code of laws which I suppose it will be necessary for you to make, I desire you would remember the ladies and be more generous and favorable to them than your ancestors. Do not put such unlimited power into the hands of the husbands.

Men of sense in all ages abhor those customs which treat us only as the [servants] of your sex; regard us then as being placed by Providence under your protection, and in imitation of the Supreme Being make use of that power only for our happiness.

Although they did declare that government is legitimate only when there is "consent of the governed," John Adams and his fellow colonists did not heed Abigail Adams's advice.

See also Child Custody; Divorce; The Early Women's Movement; Feminism; Marital Rape; Married Women's Property Acts.
References Peregrine Bingham. 1980. *Law of Infancy and Coverture.* New York: Fred B. Rothman; William Blackstone and Stanley N. Katz. 1979. *Commentaries on the Laws of England: A Facsimile of the First Edition of 1765–1769.* Chicago: University of Chicago Press.

The Early Women's Movement
Although calls for women's equality appeared in newspapers following the American Revolution and feminists like Mary Wollstonecraft and educators like Catharine Beecher called for the increased independence and education of women beginning in the late 1700s, most demands hoped to save abused wives from drunken spouses or end prostitution, matters pertaining to individuals rather than social and political movements. It was not until the early nineteenth century that women's groups organized for the larger cause of sexual equality.

The first women's movement in the United States emerged from the antislavery movement. The American Anti-Slavery Society welcomed women into its ranks and introduced them to politics. Women such as Lucretia Mott, Angelina and Sarah Grimké, Elizabeth Cady Stanton, and Lucy Stone were active proponents of abolition and women's suffrage and learned the political tactics necessary to push for change among the male politicians of the time. Mott and Stanton organized the first women's rights meeting, held in 1848 at Seneca Falls, New York. The "Declaration of Sentiments" that came out of the convention articulated the concerns of the movement; modeled on the Declaration of Independence, it presented demands for equal rights of women in marriage, education, religion, employment, and politics. Later led by Susan B. Anthony, this movement urged women's suffrage and pushed for the overturn of coverture via the Married Women's Property Acts that equalized property distribution upon dissolution of marriage.

The basis for giving women the vote rested on a key principle established by the American colonists during the Revolutionary War: no taxation without representation. John Stuart Mill linked the concepts of taxation and representation in *On the Subjection of Women* (1869), in which he argued that—if a man "is compelled to pay [taxes,] . . . if he is required implicitly to obey, he should be legally entitled to . . . have his consent asked." Women's groups found it inherently unfair that women in St. Louis, for example, owned property worth approximately $14.5 million in 1867 and were required to pay taxes on it, yet could not have their political interests represented. As one newspaper reported at the time, this was precisely the colonists' argument for war. "Why tax without representation should be tyranny with respect to England but not tyranny in Massachusetts was a mighty shrewd question" (Kerber, Kessler-Harris, and Sklar 1995, 94).

But the concept of coverture made political representation nearly impossible. A woman had no obligation to any entity but her husband. She was given a prominent duty in her role as a wife; as such, she was exempted from political life. This first women's movement argued that women deserved full citizenship. After the Emancipation Proclamation of 1863, which abolished slavery, women activists unsuccessfully pushed for women's inclusion in the Civil War amendments guaranteeing the rights of freed slaves. Following the passage of these amendments, which specifically excluded women from their protection, the women's movement broke into two disparate groups. The National Woman Suffrage Association, led by Stanton and Anthony, accepted only women and opposed the exclusionary wording of the Fifteenth Amendment. In a series of court cases, they tried unsuccessfully to include women in the protections of not only the Fifteenth Amendment but also the Fourteenth Amendment (guaranteeing equal protection of the law). The American Woman Suffrage Association, led by Lucy Stone, supported black suffrage as a step in the right direction, even though women were left out. These two groups continued in separate directions for over two decades and by the end of the century had succeeded in creating a powerful political constituency. Yet women's suffrage proved elusive; by 1890 only two states had given women the

right to vote. By 1900, when Carrie Chapman Catt took over the leadership of the National American Woman Suffrage Association (later to be called the League of Women Voters), that organization had become the more politically benign of the women's groups. Alice Paul's more militant National Woman's Party waged hunger strikes and picketed the White House.

In August 1920, the states ratified the Nineteenth Amendment and women were finally given the right to vote. But once they gained the right to vote, these groups were faced with a problem: the movement for women's suffrage nearly obliterated other issues related to women's full acceptance into political life. Economic independence, for example, as well as liberation from social convention had been nearly removed from the women's rights agenda. As a result, there was little coherence to the movement, and women failed to become a substantial political constituency. By the 1930s the first feminist movement had nearly vanished from the political spectrum.

But following World War II, developments returned feminists from their long absence from political life. First, the number of female college students rose dramatically, providing a nucleus for women's organizations to evolve. Second, there was an increase in women entering the workforce as part of the war effort. And third, birth control became more easily accessible than it had been in decades past. By the 1960s the publication of a single book roused the sleeping women's movement.

The Feminine Mystique (1963) by Betty Friedan called for a change in society's belief in "domestic bliss" for women and quickly ushered in the second feminist movement. This new movement was organized by educated, middle-class, white women, who under Friedan's leadership eventually called themselves the National Organization for Women (NOW). A politically moderate group, it patterned itself largely after the NAACP, which had successfully used the courts instead of more expensive (and often unsuccessful) legislative lobbying efforts to bring about changes in discriminatory policies in education and employment. President John F. Kennedy in 1961 established the President's Commission on the Status of Women, which documented the status of women in the economy, the legal system, and the family. NOW then successfully pushed for Title VII of the Civil Rights Act of 1964, which banned employment discrimination on the basis of race, sex, religion, and national origin and created the Equal Employment Opportunity Commission (EEOC) to enforce that act.

In the 1970s NOW and other women's rights groups focused on abortion rights and the Equal Rights Amendment (ERA). The Court's ruling in *Roe v. Wade* in 1973, legalizing abortion rights, and the ERA ratification effort tripled NOW's membership. But with the expiration of the ratification deadline in 1982, membership dropped considerably. A new women's liberation movement opposed NOW's moderate policies of reform through legislation and lobbying; instead, its adherents sought a radical restructuring of society. Writers and activists like Shulamith Firestone, followed by others like Simone de Beauvoir, argued that gender discrimination was a product of social construct and not biological necessity. They moved for building a woman's counterculture based on female values and lacking in male values and became known for their controversial stance on lesbian and gay rights, a position NOW eventually took up.

This second wave of the women's movement as a whole has been successful in changing women's political and legal rights since the 1960s. It has provided important seed money for potential political candidates, helping to elect more women to political office. It has been instrumental in the passage of legislation that ensures some maternity leave (albeit unpaid) and promises equal pay (although the disparity in pay still exists). Education opportunities for women have exploded under this second women's movement, so that in some professions like law and medicine women now make up more than half of all incoming students. The movement has also brought about changes in rape laws to favor female victims, abortions rights, and easily accessible birth control.

See also Anthony, Susan B.; Catt, Carrie Chapman; Common Law; Coverture; Feminism; Married Women's Property Acts; Mott, Lucretia; National American Woman Suffrage Association (NAWSA); National Woman Suffrage Association (NWSA); Nineteenth Amendment; Seneca Falls Convention; Separate Spheres Doctrine; Stanton, Elizabeth Cady; Stone, Lucy.

References Sara Margaret Evans. 1991. *Born for Liberty: A History of Women in America.* New York: Free Press; Eleanor Flexner. 1976. *Century of Struggle: The Woman's Rights Movement in the United States.* Cambridge, MA: Harvard University Press; Linda Kerber, Alice Kessler-Harris, and Kathryn Sklar, 1995. *U.S. History as Women's History.* Raleigh-Durham: University of North Carolina Press.

Feminism

Feminism has taken many forms but has generally always been controversial. Essentially, feminism is the idea that women should have equal rights to men but are oppressed by either society or individuals. Yet it is incorrect to see feminism as one unified theory beyond this generalized description. There are several strands of feminist thought that have predominated at various times in U.S. history. The "ideal" of feminism can be distinguished by the following characteristics.

Liberal feminism, the oldest form, is rooted in the same standards the colonists used to criticize repression by the English monarchy during the Revolutionary War. The "Declaration of Sentiments," issued at the first women's convention in Seneca Falls, New York, in 1848, stressed the principle of individual autonomy over the government.

Liberal feminism can be seen most easily in the earliest feminist movement, which stressed women's right to education, to vote, to practice their chosen professions, and to have political representation if they are obligated to pay taxes to the state. More recently, the second feminist movement stressed the need for the Equal Rights Amendment to ensure equal political and legal participation for women. Although they were largely unsuccessful in obtaining legislative victories to give women the same legal rights as men, liberal feminists have used the court system in opposing any law that distinguishes on the basis of sex. They argue that such laws are based on outdated stereotypes and typically only diminish women's equality. In general, liberal feminists focus on the macrolevel forces in society that limit women's equality; they are criticized by conservatives for concentrating on the public sphere of women's work and virtually ignoring the more private sphere that women traditionally have been involved in. That is, liberal feminists do not address domestic violence and other issues that face women who work within the home and are the primary caretakers of their children, even though these issues have a greater impact on women's day-to-day lives.

Gender feminists focus on the differences inherent in the sexes. They believe that women are different from men and that this difference is positive and could change society for the better. Furthermore, say gender feminists, these differences between the sexes can indicate superiority of one gender over another. Women's moral development, for example, is inherently superior to men's. Carol Gilligan's call for acknowledging women's special and/or superior perceptions of justice has largely defined gender feminism. If women had been involved in the framing of the Constitution, their perspective would have altered the male perception of freedom that appears not only in the document itself but also in later interpretations. Liberty and due process represent guarantees of protection from the government, issues important in a masculine theory of justice. Women would have emphasized not individual liberties but feminist theories of justice, such as responsibility of the government to ensure political participation in the form of enfranchisement or employment. Others have argued that women's exclusion from the legal system has created our modern jurisprudence of objectivity, rights, and autonomy instead of a jurisprudence based on responsibility and communitarianism, issues of more importance for women. Critics of this theory contend that focusing on women's special nature simply reinforces society's belief that women are not as strong as men and lack the autonomy necessary for full inclusion in societal power. Other critics argue that this notion of women as the sex best suited for responsibility means that men should not be held to the same obligations of nurturing the family; essentially, if women have to learn how to work in a man's world (e.g., the contemporary workplace and political marketplace), then men should learn how to operate in a woman's world (e.g., the raising of children).

Radical feminism dismisses the idea that women can work within the current system and essentially force the male power structure to give women equal rights. Like liberal feminists, radical feminists are largely concerned with macrolevels of power (e.g., the legal and political system), but they support a revolution by women that will not merely reform the system but dramatically transform it. Women should not copy male practices such as hierarchical power dynamics because they will not gain equality by becoming more like men. Rather, female characteristics should prevail; women's equality will happen when society is completely overhauled and interdependence of the genders is recognized. Often this theory is criticized because it promotes a type of separatism between the sexes. Traditional biological motherhood is an integral part of society, critics urge, and eradicating that fact will not make society better.

Marxist-socialist feminism proposes that capitalism promotes a patriarchal system that in turn discriminates against women. Because women are economically dependent on men, their political and legal rights are diminished since they have less bargaining power. Women either do not work outside the home, work in the lowest-paying jobs, or are universally paid less for the same work as men. They will not gain equal power to men until these circumstances are remedied. Marxist-socialist feminists call for a redistribution of wealth in society and comparable worth remedies in the courts. Critics zero in on the voluntary aspect of a free market economy, saying that women choose lower-paid occupations or stay out of the workforce out of economic necessity in order to care for their children. Women are not oppressed by a capitalist system, critics of Marxist-socialist feminism contend, if they voluntarily enter occupations (including full-time motherhood) that diminish their earning potential.

> *See also* Addams, Jane; Anthony, Susan B.; Catt, Carrie Chapman; Civil Rights Act; Contraception; Coverture; Equal Employment Opportunity Commission (EEOC); Equal Rights Amendment (ERA); Friedan, Betty; Married Women's Property Acts; National Organization for Women (NOW); National Woman Suffrage Association (NWSA); Nineteenth Amendment; Right to Privacy; Sanger, Margaret; Seneca Falls Convention; Stanton, Elizabeth Cady; Steinem, Gloria; Stone, Lucy.
>
> *Reference* Carole R. McCann and Seung-Kyung Kim, eds. 2002. *Feminist Theory Reader: Local and Global Perspectives.* New York: Routledge.

Labor Rights

Directly following the turn of the twentieth century, the right to contract was included in the Fourteenth Amendment's prohibition to the states from depriving any person of "life, liberty, or property without due process of law." But men's right to contract was held to a different level of importance than women's. Where men were involved, the Court held in several cases (predominately *Lochner v. New York* in 1905) that sixty-hour limits on the workweeks of bakers was an unconstitutional interference with their right to contract. But protective labor legislation that involved a woman's right to contract was not prohibited. In this case the Court held that in the interest of preserving women's health, states could regulate the maximum weekly hours that women worked.

On February 19, 1903, the legislature of the state of Oregon passed an act, the first section of which stated that:

> no female [shall] be employed in any mechanical establishment, or factory, or laundry in this State more than ten hours during any one day. The hours of work may be so arranged as to permit the employment of females at any time so that they shall not work more than ten hours during the twenty-four hours of any one day.

Oregon had set a maximum ten-hour workday for women who were employed in factories and laundries, similar to many other states. Joe Haselbock, the foreman of a laundry, required one Mrs. Gotcher to work more than ten hours and was found guilty by a state court of violating the ten-hour limit for female employees. But shortly after his conviction, the Supreme Court handed down the *Lochner* decision, which ruled that "freedom of contract" prevented states from setting hour requirements on male employees, and Haselbock appealed. He argued that female employees should be included in the *Lochner* prohibition against limiting one's right to contract. Oregon hired Louis D. Brandeis, who would later become a Supreme Court justice, to defend the law before the Supreme Court. His "Brandeis Brief" used statistical evidence to demonstrate a connection between women's health and long workdays to support the state's assertion that too many hours of paid labor were unhealthy for women.

The Court was asked whether the statute in Oregon was unconstitutional in that it affected only female employees. The Court ruled that the right to contract in relation to one's business is part of the "liberty" of individuals and thus protected by the Fourteenth Amendment. Yet this liberty was not absolute, the Court warned, and did not necessarily extend to all contracts. In some situations it may be necessary for a state to restrict the individual's right to contract, particularly if it involved the hours worked by women:

> That woman's physical structure and the performance of maternal functions place her at a disadvantage in the struggle for subsistence is obvious. This is especially true when the burdens of motherhood are upon her. Even when they are not, by abundant testimony of the medical fraternity, continuance for a long time on her feet at work, repeating this from day to day, tends to injurious effects upon the body, and as healthy mothers are essential to vigorous offspring, the physical well-being of woman becomes an object of public interest and care in order to preserve the strength and vigor of the race.

The Court went on:

> Differentiated by [various] matters from the other sex, she is properly placed in a class by herself, and legislation designed for her protection may be sustained, even when like legislation is not necessary for men and could not be sustained . . . . The two sexes differ in structure of body, in the functions to be performed by each, in the amount of physical strength, in the capacity for long-continued labor, particularly when done standing, the influence of vigorous health upon the future well-being of the race, the self-reliance which enables one

to assert full rights, and in the capacity to maintain the struggle for subsistence. This difference justifies a difference in legislation and upholds that which is designed to compensate for some of the burdens which rest upon her.

Although at the time the Court allowed such distinctions on the basis of gender, 100 years later it would hold that gender distinctions that are based on sexual stereotypes are not constitutional.

During this period, states could systematically exclude women from serving on juries, deny married women the right to make contracts, set an earlier age of majority for females, provide working women with fewer benefits for paid employment, and restrict hours for women students and not for male students.

Married Women's Property Acts

Following the Civil War, feminists failed to gain the same protections for women that were granted to freed male slaves with the Civil War amendments—the Thirteenth (banning slavery), the Fourteenth (guaranteeing equal rights for freed slaves), and the Fifteenth (allowing freed blacks the right to vote). They then launched a separate campaign for women's rights, namely, a reform of the common-law rules of coverture that severely limited married women's right to own property. Under coverture, based on English common law, women were subsumed under their husband's legal identity; a husband owned whatever property his wife brought into the marriage or inherited later, owed support to his wife, and was responsible not only for her debts but also for her discipline. A married woman lost her legal identity and owed services and sexual fidelity to her husband. Rape was thus considered a property crime and not a crime against a person; that is, it was a crime perpetrated against the husband because his property (i.e., his wife) had been damaged.

The Married Women's Property Acts

were state laws passed largely not to improve women's rights but rather to protect family property from creditors. Mississippi became the first state to enact a Married Women's Property Act in 1839, followed by Maryland in 1843. By the end of the Civil War, a total of twenty-nine states had passed such acts, which at first glance seem to herald a revolution in the legal and economic relationship between husband and wife. Yet the first acts had little to do with either feminist agitation or concern for female equality. Instead, most pertained mainly to a wife's control over slaves she had received from her birth family, protecting them from any attachments by creditors of her husband's. In 1844 Michigan enacted a law that stipulated that any personal or real property a woman received either before or after her marriage remained in her control. Within the next two years, Ohio, Indiana, and Iowa followed with legislation preventing a husband's debts from being attached to his wife's real estate. By 1900 most states had liberalized their acts somewhat, in some cases even allowing women to retain wages from work they had done outside the home.

The greatest benefit of these acts was that they diminished many of the handicaps women faced under coverture laws and made it easier for women to escape troubled marriages, for a divorce would no longer leave them legally penniless. The problem remained, however, that a husband retained the right to manage and control the property, as well as enjoy any profits from selling that property (without the wife's consent). This would not change until 1981 (see *Kirchberg v. Feenstra*).

> *See also* Common Law; Coverture; Fourteenth Amendment; *Kirchberg v. Feenstra*; Patriarchy.

Mott, Lucretia (1793–1880)

Born in Massachusetts, Lucretia Mott was a Quaker minister who was active in antislavery campaigns. She traveled with Elizabeth Cady Stanton to London for the World Anti-

Lucretia (Coffin) Mott (Library of Congress)

Slavery Convention, and after being denied seats on the floor of the convention solely because of their sex, the two began to draw parallels between women's status in the United States and those of slaves. In 1848 Mott and Stanton organized the first women's rights convention, held in Seneca Falls, New York, which was attended by approximately 300 people. The convention drafted the "Declaration of Sentiments," generally regarded as the most famous document in the history of feminism. The declaration called for expanded political and legal rights for women. It reflected the convention's dissatisfaction with divorce and criminal laws regarding women, moral codes concerning the educational opportunities of women, and other discrimination women faced in society. It pointed out that women's legal rights diminished upon marriage yet they were still taxed by the government and argued that either women should be treated as full citizens or they should not be required to pay taxes. The declaration criticized a system fraught with injustices for women: they could not enter into various professions and educational facilities; they were denied custody of their children upon divorce; they were restricted from full participation in churches. The declaration, finally, called for all women to band together to effect change. Surprisingly, one resolution that was voted on but not passed was a claim for women to be given the franchise; it was considered too controversial.

See also Anthony, Susan B.; Feminism; Fourteenth Amendment; National Woman Suffrage Association (NWSA); Nineteenth Amendment; Stanton, Elizabeth Cady.
Reference Lucretia Mott. 2002. *Selected Letters of Lucretia Coffin Mott.* Edited by Beverly Wilson Palmer, Holly Byers Ochoa, and Carol Faulkner. Chicago: University of Illinois Press.

National American Woman Suffrage Association (NAWSA)

The National American Woman Suffrage Association was formed in 1890 as the result of a merger between the National Woman Suffrage Association (NWSA) led by Elizabeth Cady Stanton and Susan B. Anthony and the American Woman Suffrage Association (AWSA) led by Lucy Stone, Henry Blackwell, and Julia Ward Howe. These opposing groups had been organized in the late 1860s partly as the result of disagreement over strategy: NWSA favored women's enfranchisement through a federal constitutional amendment, whereas AWSA believed success could be more easily achieved through state-by-state campaigns granting women the right to vote. NAWSA combined both state-focused and federally focused tactics.

In a series of well-organized campaigns led largely by Carrie Chapman Catt, NAWSA secured passage of the Nineteenth Amendment in 1920. Once NAWSA's primary goal of women's enfranchisement became a reality, the organization became the League of Women Voters.

See also Anthony, Susan B.; Catt, Carrie Chapman; Equal Rights Amendment (ERA); Feminism; Fourteenth

Amendment; National Women Suffrage Association (NWSA); Nineteenth Amendment; Stanton, Elizabeth Cady; Stone, Lucy.
Reference Kristina Dumbeck. 2001. *Leaders of Women's Suffrage.* San Diego, CA: Lucent Books.

National Woman Suffrage Association (NWSA)

The National Woman Suffrage Association was formed in 1871 by women who were frustrated with women's lack of rights. The members of NWSA campaigned for George Francis Train, a Democratic candidate for governor of Kansas who supported women's suffrage but was against suffrage for freed slaves. Initially, women's suffrage was not the group's primary issue; they addressed many concerns, including the unionization of women workers. In 1872 NWSA supported the first woman candidate for president of the United States, Victoria Woodhull.

After Susan B. Anthony's arrest for voting in the 1872 election, the political differences between NWSA and the American Woman Suffrage Association (AWSA), which limited its efforts almost solely to securing for women the right to vote and tied itself closely to the Republican Party, began to fade. By 1890 the two groups merged, becoming the National American Woman Suffrage Association (NAWSA). Despite factionalism and changes in the political climate that delayed the progress of the suffrage movement, the NWSA set a precedent for women interested in organizing independently of male-dominated political institutions. Building on the successes of the NWSA, the members of the newly formed NAWSA emulated its strategies and eventually secured passage of the Nineteenth Amendment in 1920.

See also Anthony, Susan B.; Catt, Carrie Chapman; Equal Rights Amendment (ERA); Feminism; Fourteenth Amendment; National American Woman Suffrage Association (NAWSA); Nineteenth Amendment; Stanton, Elizabeth Cady; Stone, Lucy.

Table 1.1: Women and Men Who Voted in the 1968–2000 Presidential Elections

	Women Voting (%)	Men Voting (%)	Women	Men
2000	56	53	59.3 million	51.5 million
1996	56	53	56.1 million	48.9 million
1992	62	60	60.6 million	53.3 million
1988	58	56	54.5 million	47.7 million
1984	61	59	54.5 million	47.4 million
1980	59	59	49.3 million	43.8 million
1976	59	60	45.6 million	41.1 million
1972	62	64	44.9 million	40.9 million
1968	67	72	39.2 million	37.5 million

Source: Data from Center for American Women and Politics Web site at http://www.rci. rutgers.edu/~cawp

Nineteenth Amendment

Finally passed in 1920, the Nineteenth Amendment gave women full suffrage with men. Although there were states that had allowed women to vote in certain elections (such as those for school boards), the Nineteenth Amendment marked the legalization mention of women's suffrage on a national level, except for Native American women, who did not gain the vote until 1923. Much of the pressure for women's suffrage came from western states, which were motivated by their need to get enough voters to qualify for statehood. Wyoming and Utah became the first states to grant women complete suffrage (in 1869 and 1870, respectively); Kansas (1885) and Colorado (1893) followed.

The Nineteenth Amendment was passed when the thirty-sixth state, Tennessee, ratified it in August 1920. Women could vote for the first time in the presidential election that November. Following passage, the selection of women to national office became more realistic. The first woman in the U.S. House of Representatives, Jeanette Rankin of Wyoming, had been elected shortly before passage of the amendment, in 1917. In 1922 Rebecca Felton became the first U.S. senator, but only for a short time, to fill an empty seat. No woman has ever served as U.S. president (and curiously, the first woman to run for the office, Victoria Claflin Woodhull, did so in 1872, before she was legally allowed to vote).

> *See also* Addams, Jane; American Woman Suffrage Association (AWSA); Anthony, Susan B.; Catt, Carrie Chapman; Feminism; Fourteenth Amendment; Intermediate Scrutiny Standard; National American Woman Suffrage Association (NAWSA); National Woman Suffrage Association (NWSA); Seneca Falls Convention; Stone, Lucy.
>
> *References* Aileen S. Kraditor. 1981. *The Ideas of the Woman Suffrage Movement, 1890–1920.* New York: W. W. Norton; Rosalyn Terborg-Penn. 1998. *African American Women in the Struggle for the Vote, 1850–1920 (Blacks in the Diaspora).* Bloomington: Indiana University Press.

Patriarchy

Patriarchy (from *patri-*, meaning "father," and *arche-*, meaning "rule") is the manifestation and institutionalization of male dominance over women and children in the family and in society generally. Patriarchy is pervasive not only in the United States but throughout the world. Most historians date the rise of patriarchy from 3100 to 600 B.C.E.

One of the main vehicles of instilling and preserving this practice is religion, but the political system now also perpetuates it. In the United States the courts were largely responsible for encouraging patriarchy through various rulings in the beginning of the twentieth century that posited that men and women naturally occupied "separate spheres." That is, because of women's reproductive capabilities, they are best suited to occupy the private sphere of the home while men occupy the more public sphere of employment outside the home and in politics.

Gender-based divisions of labor became part of the legal and cultural norm in the United States as well as modern Europe. Although women made crucial economic contributions through household production, they were rarely allowed to participate significantly in the decision making of legal, political, economic, and social institutions. Before the American Revolution, patriarchy was further ensured when the colonists adopted the English tradition of coverture, which viewed husband and wife as one person (that person being the husband). Women had no legal identity apart from their husbands; they could not vote, hold property, or act in their own names.

But by the Civil War era, feminists launched the first women's movement in their campaign for greater rights, culminating in the Married Women's Property Acts. These acts gave women more legal rights (although this varied by region of the country), including the right to own their own property. Women continued to press for the abolition of coverture laws across the country; they gained the right to practice some professions and the right to vote. By the late 1960s, more women than ever had entered the workforce, and women used the court system to eradicate certain vestiges of patriarchy. They gained the right to obtain birth control information through the courts, the right to constitutionally protected abortions, the right to equal pay, and protections against sexual harassment in the workplace. Yet even at the start of the twenty-first century, patriarchy remains firmly in place in politics: no woman has ever occupied the U.S. presidency, there are only two women on the U.S. Supreme Court, and

there are only a few women in the Senate and the House. And patriarchy can also be seen in the workforce, as women continue to earn approximately 25 percent less than men in the same occupations, and the glass ceiling limits women from assuming top positions.

See also Contraception; Coverture; Glass Ceiling; Marriage; Married Women's Property Acts; National Organization for Women (NOW); National Woman Suffrage Association (NWSA); Nineteenth Amendment; Right to Privacy; Sexual Harassment.

Reference Gerda Lerner. 1987. *The Creation of Patriarchy.* New York: Oxford University Press.

Seneca Falls Convention of 1848

The first conference on women's rights, in Seneca Falls, New York, in 1848, was held to "discuss the social, civil and religious condition and rights of women." The convention was organized by Lucretia Mott and Elizabeth Cady Stanton, two women who had met eight years earlier at the World Anti-Slavery Convention in London. The women became enraged that the organizers of an antislavery meeting refused to recognize women as legitimate delegates and denied them entry onto the floor of the convention hall. They did hear the speeches from the sidelines, however, and decided to capitalize on the lessons they learned there. They resolved to organize their own conference upon their return to the United States to discuss how women could secure equal rights to men. The Seneca Falls convention is now seen as the beginning of a movement that ultimately revolutionized the social, legal, economic, and political lives of American women and ushered in the first women's rights movement in the United States.

Although the plight of women had received little national attention, Mott and Stanton had plenty of incentive and justification to call for a forum on women's rights. Either by law or by custom, unmarried women were not permitted to vote, speak in

Yᴱ MAY SESSION OF Yᴱ WOMAN'S RIGHTS CONVENTION—Yᴱ ORATOR OF Yᴱ DAY DENOUNCING Yᴱ LORDS OF CREATION.

Representation of a feminist speaker being booed by men at the first women's rights convention at Seneca Falls, New York, on July 19–20, 1848. (Library of Congress)

public, hold office, attend college, or earn a living other than as a teacher, seamstress, domestic, or millworker. Married women lived under these limitations and more under the laws of coverture. Alexis de Tocqueville, the French author and statesman, observed in 1856 that "in America a woman loses her independence completely and forever with the bonds of matrimony." A married woman, for example, was prohibited by law from making and signing contracts, entering into litigation in court, divorcing a husband (even an abusive one), maintaining custody of her children upon a husband's dissolution of the marriage, or even owning property. To many women who learned of the Seneca Falls convention, the call for a discussion of women's rights legitimized their dissatisfaction with their inferior status.

The western area of New York State was also ripe for a convention questioning practices and mores. Beginning in the 1830s and throughout the Civil War era, a large reform community had emerged in the region; many of the reformers were involved in the abolitionist movement and various religious movements. And possibly even more important was that in many of these reform movements, women had active roles. As such, although the leadership was predominately male, Mott and Stanton had no trouble gaining support for their call for a conference to promote women's equality.

As mentioned, the organizers of the convention were primarily Stanton and Mott. But Martha White, Mary Ann McClintock, and Jane Hunt and others were also involved. Men were not excluded from the proceedings; in fact, the women organizers believed the prominent men that attended would provide the convention with more publicity. And publicity was the key to success; the ills facing women would not change until they were addressed publicly.

One of the goals of the convention was to draft something similar to the Declaration of Independence, which, to the organizers, was a hypocritical document since it had failed to give women the same rights as men. They named their manifesto the "Declaration of Sentiments," and its writing fell largely to Stanton. She proposed that "all men and women had been created equal" and defined eleven resolutions that argued that women had a natural right to equality in all spheres. She then discussed eighteen specific "injuries and usurpations on the part of man toward woman."

The convention took place on July 19 and 20 at a Methodist church (the Wesleyan) that had been quite sympathetic to the organizer's goals. Ironically, the entire convention was chaired by James Mott, husband of Lucretia, since women were not allowed to conduct public meetings on their own; speaking in public was thought to diminish a woman's chaste and feminine demeanor. The first day of the convention began with Stanton's reading the "Declaration of Sentiments" and the grievances the organizers had with the legal, political, and religious treatment of women. The following day was spent debating issues and rewording the resolutions in preparation for a vote of acceptance by all attendees of the convention. Each of the resolutions passed easily and unanimously with the exception of one: the resolution calling for women to secure the right to vote was vehemently challenged on strategic grounds. The fear was that demanding the vote was too radical for the (largely male) political establishment, and thus other resolutions that were less controversial would also fail to gain acceptance. The strategists warned that pursuing women's enfranchisement would make the women's movement as a whole subject to ridicule and eventual dismissal from general public discourses. In the end, however, the resolution passed by a small majority after Stanton and Frederick Douglass persistently advocated its importance.

Following the convention in Seneca Falls, a series of seemingly small but relatively revolutionary improvements in women's rights occurred. Over time, women were allowed to speak publicly, and individual states adopted laws to protect the rights of married women, including granting the right to own property in their own name, retain their earnings, and keep guardianship of their children in the case of divorce.

See also Coverture; Feminism; Mott, Lucretia; Stanton, Elizabeth Cady.
Reference Mariam Gurko. 1987. *The Ladies of Seneca Falls: The Birth of the Woman's Rights Movement.* New York: Random House.

Separate Spheres Doctrine

As life in the early years of the republic came to center on capitalism, men went out to work and women remained at home. Although women continued to be subservient to men, the doctrine of "separate spheres" began to take shape. Women's role within the home was glorified; their paid labor outside, such as teaching (which was seen as a "woman's occupation"), and unpaid charitable duties were considered an extension of their domestic duties. Today the separate spheres doctrine seems nothing other than a constraint, but at the time women developed a type of autonomy under the doctrine, especially in organizing into religious and welfare associations. Through it all, women found a source of strength and identity in their separate world.

This doctrine defined a male sphere that was public—one concerned with the regulated world of government, trade, business, and law, from which women were largely excluded—and a women's sphere that was private—encompassing the unregulated realm of home, family, and child rearing. Women attained what status they had through the legally sanctioned family, and without it, they could expect economic hardship, pity, and suspicion. Yet it was woman's place in the private sphere that justified her exclusion from the public sphere, and under the marital unity doctrine her husband retained ultimate authority over her even in that domain. The separate spheres ideology not only rationalized women's exclusion from political and economic self-rule and their assignment to dependent and subservient roles but also helped to obscure that subordination by defining women's confinement to matters of home and family as "natural."

The law of coverture, in place at the time, played a covert part in supporting this doctrine and may have had a role in establishing it at the outset. Based on Blackstone's *Legal Commentaries,* the English law imported by the colonists, coverture ensured that husband and wife became one person and that one person (both literally and figuratively) was the husband. Before a woman married, her father or other male relative was her "legal" identity.

Despite passage of the Nineteenth Amendment giving women the vote in 1920, the separate spheres doctrine continued. For example, women were routinely excluded from serving on juries well into the 1960s, and women's participation in the military is still limited to noncombat positions (seemingly out of danger). Since women were traditionally barred from public roles, they were systematically discouraged from obtaining higher education, joining certain professions, and running businesses except as helpmates to their husbands. In an attempt to remedy this situation, Congress passed Title IX of the education amendments in 1972 to support women in obtaining professional degrees and ushered in an era during which U.S. women entered the workforce at higher levels than ever before in history.

See also Civil Rights Act; Coverture; Feminism; Married Women's Property Acts; Nineteenth Amendment; Patriarchy; Title IX.

Reference Rosalind Rosenberg. 1986. *Beyond Separate Spheres.* New Haven, CT: Yale University Press.

Stanton, Elizabeth Cady (1815–1902)

Elizabeth Cady Stanton was the daughter of a well-known attorney and judge in New York State. Although she did not attend college, she worked in her father's law office; it was there that she became acutely aware of the legal discrimination against women. Against her father's wishes, she married a politically active journalist and abolitionist, Harry Stanton, who supported her rather liberal tendencies; the word "obey" was dropped from their wedding vows. She had seven children and throughout her life lectured on the difficulties women faced by having large families.

Stanton's husband introduced her to the abolitionist movement when he brought her to London to attend the World Anti-Slavery Convention, the first meeting of its kind. It was here that Stanton met Lucretia Mott and began a lifelong friendship with her. The organizers of the convention did not recognize women as legitimate delegates and refused them entry onto the floor of the convention. The two women were so outraged that an organization that purported to equalize the rights of slaves had failed to recognize the rights of women that they resolved, together, to call a women's rights convention after returning to the states.

Eight years later, in 1848, they organized the Seneca Falls, New York, conference intended to discuss "the social, civil, and religious condition and rights of women." It was Stanton who wrote the convention's "Declaration of Sentiments." Patterned after the Declaration of Independence, the Seneca Falls declaration included a woman's bill of rights and listed demands for social equality, including women's suffrage. The "Declaration of Sentiments" has been credited with initiating the long-running struggle toward women's rights and suffrage.

Although the Seneca Falls conference did not change public opinion toward women's rights, it did focus national attention on the issue of gender equality. Following the Civil War, Stanton and Susan B. Anthony founded the National Woman Suffrage Association (NWSA), hopeful that the proposed amendments to the Constitution giving freed slaves equal rights before the law would be extended to include women as well. The NWSA foundered in this endeavor.

This is not to say that the women's movement failed to change society at all. Stanton was extremely successful in ensuring other legal rights for women. She promoted the view that the best way to improve the lives of women was to change the laws that denied them equal legal rights. She thus helped win property rights for married women, give women equal guardianship of children, and liberalize divorce laws so that women could leave abusive marriages. Today these laws seem relatively mundane, but during Stanton's lifetime, changing these laws challenged the basic beliefs of society; the media and the public at large regularly and soundly criticized and ridiculed her work and actions.

Stanton was thus known as more of a radical than her feminist contemporaries. This was especially true in 1895 after the publication of her work *The Woman's Bible*, a commentary on women in the Bible that alienated her even from the NWSA. It is fitting that a woman who spent her life fighting for equal rights of women wrote the words that eventually made up the Nineteenth Amendment to the Constitution. Unfortunately, Stanton did not live to enjoy the privileges of women's suffrage, dying eighteen years before the amendment was passed.

See also Addams, Jane; Anthony, Susan B.; Catt, Carrie Chapman; League of Women Voters; National American Woman Suffrage Association (NAWSA); Nineteenth Amendment; Stone, Lucy.

Reference Geoffrey C. Ward and Ken Burns. 2001. *Not for Ourselves Alone: The Story of Elizabeth Cady Stanton and Susan B. Anthony.* New York: Knopf.

Stone, Lucy (1818–1893)

Lucy Stone was the eighth of nine children in a Massachusetts farming family. Her authoritarian father forced his wife to beg him for money to feed her children. Like most girls of the time, Stone was not encouraged to pursue higher education. Stone nevertheless became one of the best-known feminist speakers of her time and gained an education and measure of fame that none of her brothers would ever achieve.

After saving money she earned by teaching, Stone began her formal studies when she was twenty-five, at Oberlin College in Ohio, the first college in the country to admit females and African Americans. She graduated in 1847 and declined to write the commencement address for her graduating class because she realized someone else would deliver her speech, as women were not permitted to give public addresses.

Despite this prohibition, following her college graduation Stone began making a series of public speeches. The only female college graduate in the state at the time, she delivered her lectures from the pulpit of her brother's church; her talks usually involved the rights of women and slaves. She was such a popular lecturer that the Anti-Slavery Society hired her almost immediately to travel around the country speaking on the abolition of slavery. She occasionally peppered her speeches with calls for increased rights of women, eventually causing controversy and reprimand from her employers at the Anti-Slavery Society. She remained with the society, agreeing to speak on slavery during her paid weekdays and reserving the topic of women's rights for her own time during weekends. Enormous, often hostile crowds greeted Stone, and she was sometimes pelted with prayer books and other objects.

She brought many converts into the newly emerging women's movement. In 1850 she organized the first truly national woman's rights convention, held in Worcester, Massachusetts. Although the Seneca

Lucy Stone (Library of Congress)

Falls convention in 1848 had been an important and radical step, the majority of attendees at that convention were from the surrounding area. Stone believed that it was time to hold a convention more national in scope. Her speech at the Worcester convention is credited with converting Susan B. Anthony to the women's suffrage cause and influencing several other powerful leaders, including John Stuart Mill, Julia Ward Howe, and Frances Willard.

Stone's radicalism extended beyond the podium. In 1855 she married Cincinnati businessman Henry Blackwell after he agreed that she could keep her name. The letter she wrote him before her acceptance of his marriage proposal stated: "A wife should no more take her husband's name than he should hers. My name is my identity and must not be lost." Henry responded: "I wish, as a husband, to renounce all the privileges which the law confers upon me, which are not strictly mutual. Surely such a marriage will not degrade you, dearest."

Two children resulted from the marriage,

one of whom died at birth. Upon the birth of her second child, Stone retired from active touring and public speaking to devote her full attention to raising her child. She returned to her speaking tour following the Civil War in 1867, again calling for revised laws on the treatment of women and, now, freed slaves. Stone's speeches remained extraordinarily controversial, but this time for a different reason. Following the Civil War, Congress began debates on the addition of three amendments to the U.S. Constitution: the Thirteenth, which banned involuntary servitude (i.e., slavery); the Fourteenth, which ensured equal rights for the freed slaves; and the Fifteenth, which ensured voting rights for the freed slaves. By merging the dual concerns of women's rights and the rights of freed slaves, Stone opened up a Pandora's box that eventually split the women's movement.

Although all of the women activists supported equal rights of both women and freed slaves, the women differed in how to achieve that goal. The women who opposed the Fifteenth Amendment because it excluded women from the vote formed the National Woman Suffrage Association led by Susan B. Anthony and Elizabeth Cady Stanton. These women believed that the time to push for the enfranchisement of women was during the debates about the rights of freed slaves. Others argued against the wisdom of linking the women's movement with the debates over constitutional rights of freed slaves; the topic of freed slaves was in itself too divisive, they believed, and combining it with the voting rights of women would cause both groups to lose. These women founded the American Woman Suffrage Association in 1869. The groups reunified in 1890 to form the National American Woman Suffrage Association.

By failing to keep its two factions together, the women's movement saw its political power weaken; ultimately, both sides lost. In response to criticism that her speeches had contributed to the faltering of the women's movement, Stone ended her speaking career and along with her husband began editing the weekly suffrage newspaper the *Woman's Journal.*

> ***See also*** Anthony, Susan B.; Feminism; National Woman Suffrage Association (NWSA); Nineteenth Amendment; Stanton, Elizabeth Cady.
> ***Reference*** Andrea Moore Kerr. 1992. *Lucy Stone: Speaking Out for Equality.* New Brunswick, NJ: Rutgers University Press.

Truth, Sojourner (1797–1883)

Born into slavery as Isabella Baumfree in a Dutch settlement in New York State, Sojourner Truth was one of thirteen children. She was sold away from her family by the age of eleven, but she never forgot her mother's devout Christianity, and it would influence her throughout her life. Although her new owner was violent, her move enabled her to learn English.

She was forced to marry Thomas, an older slave, and the couple had five children, three of whom were sold to other owners. Her third master, John Dumont, promised he would free her from slavery; when he failed to do so, she fled the state in 1928 with her infant son. Only months later New York abolished slavery. She found work in New York City as a domestic in various religious communes dedicated to assisting impoverished women.

She changed her name to Sojourner in 1843 after a "spiritual revelation" that led her to embrace evangelical religion This revelation also directed her career path; she became an itinerant preacher in Long Island and Connecticut and eventually joined the utopian community of the Northampton Association for Education and Industry. Although she was illiterate, she managed to acquire a vast knowledge of the Bible and became a successful preacher who sang gospel songs and told stories with a strong moral message. She met abolitionists such as William Lloyd Garrison, Frederick Douglass, and Olive Gilbert and became active in

Sojourner Truth with President Abraham Lincoln (Library of Congress)

the antislavery movement. By 1850 she had published her memoirs, *The Narrative of Sojourner Truth: A Northern Slave* and settled in Michigan. She continued to be known as a radical abolitionist and women's suffrage activist, traveling most of the year to give speeches in which she linked the oppression of slavery with that of women. Harriet Beecher Stowe said of her: "[I have never] been conversant with anyone who had more of that silent and subtle power which we call personal presence than this woman."

In 1851 Sojourner Truth delivered her best-known public address, "Ain't I a Woman?" and received wide acclaim not only from fellow abolitionists and suffragists but from the public at large. This publicity gave her the courage to become even more radical in her responses to policies she deemed oppressive to her status as former slave and woman. While in Washington, D.C., for example, she refused to leave a streetcar after the driver ordered her off because she was black. As did Rosa Parks a century later, Truth was able to end the segregation of public transportation during the Civil War.

During the Civil War Truth traveled the roads of Michigan dispensing food and clothing to black regiments. She petitioned Congress to give former slaves land in the West to establish a "Negro State" and met with Abraham Lincoln to lobby for relief efforts for the freed slaves during Reconstruction. "It is hard for the old slaveholding spirit to die," she said, "but die it must." She worked closely with former slaves and continued her public speeches until forced to retire because of poor health. She died in Battle Creek, Michigan, in 1883.

Reference Bernard, Jacqueline. 1990. *Journey Toward Freedom: The Story of Sojourner Truth.* New York: The Feminist Press.

Harriet Tubman (Library of Congress)

Tubman, Harriet (1818 or 1820–1913)

Born into slavery in Maryland, Harriet Ross was severely injured as a young teen when a white overseer struck her on the head for refusing to tie up an escaped slave. The injury apparently caused lifelong narcolepsy. At twenty-five she married John Tubman, a free black, but the marriage did not free her from slavery, and at the age of thirty she fled, fearing she would be sold to an owner in the Deep South, a region known for its especially brutal treatment of slaves. Tubman left behind not only her husband but also her parents and siblings. She was known throughout her life as a determined woman, more militant than most to be freed from the bondage of slavery. "My people must go free," she said.

A sympathetic white neighbor helped Tubman escape to Canada. Tubman settled temporarily in Pennsylvania and met William Still, one of the predominate leaders of the Underground Railroad, the system to help slaves fleeing to Canada and elsewhere and their eventual freedom from bondage. In 1851 Tubman began relocating family members and others to Ontario, Canada. She continued shuttling fugitives

on the Underground Railroad until about 1857; she is credited with leading at least 300 slaves to freedom. It is estimated that Tubman returned to the South at least nineteen times, demonstrating remarkable courage and intelligence in eluding the multitudes of bounty hunters searching for escaped slaves and never losing one of her fugitives. Bounty hunters nicknamed her "Moses" and a $40,000 reward was offered for her capture.

Tubman was known also throughout abolitionist circles. She worked with fellow abolitionists Frederick Douglass, Jermain Loguen, Gerrit Smith, and even John Brown, who led the infamous Harper's Ferry raid, arguably the spark that began the Civil War. In fact, she collaborated with Brown prior to the raid and missed it only because of illness. During the Civil War she garnered publicity through accounts of her work as a soldier, spy, and nurse. Whether she actually served in these capacities is unclear, but it is known that she was recruited by the Union government and paid $200 over a three-year period (so paltry a sum that she supported herself by selling baked goods). Part of the reason the Union was so interested in her help was that she was able to move unnoticed through rebel territory and deliver valuable information to Union leaders about rebel resources.

It is uncertain what happened to John Tubman, her first husband, but following the Civil War she married Nelson David, a black veteran, and the couple settled in upstate New York. At the time, upstate New York was an extremely progressive area known for its egalitarian-minded religious communities; it was also the heart of the first women's movement. Tubman turned her own residence into the Home for Indigent and Aged Negroes and supported herself and her family by giving speeches. She continued to lobby for the advancement of women, in 1896 organizing the National Association of Colored Women to struggle for equal rights for all.

Reference Bradford, Sarah Elizabeth. 1993. *Harriet Tubman, the Moses of Her People.* Bedford, MA: Applewood Books.

Women as Jurors

Since the passage of the English Magna Carta in 1215 and the American colonists' adoption of the English common law, the right to a jury trial by one's peers has been viewed as a basic protection against tyranny of the majority and a way to educate the citizens about the judiciary. The right to a trial by jury is guaranteed to every citizen of the United States through the Sixth Amendment of the Constitution, which states that in a criminal case an accused person has the right to a speedy and public trial by an impartial jury. The Seventh Amendment preserves the right of trial by jury in all civil cases in which "the value in controversy" exceeds $20.

Juries are intended to be a representative cross-section of the community, and few citizens are exempt from jury duty. In the eighteenth and nineteenth centuries, however, women participated in juries only as "matrons" in specific cases involving women defendants. In the early part of the twentieth century, states either absolutely excluded women from jury duty, excluded them but gave them the option of volunteering for service, or gave child care exemptions. And even after passage of the Nineteenth Amendment in 1920, when no governmental entity could deny women the right to vote, few states allowed women to participate in other civic activities such as serving on juries. Those few states that did were not required to treat women and men equally in establishing the pool from which jurors were drawn.

After suffrage was granted, women's rights activists claimed that their new position as voting citizens entitled them to other rights (or obligations), including the right to serve on juries. Their arguments paralleled those of the early suffragists who criticized the Civil War amendments (known as the Reconstruction amendments) for protecting the citizenship rights only of freed male slaves and not women. To them, jury service was a privilege of citizenship, as was voting. To this day, jury service is tied to voting since in most states the jury pool is selected from citizens who are registered to vote. The suffragists, therefore, argued that not only voting but also jury service was a significant right of citizenship.

The idea of giving women jury duty was controversial at best. It was feared that women's public duties would affect their ability to meet their private obligations in the domestic realm; insulting women's tender sensibilities would possibly harm their home life and thus the entire human race. Most scholars, however, point to three additional reasons why women were prevented from serving on juries even after they won suffrage. First was common law. According to Blackstone's *Commentaries*, the guide to the English law that the colonists adopted as their own, a jury was composed of "twelve free and lawful men," not women. Second, because of the common-law tradition of coverture, women were not legal identities but instead were subsumed under their husbands' identities; they could not act in a legal capacity since they had no legal existence. Third, most states had specific laws that limited eligible jurors to men and in some cases explicitly prevented women from serving. But women activists had a very simple basis for putting women on juries: the U.S. Constitution ordained that every criminal defendant be tried by a jury of his or her peers. Without women jurors, who would decide cases of women defendants? If a woman was convicted of a crime and sentenced to death but claimed she was pregnant, common law called for a jury of twelve "matrons" to determine whether she was actually pregnant. If she was, her death sentence was delayed until the birth of her child. Thus the common law had already deemed that women jurors were sometimes necessary.

In 1961 Gwendolyn Hoyt appealed her conviction by an all-male jury of second-degree murder of her husband. In *Hoyt v. Florida* she argued that a Florida statute that automatically registered men for jury duty but required women to make a trip to the courthouse to register effectively limited juries to males and was therefore a violation of the Fourteenth Amendment. According to Hoyt, women jurors would have been "more understanding or compassionate than men" in assessing her actions as well as her defense of temporary insanity. But the Court upheld the statute, saying a defendant is not entitled to "a jury tailored to the circumstances of the particular case." Because Florida allowed women to volunteer for jury service, the Court ruled, the state was acting in good faith and not attempting to exclude women from that duty—although the Court also observed that women are "still regarded as the center of home and family life."

In *Taylor v. Louisiana* in 1975 the Court addressed the issue again and came to a different conclusion. In the case of a male defendant who was charged with aggravated kidnapping and rape, the Court ruled that the state's all-male jury selection procedure was unconstitutional. The two rulings seemed inconsistent, since the facts in both cases were nearly identical, both defendants having been charged with violent assault against a member of the opposite sex. And the rights to an impartial jury and equal protection of the law were implicated in both cases. As Justice William Rehnquist pointed out in his dissent in *Taylor,* the male defendant had less claim to unconstitutional treatment than did the female defendant in *Hoyt.*

The difference in the two rulings seemed to center on the legal rights the two defendants claimed. Taylor relied on his fundamental right to a trial by jury guaranteed by the Sixth Amendment, whereas Hoyt relied on her equal protection rights guaranteed by the Fourteenth Amendment. It is a good example of the lack of deference paid by the Court to rights under the Equal Protection Clause (on which most gender discrimination cases rely) compared to more "fundamental" rights of trial. Largely as a result of this case, the ACLU—Women's Rights Project was founded.

The precedent of *Hoyt* stands today. Women now have the right and obligation to have their names automatically included in jury pools. Courts have, however, ruled that it is "reasonable" to exempt from federal jury service people who are primarily responsible for the aged, the infirm, or children under ten years of age.

Women as Lawmakers

Nancy Pelosi was the first women to be elected by her colleagues as the House Democratic leader. She served as a reminder to the American public that although women leaders have not reached parity with men, more women than ever before are holding elective office. For example, in 2003 seventy-three women were in the U.S. Congress (14 percent), representing twenty-five states; fourteen served in the Senate (14 percent) and fifty-nine in the House (14 percent). Of the women in Congress in 2003, 25 percent were women of color (eleven African Americans and seven Latinas).

The women in the U.S. Senate in 2003 were: Barbara Boxer (D-CA), Maria Cantwell (D-WA), Hillary Rodham Clinton (D-NY), Susan Collins (R-ME), Elizabeth Dole (R-NC), Dianne Feinstein (D-CA), Kay Bailey Hutchison (R-TX), Mary Landrieu (D-LA), Blanche Lincoln (D-AR), Barbara Mikulski (D-MD), Lisa Murkowski (R-AK), Patty Murray (D-WA), Olympia Snowe (R-ME), and Debbie Stabenow (D-MI).

Additionally, seventy-nine women hold elective executive positions at the state level (accounting for 25 percent of all such offices), and women fill 22.3 percent of the seats in state legislatures. These figures are simply extraordinary when put into historical context. In 1969 only 4 percent of all state legislative posts were held by women, and in 1970 there were only three female governors compared to ten in 2003. Women of color have not seen the same proportionate increases; only 6 percent of all women serving in statewide executive office and only 18 percent of women state legislators in 2003 were women of color. This figure is even more discouraging when compared to the makeup of the legislatures as a whole (not just the proportion of women legislators): women of color constitute only 4 percent of all state legislators.

Some states elect more women to office than others. As Table 1.2 demonstrates, western and eastern states have the highest number of women in elected offices. Forty-eight states have at one time elected women to executive office; only Maine and West Virginia have never had female governors.

Part of the reason there have been more women holding elective office in recent years may be term limits that have forced

Table 1.2 States with Highest Percentage of Women Holding State Offices

Washington	36.7
Colorado	36.7
Maryland	33.0
Oregon	31.1
Vermont	31.1
California	30.0
New Mexico	29.5
Connecticut	29.4
Delaware	29.0
Nevada	28.6

Source: Center for American Women and Politics (http://www.rci.rutgers.edu/~cawp/index.html)

entrenched incumbents from legislative seats. But term limits exist only at the state level, not the national level. Will this make it more difficult for a woman to become president of the United States? The United States has, of course, never had a female executive. But several women have indicated plans to pursue their parties' nomination for president in the 2004 election or possibly beyond that. It is highly likely that a woman Democrat will run (if not win); of all women who have held federal elective office in the United States, the majority have been Democrats. Of the thirty-three women who have served in the Senate, for example, twenty were Democrats and thirteen were Republicans.

But the largest problem a woman faces in a bid for the White House is money. Although male candidates have been able to rely on political action committees (PACs) to finance costly campaigns, until the 1980s there were few PACs that contributed to women candidates' war chests. In general, partisan PACs give only to candidates running for a particular party, and issue PACs tend to give to candidates supporting particular issues (especially with regard to abortion). Issue PACs are important to the success of women running for high political office, and because there are more PACs supporting pro-choice issues than pro-life issues, pro-choice women candidates have a greater likelihood of receiving money, and more of it.

One recent PAC strategy that has been extremely beneficial to women candidates has been the increase of donor networks, or PACs that bundle together money from individual donors. Traditional PACs (like the National Organization for Women) raise money from individuals who contribute directly to the PAC; the PAC then forwards that money to a candidate. But campaign finance laws limit contributions to $5,000 per individual per election to each candidate. A bundling strategy benefits women candidates because a large group of individuals can contribute individually a set amount, then the PAC bundles the individuals' checks together and sends the money off to a candidate, thereby skirting Federal Election Commission contribution rules. An example of this type of PAC is EMILY's List (from "Early Money Is Like Yeast" because it "makes the dough rise"), organized by philanthropist Ellen Malcolm in 1985. Malcolm used direct mail to appeal to women for help in electing Maryland's Barbara Mikulski to the U.S. Senate. Mikulski became the first Democratic woman ever to be elected in her own right to the U.S. Senate, largely because of the enormous amount of start-up money that EMILY's List was able to provide. Although women are less likely to contribute to a political campaign than men are, they are more likely to respond to direct mailings; in 1998 EMILY's List contributed over $7.5 million to pro-choice Democratic women candidates. In 1992 Republican women followed the Democrats' example by creating WISH List (Women in the Senate and House). Both PACs contribute to women candidates early in their campaigns, helping them to win nomination in contested primaries and providing start-up labor for further fundraising.

These women's PACs are one of the most important resources for increasing the numbers of women in political office. Since 1992 the WISH List has supported the elections of three women Republican senators, one governor, and ten House members. EMILY's List has helped eleven Democratic women senators, four governors, and fifty-three House members.

Women as Presidential Candidates

A woman first ran for the U.S. presidency in 1872, and since that time twenty-one other women have run for the presidency, twelve of them in 1996:

1872	Victoria Woodhull (Equal Rights Party)
1884	Belva Lockwood (Equal Rights Party)
1888	Belva Lockwood (Equal Rights Party)
1964	Margaret Chase-Smith (Republican Party)
1972	Shirley Chisholm (Democratic Party)
	Toni Nathan (Libertarian Party)
1988	Patricia Schroeder (Democratic Party)
1992	Lenora Fulani (New Alliance Party)
1996	Georgiana Doerschuck (Republican Party)
	Susan Ducey (Republican Party)
	Heather Harder (Democratic Party)
	Mary Hollis (Socialist Party)
	Ann Jennings (Republican Party)
	Caroline Killeen (Democratic Party)
	Mary Le Tulle (Republican Party)
	Elvina Lloyd-Duffie (Democratic Party)
	Isabell Masters (Republican Party)
	Monica Moorehead (Workers' World Party)
	Joann Pharr (Republican Party)
	Diane Templin (Reform Party)
2000	Elizabeth Dole (Republican Party)
2004	Carol Moseley-Braun (Democratic Party)

Although none of these women has won her party's primary, there has been an increased interest in electing a woman to the country's two highest offices. In 1984 Geraldine Ferraro was the first woman ever on the vice-president's ticket; she and her running mate, Walter Mondale, did not win, but they were more successful than any other "women's" ticket.

The biggest problem facing women candidates for high office is money. Male candidates tend to receive contributions from business interests, which give more than the social groups that generally support women. And the factor that most helps women presidential hopefuls is name recognition: both Elizabeth Dole and Hillary Rodham Clinton (a rumored contender for the 2004 race) had husbands who ran for president in the 1996 election, Bob Dole and Bill Clinton. By 2003 it was their wives who were in the spotlight. Hillary Rodham Clinton won a Senate seat for New York in 2000, and Elizabeth Dole won a North Carolina Senate seat in 2002. Once again, it is Clinton versus Dole, but this time in the Senate. Although they represent opposing views and party platforms, both were originally known as helpmates for their husbands and later won political positions in their own right. Both graduated from law school (Clinton from Yale, Dole from Harvard) at a time when women were underrepresented in their classes. The similarities, however, end there. Clinton went on to become a well-known lawyer, whereas Dole served in various political positions, including secretary of transportation and president of the American Red Cross. Will they be the first two women to run against each other for president some day? Possibly.

Women in the Legal Profession

At the turn of the twentieth century, judges and lawyers viewed the female character as too delicate for the legal profession. As one prominent judge explained, it is filled with "unclean issues and collateral questions of sodomy, incest, rape, seduction, fornication, adultery, pregnancy, bastardy, legitimacy, prostitution, lascivious cohabitation, abortion, infanticide, obscene publications, libel and slander of sex, impotence and divorce."

But critics were also concerned about the independence education would grant women and the resulting threat it posed to traditional relations between the sexes. Additionally, medical studies at the time suggested that women were biologically inferior to men and could not withstand the physical and mental demands of higher education. Women who expanded their intellect too much would experience physical weakness, emotional breakdown, sterility, and even death. A leading medical scholar at the time warned that if women undertook the same rigorous intellectual training as men, it would "divert energy from female reproductive organs to the brain, causing a breakdown in women's health and threaten the health of future generations."

Legal precedent upheld the social conventions that restricted women from professional roles, particularly as lawyers. Essentially, lawyers were officers of the court; under coverture, women could neither vote nor had any legal identity, so were thus unfit to be officers of the court. Adoption of the Fourteenth and Fifteenth Amendments, however, gave many women hope since they extended equal political rights to freed male slaves. Women argued for an expansive interpretation of the Fourteenth Amendment to allow them to share the political rights granted to the freed slaves. Among these women was Myra Bradwell, who in *Bradwell v. Illinois* (1872) argued that the state's refusal to license her to practice law was an infringement on her right to enter into the legal profession, a privilege of citizenship protected by the Fourteenth Amendment. Like most attorneys at the time, Bradwell trained for the Illinois bar under a practicing attorney (who happened to be her husband) and met the statutory requirements of admission (e.g., proper age, good moral character, and proper training): the word "he" in the attorney licensing statute, Bradwell said, presumably included women. The Supreme Court upheld the state's decision to deny Bradwell the opportunity to take the state bar exam (which was required to practice law in that state) simply because she was a woman. Illinois officials apparently considered Bradwell's petition so trivial that they did not even send a lawyer to the U.S. Supreme Court to present their side of the case. The U.S. Supreme Court agreed with social mores of the time in holding that the Constitution protects only national citizenship and not state citizenship privileges. Thus the practice of law was properly governed by states, who could restrict membership on whatever basis they so chose. Indeed, in a now famous concurring opinion in the *Bradwell* case, Justice Joseph Bradley wrote, "Man is, or should be, woman's protector and defender. The natural and proper timidity and delicacy which belongs to the female sex evidently unfits it for many of the occupations of civil life. . . . [A] married woman is incompetent fully to perform the duties and trusts that belong to the office of an attorney and counselor."

Myra Bradwell was eventually given a license to practice law, and both of her children, a boy and a girl, would later obtain their licenses to practice law in Illinois. By the early 1990s, there were two women on the U.S. Supreme Court, and 20 percent of the lower federal court judges were women. By 2001, women made up over 50 percent of incoming law school students. Yet the landscape for female attorneys has not changed entirely; they are paid less and are far less likely to receive promotions to partner.

Women in the Military

The Military Selective Service Act empowers the president to require the registration of "every male citizen" and male resident aliens between the ages of eighteen and twenty-six for the military draft. Congress has the power to carry out the president's order.

Registration for the draft was discontinued in 1975 but was reactivated by President Jimmy Carter in early 1980 after the Soviet Union invaded Afghanistan. Carter also recommended that Congress amend the act to permit the registration and conscription of both genders. Although Congress agreed to reactivate the draft registration process, it allocated only the funds necessary to register males and refused to permit the registration of women. When several men challenged the constitutionality of the Military Selective Service Act, a U.S. district court applied the intermediate scrutiny standard and invalidated the male-only registration, holding that the "availability of women registrants would materially increase flexibility, not hamper it."

But in *Rostker v. Goldberg* (1981), the Supreme Court disagreed. Although the Court did not address the appropriate standard of review of such cases (e.g., whether a case such as this should be held to the rational basis standard or the intermediate scrutiny standard), it did address whether Congress had exceeded its power to manage the draft. The Court ruled that the Constitution explicitly gives Congress the power to raise armies, clearly an important objective. Further, Congress is given great deference to legislate in areas of national defense and military affairs, and limiting registration to men only is necessary (according to Congress) to obtain combat-ready troops; Congress does not have to be concerned with equity between the sexes. Men are not discriminated against (by being required to register) because it is reasonable for Congress to conclude that combat-readiness precludes registration of women. In sum, the Court did not view this case as a matter of affirmative action but rather military necessity. In dissent, Justice Thurgood Marshall argued that the question should not be whether Congress had the power to exclude women from the draft but rather whether the Constitution prohibits such gender-based classifications. Critics of the decision viewed the Court's ruling as an act of "benign" sex discrimination. Additionally, denying women a "fundamental civic obligation" of draft registration, as Marshall claimed in his dissent in *Rostker*, has many legal consequences. For example, the Court has allowed men but not women to be required to declare whether they have registered for the draft in order to be eligible for student loans. The Court has also allowed hiring preferences for veterans even though most women are excluded from military duty. Today over 15 percent of active military personnel are women, and thousands of women have volunteered for military duty since World War II.

Schlesinger v. Ballard (1975) involved a Navy lieutenant who had filed suit after his discharge from service; whereas the Navy claimed he was fired because he had been denied promotion a second time, Ballard argued that he would have been promoted if he had been a woman. After thirteen years of commissioned service, a woman service member received a mandatory discharge if she was denied promotion. But male service members were discharged after only nine years of active service. This, said Ballard, was discrimination and violated the Due Process Clause of the Fifth Amendment.

At the federal district court, Ballard was successful. The court held that the military statute was unconstitutional because the thirteen-year tenure provision discriminated in favor of women without sufficient reason. That court issued a temporary restraining order prohibiting Ballard's discharge and directing the Navy to allow Ballard the full thirteen years of commissioned service before discharge. Under the Navy's rules, the secretary of the Navy is required periodically to convene selection boards to consider and recommend for promotion male officers in each of the separate ranks. Recommendations for promotions are based on merit, and the promotions take place as vacancies occur. Because the number of commanders in the Navy is set by

statute, the number of lieutenants who are recommended for promotion in any year depends upon the number of existing vacancies estimated for the coming year.

The Navy's argument for setting a different standard for male and female officers was that fewer officers were needed at each higher rank than the rank below. Only by mandatory attrition of officers, like the policy used in Ballard's case, are promotion positions opened up. If the Navy failed to set a mandatory attrition number, the promotion of younger officers would stagnate and create a disincentive to join the Navy. The Navy's policy of "up or out" was needed to maintain the quality of officers by heightening competition for the high ranks while providing junior officers with an opportunity for promotion. So the policy was not needed merely because of administrative convenience.

The Supreme Court accepted the case for review and reversed the lower court's decision. Under the Due Process Clause of the Fifth Amendment, the Court held, male and female officers could be treated differently since the statute under question was completely rational. There are two specific references to "due process" in the U.S. Constitution. The Fifth Amendment specifies the term but does not promise "equal protection of the law" as does the Fourteenth Amendment. But the Fifth Amendment's Due Process Clause prohibits the federal government from engaging in discrimination that is unjustifiable. The gender distinctions made by the Navy in this policy were, presumably, justifiable. Dissenters on the Court argued that they would have affirmed the lower court's decision since the government had advanced no justifiable interest in making such a gender-based classification.

Women on the U.S. Supreme Court

Sandra Day O'Connor and Ruth Bader Ginsburg are the only two women ever to sit on the U.S. Supreme Court. Although nominated by a conservative president,

Ronald Reagan, O'Connor has voted relatively moderately on abortion and issues involving gender rights. Nominated by a liberal, President Bill Clinton, Ginsburg came to public prominence as an attorney with the American Civil Liberties Union—Women's Rights Project and has consistently voted as one of the most liberal members of the Court.

Both O'Connor and Ginsburg faced gender discrimination in their careers, bringing a new perspective to the justices deciding discrimination cases. Both graduated near the top of their class from prestigious law schools yet had difficulty finding work at the top firms their male counterparts joined. O'Connor was offered a job as a legal secretary after graduation from Stanford Law School, and Ginsburg applied for a clerkship with Supreme Court Justice Felix Frankfurter, only to be told that he was not ready to hire a female at the time.

Women's Suffrage

Following passage of the Fourteenth and Fifteenth Amendments guaranteeing rights of citizenship and the vote to freed male slaves, women's groups rallied to win women the right to vote. The idea was extremely controversial, and the suffragists were routinely criticized by newspapers and even former president Grover Cleveland. But in 1872 Virginia Minor attempted to register to vote in Missouri for the upcoming federal elections. The registrar of voters refused her registration because she was not a male citizen of the United States. Because she was a women and under the laws of coverture could not sue in court, her husband, Francis, had to challenge the law on her behalf. Francis Minor was an attorney and an active member of the National Woman Suffrage Association (NWSA), which had actively pursued women's suffrage for over a decade. Many of the members of that organization saw the courts as a better avenue for legal change than the legislature; they lobbied for the Fourteenth Amendment's guarantee of

"equal protection of the law" as including women's suffrage.

In deciding *Minor v. Happersett*, the Supreme Court held that those who wanted to vote in any election must have registered properly in the state in which they intended to cast their votes. Minor argued that the Fourteenth Amendment established the privileges and immunities of citizenship, presumably for all American citizens. Virginia Minor wished to exercise her citizenship rights by voting in federal elections, and the state of Missouri, by refusing her this citizenship right, was violating her constitutional rights. The Court disagreed. There is no doubt, its decision proclaimed, that women may well be citizens; they are persons, and the Fourteenth Amendment states that "all persons born or naturalized in the United States and subject to the jurisdiction thereof" are expressly declared to be "citizens of the United States and of the State wherein they reside." But women do not need the Fourteenth Amendment to give them this right. Before its adoption, the Constitution did not determine who should be citizens, and yet we accepted the fact that citizenship did exist. There cannot, after all, be a nation without citizens: "Certainly, if the courts can consider any question settled, this is one."

But the Fourteenth Amendment relates only to federal citizenship and not state citizenship. The Court was unable to require that states allow women the right to vote, and at the time, no state granted women suffrage (although women could vote in the territories of Utah and Wyoming). As such, although the Constitution does confer citizenship, the Court said, it does not necessarily confer the right of suffrage. The Court's task was not to decide whether or not this was the correct practice; it was tasked only with determining what the law is, not declaring what it should be. Thus the Court could not decide whether women should be given the right to vote but only decide whether their right to vote is given in the Constitution.

FRANK LESLIE'S
ILLUSTRATED
NEWSPAPER

Entered according to Act of Congress, in the year 1888, by Mrs. FRANK LESLIE, in the Office of the Librarian of Congress at Washington.—Entered at the Post Office, New York, N. Y., as Second-class Matter.

No. 1,732.—Vol. LXVII.]   NEW YORK—FOR THE WEEK ENDING NOVEMBER 24, 1888.   [PRICE, 10 CENTS.

"Woman Suffrage in Wyoming Territory: Scene at the Polls in Cheyenne," published in Frank Leslie's Illustrated Newspaper *on November 24, 1888. (Library of Congress/Alexandria)*

Minor helped spur campaigns to introduce a constitutional amendment granting suffrage rights to women, but women would not be given the right to vote for forty-five more years with passage of the Nineteenth Amendment. But the case does serve two purposes today. First, it demonstrates the "original intent" of the framers of the Fourteenth Amendment, since the Court held that that amendment protected the rights of freed slaves and not women. Second, the decision is still viable precedent today. Although this interpretation of the amendment was largely abandoned in *Reynolds v. Sims* (1964) and *Harper v. Virginia State Board of Elections* (1966), the Court quoted this opinion in 1980 in a case regarding the possible dilution of voting strength of African Americans: "the Constitution of the United States does not confer the right of suffrage upon any one."

By the time the Nineteenth Amendment was passed, the only countries in the world that had already given women suffrage rights were New Zealand, Australia, Finland, Norway, Iceland, Austria, Canada, Germany, and Great Britain. By the end of the 1960s, Afghanistan and a handful of other countries had given women suffrage. It was not until the 1970s that Switzerland and Portugal granted women this right and not until 1994 that South Africa gave black women the right to vote in any election.

References and Further Reading

Baer, Judith A. 1996. *Women in American Law: The Struggle Toward Equality From the New Deal to the Present*. 2d ed. New York: Holmes and Meier.

Cushman, Clare, ed. 2001. *Supreme Court Decisions and Women's Rights: Milestones to Equality*. Congressional Quarterly Press.

Friedman, Lawrence M. 1985. *A History of American Law*. 2nd ed. New York: Simon and Schuster.

Hymowitz, Carol, and Michaele Weissman. 1978. *A History of Women in America*. New York: Bantam Books.

Langley, Winston E., and Vivian C. Fox, eds. 1994. *Women's Rights in the United States*. Westport, CT: Greenwood Press.

Library of Congress, National Woman Suffrage Association Collection 1848–1921 Web site: http://lcweb2.loc.gov/ammem/nawshome.html.

Lunardini, Christine. 1994. *What Every American Should Know About Women's History*. Holbrook, MA: Bob Adams.

National Women's Hall of Fame and the Seneca Falls convention Web site: http://www.greatwomen.org.

Rosen, Ruth. 2001. *The World Split Open: How the Modern Women's Movement Changed America*. New York: Penguin.

Sterling, Dorothy, ed. 1984. *We Are Your Sisters: Black Women in the Nineteenth Century*. New York: W. W. Norton.

Sixty-sixth Congress of the United States of America;

At the First Session,

Begun and held at the City of Washington on Monday, the nineteenth day of May, one thousand nine hundred and nineteen.

JOINT RESOLUTION

Proposing an amendment to the Constitution extending the right of suffrage to women.

Resolved by the Senate and House of Representatives of the United States of America in Congress assembled (two-thirds of each House concurring therein), That the following article is proposed as an amendment to the Constitution, which shall be valid to all intents and purposes as part of the Constitution when ratified by the legislatures of three-fourths of the several States.

" Article —————.

"The right of citizens of the United States to vote shall not be denied or abridged by the United States or by any State on account of sex.

"Congress shall have power to enforce this article by appropriate legislation."

F. H. Gillett

Speaker of the House of Representatives.

Thos. R. Marshall

Vice President of the United States and
President of the Senate.

House Joint Resolution 1 proposing the 19th amendment to the states. (National Archives)

CONSTITUTIONAL EQUALITY

Abzug, Bella (1920–1998)

Born to Russian Jewish immigrants in the Bronx, Bella Savitzky would become a staunch activist for the rights of women and gays and lesbians. She graduated from Hunter College in 1942 and attended Columbia University Law School, where she held the prestigious position of editor of the *Columbia Law Review*. She married Martin Abzug and for the next twenty-three years practiced civil rights and labor law and defended those accused of "anti-American activity" during the McCarthy era. In the 1960s she founded Women Strike for Peace, in 1968 campaigned for Eugene McCarthy, and in 1970 ran for the U.S. House; she became the first Jewish woman elected to Congress. Her aggressive campaigns for the Equal Rights Amendment, abortion rights, child care legislation, an end to the war in Southeast Asia, and an investigation into the competence of FBI director J. Edgar Hoover earned her the nickname "Hurricane Bella."

Abzug introduced a bill to add sexual orientation in 1975 to amend the Civil Rights Act of 1964 to gays and lesbians. By 1995, confined to a wheelchair, she still spoke out against inequalities throughout American society. "Women have been trained to speak softly and carry a lipstick," she said. "Those days are over!" She died in New York City in 1998.

> *Reference* Abzug, Bella S., and Mim Kelber. 1984. *The Gender Gap: Bella Abzug's Guide to Political Power for American Women*. Boston: Houghton Mifflin.

American Civil Liberties Union—Women's Rights Project (ACLU—WRP)

In the early 1960s, the Supreme Court upheld the constitutionality of a jury selection system that excluded women from potential jury pools on the grounds that "women are the center of home and family life." More than a decade later, the American Civil Liberties Union (ACLU) established its Women's Rights Project (WRP) in representing the plaintiff in a case that challenged the automatic preference of men over women as administrators of estates. Congress had already passed several laws barring some forms of sex discrimination (e.g., the Equal Pay Act, Title VII of the Civil Rights Act), but in this case, *Reed v. Reed* (1971), the Court would further define sex discrimination; a classification based on sex, it ruled, was unconstitutional and in violation of the Equal Protection Clause of the Fourteenth Amendment. The case was significant, though, not only because it clarified gender discrimination but also because it was the first case argued before the U.S. Supreme Court by future Supreme Court justice Ruth Bader Ginsburg.

The goal of the WRP was to urge the courts to hold sex discrimination to the same level of constitutional scrutiny as race discrimination, to attack the various forms of sex discrimination that were permitted by law, and to design strategies to overcome practices that effectively denied true equality to women. The WRP remains the principal group responsible for systematic legal reform through the courts in the areas of women's equality and economic rights. Ironically, many of the cases that eventually defined gender discrimination law in the United States involved male litigants. "Women's Rights Project" is a bit of a misnomer, then; "Gender Rights Project" would probably have been a better name.

Although gender discrimination still is not held to the same level of scrutiny required in race discrimination cases, the WRP was finally successful in holding gender discrimination to a heightened level of constitutional scrutiny in the 1976 case of *Craig v. Boren*. In this case the Court established the "heightened scrutiny" standard for measuring the constitutionality of sex-based classifications. The case involved an Oklahoma statute that allowed young women to purchase 3.2 percent beer at age eighteen but required young men to wait until they were twenty-one. The WRP won another victory in 1977 in *Califano v. Goldfarb*, in which the Supreme Court struck down discriminatory Social Security regulations, finding that the "accidental by-product of [legislators'] traditional way of thinking about females" was still unconstitutional. *Goldfarb* concerned regulations that favored male workers by automatically granting survivors' benefits to their widows but granted them to the widowers of female workers only if the husband could prove that they had been financially dependent on their wives.

The WRP has also been involved in enforcing women's statutory rights, predominately concentrating on cases that involve poor women and/or women of color in nontraditional jobs, such as truck driving, skilled trades, and production-line work. More recently, the group has taken up several pregnancy discrimination cases, an issue that (the WRP argues) is the focus of most employment discrimination against women. Its work with pregnancy discrimination culminated in *United Auto Workers v. Johnson Controls* (1991), in which the Court

gave women the right to equal employment opportunity without regard to their childbearing capacity.

See also Bona Fide Occupational Qualification (BFOQ); *Califano v. Goldfarb*; Civil Rights Act; *Craig v. Boren*; Equal Pay Act; Ginsburg, Ruth Bader; Intermediate Scrutiny Standard; *Reed v. Reed*; *United Auto Workers v. Johnson Controls*; *Weinberger v. Wiesenfeld*.
Reference American Civil Liberties Union Web site: www.aclu.org.

Boxer, Barbara (1940–)

Born in Brooklyn, Barbara Boxer graduated from Brooklyn College in 1962 with a degree in economics. She worked as a stockbroker and a journalist before she was elected by California to the U.S. Senate in 1993 after ten years in the U.S. House. She is best known for her advocacy of women's rights and the environment but has also advocated for human rights, election reform, and health care reform. She gained national media attention in 1991 when she sought to derail the Supreme Court nomination of Clarence Thomas after sexual harassment allegations arose. She is also known for publicizing government corruption; in 1984 she exposed the Air Force purchase of a $7,622 coffeemaker.

Boxer is probably one of the most outspoken senators. In 1996 she was one of only fourteen senators to oppose the Defense of Marriage Act, which allows states to withhold marital rights from new residents who relocate from a state where same-sex marriage is recognized. (Congress eventually passed the act.) She also wrote the Employment Non-Discrimination Act, which, had it passed, would have prohibited job discrimination on the basis of sexual orientation. Boxer was critical of President Bill Clinton's "don't ask, don't tell" policy for homosexual military members, pointing out that Congress failed to pass antiheterosexual laws when a minority of heterosexual males engaged in sexual misconduct in the Navy's Tailhook scandal in 1991.

Although she is sometimes named as a potential presidential candidate, she would face serious obstacles in her candidacy; she is not only a woman but also Jewish and tied closely to Bill and Hillary Clinton.

Califano, Secretary of Health, Education, and Welfare v. Goldfarb (1977)

In *Goldfarb* the Supreme Court ruled that Social Security provisions amounted to unconstitutional sex discrimination. The provisions allowed male workers to leave survivors' benefits to their widowed spouses but allowed female workers to leave benefits to their husbands only when they could prove their husbands were financially dependent on them. This eligibility provision presumed that in two-parent families fathers were responsible for the support of their families. Goldfarb, a widower who had been denied the widower's benefit because of the support requirement, challenged the sex-based distinction in the act.

Goldfarb had to show that he provided less than a quarter of his family's income in order to get widower's benefits. He argued that his wife had paid Social Security taxes at the same rate as male workers, yet he was not subject to the same economic benefits as he would be if he were a woman. The Supreme Court agreed that the sex-based distinction violated the Equal Protection Clause of the Fourteenth Amendment, since the efforts of female workers who were required to pay Social Security taxes produced less protection for their spouses than did the efforts of men. The Court held that the gender classification was not related to the attainment of any important and/or valid goal but rather was part of the "baggage of sexual stereotypes." The dissent in *Goldfarb* disagreed. Four justices argued that the challenged classification was justified because of administrative convenience and did not promote economic discrimination on the basis of sex.

But in previous cases the Court had ruled similarly. In *Weinberger v. Wiesenfeld* (1975), for example, the Court had overruled presumptions that the father had the "primary responsibility to provide a home [for his family] and its essentials." It was not only men who supported families and women who took care of the children; in many cases the reverse was true. In *Weinberger* the Social Security provision in question allowed a widow, after her husband died, a government payment or subsidy to enable her to stay home and care for the children rather than to find a paying job. But if a female worker died, the provision did not entitle her widower this same benefit. The Social Security Act simply assumed that widowers would not wish to stay home. But the Court ruled, as it had in *Goldfarb,* that this provision is unconstitutional and said that it was based on outdated sexual stereotypes.

See also Califano v. Webster; Fourteenth Amendment; Kahn v. Shevin; Orr v. Orr; Weinberger v. Wiesenfeld.

Califano v. Webster (1977)

In *Webster* the Court unanimously upheld a Social Security Act provision that, in computing a wage earner's "average monthly wage," allowed women to exclude three more lower-earning years than men. This would result in a slightly higher "average monthly wage" and correspondingly higher monthly old-age benefits for the retired female wage earner than for a man of the same age and with the same earnings record. Under the Social Security Act (which was amended in 1972), the formula for computing benefits was altered so that the previous distinction between men and women was eliminated, however, it pertained only to men reaching the age of sixty-two before 1975 or later. Robert Lee Webster had turned sixty-two prior to 1975 and was dissatisfied with the amount of the benefits he was to receive. After pursuing administrative remedies, the ACLU-WRP challenged the law on his behalf, arguing that the distinction in benefits violated the Equal Protection Clause of the Fourteenth Amendment.

But the Supreme Court disagreed. The law did not violate equal protection, it said, because the more favorable treatment of female wage earners was not the result of archaic stereotypes about gender. Rather, the law served the permissible purpose of redressing society's longstanding disparate treatment of women, which barred most women from all but the lowest-paying jobs in society. Further, there was verifiable and objective proof that it operated directly to compensate women for past economic discrimination. In a concurring opinion, Chief Justice Warren Burger and Justices Potter Stewart, Harry Blackmun, and William Rehnquist also disagreed with Webster but for a different reason; the challenged classification, they said, was rationally justifiable on the basis of administrative convenience.

The Court's opinion set out little new ground because it relied mainly on recent decisions it had handed down. But it reclarified that any classifications by gender had to serve important governmental objectives and had to be substantially related to the achievement of those objectives, as the Court had previously held in *Craig v. Boren* (1976). In *Califano v. Goldfarb* (1977), the Court had ruled that redressing society's longstanding disparate treatment of women was a worthy goal and not necessarily the by-product "of a traditional way of thinking about females."

> *See also* American Civil Liberties Union— Women's Rights Project (ACLU—WRP); *Califano v. Goldfarb; Craig v. Boren;* Fourteenth Amendment; *Kahn v. Shevin; Orr v. Orr; Weinberger v. Wiesenfeld.*

Chisholm, Shirley (1924–)

Shirley Anita St. Hill was born in Brooklyn, graduated from Brooklyn College in 1946, and received an M.A. from Columbia in 1952. After working as a nursery school teacher and director of a child care center until the early 1960s, she was elected to the New York legislature. In 1968 she became the first woman of color elected to the U.S. Congress. She became known as an outspoken critic of gender discrimination policies: "Tremendous amounts of talent are being lost to our society just because that talent wears a skirt," she said.

Immediately after her election, she joined fifteen other representatives in introducing a bill to end the draft. She advocated for better day care, fought for inclusion of domestics in minimum-wage legislation, and sponsored the Adequate Income Act (1971) that guaranteed a minimum income to all Americans. In 1971 she campaigned for the Democratic presidential nomination and faced some surprising resistance from black men who opposed her candidacy because, they argued, the first black president should be a man. Her response was, "Of my two 'handicaps,' being female put more obstacles in my path than being black"; she was undeterred by their lack of support, but only one African American woman since has sought the presidential nomination: Carol Moseley-Braun.

Chisholm retired from Congress in 1982 and was elected chair of the National Political Congress of Black Women in 1984. President Clinton nominated her to serve as ambassador to Jamaica.

> *Reference* Nancy Hicks. 1971. *The Honorable Shirley Chisholm, Congresswoman from Brooklyn.* New York: Lion's Books.

Clinton, Hillary Rodham (1947–)

Born in Chicago, Hillary Rodham graduated from Wellesley College in 1969 and Yale Law School in 1973. She was extraordinarily successful at Yale, serving on the board of editors of the *Yale Law Review* and the group Social Action and interning with children's advocate Marian Wright Edelman. Shortly after graduation, she married classmate William Jefferson Clinton, and they moved to Arkansas. She joined the faculty of the University of Arkansas Law School in 1975 and the Rose Law Firm in

U.S. Senators (left to right) Hillary Rodham Clinton, D-NY, Elizabeth Dole, R-NC, and Kay Bailey Hutchison, R-TX gather for a photo of newly elected women members of the 108th Congress, January 9, 2003, on Capitol Hill. (Reuters NewMedia, Inc./Corbis)

1976. By 1978 her husband became governor of the state, and Hillary Rodham Clinton worked in education and children's initiatives as the first lady of Arkansas for the next twelve years. Their daughter, Chelsea, was born in 1980.

When her husband became president of the United States, Clinton became one of the most public first ladies in history. She chaired the national task force on health care reform, led several initiatives on women's and children's issues, and played a leading role in the passage of the Family and Medical Leave Act. Critics were harsh; she had created a new role for the first lady yet seemed to be immersing herself in the most unpopular issues of the day. She wrote a weekly newspaper column called "Talking It Over," which focused on her experiences as first lady and her observations of women, children, and families she had met around the world. In 1996 she published *It*

Takes a Village and Other Lessons Children Teach Us, which became a best-seller and earned Clinton a Grammy Award for her audio version of the book.

She again made history in November 2000 when she became the first lady ever to be elected as a U.S. senator; she won as a Democrat from the state of New York. There, she has served on the Senate Committees for Environment and Public Work (her subcommittee assignments are Clean Air, Wetlands, Private Property, and Nuclear Safety; Fisheries, Wildlife, and Water; Superfund, Waste Control, and Risk Assessment); Health, Education, Labor, and Pensions (her subcommittee assignments are Aging and Public Health); and the Armed Services Committee (her subcommittee assignments are Airland, Emerging Threats and Capabilities, and Readiness and Management Support). She supported the 2002 Farm Bill as well as legislation intended to rebuild schools. Following the terrorist attacks of September 11, 2001, she secured $21.4 billion in funding for cleanup and recovery of her state. She continues to travel across the world much as she did as first lady; she regularly meets with leaders of foreign nations to discuss democracy, religious tolerance, and human rights and is known as a public advocate for issues that affect women's access to education, economic opportunity, and family planning.

In 2003 a CNN poll indicated that registered Democrats supported her potential bid for the presidency. Although she has indicated that she will not be a candidate for the White House in 2004, some believe she has the best chance of being the first woman to land that position, not only because of her name recognition but also because of her success in fundraising. For her Senate race, for example, she managed to raise more than $31 million. And her main contributors are different from those of other Democrats; whereas most Democrats find support from labor unions and the industries that make up the economic base of their home states, Clinton raised a good portion of her money from individuals, suggesting that a presidential run may allow her to capitalize on her celebrity to raise even more money. She is considered one of the best contenders for the 2008 presidential race.

Craig v. Boren (1976)

In this landmark gender discrimination case, the Supreme Court established the legal principle that such cases deserve a heightened level of scrutiny. Although gender discrimination cases did not receive the highest level of scrutiny afforded to race-based claims, gender cases were given an intermediate level. This was an improvement from the past; until Craig, gender discrimination cases received the lowest level of scrutiny by the courts.

Craig v. Boren involved two brothers who had challenged an Oklahoma law that restricted men from purchasing 3.2 percent beer until they were twenty-one years of age, whereas women could buy the beer at the age of eighteen. The case was ridiculed by the press at the time, but the issues were more substantive than they seem. In essence, establishing differences in age limits between the genders institutionalized sex stereotypes that had no place in the law. Ruth Bader Ginsburg, then a young professor at Columbia University School of Law and now a Supreme Court justice, offered an amicus curiae brief (a "friend of the court" brief) for the young brothers. In it, she argued that the discrimination suffered by the brothers in this case revealed traditional "attitudes and prejudices about the expected behavior and roles of the two sexes in our society, part of the myriad signals and messages that daily underscore the notion of men as society's active members, women as men's quiescent companions, members of the 'other' or second sex." The state of Oklahoma, in contrast, argued that young men were more likely to be involved in alcohol-related driving offenses; they offered proof that .18 percent of females compared to 2 percent of males from eighteen to twenty years old had been arrested for drunk driving offenses.

Although a lower court declared the Oklahoma law constitutional, the Supreme Court reversed that finding. Any classifications by gender, it held, must serve important governmental objectives and must be substantially related to achievement of those objectives. The state law in question constituted a denial of equal protection of the law to males between the ages of eighteen and twenty. That is, distinguishing between males and females in this situation was not shown to be substantially related to the achievement of the legitimate governmental objective of enhancing traffic safety, since the statistical surveys offered did not demonstrate a substantial difference between the sexes. Administrative ease and stereotypes did not justify gender-based laws that ultimately discriminated against a person on the basis of sex. Further, and more fundamental, the Court held that any laws with gender-based classifications would in the future be examined under a heightened, intermediate level of scrutiny.

> *See also* American Civil Liberties Union—Women's Rights Project (ACLU—WRP); Fourteenth Amendment; *Frontiero v. Richardson; Geduldig v. Aiello;* Ginsburg, Ruth Bader; Intermediate Scrutiny Standard; *Reed v. Reed.*

Dole, Elizabeth (1936–)

Born in North Carolina, Elizabeth Dole graduated from Duke University in 1958 and Harvard Law School in 1965. She also holds a master's degree in education and government from Harvard.

She has been an active public servant. From 1969 to 1973, she served as deputy assistant of consumer affairs for the administration of Richard Nixon; she was a member of the Federal Trade Commission from 1973 until 1979; and she was an assistant to President Ronald Reagan for two years before joining his cabinet as secretary of transportation in 1983, the first woman to hold that position. She became secretary of labor in 1989, then president of the American Red Cross in 1991, a position she held until seeking the Republican presidential nomination in 1999.

Dole left the race before the primaries. Part of her problem was money, but she was also dogged by criticism that she had never held elected office but simply supported her husband, former senator Robert Dole, through his successful Senate bids and one unsuccessful presidential bid. But in 2000 she was elected to the U.S. Senate from her home state of North Carolina. Her campaign was extremely successful, and she received much public attention from the socially conservative wing of her party; in public appearances she told audiences that religious faith was the center of her life, and she called on supporters to act as her "prayer warriors." Whatever advantage that may gain

Dole in her home state, it is unlikely to give her the national backing she would need to win the presidential bid. Specifically, her positions on abortion (which she opposes) and religion in schools (she advocates posting the Ten Commandments in all public schools) would draw little support from the well-educated, politically active women voters she needs to attract.

Equal Rights Amendment (ERA)

The Equal Rights Amendment was intended to bar sex-based classifications by the state and federal government. Despite its approval by the requisite two-thirds vote of both houses of Congress, it was never fully ratified by the states and therefore never became an amendment to the Constitution. The amendment read: "Equality of rights under the law shall not be abridged by the United States nor by any State on account of sex." Supporters of the ERA, such as the National Organization for Women (NOW), argued that a constitutional amendment banning gender discrimination was a more swift, economical, and thorough means to enforce gender equality than other alternatives (such as statutes).

The ERA would have banned the use of any sex-based classifications in law except in rare and readily identifiable situations involving physical characteristics unique to one sex or privacy rights that are independently protected by the Constitution. Had it been passed by the states, the ERA would have used a standard of review for gender-based discrimination cases even more stringent than the strict scrutiny test developed by the Court for race-based classifications. The ERA would also have brought major changes to the structure of government programs and agencies as well as major changes to the structure of criminal and family law. Finally, it would have eliminated protective labor laws that had proliferated from the early years of the twentieth century.

After passage by Congress, the amendment received much early support: thirty states ratified it within one year of its Senate approval. Hawaii was the first to ratify it, followed by Delaware, Nebraska, and New Hampshire the next day. But ratification was compromised when in 1973 the Supreme Court handed down its controversial decision in *Roe v. Wade*. After *Roe* legalized abortion, ratification of the ERA became linked politically with the more radical arms of the women's movement, garnering heated debate among conservatives and provoking more public controversy than ever before. Largely as a result, the ERA ultimately failed to achieve ratification by the required thirty-eight states, even though the deadline for ratification was extended to 1982. It was three states short when the deadline expired.

Originally written by Alice Paul, a suffragist leader, the ERA has been introduced into every session of Congress since 1921. As late as 1976, support for its passage was included in the platforms of both major political parties, although it remains controversial. Proponents argue that the ERA provides guarantees that women will be treated fairly by the government and given the same rights as men. Opponents argue that it will cause a parade of horribles, including legalized rape and prostitution, sexually integrated public restrooms, and the sharing of dorm rooms by single men and women in public colleges.

Such fears have not materialized in the several states that have incorporated into their own constitutions amendments expressly prohibiting discrimination on the basis of sex. Ironically, for many of the states with ERAs (e.g., Washington, Pennsylvania, and Massachusetts), any statute that discriminates on the basis of sex is subject to strict scrutiny, yet laws are rarely declared not discriminatory. In states with no Equal Rights Amendment, women are often protected against sex discrimination by being regarded as "citizens" and "persons" in gender-neutral terms and statutes are given a similar, heightened level of scrutiny that

eradicates discriminatory laws. Supporters of a national ERA continue to point out that under the federal Constitution (and most state constitutions), women do not yet have the same level of constitutional protection enjoyed by men.

In the original ratification process, the ERA was three states short of the thirty-eight states needed to formally ratify the amendment. But in March 2001, Representatives Carolyn Maloney (D-NY) and Stephen Horn (R-CA) and Senator Edward Kennedy (D-MA) reintroduced the ERA, and by 2002 another bill sponsored by Representative Robert Andrews (D-NJ) was proposed. This bill allowed the ERA to be ratified if three previously unratified states agreed to the ratification. Several interest groups are currently seeking support to finally ratify the ERA and Congress is currently holding hearings on the issue. Passage of this amendment would ensure that women have equal rights in virtually every realm of public life, including public education, the criminal justice system, and government benefits.

See also Feminism; Fourteenth Amendment; Friedan, Betty; *Frontiero v. Richardson*; Intermediate Scrutiny Standard; National Organization for Women (NOW); Right to Privacy; *Roe v. Wade*.
Reference Steven M. Buechler. 1990. *Women's Movements in the United States: Woman Suffrage, Equal Rights, and Beyond.* New Brunswick, NJ: Rutgers University Press.

Feinstein, Dianne (1933–)

Born in California, Feinstein graduated from Stanford University in 1955 with a degree in history. In 1960 she was appointed to the women's parole board and by 1969 had won her first election to the San Francisco County Board of Supervisors, where she served two terms as president.

In 1978 following the assassination of Mayor George Moscone, she became mayor of San Francisco and in 1979 won election to that post in her own right; she served four terms as San Francisco's first female mayor and won widespread public acclaim for her management of the city. In 1984 she was first mentioned as a contender for a presidential ticket when candidate Walter Mondale considered her as a running mate; he decided against her when questions surfaced about her husband's business dealings.

In 1992 Feinstein was elected to the Senate, finishing out Pete Wilson's term after he resigned to become governor, and in 1994 she was elected to serve her first full term; she won again in 2000. She is not only extremely popular in her home state but also well known nationally; she was the first woman to serve on the Senate Judiciary Committee, is the ranking member of the Technology and Terrorism Subcommittee, and serves on the Senate Appropriations Committee. She has introduced legislation to create a comprehensive national plan for combating cancer; her bill calls for the modernization of treatments to combat the deadly disease.

Although a liberal Democrat, she distanced herself from the administration of Bill Clinton by voting against the North American Free Trade Agreement (NAFTA) and the Clinton health care plan in 1994. In 2002 her office indicated that she was exploring a 2004 bid for the presidency. Many commentators argue that she is the most viable woman presidential candidate (or possibly a vice-presidential candidate on the 2004 ticket). She brings the enormous number of California's electoral votes to any presidential election, assuming she would maintain her popularity in a national election. Yet she faces the same problem other women candidates face: raising enough money to enter into the presidential fray; her 2000 Senate campaign raised less than $10 million. Additionally, by 2004, she will be seventy-one years old and may have to deal with doubts about her health and age.

Fourteenth Amendment

Directly following the Civil War, three amendments were passed that severely constrained state power: the Thirteenth prohib-
ited slavery, the Fifteenth protected the right to vote, and the Fourteenth protected due process and equal protection of the laws. Although women were active in attempting to have gender explicitly included in the protections afforded freed slaves in these amendments, they were unsuccessful. One clause in particular in the Fourteenth Amendment gave women hope that they would be given the same citizenship as black Americans, as well as the same benefits such citizenship would provide: "All persons born or naturalized in the United States are citizens of the United States and of the state wherein they reside." Early on, however, the Court decided that although women were indeed citizens of the national government, citizenship rights did not include the right to vote or practice a profession. Instead, it was legal for states to restrict women in various endeavors.

But women's rights would expand with another clause in this amendment. Equal protection of the law, or the Equal Protection Clause, reads: "Nor shall any state . . . deny to any person within its jurisdiction the equal protection of the law." Today, interpretations of the Fifth Amendment and various state constitutional provisions also guarantee equal protection of the law, but women have used the Fourteenth Amendment to push many issues through the courts. Since 1971 the Supreme Court has extensively applied this clause in challenges to sex-based laws and government practices.

The limitation to this clause is that the amendment, and therefore equal protection of the law, addresses the conduct only of state and federal government. Private parties (e.g., individuals, groups, corporations) cannot violate it and are presumably free to violate it. In race discrimination cases "government conduct" has been interpreted widely and now encompasses the actions of public schools and universities as well as various governmental entities. But definitions of the word "equality" in gender discrimination cases have not been so broad.

The Supreme Court has ruled that the word "equality" does not require that people of different genders be treated in the same way. Instead, in gender discrimination cases, the Fourteenth Amendment has been interpreted to mean that women be placed in more equal positions, as well as that like cases be treated alike. There are instances, then, in which women can be treated differently from their male counterparts, unlike race cases, in which people of different races must be treated the same.

In determining how to examine whether laws are not equal in race and gender discrimination cases, the Supreme Court has formulated three standards of review. These contrasting equal protection standards now used in discrimination cases range on a continuum from lenient to stern; the most lenient is the "rational basis standard," and at the stern end is the "strict scrutiny standard." The vast majority of laws are reviewed under the lenient, rational basis standard and are rarely declared discriminatory. Essentially, courts will presume the validity of a state statute if there is any rational basis for it; this test requires that the purpose of a law must be constitutionally legitimate and the means selected to achieve this purpose must be rationally related to accomplishing this end. Only when a law is suspected of discriminating against a traditionally disadvantaged group (e.g., race) is the strict scrutiny standard used. A law subject to the strict scrutiny test must serve a compelling government interest, and the specific provisions of the statute must be "strictly tailored" to the achievement of the compelling purpose, with no less invasive means available. Very rarely are laws *not* declared discriminatory when this standard is used.

Since the 1950s, women have attempted to persuade the courts that gender discrimination is analogous to race discrimination and should be held to the same strict scrutiny standard. The Supreme Court has consistently relegated sex discrimination to the lower rational basis standard. But by the 1970s the Court became much more critical in gender discrimination cases of both the importance of a discriminatory law's purpose and the means by which the statute proposed to accomplish this purpose. In 1976 (*Craig v. Boren*) the Court articulated an "intermediate" level of review for sex-based discrimination claims; sex-based laws must now meet a higher standard than rational basis but a lower standard than strict scrutiny. In this intermediate category the law must be substantially related to the achievement of an important governmental objective. Equal protection challenges focus only on whether a benefit or a burden is imposed equally on both men and women; the courts do not address the content of the law, that is, that the law does not treat equally men and women who are similarly situated.

> *See also Craig v. Boren*; Feminism; *Frontiero v. Richardson; Geduldig v. Aiello*; Ginsburg, Ruth Bader; Intermediate Scrutiny Standard; *Reed v. Reed*.
> *Reference* Nancy E. McGlen and Karen O'Connor. 1983. *Women Rights*. New York: Praeger; David M. O'Brien. 1997. *Constitutional Law and Politics: Civil Rights and Liberties*. 3d ed. New York: W.W. Norton.

Friedan, Betty (1921–)

Betty Friedan is known as the catalyst and arguably the most prominent leader in the second feminist movement. Born in Peoria, Illinois, she graduated from Smith College, immediately married, became the mother of three children, and worked as a freelance magazine author. In 1957, after attending her fifteenth college reunion, she sent questionnaires to members of her class asking them to describe their lives and feelings of happiness with their families and career choices since college. Her book *The Feminine Mystique*, published in 1963, was largely the result of the survey and further research; it became an international best-seller and made her an international celebrity. Her ideas, called revolutionary, ushered in the

Betty Friedan (Library of Congress)

second feminist movement and articulated to millions of wives and mothers the "problem that has no name."

The book's thesis was that suburban, middle-class housewives were not necessarily fulfilled by their lives as homemakers with children. She called this "the feminine mystique" and criticized society (e.g., psychiatrists, social scientists, and educators) for encouraging women to live segregated lives in "suburban ghettos." Friedan (along with various other feminists later) criticized the social convention that women play the role of primary caretaker of the family—the belief that women could achieve fulfillment only through work inside the home. The book struck a resounding chord with well-educated, bored housewives and mothers who were no longer happy with their lives. They wanted to expand their world to work outside the home, and Friedan articulated this need. Many feminists today point to her

book as a partial reason women flooded into the workplace in the late 1960s and 1970s.

In 1966 Friedan helped found the National Organization for Women (NOW) and wrote its founding statement demanding full equality for women in America. She also helped lead the organization in its support of the Equal Rights Amendment and abortion rights. Upon leaving the presidency in 1969, she called for a national strike in 1970 to commemorate the fiftieth anniversary of the Nineteenth Amendment that gave women the right to vote. The success of the rallies promoting such a national strike was impressive; 50,000 women attended the New York rally alone.

By the 1980s Friedan was advocating her belief that both women and men desire the prestige and fulfillment that come from work outside the home but also want the love and identity gained through marriage and children. In 1981 her book *The Second Stage* argued that feminism had polarized the sexes and urged feminists to join with men and even conservatives on new issues influencing the family and work outside the home.

> *See also* Equal Rights Amendment (ERA); Feminism; National Organization for Women (NOW).
> *Reference* Betty Friedan. 2001. *The Feminine Mystique.* New York: W.W. Norton.

Frontiero v. Richardson (1973)

The case of *Frontiero v. Richardson* involved a servicewoman whose request for an increase in her housing allowance as well as medical and dental benefits for her husband (who was her dependent), was turned down. The U.S. military rule at the time was that servicemen could automatically include their wives as dependents but that servicewomen had to prove that their husbands were dependent on them for at least one-half of their financial support before being classified as dependents. Frontiero sued, claiming sex discrimination had occurred because a serviceman could claim his wife as a dependent without regard to whether she was financially dependent on him, whereas a servicewoman could not do the same for her husband.

The Supreme Court agreed with her and made more stringent the "mere rationality" standard for use in gender discrimination cases that had previously been established in *Reed v. Reed* (1971). "Traditionally," Justice William Brennan said in his concurring opinion, "[sex] discrimination was rationalized by an attitude of romantic paternalism which, in practical effect, put women not on a pedestal, but in a cage."

See also *Craig v. Boren;* Fourteenth Amendment; *Reed v. Reed.*

Geduldig v. Aiello (1974)

In *Geduldig v. Aiello,* the Court ruled that states are free to distinguish between pregnancy and other temporary physical disabilities. For almost thirty years, California had offered state employees a disability insurance system that paid benefits to persons in private employment who were temporarily unable to work because of a disability not covered by workmen's compensation. Yet the disability insurance system excluded disabilities that "accompani[ed] normal pregnancy and childbirth." Such disability insurance was funded entirely through deductions from workers' wages. Carolyn Aiello and Elizabeth Johnson had suffered ectopic and tubal pregnancies, Augustina Armendariz suffered a miscarriage, and Jacqueline Jaramillo experienced a normal pregnancy; all claimed pregnancy was the sole cause of their disabilities. The women challenged the constitutionality of the California program that defined "disability" yet excluded coverage for pregnancy-related disabilities. They argued that since only women could become pregnant, the program sexually discriminated against women.

The lower federal court found that "the exclusion of pregnancy-related disabilities is not based upon a classification having a rational and substantial relationship to a legitimate state purpose" and ruled the exclusion unconstitutional. On appeal, the Supreme Court was asked to answer the following question: Was the California disability insurance program invidiously discriminating (under the Equal Protection Clause of the Fourteenth Amendment) against women by not paying insurance benefits for a disability that accompanies normal pregnancy and childbirth? The Court, of course, ruled that it was not invidious discrimination.

The majority ruled that the program did not exclude anyone from eligibility of this benefit because of gender but merely removed "one physical condition—pregnancy—from the list of compensable disabilities." Although it may be true, the Court held, that only women can become pregnant, not every classification concerning pregnancy is a sex-based classification that is discriminatory. That is, benefit programs that categorize on the basis of pregnant employees would involve only women, of course. But because they also categorize on the basis of nonpregnant employees (who would be both men and women), they are not discriminating on the basis of gender. Thus lawmakers are free to include or exclude pregnancy from coverage of benefits.

Furthermore, for discrimination claims arising under a state employment medical program like this one (which excluded pregnancy), the rational basis test can be used; and presumably the Court would continue to find the state program rationally served a legitimate state purpose. A disability program is an economic "benefit" rather than a state-imposed "burden" on the fundamental right of a woman to be pregnant. The dissenters, William Brennan, William Douglas, and Thurgood Marshall, in contrast, argued that a pregnancy exclusion was based on physical characteristics inextricably linked to one gender and thus constituted sex discrimination.

See also *California Federal Savings and Loan Association v. Guerra;* Family and Medical Leave Act (FMLA); Fourteenth Amendment; *Frontiero v. Richardson; General Electric v. Gilbert;* Intermediate Scrutiny Standard; Maternity Leave; *Reed v. Reed; United Auto Workers v. Johnson Controls.*

Ruth Bader Ginsburg (U.S. Supreme Court)

Ginsburg, Ruth Bader (1933–)

Appointed in 1993 as the 107th justice of the U.S. Supreme Court, Ruth Bader Ginsburg is only the second woman to serve on that bench. Although she has been involved in many areas of the law, before her confirmation she was best known for her groundbreaking legal work in the area of women's rights in the 1970s. Born in Brooklyn, New York, she graduated Phi Beta Kappa from Cornell in 1954 and married her classmate Martin Ginsburg that same year. In 1956, with a fourteen-month-old daughter, Ginsburg entered Harvard University Law School as one of only nine women in the freshman law class of 400. She did exceptionally well.

She moved to New York one year short of her graduation to allow her husband to accept a job offer and finished her last year of law school at Columbia Law School in 1959. She was the first person ever to make law review at both Harvard and Columbia, two of the country's most prestigious law schools. Despite her successes, however, she was denied a job at every firm she applied to. She was finally hired as a law clerk by a U.S. district court judge, represented litigants for the ACLU, later became a professor of law at Rutgers University Law School, and then moved to a professorship at Columbia Law School.

The ACLU—Women's Rights Project had existed for some time, but not until the 1970s did the number of sex discrimination cases increase to such an extent that the organization needed a legal director. Ginsburg became that director in 1970 and immediately brought several high-profile cases to the Supreme Court. Probably the most impor-

tant case during her seven-year tenure at the ACLU was *Reed v. Reed* (1971), a challenge to an Idaho law that gave automatic preference to fathers in designating executors of estates. For the first time in history, Ginsburg asked the Court to declare gender a suspect class that warranted the same heightened level of scrutiny given to race discrimination claims. The Court denied this request but did declare the Idaho law unconstitutional. As she recalled at her confirmation hearings: "Race discrimination was immediately perceived as evil, odious, and intolerable. But the response I got when I talked about sex-based discrimination was 'What are you talking about? Women are treated ever so much better than men.' I was talking to an audience that thought . . . I was somehow critical about the way they treated their wives . . . [and] daughters." During her tenure at the ACLU, Ginsburg promoted the view that sex stereotyping unfairly limited not only women's opportunities but also society generally.

Ginsburg argued five other key sex discrimination cases before the Court, including *Frontiero v. Richardson* (1973), which not only gave sex heightened scrutiny in equal protection cases but also overturned stereotypes of men and women service members. She was also successful in *Weinberger v. Wiesenfeld* (1975), which equalized Social Security benefits for widows and widowers alike.

Ginsburg did not exclusively represent women in these cases; in fact, a large number of her clients were men asking for equal treatment of the law. And it also is interesting to note that although she has been a champion of women's rights in the courts, Ginsburg has criticized what is arguably the most important case for women's rights in this century, *Roe v. Wade* (1973). That case, Ginsburg has said, should have been challenged on equal protection grounds, not privacy grounds. With that case based on a fundamental right to privacy (a word not present in the Constitution), the debate over abortion has focused on an implied right instead of an explicit one. A woman's right to an abortion would still be constitutional, she has argued, but the political debate would be different.

After her tenure at the ACLU, in 1980 Ginsburg was appointed by President Jimmy Carter to the U.S. Courts of Appeals for the District of Columbia Circuit, a position she held for thirteen years. Calling her the "Thurgood Marshall of gender equality law," President Bill Clinton nominated her to the Supreme Court in 1993 to replace retiring justice Byron White. Clinton's nomination met with skepticism from feminists largely because of Ginsburg's reservations about *Roe v. Wade*. Yet that stance probably helped her Senate confirmation by making her seem like more of a political moderate rather than the ardent feminist she proved to be once on the bench. She was confirmed by a nearly unanimous vote and has been one of the most liberal justices currently sitting on the Court.

See also American Civil Liberties Union—Women's Rights Project (ACLU—WRP); *Califano v. Goldfarb; Frontiero v. Richardson; Griswold v. Connecticut; Reed v. Reed;* Right to Privacy; *Weinberger v. Wiesenfeld;* Women in the Legal Profession.
Reference Clare Cushman, Ruth Bader Ginsburg, and Talbot D'Alemberte, eds. 2002. *Supreme Court Decisions and Women's Rights: Milestones to Equality.* Washington, DC: Congressional Quarterly Press.

Guinier, Lani (1950–)

Born in New York City, Lani Guinier graduated from Radcliffe College (1971) and Yale Law School (1974). Following her graduation from law school, she headed the voting rights project of the National Association for the Advancement of Colored People (NAACP) and served in the Civil Rights Division of the Department of Justice under President Jimmy Carter. She rose to national prominence, however, following her nomination by President Bill Clinton to head the Civil Rights Division in 1993. She would have been the first black woman to hold the post. Clinton withdrew her nomination, however, after controversy arose over her views on democracy. But her book about the incident (*Lift Every Voice: Turning a Civil Rights Setback into a New Vision of Social Justice*) was published to wide acclaim. Guinier went on to become the first tenured black woman at Harvard Law School (in 1998).

Most of Guinier's scholarship focuses on democratic theory, political representation, educational equality, and race and gender issues. One of her most popular publications was the book *Becoming Gentlemen: Women, Law School and Institutional Change* (1995), in which she described how male and female students came to law school with virtually identical credentials yet women did not graduate with comparable grades to men, did not have comparable experiences during law school, and did not find comparable jobs following graduation. Her analysis indicated that male students (and their male professors) interacted differently than female students and were judged (by their male professors) more favorably.

See also Women in the Legal Profession.
Reference Lani Guinier. 2003. *Lift Every Voice: Turning a Civil Rights Setback into a New Vision of Social Justice.* New York: Simon and Schuster.

Hutchison, Kay Bailey (1943–)

Born in Galveston, Texas, Kay Bailey Hutchison graduated from the University of Texas Law School in 1967. Unable to find a job in the legal field, she worked as a political and legal correspondent for a Houston television station. But in the early 1970s she was elected to the Texas House of Representatives. She entered the national scene in 1976 when she became vice-chair of the National Transportation Safety Board, a post she held until 1979. In 1990 she was elected Texas state treasurer and in 1993 was elected to the U.S. Senate as the first women to represent Texas in that office. In 2000 she won reelection with the largest number of votes ever recorded in Texas, and in 2001 she became vice-chair of the Senate Republican Conference, making her one of the top five leaders of Senate Republicans and, of course, the only woman among them.

Hutchison has served as chair of the Military Construction Subcommittee, a member of the Defense Subcommittee of the Senate Appropriations Committee, and a member of the Veterans' Affairs Committee (advocating recognition of Gulf War syndrome). She is currently chair of the Surface Transportation and Merchant Marine Subcommittee, setting policies on Amtrak and ports and railroad shipping issues. She has been relatively active in women's issues as well, introducing the marriage penalty tax relief bill (signed into law in 2001) and the homemaker IRA legislation, which significantly expanded retirement opportunities for stay-at-home spouses. She also authored the first federal antistalking statute, which made stalking across state lines a federal crime.

As a potential presidential contender, Hutchison would face enormous criticism from feminist groups. Although she is pro-choice, she has also opposed taxpayer funding for abortions, the Freedom of Choice Act that would wipe out state parental consent laws, and she supports the partial-birth abortion ban. In her 2000 re-election bid, she was able to raise only approximately $6 million.

Intermediate Scrutiny Standard

In legal challenges to the Fourteenth Amendment, the Court has treated claims based on race differently than claims based on gender. In *Craig v. Boren* (1976), the Court specified that the Fourteenth Amendment claims for sex discrimination be subjected to a more stringent review than is provided by the rational basis test. In determining whether a gender-based law is discriminatory, the Court will hold the law up for "intermediate" scrutiny. That is, a law is allowed to distinguish on the basis of gender if it is substantially related to the achievement of an important government objective. Usually, laws that classify on the basis of gender, alienage, and illegitimacy are examined in light of intermediate scrutiny.

Laws that classify on the basis of race are not necessarily unconstitutional; motive or discriminatory purpose must be shown. But the standard is much stricter for laws distinguishing on the basis of race than for laws classifying on the basis of gender, and race-based laws are rarely upheld. Indeed, these laws are allowed only if they are necessary to achieve a compelling governmental objective. So it is far easier for laws that categorize on the basis of gender to pass constitutional muster.

The Supreme Court, however, has not been in complete agreement as to the appropriate method of review in all gender cases. In the first state case decided in this area, a California law provided that only males could be held criminally liable for statutory rape ("an act of sexual intercourse accomplished with a female not the wife of the perpetrator where the female is under the age of 18 years"). The state claimed that the law was needed to prevent illegitimate births, the harmful consequences of such falling on the young females; thus the law acted as a deterrent to males from engaging in sex at such a young age. When it took up the case, *Michael M. v. Superior Court of Sonoma County* (1981), the Supreme Court held that a criminal sanction imposed solely on males served to "equalize the deterrents on the sexes" so did not constitute sexual stereotyping by which men needed special "solicitude of the courts." The Court held similarly in a male-only draft registration case that equal protection did not require subjecting women to draft registration because women are not situated similarly to men. Further, Congress has been given great deference in areas of national defense; the purpose of excluding women was not to discriminate against men but rather to focus on the military need of combat-ready troops.

One principle that is generally agreed upon, however, is that gender-neutral statutes that have an unintended disparate impact against one sex are subject solely to the rational basis test. The only way to establish discrimination in such cases is to demonstrate a discriminatory purpose on the part of the state legislature.

An example of a gender-neutral statute that has unintended consequences for women can be found in *Geduldig v. Aiello* (1974). In that case, the Court held that California's state employees disability insurance system could refuse to cover disabilities that accompanied normal pregnancy. The litigants had argued that since only women could become pregnant, the program discriminated against women only. The Court, however, held that it was not the purpose of the state to discriminate against women, but rather women were simply not covered under the disability system for pregnancy-related disabilities; in other words, the lack of coverage for pregnancy-

related difficulties had the unintended consequence of just impacting women.

In 1981 the Court was joined by the first woman justice, Sandra Day O'Connor. Shortly thereafter the Court faced another male discrimination claim, *Mississippi University for Women v. Hogan* (1982). This case involved a state policy that restricted enrollment in one state-supported nursing school to females; in an opinion written by O'Connor, the Court noted that when the purpose of a statute was to "exclude or protect members of one gender because they are presumed to suffer from an inherent handicap or to be innately inferior, the objective itself is illegitimate." She even suggested that sex should in the future be treated as a suspect classification.

> *See also* Craig v. Boren; Fourteenth Amendment; *Geduldig v. Aiello*; Ginsburg, Ruth Bader; *Mississippi University for Women v. Hogan*; United States v. Virginia.
> *References* Lee Epstein and Thomas G. Walker. 2003. *Constitutional Law for a Changing America: Institutional Powers and Constraints*. 4th ed. Washington, DC: Congressional Quarterly Press; O'Brien, David M. 1997. *Constitutional Law and Politics: Civil Rights and Liberties*. 3d ed. New York: W.W. Norton.

Ireland, Patricia (1945–)

Patricia Ireland graduated from the University of Tennessee in 1966. After she became a flight attendant, she sued her employer, Pan American World Airways, for sex discrimination regarding her health insurance coverage: her husband was not covered on her dental policy whereas wives of employees were automatically covered. With the help of the local chapter of NOW, she won her suit. Ireland immediately enrolled in law school, volunteered at NOW, and later worked to promote Florida's ratification of the ERA as an officer of the Florida NOW chapter. In 1983 she was elected to chair NOW's lesbian rights task force in Florida; although she was low-key about her private affairs, she admitted companionship with a woman while staying married to her second husband. In 1987 she won the vice-presidency of NOW and in 1991 became NOW's ninth president.

As president of NOW, she managed to increase membership in the organization, particularly during the 1991 Senate confirmation hearings of Supreme Court nominee Clarence Thomas that brought up his alleged sexual harassment of Anita Hill. In 1992 she helped organize a pro-choice demonstration in Washington, D.C., that was attended by nearly 1 million people. But possibly her biggest victory was in 1998 in a series of class-action lawsuits against several antiabortion groups, including the largest and most militant, Operation Rescue. A jury unanimously found Operation Rescue guilty of racketeering, but the Supreme Court overturned this verdict in March, 2003.

See also National Organization for Women (NOW).

Reference National Organization for Women Web site: http://www.now.org.

Jordan, Barbara (1936–1996)

Born in Houston, Texas, into a poor preacher's family, Barbara Jordan became the first black woman to be elected as a Texas state senator and the first black woman to be elected to Congress from the South (in 1972); the *Washington Post* described her as "the first black woman everything." She graduated from Texas Southern University, then received her law degree in 1959 from Boston University.

She was considered a likely candidate for the White House and became known as a pragmatic politician; she raised money for Democratic candidates yet advocated strict measures to limit illegal immigration. She rose to national prominence after her public summation as she prepared to vote for articles of impeachment against President Richard Nixon: "'We the people'—it is a very eloquent beginning. But when the Constitution of the United States was com-

pleted on the 17th of September in 1787, I was not included in that 'We the people.' I felt for many years that somehow George Washington and Alexander Hamilton just left me out by mistake. But through the process of amendment, interpretation and court decision, I have finally been included in 'We the people.'" Because of the power of her words, she was invited as the keynote speaker at the 1976 Democratic National Convention, becoming the first black woman to make a keynote address to the national convention of a political party. She also spoke at the Democratic convention in 1992.

In 1976 she was on presidential candidate Jimmy Carter's list of fourteen potential running mates. But she was offended by any notion of using her as a symbol of diversity and later rejected Carter's nomination of her as U.S. ambassador to the United Nations. She was extremely successful during her tenure in Congress, expanding the Voting Rights Act to bring under its protection those who did not speak English.

In the late 1970s, she left Congress and public life to teach at the University of Texas Lyndon B. Johnson School of Public Affairs. President Bill Clinton awarded Jordan the Presidential Medal of Freedom in 1994. She died in 1996.

References National Women's Hall of Fame Web site: http://www.greatwomen.org; Rogers, Mary Beth. 2000. *Barbara Jordan: American Hero.* New York: Bantam Doubleday.

Kahn v. Shevin (1974)

In *Kahn v. Shevin* the Court first defined "benign" sex classifications as remedial measures to correct economic imbalances between the sexes. The Court held, however, that it would insist on considerable proof that the benign classification was rooted in the actual purpose of a law. *Kahn v. Shevin* concerned a Florida statute that granted widows but not widowers an annual $500 property-tax exemption; a widower had sued to be allowed the exemption. The Supreme Court ruled that the classification was overty sex based but was valid because it had a substantial relation to the object of the legislation, which was the reduction of the disparity between the economic capabilities of men and women. That is, the Court readily accepted the state's compensatory rationale that the law helped to cushion the financial impact of spousal loss upon the sex for which that loss imposes the disproportionately heavier burden. In such cases, the Court will give only minimal scrutiny to the law.

> *See also* Craig v. Boren; Intermediate Scrutiny Standard; *Weinberger v. Wiesenfeld*.

Kennedy, Florynce (1916–2000)

Florynce Kennedy was born in Kansas City. Following her high school graduation in 1934, she worked various jobs before moving to New York City and enrolling at Columbia University. She graduated with top honors in 1948 but was originally denied admission to Columbia Law School because she was African American. The school finally admitted her after being threatened with a lawsuit for blatant race discrimination. She graduated in 1951 and worked as a law clerk before opening her own law firm in 1954.

By the early 1960s Kennedy was politically active, eventually joining with other women to found the National Organization for Women and the Media Workshop dedicated to fighting gender and race discrimination. She later became active in the antiwar movement and the more radical wing of the women's movement; she was among the bra burners at Atlantic City's Miss America Pageant in 1967. She formed the Feminist Party in 1971 supporting Shirley Chisholm for president and the National Black Feminist Organization in 1975. She died in San Francisco at the age of eighty-four.

> *See also* National Organization for Women (NOW).
> *Reference* National Organization for Women Web site: http://www.now.org

Florynce Kennedy (Bettman/Corbis)

League of Women Voters

The League of Women Voters was founded in 1920 by Carrie Chapman Catt directly following passage of the Nineteenth Amendment that granted women suffrage rights. The league was organized to encourage women to use their new voting power to shape public policy in issues that were of direct interest to women and their families. It was Catt's vision to form "a union of all intelligent forces within the state" to attack "illiteracy, social evils, and industrial ills."

Originally, the league provided citizens with well-researched and politically unbiased information to help them make policy decisions for their communities and nation. That is still its mission today, and the league is generally seen as an unbiased organization, allowing it to play an influential role in shaping public policy. Since 1999, however, the league has focused much of its attention on enhancing voter participation, although it continues to act as a grassroots activist organization.

In the first few decades of its existence, the league tended to concentrate on such issues as support for college bargaining, child labor laws, minimum-wage laws, a joint federal and state employment service, compulsory primary and secondary education, maternity leave, and equal opportunities for women in government industry. Only by enacting such policies, the organization believed, would women gain independence. Most of the policies passed into law in the league's early years remain in effect today.

In the 1930s the league shifted strategy somewhat and began a campaign for global disarmament and implementation of the Kellogg-Briand Pact, which renounced war as an instrument of national policy. It also entered into a campaign to stamp out government corruption and political patronage in federal and state government jobs. By the 1940s legislation was finally passed removing hundreds of federal jobs from the spoils system and enacting the merit system for selection of government employees.

Also during this time, the league began its foray into environmental concerns, taking on the issues of water and air pollution, water and waste management, land use, and energy policy. Through grassroots mobilization and citizen education, the group backed legislation requesting the development of the Tennessee River basin as the site of a publicly owned power facility. The massive citizen education effort was accomplished by forums and conferences nationwide, lectures at universities, and even a debate in Washington, D.C., on the use of hydroelectric power. Also during this time the league confronted problems of public transportation, environmental violations by power plants, solid waste disposal, disposal of hazardous substances, and ways to encourage conservation. Its grassroots network has worked ceaselessly for effective implementation of the Clean Air and Clean Water Acts.

In the 1950s and 1960s, the league again reshaped its focus to uphold civil rights and liberties. The organization studied poverty and discrimination, looking in particular at unemployment and inequalities in public education. By the 1960s it became more international, urging the United States to normalize its relations with the People's Republic of China by ending its opposition to China's membership in the United Nations.

The league views "equal rights for all regardless of sex" to be fundamental and necessary in its long-term support for equal opportunity in education, employment, and housing. It therefore overwhelmingly supported ratification of the Equal Rights Amendment. When the ERA failed passage, the league channeled its energies into reproductive choice in the 1980s. In the 1990s it began an international campaign to guide the civic education of women in emerging democracies. These educational grants gave women the training needed to understand coalition building, networking, and effective participation in the democratic political process. Also during the 1990s the league began one of its broadest-based grassroots campaigns, to encourage the electorate to involve itself in the political system. The 1992 election saw the first rise in voter participation in twenty years, continuing the league's tradition of fostering greater participation in a democratic environment.

See also Catt, Carrie Chapman; Equal Rights
    Amendment (ERA); Nineteenth
    Amendment.
Reference League of Women Voters Web site:
    www.lwv.org/where.

Michael M. v. Superior Court of Sonoma County (1981)

In *Michael M.* the Supreme Court decided that California's statutory rape law did not violate the Equal Protection Clause of the Fourteenth Amendment because it made only men criminally liable for sexual intercourse with an underage female. A state may attack the problem of teenage pregnancy directly, the Court ruled, by prohibiting a male from having sexual intercourse with a minor female.

Under California's penal code, unlawful sexual intercourse is defined as "an act of sexual intercourse accomplished with a female not the wife of the perpetrator, where the female is under the age of 18 years." In 1978 Michael M. was charged with having unlawful consensual sexual intercourse with a sixteen-year-old female when he was seventeen years old. The young woman was intoxicated at the time of the incident. Michael M. asserted at trial that the penal code discriminated against him because only males could be held criminally liable for such a sexual act. The high court in California upheld the penal law, holding it to the strictest scrutiny (the law could only be justified by a compelling state interest). The court found that the classification was "supported not by mere social convention but by the immutable physiological fact that it is the female exclusively who can become pregnant." Thus, that court held, the state had a compelling interest in preventing teenage pregnancies and because males alone could "physiologically cause the result which the law properly seeks to avoid," the gender classification was justified as a means of identifying offender and victim.

The U.S. Supreme Court had held in prior rulings (Reed v. Reed [1971] and Weinberger v. Wiesenfeld [1975]) that gender-based classifications were not "inherently suspect." Instead, that Court had used an intermediate level of scrutiny when evaluating the constitutionality of gender-based discrimination claims. Specifically, the traditional minimum rationality test took on a somewhat "sharper focus" when gender-based classifications were challenged. That meant that the California legislature could criminalize acts of illicit sexual intercourse between men and minor females if it was doing so to prevent illegitimate teenage pregnancies. Preventing illegitimate teenage pregnancies was a strong interest and reason for passing such legislation.

"At the risk of stating the obvious," the Court held, "teenage pregnancies, which have increased dramatically over the last two decades, have significant social, medical and economic consequences for both the mother and her child, and the State. Of particular concern to the State is that approximately half of all teenage pregnancies end in abortion. And of those children who are born, their illegitimacy makes them likely candidates to become wards of the State." Chief Justice William Rehnquist, who wrote the majority opinion of the Court, argued that the justices "need not be medical doctors to discern that young men and young women are not similarly situated with respect to the problems and risks of sexual intercourse. Only women may become pregnant and they suffer disproportionately the profound physical, emotional, and psychological consequences of sexual activity." Further, California's law protects women from sexual intercourse at an age when those consequences are particularly severe.

Because virtually all of the significant consequences of teenage pregnancy fall on the female, it is reasonable for a legislature acting to protect minor females to exclude them from punishment. Moreover, the opinion held, the risk of pregnancy itself constitutes a substantial deterrence to young females in engaging in illicit sexual intercourse. No similar natural sanctions deter males. A criminal sanction imposed solely on males serves roughly to "equalize" the deterrents on the sexes. Further, if states were required to pass gender-neutral statutes of this kind, a female would surely be less likely to report violations if she herself would be subject to criminal prosecution. The Court also disagreed with Michael M.'s claim that the statute was unconstitutional because he, too, was under the age of eighteen at the time of the sexual incident and that the male was unfairly presumed the culpable aggressor even when both parties were underage. The statute does not assume that the male is always the aggressor, the Court ruled, but rather is an attempt by a legislature to prevent illegitimate teenage pregnancy by providing an additional deterrent for men. The age of the man is irrelevant since young men are as capable as older men of inflicting the harm the state hoped to prevent.

Dissenters from the Court's opinion argued that the only question they should answer was whether the admittedly gender-based classification in the law bore a significant relationship to the state's goal of preventing teenage pregnancies. Using the precedent of *Craig v. Boren* (1976), Justice William Brennan argued the state law was unconstitutional, but he said that preventing teenage pregnancy as a stated goal of the state was not as important as whether the sex-based discrimination in the law was substantially related to the achievement of that goal. A gender-neutral law was no more difficult to enforce than a gender-specific law; in fact, thirty-seven states had already enacted gender-neutral statutory rape laws. Although most of those laws protect young persons (of either sex) from the sexual exploitation of older individuals, the laws of Arizona, Florida, and Illinois permit prosecution of both minor females and minor males for engaging in mutual sexual conduct with minors. Obviously, these states found it possible to enforce such laws. Further, a gender-neutral statutory rape law was potentially a greater deterrent to sexual activity than a gender-specific law; if both men and women were subject to criminal sanctions, twice as many people would be subject to punishment for illicit sexual activity.

The greatest criticism the dissenters leveled at the majority was that the purpose of the law itself was flawed. That is, the law was initially enacted on the premise that young women, in contrast to young men, were deemed legally incapable of consenting to an act of sexual intercourse. Because their chastity was considered particularly valuable, young women were felt to be uniquely in need of the state's protection in protecting their "honor." In contrast, young men were assumed to be capable of making such decisions for themselves, yet the law did not offer them any special protection.

The general message of the Court in *Michael M.* was that governments were permitted to enact gender-specific statutes as long as they could show that the statutory objective was legitimate and the classification was necessary because of an identifiable physical difference between the sexes. In explaining why California was allowed to punish a male but not a female for engaging in sexual intercourse with another person who was under that age of eighteen, Justice Rehnquist said, "Only women may become pregnant" and "males alone can 'physiologically cause [that] result.'"

> **See also** *Craig v. Boren;* Date and Acquaintance Rape; Intermediate Scrutiny Standard; *Reed v. Reed;* Separate Spheres Doctrine; Statutory Rape; *Weinberger v. Weisenfeld.*

Miller v. Albright (1998)

Lorena Penero Miller challenged a federal law that allowed children born of American mothers to gain U.S. citizenship automatically but if born of American fathers to have to prove paternity. Miller was born in the Philippines and declared "illegitimate" in city records there, which gave no father's name. Her father, Charlie Miller, was a U.S. citizen who had served a military tour in the Philippines at the time of Lorena's conception. There was no evidence that he ever returned to the Philippines after completing his tour of duty, and he never married Lorena's mother.

In November 1991 Lorena applied for U.S. citizenship, and her father filed supporting documents to establish his relationship with Lorena. Although a lower court entered a "voluntary paternity decree" that found Charlie to be Lorena's "biological and legal father," she was still denied citizenship. The reason the court gave was that the

Immigration and Nationality Act (INA) provided that children born abroad and out of wedlock to citizen fathers and alien mothers had to obtain "formal" proof of paternity by age eighteen in order to acquire U.S. citizenship by right of birth. Children born out of wedlock to citizen mothers had no such requirement; their citizenship was automatic. Lorena and her father sued, alleging that the INA's different treatment of citizen fathers and mothers was a gender classification that violated fathers' right to equal protection of the law.

The Supreme Court declared that the requirement that fathers had to take an affirmative step to establish paternity, which mothers were free from, did not violate the Constitution. It was a valid governmental interest to distinguish on the basis of gender. It was not a statutory distinction that was either arbitrary or invidious. The Court recognized that mothers and fathers should be deemed to have an equal emotional and legal connection to their children but ruled against such fathers. Dissenting justices criticized the finding of the Court, arguing it was based on impermissible stereotypes of women's innate "special connection" to their children.

See also Fourteenth Amendment.

Mink, Patsy (1928–2002)

All four of Patsy Mink's grandparents emigrated from Japan in the 1800s to work as laborers on sugar plantations in Hawaii. A child during Pearl Harbor, Mink dealt with the discrimination against Japanese Americans so prevalent during World War II. She graduated from the University of Hawaii and applied to medical school in 1948; none of the twenty schools she applied to accepted women. She instead earned a law degree in 1951 from the University of Chicago, where she was accepted because she was a "foreign student," even though Hawaii was a U.S. territory at the time. Mink became the first Asian American woman to practice law in Hawaii and was elected to the state legis-

lature in 1956, right before Hawaii became the fiftieth state (in 1959). She was elected to the U.S. Congress in 1965 and served six terms.

Mink became known for her role in enacting Title IX of the education amendments, which prohibits gender discrimination in educational institutions and paved the way for so many women to obtain a college education by providing them with scholarships that had previously been awarded exclusively to male students. She made an unsuccessful attempt at an open U.S. Senate seat, resting on her record as a promoter of equal opportunity (specifically with regard to women's rights), better child care, education, and environmental issues. She died in 2002.

Reference Sue Davidson and Jeannette Rankin. 1994. *A Heart in Politics: Jeannette Rankin and Patsy T. Mink (Women Who Dared)*. Seattle, WA: Seal Press.

Mississippi University for Women v. Hogan (1982)

In *Mississippi University for Women v. Hogan*, the Supreme Court held that the policy of a state-supported university that excluded males from enrolling in its professional nursing school violated the Equal Protection Clause of the Fourteenth Amendment. In 1884 the Mississippi legislature created the Mississippi Industrial Institute and College for the Education of White Girls of the State of Mississippi and limited its enrollment to women. The charter of the school declared that

The purpose and aim of the Mississippi State College for Women is the moral and intellectual advancement of the girls of the state by the maintenance of a first-class institution for their education in the arts and sciences, for their training in normal school methods and kindergarten, for their instruction in bookkeeping, photography, stenography, telegraphy, and typewriting, and in designing, drawing, engraving, and painting, and their industrial application, and for their instruction in fancy, general and practical needlework, and in such other industrial branches as experience, from time to time, shall suggest as necessary or proper to fit them for the practical affairs of life.

The school had instituted a nursing program in 1971. Men were allowed to audit classes but not to take classes for credit; the school believed that it was not in the best interests of the female students to have males in their midst.

Joe Hogan was a registered nurse but did not hold a degree in nursing. With a baccalaureate degree, Hogan would be able to earn a higher salary and would be eligible to obtain specialized training as an anesthetist. He applied for admission to the Mississippi University for Women and although he was otherwise qualified was not admitted because of his gender. There were nursing programs in other coeducational institutions in the area, but Hogan would have had to commute a long distance to attend. He challenged the school's policy, arguing that it violated the Equal Protection Clause of the Fourteenth Amendment. A lower federal court concluded that the university's policy as a single-sex school was rationally related to the state's interest in providing a range of educational opportunities for the female student population; further, that court held that the admissions policy was not arbitrary because providing single-sex schools is consistent with the respected, though by no means universally accepted, educational theory that single-sex education affords unique benefits to students. Further, Congress had enacted Title IX of the education amendments of 1972 and expressly authorized universities such as this one to continue its single-sex admissions policy by exempting from the discrimination prohibition of the act public undergraduate institutions that have traditionally had single-sex admissions policies. Thus Congress had limited the abilities of plaintiffs like Hogan to use the Equal Protection Clause for discrimination cases.

In her first opinion for the Court, Sandra Day O'Connor wrote the opinion that disagreed with the lower court's finding. The Court applied the intermediate scrutiny standard established in *Craig v. Boren* (1976) in judging the "important interest" the state had in compensating for previous discrimination against women. The Court held that in cases such as this one, states seeking to use a classification that distinguishes individuals on the basis of their gender must show an "exceedingly persuasive justification" for the classification. The burden is met only by demonstrating at least that the classification serves "important governmental objectives and that the discriminatory means employed" are "substantially related to the achievement of those objectives." The single-sex admissions policy of the school could not be justified on the grounds that it compensated for discrimination against women and therefore constituted a type of educational affirmative action. A state could justify such a distinction only if members of the gender benefiting from the policy (e.g., women) actually suffer a disadvantage related to the classification. And clearly this was not the case. For one thing, this policy would not encourage women's entry into a profession that had previously been denied to them, since women already made up 98 percent of all nurses in the country. Excluding males merely served to "perpetuate the stereotyped view of nursing as an exclusively woman's job." Further, the state policy did not "substantially further" the alleged objective of compensating for past discrimination since men were already allowed to audit classes there.

Finally, the state had even failed to show that the gender-based classification was necessary: since the school already permitted men to attend classes as auditors, it was obvious the school did not believe that women were adversely affected by the presence of men in the classroom. As to the intentions of Congress, Title IX did not limit the range of the Equal Protection Clause. Rather, Title IX simply sets out the limitations upon that statute and not the Constitution. Thus the school's policy of excluding men from its program of nursing was a violation of the Equal Protection Clause.

This case established the principle that an "exceedingly persuasive justification" must be shown for any sex-based classification in a single-sex school. Later cases involving the entry of women into male-only institutions would not reach the courts until the late 1990s.

> *See also* Faulkner, Shannon; Fourteenth
> Amendment; Title IX; *United States v.*
> *Virginia*; *Williams v. McNair*.

Morgan, Robin (1941–)

A poet, journalist, political theorist, and radical feminist activist of the 1960s, Robin Morgan is best known as the editor of *Ms.* magazine from 1990 to 1994. She, along with Gloria Steinem, founded the feminist publication in 1972. She also founded the Sisterhood Is Global Institute, an international women's think tank that compiles data on the plight of women across the globe. In 1990 she was awarded the Feminist Majority Foundation Woman of the Year award. In 2001 she was credited with organizing the partnership between *Ms.* and the Feminist Majority. Her publications include *Sisterhood Is Powerful* (1970), *Sisterhood Is Global* (1984), and *Sisterhood Is Forever* (2003).

> *See also* National Organization for Women
> (NOW).
> *Reference* National Organization for Women
> Web site: http://www.now.org

Moseley-Braun, Carol (1947–)

Born to a Chicago policeman and his wife, Carol Moseley-Braun received an undergraduate degree from the University of Illinois at Chicago and a law degree from the University of Chicago. Directly following her graduation from law school, she began working as an assistant U.S. attorney, a post she held for three years. In 1978 she was elected to the Illinois legislature as the only women of color; a charismatic speaker, she almost immediately became assistant majority leader. She was popular among her colleagues and the public alike.

After years of involvement in education reform, she won acclaim from parents and statewide attention in 1985 for sponsoring the Urban School Improvement Act, which created parents' councils in Chicago public schools. She also became known as a protector of the less fortunate, sponsoring a bill, for example, that allowed public assistance recipients to attend college without losing their benefits. She was also actively involved in antidiscrimination initiatives, including a bill that barred the state of Illinois from investing in South Africa during apartheid.

In 1987 Moseley-Braun was elected Cook County recorder of deeds, making her the first black female executive in Cook County, Illinois. She gained notoriety by cutting the budget and modernizing the role of the office. But it was in 1992 that she gained national prominence. That year she became the second African American elected to the U.S. Senate, and she won her race even though her opponent outspent her 20 to 1. She later became the first woman to serve on the Senate Finance Committee and also served on the Judiciary Committee; the Banking, Housing, and Urban Affairs Committee; the Small Business Committee; and the bipartisan Commission on Entitlements and Tax Reforms. Her policies were not completely without controversy; for example, she campaigned vehemently against a Confederate flag patent. When she left the Senate in 1998, she became ambassador to New Zealand. In late 2003 she announced her run for the Democratic Party presidential nomination in 2004.

President Ellie Smeal raises her fist in the air during her opening speech at a 1986 National Organization for Women rally on the state capitol steps in Denver. (Bettmann/Corbis)

See also Women as Lawmakers.

Reference University of Maryland Women's Studies Web site: http://www.mith2.umd.edu/WomensStudies/GovernmentPolitics/WomeninCongress/Biographies/Senate/moseley-braun-carol.

National Organization for Women (NOW)

The National Organization for Women (NOW), the largest feminist organization in the United States, has the following objectives: to increase educational, political, and employment opportunities for women; to secure abortion and reproductive rights for women; to end all violence against women;

and to abolish discrimination based on sex, race, and sexual orientation. Founded in 1966 by several women (including Betty Friedan), began as a group of educated, middle-class, predominately white women whose goal was to bring "women into full participation in the mainstream of American society[,] exercising all privileges and responsibilities thereof in truly equal partnership with men." NOW largely ushered in the second feminist movement of the United States.

The organization's members consist mainly of politically moderate professionals. NOW has patterned itself after the National Association for the Advancement of

Colored People (NAACP), adopting a legal approach in bringing cases to the courts in order to change existing laws that discriminate against women—a much less expensive way to change laws than lobbying state and federal legislatures. NOW has been extremely active in enforcing Title VII of the Civil Rights Act of 1964 and has lobbied against laws that prohibit the employment of women in certain occupations, sex-segregated advertising (newspaper employment advertisements that showed preference for one sex, thus excluding women from some higher-paying jobs), abortion rights, and equal rights for lesbians and gay men. It has also been very active in the ERA movement and other grassroots organizing.

NOW has become less focused on issues it began with, such as child care and the feminization of poverty, turning its attention instead to more controversial, less mainstream problems, such as equal benefits for gay and lesbian partners. It is still, however, active in electoral politics, legislation, and lobbying and has been a pivotal force in the women's movement, pushing for increased political, employment, and education opportunities for women, equal pay, the acceptance of two-career families, and the use of "Ms." as a salutation. NOW has more than 550 chapters throughout the fifty states and in the District of Columbia.

> *See also* Civil Rights Act; Equal Pay Act;
> Equal Rights Amendment (ERA);
> Feminism; Friedan, Betty; Ireland,
> Patricia; National American Woman
> Suffrage Association (NAWSA); *Roe v.
> Wade.*
> *Reference* National Organization for Women
> Web site: http://www.now.org.

New York v. Santorelli and Schloss (1992)

Five women were arrested for removing their blouses in a public park in Rochester, New York. All five agreed that they did not intend to be lewd or annoy other park patrons. Two of the women, Ramona San-

torelli and Mary Lou Schloss, later sued the state, claiming the penal law under which they were charged offended the Equal Protection Clause of the Fourteenth Amendment. They argued that the statute discriminated against women because it defined "private or intimate parts" of a woman's body but not a man's. The women had been prosecuted, they argued, for doing something that would have been permissible, or at least not punishable, if they had been men. The law under question in this case specified that a person was guilty of "exposure" when she appeared "in a public place in such a manner that the private or intimate parts of his [or her] body were unclothed or exposed."

Because the statute specified that "the private or intimate parts of a female person shall include that portion of the breast which is below the top of the areola," the statute triggered scrutiny by the court for its gender-based classification. At trial the state had the burden of proving that the gender classification was substantially related to the achievement of an important state objective, since the statute demonstrated that the state assumed that the sight of a female's uncovered breasts in a public place is offensive to the average person in a way that the sight of a male's uncovered breasts is not.

The state was able to defend the statute only by arguing that the explicit purpose of the law was to protect parents and children who use the public beaches and parks "from the discomfort caused by unwelcome pubic nudity." The implicit purpose of the law was to prevent nude sunbathing. Prurient interest was aroused in society by viewing the female breast and not the male breast, the state said; although many communities in the world do not link naked female breasts to prurient thoughts, New York was not one of those communities. The state was unable, however, to provide evidence to demonstrate that exposure of the female breast was harmful to the public's health or well-being.

When the penal code under question was enacted, it was aimed "at discouraging 'topless' waitresses and their promoters." The Supreme Court pointed to several prior state cases in which courts held that a woman on a street wearing a fishnet, transparent blouse did not violate the statute because the statute was not intended to be "applied to the noncommercial, perhaps accidental, and certainly not lewd, exposure." The Court thus held that the state had not succeeded in proving there was an important governmental interest obtained in this gender classification and, further, that the law was not applicable to the conduct of the two women in this case. All the state had done was to demonstrate that law that classifies exposure on the basis of gender violates the Fourteenth Amendment.

See also Fourteenth Amendment; Intermediate Scrutiny Standard.

Norton, Eleanor Holmes (1937–)

Eleanor Holmes Norton received an undergraduate degree from Antioch College in Ohio and then simultaneously earned a law degree and a master's degree in American studies from Yale University. Norton has worked as an attorney for the American Civil Liberties Union (1965–1970) and for New York City's Human Rights Commission (1970–1977) and was named by President Jimmy Carter as the first woman to chair the federal Equal Employment Opportunity Commission (1977–1983). During her tenure at the EEOC, she issued the first set of federal guidelines on sexual harassment. These guidelines specified that sexual activity as a condition of employment or promotion was a violation of Title VII, and the creation of a hostile or offensive working environment would be considered such a violation. These guidelines urged corporations and other business to educate their employees of federal regulations.

She has been a board member of three Fortune 500 companies, taught at Georgetown University Law School, and is cur-

rently one of the most powerful women in Washington, D.C. Since 1991 Norton has been the District of Columbia's elected, nonvoting delegate to the U.S. Congress. During her time in Congress, she has served as the Democratic chair of the women's caucus.

In the 1990s Norton became known for her management of Washington during the city's most serious financial crises in a century; she gained recognition as well for her success in pushing for a two-day debate and the first vote on D.C. statehood.

> *Reference* Joan Lester. 2002. *Eleanor Holmes Norton: Fire in My Soul.* New York: Atria Books.

O'Connor, Sandra Day (1930–)

Born on a remote ranch in El Paso, Texas, Sandra Day O'Connor graduated third in her class from Stanford Law School in 1952 and immediately married. She was unable to find employment as a lawyer at the law firms she applied to because she was a woman; she received only one job offer, as a legal secretary. (The classmate who graduated first in her class, William Rehnquist, later to become chief justice of the U.S. Supreme Court, was hired as a law clerk by Supreme Court justice Robert Jackson.)

O'Connor later became a county attorney in California and then followed her husband to Germany (he was in the Army) and worked as a civilian lawyer for the U.S. government. While raising her three children, she was a full-time mother and active volunteer, particularly for the Republican Party. She became assistant state attorney general in 1965 and later an interim replacement for a state senator from Arizona who resigned. She won reelection to that senate seat twice and was elected majority leader in 1972, becoming the first woman to hold such an office in the United States. She voted as a moderate Republican, supporting the Equal Rights Amendment (which was a moderate to liberal position) but also backing Nixon's campaign for the presidency (which was very conservative). This moderate stance helped her appointment (by a Democratic governor) to the state court of appeals in 1979.

In 1981 newly elected president Ronald Reagan nominated her to fill a seat vacated by Justice Potter Stewart on the Supreme Court. During his presidential campaign, he had promised women's groups that he would appoint a woman to the Supreme Court. The Senate unanimously confirmed her in a vote of 100–0. Although she was called a conservative, she is probably best known for one of the most liberal decisions of her career: she voted with the liberals of the Court in ruling that Mississippi could not exclude men from its school of nursing. She also called for a heightened scrutiny standard for gender discrimination claims arising from the Fourteenth Amendment.

More recently, she has become known for her swing votes in abortion decisions. She has criticized the trimester approach for pregnancy defined in *Roe* (1973) yet has not explicitly voted to overrule it—she has actively upheld state regulations that are not "unduly burdensome" to the woman wishing to get an abortion. In 1988 she was diagnosed with breast cancer but was back on the bench within ten days of surgery, missing an oral argument. In 2000 she was soundly criticized for voting with the majority in *Bush v. Gore,* the pivotal case that decided the 2000 presidential race; all Republican appointees voted in the majority, and all Democratic appointees to the Court dissented. Shortly after the decision, several comments attributed to her or her advisers became public and controversial. First, several people close to her indicated her wish to retire from the bench and her relief that a Republican had won the election and was therefore able to replace her. Second, she commented at a state bar lunch in Minnesota that she was having "second thoughts" on whether the death penalty could be fairly administered. This outraged supporters of the death penalty, who have been able to count on O'Connor in the death

Sandra Day O'Connor (Library of Congress)

penalty cases that made it to the Supreme Court.

> ***See also*** Ginsburg, Ruth Bader; *Planned Parenthood of Southeastern Pennsylvania v. Casey;* Women in the Legal Profession.
> ***References*** O'Connor, Sandra Day, and Craig Joyce. 2002. *The Majesty of the Law: Reflections of a Supreme Court Justice.* New York: Random House; O'Connor, Sandra Day, and H. Alan Day. 2002. *Lazy B: Growing Up on a Cattle Ranch in the American Southwest.* New York: Random House.

Paul, Alice (1885–1977)

Born 1885 in Moorestown, New Jersey, Paul received her M.A. and Ph.D. from the University of Pennsylvania and was known as an ardent feminist and social reformer. She was active in getting the Nineteenth Amendment passed, giving women the right to vote.

Paul became publicly known as a militant feminist in 1906 when she and her colleagues protested on the streets of England and she

Alice Paul (Library of Congress)

was arrested three times there for "suffragist agitation." When she returned to the United States in 1909, she helped form the Congressional Union for Woman Suffrage in 1913, which later merged with the Woman's Party to form the National Woman's Party in 1917. Their militant protests involved picketing the White House to protest a government that promised democracy while denying half its citizens the right to vote. During the 1920s and 1930s, she focused her energies on international women's rights and, in 1928, helped found the World Party for Equal Rights for Women.

Paul also fought for the failed Equal Rights Amendment that was originally introduced into Congress in 1923. She worked on the amendment until her death in 1977.

See also Feminism; Fourteenth Amendment; Nineteenth Amendment.
Reference Kristi Andersen. 1996. *After Suffrage: Women in Partisan and Electoral Politics before the New Deal.* Chicago:

University of Chicago Press; Amy E. Butler. 2002. *Two Paths to Equality: Alice Paul and Ethel M. Smith in the ERA Debate, 1921–1929.* New York: State University of New York Press.

Pelosi, Nancy (1940–)

Born in Baltimore, Nancy Pelosi graduated from Trinity College in 1962. She began her political career volunteering for the Democratic Party, serving as the chair of the California Democratic Party and the 1984 Democratic National Convention Host Committee.

In 1987 she was first elected to the U.S. House to fill a seat created by the death of Sala Burton of California. She later served for a year as House Democratic whip. Pelosi gained widespread national exposure in 2002, when she was elected Democratic leader of the U.S. House of Representatives, making her the highest-ranking woman in the history of the U.S. Congress and the first woman to lead a major political party.

Pelosi has been extremely active in supporting or sponsoring legislation to ensure the government's assistance in the AIDS crisis. As a representative for the San Francisco Castro District, she has been involved in several pieces of legislation supporting gay rights. She is pro-choice and has voted against display of the Ten Commandments in public schools and has sponsored legislation to provide housing for low-income communities. Though hailed by many as a serious contender for the White House in the 2002 election, she managed to raise just $1 million in campaign funds.

Reference Congressional Caucus for Women's Issues Web site: www.house.gov/Pelosi/womcauc.htm

Personnel Administration of Massachusetts v. Feeny (1979)

In *Feeny* the Supreme Court examined whether sex discrimination can occur when gender-neutral terms are used in a law and therefore discrimination is an unavoidable consequence against a particular gender.

This is an important case because the Court held that a classification that is not gender based but has the unintended impact of excluding one gender from a benefit will be subjected only to the rational basis test and not the more stringent intermediate scrutiny standard.

The case involved a woman who challenged Massachusetts' civil service statute for giving absolute and lifetime hiring preferences to any veteran who passed a competitive exam. Feeny passed with higher scores on civil service examinations than other male veterans yet was repeatedly passed over for employment and promotion in favor of veterans. She claimed that the law discriminated against her on the basis of gender because 98 percent of the veterans in Massachusetts were male, that the veteran preference applied to approximately 60 percent of the public jobs in the state, and that its impact on public employment opportunities for women was severe: since women tended not to be veterans, they were excluded from most jobs in the state.

The Supreme Court, however, ruled that the law was not intentionally gender based. The statute may well favor men, but this did not indicate an intent to discriminate against women because the class of non-veterans included many males as well as females. The statute was valid because it rationally served a state goal of assisting veterans in their return to civilian life after military life. The constitutional standard to be used in such cases, furthermore, required showing that a discriminatory "purpose" took place, not merely a disproportionate "impact." So even if discriminatory results were foreseeable, a law would stand up to constitutional scrutiny unless it could be found that the legislature acted because of these foreseeable discriminatory results.

That is, if the legislature had passed the measure "because of" an admitted discriminatory impact against women, the policy would be unconstitutional under the Fourteenth Amendment. But the effect of this ruling is that anyone alleging discrimination under the amendment must prove discriminatory intent in addition to impact. Equal protection of the law does not require that the government refrain from actions that have a disparate negative impact on a group, only prejudice that is ordinarily thought of as a willingness or intention to inflict injury on a group. Intent, however, is extremely difficult to prove; legislation may result from mixed motives of its framers, some with an intent to discriminate and some without. Essentially, a veterans' preference program is a form of affirmative action and is therefore allowed.

See also Affirmative Action; Disparate Impact; Fourteenth Amendment.

Reed v. Reed (1971)

In *Reed v. Reed* the Court struck down a mandatory provision of Idaho law that gave preference to men over women for appointment as administrators of estates. Cecil and Sally Reed were divorced, but both applied to become administrators over the estate of their dead son. Sally filed suit when Cecil was named administrator. The state argued that it was administratively convenient automatically to make men administrators and thus limited the conflict among surviving family members.

But the Supreme Court disagreed with the state: "To give a mandatory preference to members of either sex . . . merely to accomplish the elimination of hearings on the merits, is to make the very kind of arbitrary legislative choice forbidden by the Equal Protection Clause of the Fourteenth Amendment."

See also Frontiero v. Richardson; Ginsburg, Ruth Bader; Intermediate Scrutiny Standard; *Williams v. McNair.*

Richmond v. J. A. Croson Company (1989)

Richmond v. J. A. Croson Company involved a "minority business utilization plan" enacted in Richmond, Virginia, that required construction contracts funded by the city to subcontract at least 30 percent of the jobs to one or more minority business enterprises (MBEs). To be an MBE, a business had to be at least 51 percent owned by a minority-group member. Waivers would be given to contractors only if it could be shown that there were no qualified MBEs available and willing to participate. The program had been enacted because of statistics showing that although the city was 50 percent black, less than 1 percent of construction contracts were given to minorities. Additionally, local contractor associations had no minority representation in their membership.

Croson was a white contractor seeking a contract to install toilets in the city jail who claimed there were no MBEs available to participate in the contract. He filed suit stating that the set-aside program violated his right to equal protection under the law. Under precedent set by the Supreme Court, Croson argued, "any government action that is explicitly race-based must be necessary to achieve a compelling government interest" because race-based affirmative programs are subject to strict scrutiny (unlike gender-based programs, which are subject to intermediate scrutiny). Further, Croson argued, there was no evidence of discrimination by anyone in Richmond, there was no evidence that there would be more minority contracting firms had there not been past societal discrimination, and there was no showing of how many MBEs in the local labor market could have done the work.

The Court agreed with him largely because the city had been unable to show clear past race discrimination. Although Congress had concluded that there was race discrimination in the United States, this was irrelevant because the degree of discrimination varied so much from market to market.

See also Fourteenth Amendment; Intermediate Scrutiny Standard.

Sanchez, Loretta (1965–) and Linda (1968–)

In 2002 the Sanchez sisters made history when both were elected to represent California in the U.S. House. Loretta Sanchez, the elder sister, was thirty-six when she won her fourth term representing Orange County as a Republican. After receiving an MBA from American University, she had worked as a financial manager before running for national office. Linda Sanchez was a newly elected Democrat, serving Los Angeles County at age thirty-three after receiving a law degree at UCLA and working as a civil rights attorney and labor leader. Their mother had come to the United States from Mexico. She had seven children before graduating from college and becoming a teacher; she was active on behalf of immigrant families and campaigned for her two daughters in their separate bids to the House.

When the sisters began their terms in 2002, each had a different agenda. Linda, the Democrat, planned to focus on education, health, and retirement, whereas Loretta, the Republican and the highest-ranking women on the House Armed Services Committee and a member of the Committee on Education and the Workforce, intended to concentrate on retraining unemployed workers.

The Sanchezes made history with their elections to the House because they were sisters, but their story received all the more coverage because of the difficulty women faced in the 2002 House race. Women had a 54 percent chance of winning open seats but only a 12 percent chance of unseating incumbents, who are typically men with more money to spend on election campaigns. The majority of races in 2002 were against incumbents. Many hoped that 2002 would mirror 1991, when ninety-one seats opened up following the Anita Hill–Clarence Thomas confirmation hearings. But the number of women in the House remained steady in the 2002 election, with only fifty-nine women (out of 425 total members).

Representative Loretta Sanchez (right) and her sister Representative Linda Sanchez raise their arms during an election night party in Lakewood, California, on November 5, 2002. (Reuters NewMedia, Inc./Corbis)

Reference Center for American Women and Politics at Rutgers University Web site: http://www.rci.rutgers.edu/~cawp/index.html

Schroeder, Patricia (1941–)

Although Pat Schroeder was born in Portland, Oregon, her father was a pilot, so the family moved constantly. She graduated from the University of Minnesota and went on to Harvard Law School, graduating in 1964 in a class of fifteen women and 500 men. After earning her law degree, she married Jim Schroeder; they moved to Colorado and had two children. In 1972 she was elected to the U.S. Congress, as a member of the first generation of female legislators.

The average campaign contribution during her first bid was $7.50.

During her tenure in Congress, Schroeder was known as an outspoken advocate for women's rights and equal opportunity; she lobbied for the Equal Rights Amendment and was a staunch supporter of reproductive freedom, introducing legislation that made it a federal crime to obstruct access to abortion clinics. The first woman to be appointed to the Armed Services Committee, she also lobbied for a vote to allow women to fly in combat missions in the military in 1991. On the House Select Committee on Children, Youth, and Families, she ushered in the Family and Medical Leave Act. Yet she was quick to disregard those who focused on her as a woman and not a member of Congress: "When people ask me why I am running as a woman, I always answer, 'What choice do I have?'"

Schroeder was considered a promising presidential candidate in the 1988 election but did not run. After twelve terms in Congress (twenty-four years), she retired in 1996 without ever having lost a campaign. Since retirement, she has worked as a lobbyist for the Association of American Publishers, advocating for First Amendment issues.

See also Fourteenth Amendment; Women as Lawmakers.

References Center for American Women and Politics Web site: http://www.rci.rutgers.edu/~cawp/index.html; Patricia Schroeder. 1999. *24 Years of House Work and It's Still a Mess.* Kansas City, MO: Andrews McMeel Publishing.

Smeal, Eleanor (1939–)

As president of the National Organization for Women for three terms, Ellie Smeal was active in the campaign to ratify the Equal Rights Amendment, as well as the initiation of the Supreme Court case *NOW v. Scheidler,* a suit that used the Racketeer-Influenced and Corrupt Organizations Act (better known as the RICO Act) to punish coordinated violence and protest efforts by the Pro-Life Action Network and Operation Rescue against women entering abortion clinics. The Supreme Court ruled against NOW in 2003.

In 1987 Smeal cofounded and assumed the presidency of the Feminist Majority, an organization that encouraged women to increase their political representation. The group led the first abortion rights march in Washington, D.C., in 1986 and the first national feminist exposition in 1996. In 2002 Smeal spearheaded a merger between the Feminist Majority and Liberty Media for Women, the publisher of *Ms.,* the preeminent feminist publication in the country. Launched in 1972, the magazine went ad-free in 1990, and the loss of advertising revenue had forced it into economic difficulties.

References Feminist Majority Web site: www.feminist.org; *Ms.* Web site: www.msmagazine.com; National Organization for Women Web site: http://www.now.org.

Snowe, Olympia (1947–)

Born in Maine and raised by relatives after the death of her parents, Olympia Snowe received a political science degree from the University of Maine in 1969 and later married former Maine governor John R. McKernan Jr. Following the death of her first husband, she took over his post as a member of the state house of representatives. She was first elected to the U.S. House of Representatives in 1978 at the age of thirty-one; she was the youngest Republican woman ever elected to Congress. She held that office until 1994, when she was elected to the U.S. Senate. She was reelected in 2000 with over 64 percent of the vote. She is the fourth women in history to be elected to both houses of Congress and has won more federal elections (in her state) than any person since World War II.

In 2001 Snowe served on the Senate Finance Committee (the first Republican woman to do so) and the Senate Armed Services Committee. Her critics and advocates alike see her as a centrist, and in fact she cochairs the Senate Centrist Coalition. This has allowed her to work on a wide range of issues of particular interest to women, including education (e.g., student financial aid and education technology), women's reproductive rights, health care (e.g., prescription drug coverage for Medicare recipients), child support enforcement, and campaign finance reform. She was one of the most outspoken critics of the Republican Party's anti-abortion plank at the 1996 national convention and was one of the few Republican senators to vote against impeaching President Bill Clinton in 1998.

Like many other women who are potential contenders for the presidency, she faces challenges in fundraising; she raised only $2.5 million in the last election.

Steinem, Gloria (1934–)

Gloria Steinem, cofounder (in 1972) of *Ms.* magazine, is probably the best-known feminist leader today. Born in Toledo, Ohio, she later graduated from Smith College, majoring in government. After witnessing female oppression and nonviolent protests on a trip to India, she returned to the United States and wrote several articles for *Help!* and *Esquire* magazines. She was working full-time as a freelance writer, but she did not enter the public eye until 1963, with the publication in *Esquire* of "A Bunny's Tale," profiling her undercover work as a Playboy bunny at the Playboy Club. Steinem went on to write stories on abortion and other women's issues, as well as race and poverty, and by the 1970s had become a popular feminist figure. Women quickly identified with her because of her glamorous image and her outspokenness. *McCall's* voted her Woman of the Year in 1972.

Gloria Steinem (Ms. magazine)

Steinem was active in civil rights protests, war protests, and political campaigns during the late 1960s and 1970s, including those of George McGovern, Robert Kennedy, Eugene McCarthy, and Adlai Stevenson. She founded the Ms. Foundation for Women, the National Women's Political Caucus, and Coalition of Labor Union Women. She was also well liked because of her calls for the feminist movement to open its doors and coalesce with racially based groups. She was largely successful in demonstrating that feminism was relevant to more than simply the white middle class, something no other feminist leader had done.

But she was also criticized for her disregard for marriage, which she dismissed as an institution that destroys relationships. She penned the oft-quoted maxim: "A woman needs a man like a fish needs a bicycle."

In 1983 Steinem published a book that highlighted the lives of other notable women of the twentieth century, and in 1986 she published another on Marilyn Monroe. In 1993 she was inducted into the National Women's Hall of Fame, and in 1998 she was inducted into the American Society of Magazine Editors Hall of Fame, along with Hugh Hefner and Byron Dobell; this was ironic considering she entered the public eye because of her description of the Playboy Club, owned by Hefner.

In 2000, at the age of sixty-six, the feminist icon married South African–born entrepreneur David Bale. During the wedding ceremony the word "partners" was substituted for "husband and wife."

See also Feminism; Morgan, Robin; National Organization for Women (NOW).
References *Ms.* magazine Web site: www. msmagazine.com; National Organization for Women Web site: www.now.org; National Women's Hall of Fame Web site: http://www.greatwomen.org.

Waters, Maxine (1938–)

Born in St. Louis, Missouri, as the fifth of thirteen children raised by a single mother, Maxine Waters worked in factories and restaurants throughout her teens before moving to California and graduating from California State University at Los Angeles. She was a teacher in the Head Start program before marrying and having two children. She served fourteen years in the California State Assembly, becoming Democratic caucus chair. In 2000 she began her sixth term in the U.S. House representing South Central Los Angeles.

She has been the chair of the Congressional Black Caucus (1997–1998) and was chief deputy whip of the Democratic Party. She has served on various committees in the House, including the Committee on Financial Services and the Subcommittee on Financial Institutions and Consumer Credit. Following the 2002 presidential election, she chaired the Democratic Caucus Special Committee on Election Reform to establish minimum federal standards for election practices.

Weinberger v. Wiesenfeld (1975)

In *Weinberger v. Wiesenfeld* the Court invalidated a Social Security provision that allowed that upon the death of a husband and father, benefits were payable to the widow and the couple's minor children, but upon the death of a wife and mother, benefits were payable only to the minor children and not the widower.

The case concerned a widower whose wife had died in childbirth and who wanted to stay home and take care of his infant son. Had his wife survived him, she would have been automatically entitled to Social Security benefits based on his salary. But even though she had paid the same Social Security taxes as a man, she was not able to obtain the same level of protection for her family. Justice Ruth Bader Ginsburg, in her position as counsel for the ACLU—Women's Rights Project, argued that the law was based on the stereotype that husbands are always the wage earners. In her new role as counsel for the group, Ginsburg had been on the watch for Social Security and jury selection cases that specifically discriminated against women. This was a good example, to Ginsburg, of discriminatory action by the government; it involved a father whose wife had died in childbirth and then was unable to stay home with his newborn because Social Security regulations provided benefits only for mothers and not fathers. "If there ever was a case to attract suspect classification [and change the standard from intermediate scrutiny], this was the one," said Ginsburg. (During the prior term, the Court had ruled in *Kahn v. Shevin*, a case involving a widower challenging a Florida statute granting tax breaks to widows who owned property but not widowers.) In *Weinberger v. Wiesenfeld* the Supreme Court indeed found the provision discriminatory against female wage earners by giving them less protection for their survivors than that provided for survivors of male wage earners. But the Court failed to raise sex discrimination to the heightened level of scrutiny enjoyed in race discrimination cases.

> *See also* American Civil Liberties Union— Women's Rights Project (ACLU—WRP); *Califano v. Goldfarb; Califano v. Webster;* Fourteenth Amendment; Ginsburg, Ruth Bader; Intermediate Scrutiny Standard; *Kahn v. Shevin.*

References and Further Reading

Center for American Women and Politics Web site: www. cawp.rutgers.edu.

Coalition for Women's Appointments Web site: www.appointwomen.com.

Congressional Caucus for Women's Issues Web site: www.house.gov/Pelosi/ womcauc.htm.

Gelb, Joyce, and Marian Lief Palley. 1982. *Women and Public Policies.* Princeton, NJ: Princeton University Press.

Godshalk, David K. 2000. "Protected Petitioning or Unlawful Retaliation? The

Limits of First Amendment Immunity for Lawsuits under the Fair Housing Act." *Pepperdine Law Review* 27: 483.

Harrison, Brigid C. 2003. *Women in American Politics: An Introduction.* Belmont, CA: Wadsworth/Thompson.

Jackson, Donald W. 1992. *Even the Children of Strangers: Equality under the U.S. Constitution.* Lawrence: University Press of Kansas.

Langley, Winston E., and Vivian C. Fox, eds. 1994. *Women's Rights in the United States.* Westport, CT: Greenwood.

League of Women Voters Web site: www.lwv.org.

Lynn, Naomi B., ed. 1990. *Women, Politics and the Constitution.* New York: Haworth.

National Women's Hall of Fame Web site: www.greatwomen.org.

U.S. court system Web site: www.uscourts.gov.

EDUCATION

American Association of University Women (AAUW)

The AAUW is a national organization that promotes education and occupational equity for women and girls. It is actually three separation corporations: the association, which lobbies and advocates for education and equity of girls and women (there are 150,000 branches nationwide); the Legal Advocacy Fund, which provides funds and other means of support for women seeking redress from the courts for sex discrimination in higher education; and the Educational Foundation, which funds research on women and girls in education and community projects.

Established in 1921, the AAUW has been influential in defining the debates on education, Social Security, sex discrimination, civil rights, reproductive choice, affirmative action, Title IX compliance, welfare reform, vocational education, the Equal Pay Act, family and medical leave, and health care reform in issues relating to women.

See also Affirmative Action; Equal Pay Act; Family and Medical Leave Act (FMLA); Right to Privacy; Title IX.

Reference American Association of University Women Web site: http://www.aauw.org.

Carnes v. Tennessee Secondary School Athletic Association (1976)

Jo Ann Carnes, a high school senior, attempted to join the boys' high school baseball team but was prohibited by state athletic association rules that barred females from playing or participating in contact sports. The association's rules stated that both sexes could not participate in interschool athletic games together, nor could boys' teams and girls' teams play against each other if the sports involved physical contact. Included in this ban were football, baseball, basketball, and wrestling. Carnes filed suit against both her high school and the voluntary athletic association where her high school retained membership, arguing she was denied the right to participate in an interscholastic sport even after agreeing to follow all the rules—in other words, that she was denied solely because of her sex.

Carnes filed a preliminary injunction to force the school to immediately allow her to participate on the team instead of a lawsuit because she claimed that by not allowing her to join the team, the association and school essentially prevented her from participation in such sports forever: Carnes was a graduating senior, and once a court ruled on the merits of her case, it was likely that both the sports season and her high school athletic career would be over.

The U.S. district court granted her preliminary injunction and ordered the school (and the association) to allow her participation. The only way a school could prohibit mixed participation in a contact or collision sport would be if it could show that such a prohibition was rational in obtaining a legitimate state purpose. In this case the association and the school argued a legitimate state purpose in preventing women from participating in collision sports was to protect them from "unreasonable risk of harm" and to protect female sports programs from male intrusion. But the court held these were not legitimate state purposes. The rule permitted males who are highly prone to injury to play baseball while barring females whose "physical fitness would make a risk of physical harm unlikely from participating in the program."

It was also evident to the court that Carnes was denied the opportunity to participate solely because of her sex and not because she may have been exposed to a risk of harm greater than that of the male players. As evidence, the court used the fact that Carnes had actively engaged in other sports without suffering any serious injuries. Additionally, by keeping Carnes from participating on a male team, the school effectively prevented her from participating in any baseball program at her high school because there had been no effort to organize a baseball program for women there. Had there been a female baseball team, the school would have been able to argue that separating female from male interscholastic competition bore a rational relation to fostering equitable competition.

There are ways, however, that a school can justify the distinction between male and female teams, as well as a rule that male teams cannot compete against female teams. A state can legitimately discriminate between the sexes when dealing with contact sports, but only if the classification of a sport as a contact sport is reasonable. Because the rules of baseball specifically prohibit body checking and base runners are generally tagged with a glove, a properly played game would make collision infrequent. It was questionable, therefore, that baseball could be reasonably classified as a contact sport.

See also Title IX; *Vorchheimer v. School District of Philadelphia.*

The Citadel and Virginia Military Institute

In 1992 Shannon Faulkner applied for admission to the Citadel, an all-male military college in Charleston, South Carolina. In her application she did not mention that she was female, and the Citadel accepted her. Once the school realized Faulkner was female, it reversed its admission decision, and Faulkner sued. She argued that the Citadel was practicing gender discrimination and could do so only if it did not receive federal funds. In 1993 a U.S. district court allowed Faulkner to attend day classes only until her case could be appealed; she was restricted from any military training.

At the same time, the Virginia Military Institute faced a similar claim and appealed to the U.S. Supreme Court. In the majority, written by Justice Ruth Bader Ginsburg, the Court held that "the United States maintains that the Constitution's equal protection guarantee precludes Virginia from reserving exclusively to men the unique educational opportunities VMI affords." VMI was forced to admit women into their corps of cadets, as was the Citadel.

Faulkner began "hell week" at the Citadel shortly after the VMI decision was handed down. After receiving death threats and keeping up with a brutal physical regimen, she was admitted to the school infirmary for exhaustion. She left the Citadel later that week, the male cadets cheering her exit. Faulkner is now a teacher in the South. She claims she never intended to change constitutional law but just wanted an equal opportunity to attend a premier military academy.

Clark v. Arizona Interscholastic Association (1982)

In *Clark v. Arizona Interscholastic Association,* the courts held that boys could be precluded from playing on girls' interscholastic teams in Arizona high schools. The policy of the association was a permissible means, via Title IX, of attempting to ensure equality of opportunity for girls in Arizona interscholastic sports and of redressing past discrimination.

The case involved a boy who wanted to be on the girls' interscholastic volleyball team. Boys were not invited on the girls' teams because, generally, "high school males are taller, can jump higher and are stronger than high school females . . . and have the potential to be better hitters and blockers than females and thus may dominate these [skills] in volleyball." The court held that the government's interest was in redressing past discrimination and was a legitimate and important interest. But was the exclusion of boys substantially related to this interest? Here, the court held that although athletic equality could be found in ways other than simply excluding boys from the team (i.e., specific physical characteristics other than sex could be a prerequisite for the team), absolute equality of opportunity to participate was not the most important goal.

> *See also* Civil Rights Act; *Cohen v. Brown University;* Title IX; *Vorchheimer v. School District of Philadelphia.*

Cohen v. Brown University (1996)

In *Cohen v. Brown University,* the Supreme Court ordered Brown University to cease eliminating or reducing funding for women's sports. The case was a class-action lawsuit that charged that Brown, its president, and its athletic director had discriminated against the women's athletic program and violated Title IX by moving its women's gymnastics and volleyball teams from university-funded varsity status to donor status.

> *See also* Civil Rights Act; *Clark v. Arizona Interscholastic Association;* Title IX; *Vorchheimer v. School District of Philadelphia.*

Deer, Ada (1935–)

Born on the Menominee Indian Reservation in Wisconsin, she became the first Menominee tribal member to graduate from univer-

Ada Deer (Bureau of Indian Affairs)

sity, receiving a degree in social work from the University of Wisconsin in 1957. She also earned an M.A. from Columbia University.

When the Menominee tribe was unable to pay property taxes and sold off many of its holdings, terminating its federal recognition as an official tribe, Deer organized a grassroots movement to stop the land sale and successfully lobbied the administration of Richard Nixon to sign the Menominee Restoration Act in 1973, which restored the reservation to its former status. She was then elected to chair the new tribal council.

President Clinton appointed Deer as the assistant secretary of the Bureau of Indian Affairs in 1992; she was the first women to serve in that position. She was extremely active and successful in this position. More than half of the Indian schools in America came under tribal council or tribal board control during her tenure, federal recognition was extended to twelve tribes, and she developed several U.S. policies regarding international human rights. She was also active in gaining congressional passage of the

Trust Fund Reform Act, a law designed to reform the Bureau of Indian Affairs' management of $2 billion in Native American trust funds.

But she was not without her critics. She was sued after leaving office for illegal conduct in regard to funds managed by the Bureau of Indian Affairs. The class action suit claimed the federal government lost billions of dollars from various tribes for oil and gas production, grazing leases, coal production, and timber sales on their lands. The suit was later dropped. After leaving her federal position, she became director of the American Indian Studies Program at the University of Wisconsin at Madison. Her focus is to encourage American Indian youth to take on leadership roles, within their communities and beyond.

Edelman, Marian Wright (1939–)

Born in South Carolina, she graduated from Spelman College in Atlanta in 1960 and Yale University Law School in 1963. She worked registering African American voters in Mississippi during the civil rights movement and became the first African American woman to pass the bar in that state. She met her husband, an assistant to Robert Kennedy, and moved to Washington, D.C., later that year. Edelman then began work as a staff attorney for the Legal Defense and Educational Fund of the National Association for the Advancement of Colored People (NAACP) in New York. In 1973 she founded the Children's Defense Fund (CDF) to advocate for the rights of disadvantaged children. The organization serves as a lobbying organization as well as a research center, yet is financed with private funds.

First lady Hillary Rodham Clinton's involvement with the CDF gave the group increased media attention. Edelman received public approbation after she advocated pregnancy prevention as a way of improving children's health; she was also vocal in promoting prenatal care, child education, and gun control.

Faulkner, Shannon (1975–)

In 1992 Shannon Faulkner was accepted into the Citadel, an all-male military academy in Charleston, South Carolina. But in 1993, once college officials learned she was female, the Citadel revoked Faulkner's admission. Faulkner immediately filed a discrimination suit against the college. She argued that the school was unconstitutionally refusing women admittance since the school received tax funds from the state; state-supported educational institutions are not allowed to restrict admissions on the basis of race or gender. Faulkner eventually won her suit against the school when an appellate court held that her civil rights were violated when she was denied admission to the college. The Citadel was then forced to eliminate gender requirements and begin accepting women into the college.

Immediately following the Citadel's decision to deny her admission, the South Carolina state legislature signed a contract with Converse College, a private South Carolina women's college, to develop and operate an Institute of Leadership for Women. At a cost of approximately $10 million, Converse was tasked with creating a leadership program for women that would allow the state to make the case that it was thus providing equal educational opportunities for both male and female students in the state. The state would then be free to limit women's enrollment in the Citadel, since the state would have a suitable parallel military-based "leadership" training facility for women.

A lower court forced the Citadel to accept Faulkner after it was determined that the program at Converse was not comparable to the "history and prestige" of the Citadel. Faulkner began her first year at the military academy in 1996. The male cadets were outraged, and Faulkner claimed that as a result she was forced to drop out a week later. During her five days as a member of the corps of cadets, she was isolated from the other male students, who refused to ac-

Citadel cadets staring at Shannon Faulkner (Mitchell Smith/Corbis)

knowledge her presence and delivered continual taunts and threats to her. Faulkner cited exhaustion and harassment when she withdrew from the corps. Her mission, she also argued, was contrary to the workings of the college's fourth-class system, in which cadets were deliberately broken down and taught to accept rules without question.

A year later the Citadel was again in the news when the Supreme Court ruled that the male-only policy of the Virginia Military Institute (VMI), similar to the one in place at the Citadel, was discriminatory. Further, the Court held that VMI's alternative Women's Leadership Institute, similar to Converse's Institute of Leadership for Women, was not comparable and thus unconstitutionally discriminatory to women. Both VMI and the Citadel were forced to accept female cadets into their student body in the 1996–1997

school year, and four female cadets enrolled at the Citadel the following year.

Faulkner received a degree in education at a nearby college and today teaches high school English. She moved away from South Carolina following her withdrawal from the Citadel because general public opinion in the state was so hostile toward her. Although she continues to deny that she is a feminist, she believes that had she not fought for her rights, women would still not be at the Citadel.

See also Mississippi University for Women v. Hogan; United States v. Virginia.

Franklin v. Gwinnett County Public Schools (1992)

While a student at a Georgia high school from 1985 to 1989, Christine Franklin alleged she had been subjected to continual sexual harassment from Andrew Hill, a coach and teacher employed by the school. She argued that Congress, in passing Title IX of the education amendments of 1972, allowed individuals to receive damage awards from school districts that violated that act. The school district, of course, disagreed.

Franklin alleged that her coach and teacher regularly entered into sexually charged discussions with her, questioning her about her prior sexual experiences and whether she would consent to sexual intercourse with an older man. Additionally, she alleged that Hill forcibly kissed her, regularly phoned her at home, and requested that she meet him socially. On three separate occasions he interrupted her in class and took her to a private office at the school where she was coerced into sexual intercourse with him. When the school was informed of her allegations, it discovered that Hill had a history of sexually harassing female students, teachers, and administrators. Nevertheless, the school district took no further action other than to attempt to dissuade Franklin from filing formal legal charges.

Franklin used Title IX of the education amendments of 1972 to support her claim that she was due monetary damages (both compensatory and punitive) from the school district for not taking further action against their employee, Hill. Title IX, of course, prohibits sexual discrimination in any educational program that receives federal funding but does not explicitly authorize monetary relief for such discrimination. In this case the school district had received Hill's resignation, which was given on the condition that all legal matters pending against him be dropped. The school district took no further action toward Hill once they received his resignation.

The Supreme Court reversed the decisions of two lower federal courts that had ruled against Franklin. "Where legal rights have been invaded, and a federal statute provides for a general right to sue for such invasion," the Court reasoned, "federal courts may use any available remedy to make good the wrong done." The Court forced the school to pay Franklin damages.

See also Title IX.

Pennsylvania v. Pennsylvania Interscholastic Athletic Association (1975)

The state of Pennsylvania filed suit against the state's athletic association, alleging that a section of its bylaws was unconstitutional: "Girls shall not compete or practice against boys in any athletic contest." The state argued that it violated the Equal Protection Clause of the Fourteenth Amendment by denying female student athletes the same opportunities available to male athletes. This case was filed prior to passage of Title IX of the education amendments that outlawed this type of prohibition permanently. But the court never decided whether or not the bylaws of the association violated the federal Constitution. Rather, Pennsylvania's constitution included an Equal Rights Amendment (ERA) that prohibited "against denial or abridgment of equality rights because of sex" and included the statement, "Equality of rights under the law shall not be denied or abridged in the Commonwealth of Pennsylvania because of the sex of the individual." As such, the state court held, it was bound to protect individuals from discrimination on the basis of their gender.

The athletic association, however, justified its bylaws by arguing that men generally possessed a higher degree of athletic ability in traditional sports offered by most schools. Therefore, female students would be given greater opportunities for participation if they competed exclusively with members of their own sex and were not required to compete against men, presumably the better athletes. But the court disagreed. The court decided that the bylaws were indeed unconstitutional under the state constitution and no justification could sustain their legality. In many schools only one sports team was in existence, and that sport's membership was limited to men. Female students wishing to compete in that sport thus were given no opportunity to do so, even if they were skilled enough to compete with the male members of the team. In some cases there were separate teams offered for both males and females, but even then the most talented girls were relegated to a girl's team solely because of their sex; thus, "equality under the law" had been explicitly violated. As to the athletic association's contention that girls were weaker athletes and thus more prone to injury if they competed with boys, the court held that if an individual is too weak or unskilled to compete, she may be excluded from participating on that basis but she could not be excluded solely because of her sex without reference to her individual skill. The court then held that beginning in 1975, girls were to be permitted to practice and compete with boys in all interscholastic athletics in the state.

See also Carnes v. Tennessee Secondary School Athletic Association; Civil Rights Act; *Clark v. Arizona Interscholastic Association; Cohen v. Brown University; Vorchheimer v. School District of Philadelphia; Williams v. McNair.*

Title IX of the Education Amendments (1972)

Although education has traditionally been the prerogative of the states, in 1972 Congress enacted Title IX of the education amendments, which allows that no person shall, on basis of sex, be excluded from participation in, be denied the benefits of, or be subjected to discrimination under any education program or activity receiving federal financial assistance. Many states enacted parallel statutes with even more stringent requirements for sex equity in education. Signed into law by Richard Nixon, Title IX was originally targeted at law schools and medical schools that had limited quotas for the number of women they accepted. But

vocational institutions (high school or college) and public undergraduate coeducational institutions have had to comply as well. Also as a direct result of Title IX, home economics, shop, and other classes offered in high schools became coeducational. These changes have, for the most part, been embraced by educators and their institutions. Any public controversy that remains surrounding Title IX tends to relate to athletics.

In 1975 Congress issued regulations that in part insisted on proportionality. That is, the number of athletes from each sex should be roughly equivalent to enrollment percentages. So if women make up half of a school's student body, about half of its athletes should be women and half of its athletic scholarships should go to women athletes. Since 1972, when Title IX was passed and signed into law, more than 400 men's teams have been dropped to make way for women's teams, garnering heavy criticism from opponents of the law. Between 2001 and 2003, 948 schools added one or more women's teams. Further, the Office for Civil Rights will rule when a school is not in compliance with Title IX if the school cannot show a history and continuing practice of adding women's sports to their athletic programs. That office will also find a school not in compliance if it cannot show that the athletic interests and abilities of women on campus are fully and effectively accommodated—in other words, if it is not offering all of the women's sports its students want and can play.

The largest problem for schools not in compliance with the act has been the disproportionate amount of money spent on men's teams. Although men and women tend to receive similar numbers of scholarships, schools still tend to spend more money on men's athletics for recruiting expenses and coaches' salaries. Overall head coaches' salaries for women's teams in 2000 were $330,000, compared to $484,900 for men's teams. Another problem is the differences in male and female sports. A football program, for example, may offer eighty-five

Figure 3.1: Title IX

Women in Athletics —How Things Have Changed!

Women as a class cannot stand a prolonged mental or physical strain as well as men. Exact it of them and they will try to do the work, but they will do it at a fearful cost to themselves and eventually to their children.

—Dudley A. Sargent, M.D., *Ladies' Home Journal,* March 1912.

There's nothing feminine or enchanting about a girl with beads of perspiration on her alabaster brow, the result of grotesque contortions in events totally unsuited to female architecture.

—Arthur Daley, Pulitzer Prize–winning sportswriter, *New York Times,* 1953

Twenty years ago, little girls interested in basketball had posters of Larry Bird or Magic Johnson. Now they have posters of Lisa Leslie or Sheryl Swoopes.

—Lesley Visser, CBS sportscaster

The attitude toward physically gifted and strong women has definitely changed for the better. I can go into a weight room, and people actually look at me and say, "Gosh you're really strong—that's so cool."

—Lisa Fernandez, 1996 Olympic gold medalist in softball; volunteer assistant coach for the UCLA Bruin women's softball team

Oppenheimer Funds/MassMutual Financial Group Survey of female business executives on the role of sports in their careers:

86 percent said sports increased their self-discipline;
81 percent said sports helped them become better players;
69 percent said sports helped them develop leadership skills that contributed to their professional success;
68 percent said their sports experiences helped them to cope with failure;
60 percent believe that those who play sports are more productive employees;
59 percent said that sports gave them a competitive edge over those who did not.

Source: MassMutual Financial Group, 2002. "From the Locker Room to the Boardroom: A Survey on Sports in the Lives of Women Business Executives."

scholarships in that program alone, whereas a woman's track program may need only ten athletes (and thus ten scholarships).

The Supreme Court has issued several rulings defining different aspects of Title IX. In *Grove City College v. Bell* (1984), the Court ruled that Title IX did not apply to programs that did not directly receive fed- eral aid. Congress essentially overruled the Court's opinion four years later in the Civil Rights Restoration Act, which mandated that Title IX applied to all operations of any school that received any federal funds. In 1992 the Court allowed female athletes to receive monetary damages in lawsuits over Title IX in *Franklin v. Gwinnett County Pub-*

Girls soccer teams like this one were made possible by Title IX (Bob/Corbis)

lic Schools. Finally, the Court decided *Cohen v. Brown University* (1996), which overruled Brown's assumption that women did not have as much interest in playing sports as men. Brown's faulty belief is evident in current statistics: before Title IX was passed, one in twenty-seven girls participated in high school sports; in 2003 more than one in three participated, an increase of 800 percent.

Not all groups are required to accept both sexes or provide separate teams. Some schools that receive federal funding may even exclude members of one sex from admission. For example, primary and secondary schools or public undergraduate schools that have been single sex since their inception are allowed to stay single sex. The YWCA, YMCA, Girl Scouts, Boy Scouts, Camp Fire Girls, and social sororities and fraternities are allowed to stay single sex as well.

Probably the largest impact of Title IX can be seen in the gender transformation in pro-

fessional schools. Largely as a result of Title IX, there has been a marked increase in women professional students, particularly in medicine and law, where women make up nearly 50 percent of the student body. Part of this is most likely due to the scholarship money that is available to female college athletes today; money for women has increased from $100,000 per year to $431 million. Before Title IX, 2 percent of collegiate sports budgets had gone to women; in 2003 it is 42 percent, allowing more women an opportunity not only to attend college but also to graduate with little or no debt and go on to professional schools. A 2001 survey of senior women business executives indicated that 82 percent of those surveyed had played organized sports in college.

See also Carnes v. Tennessee Secondary School Athletic Association; Civil Rights Act; *Clark v. Arizona Interscholastic Association; Cohen v. Brown University; Franklin v. Gwinnett County Public Schools; Pennsylvania v. Pennsylvania Interscholastic Association;*

Vorchheimer v. School District of Philadelphia; Williams v. McNair.

References Joyce Gelb and Marian Lief Palley. 1982. *Women and Public Policies.* Princeton, NJ: Princeton University Press; Brigid C. Harrison. 2003. *Women in American Politics: An Introduction.* Belmont, CA: Wadsworth/Thompson.

United States v. Virginia (1996)

The Court held in *United States v. Virginia* that gender-based schemes like the maintenance of all-male status at the Virginia Military Institute (VMI) could be sustained only if the state could show an "exceedingly persuasive justification" that the Court could examine with "skeptical scrutiny." VMI was a state-supported military college, similar to the Citadel in South Carolina. Both schools had long histories of turning out future military leaders. VMI emphasized training students for physical hardship, mental stress, and exacting regulation of behavior; the school's goal was to produce leaders with strong characters, and historically it had succeeded.

In 1990 a female student filed a complaint alleging that VMI's male-only admission policy was a violation of the Constitution's guarantee of equal protection. VMI won the first round; the lower court held that classifying students on the basis of gender served an "important governmental objective," that being to promote diversity in higher education. Further, evidence suggested that students at single-sex colleges were more academically involved and more likely to be successful later in life. Thus, excluding women from the corps of cadets was the only way to achieve such success. A higher appellate court, however, clarified matters somewhat by holding that the state could continue with its process of excluding women from VMI but only if it provided women with the same type of educational opportunity. That court suggested that VMI could either admit women, establish a parallel institution for women, or continue as a private college, which would make it free to

discriminate against women since it would not be receiving state tax dollars.

The state immediately instituted the Virginia Women's Leadership Institute, located at a local women's school. But a court held that the institute was not comparable to VMI; incoming test scores were lower, the faculty were not as well trained, and the college itself failed to offer the same benefits and services. The most egregious problem, however, was funding; VMI had an endowment of $131 million, whereas the institute was funded with only $19 million.

When the case hit the Supreme Court, women's groups around the country called for the Court to raise gender discrimination cases to the same scrutiny level as race discrimination cases. Their justification was that sex was an immutable characteristic, like race, and women had been subject to a history of discrimination. Critics argued that women were not a minority and gender discrimination cases were not in need of heightened scrutiny. The Court ultimately held that VMI had to admit women, yet failed to address the question of heightened scrutiny. A six-justice majority held that gender-based classification had to demonstrate an "exceedingly persuasive justification," which Virginia had failed to provide. Historically, schools and professions have excluded women because, they argued, their presence would undermine male solidarity or lead to sexual misconduct; neither of these occurred once women were accepted into various professions. In essence, the Court ruled, the state's claim that women would destroy the adversative system of the school was an excuse for discrimination and would not be tolerated. Further, the establishment of a parallel women's school was sorely inadequate.

In 1997 VMI was forced to admit women into its incoming classes; it made accommodations for their admission by hiring female staff, providing training on sexual harassment, and installing women's bathrooms. In 1999 VMI graduated its first female cadets.

The Court has yet to decide the question whether gender discrimination should continue to be held to the intermediate level of scrutiny instead of the heightened scrutiny used for race discrimination cases.

See also Faulkner, Shannon; Intermediate Scrutiny Standard; *Mississippi University for Women v. Hogan; Williams v. McNair.*

Vorcheimer v. School District of Philadelphia (1976)

Can a school district set aside a limited number of single-sex high schools? *Vorcheimer* involved a student who had applied to Central High School, a public school in Philadelphia. Although she had graduated from junior high with honors, she was denied admittance to high school because she was female. Philadelphia's school district had offered four types of senior high schools: academic, comprehensive, technical, and magnet. Comprehensive schools provided a wide range of courses (particularly courses required for college admission), including advanced-placement classes, and were all coeducational. Academic schools had higher admission standards and offered only college preparatory courses. Philadelphia had two academic schools, one for males and one for female students. Enrollment at either school was strictly voluntary, but students had to meet high scholastic requirements to be admitted—and had to be the correct gender, since neither school was coeducational.

A lower court determined that the courses offered by the two schools were similar in quality, the academic facilities were comparable, and thus "the education available to female students was comparable to that available to male students." But Vorcheimer argued that the standards at the female-only school were not as high as the standards available at the male-only school, thus she wished to switch schools. The trial court agreed; the gender-based classification of students at the two schools lacked a "fair and substantial relationship to the School Board's legitimate interest."

The school district appealed. The appellate court examined the legislation Congress had passed providing for equal education. The education amendments of 1972 ensured that all educational programs funded through federal monies should be available to all persons without discrimination based on sex. But this statute applied only to specified types of educational institutions and excluded coverage of secondary schools. In essence, the legislation was so equivocal that it was of no assistance to the court. Further, legislative intent did not indicate that every secondary school must be coeducational. Even in the Equal Educational Opportunities Act of 1974, Congress indicated an expressed desire to wait for more information before making a decision on the necessity for coeducational institutions. This act allowed that "all children enrolled in public schools are entitled to equal educational opportunity without regard to race, color, sex or national origin." In the absence of congressional mandate or intent, the appellate court decided to consider the constitutional issues that might shed light on the topic.

In contemporary cases that dealt with sex discrimination (see *Frontiero v. Richardson; Kahn v. Shevin; Reed v. Reed*), the Supreme Court had held that sex was not a suspect classification and thus was not subject to heightened scrutiny when the constitutionality of a law was examined. Only in race-based discrimination cases was the law held to the highest level of scrutiny. Essentially, since there is no fundamental difference between races there can be no dissimilar treatment. But there are differences between the sexes that may, in limited circumstances, justify disparity in law. These disparities in law must meet a stricter standard than the mere "rational relationship test" but a less strict standard than the "strict scrutiny" used in race claims. That is, the gender classification must bear a "fair and substantial relationship" to a legitimate governmental objective. In previous cases one gender had suffered an actual deprivation or loss of a benefit that could not be obtained elsewhere. In each instance where a statute was struck down, the rights of the respective sexes conflicted, and the benefits to one gender were found to be less than those offered to the other. Yet in none of the prior cases was equal opportunity extended to each sex (as in *Vorcheimer*), nor did any of the cases involve an educational institution. Vorcheimer did not allege that she was deprived of an education equal to that made available to males. Nor was she denied admission because of a quota system. Moreover, enrollment was solely voluntary, not mandatory. Thus, Vorcheimer could not establish discrimination in the school board's policy. If there were benefits or detriments inherent in the system, they fell on both sexes in equal measure.

The court held that "[e]qual educational opportunities should be available to both sexes in any intellectual field. However, the special emotional problems of the adolescent years are matters of human experience and have led some educational experts to opt for one-sex high schools. Although this policy has limited acceptance on its merits, it does have its basis in a theory of equal benefit and not discriminatory denial." There are, then, some legitimate reasons for a school's remaining single sex. If the primary aim of any school is to furnish a high-quality education, then innovation is allowed in methods and techniques and has a high degree of relevance. Thus, if experts theorize that adolescents may study more effectively in single-sex schools, the policy of the school seems legitimate.

Although the appellate court opinion sympathized with Vorcheimer for not having the freedom of choosing among all schools in the district, the judges also feared that abolishing all single-sex schools would not be prudent because students and parents preferring single-sex schools would be denied their freedom of choice. That there were single-sex private schools available to such people was no more relevant than it was to Vorcheimer.

In a vehement dissent, one judge on the court stated that the majority opinion had established "a twentieth-century sexual equivalent to the *Plessy* decision" (which allowed for separate facilities on the basis of race). The dissent argued that the doctrine of "separate but equal" can and will be invoked to support sexual discrimination in the same manner that it supported racial discrimination. The school district had no evidence that coeducation had an adverse effect upon a student's academic achievement. Indeed, the school could not seriously assert that argument in view of its policy of assigning the vast majority of its students to coeducational schools. So the schools' single-sex policy reflected a choice among educational techniques but not necessarily one substantially related to its stated educational objectives. One of those objectives, in fact, is to provide "educational options to students and their parents." Excluding females precludes achievement of this objective because there is no option of a coeducational academic senior high school.

> *See also* Carnes v. Tennessee Secondary School Athletic Association; Civil Rights Act; *Clark v. Arizona Interscholastic Association; Cohen v. Brown University; Pennsylvania v. Pennsylvania Interscholastic Athletic Association;* Title IX; *Williams v. McNair.*

Williams v. McNair (1971)

In *Williams v. McNair* a lower federal court ruled that a state-supported school in South Carolina, Winthrop College, could limit admissions to "girls" only. Several males had sued the state for not allowing them entrance into the all-female school, arguing that except for their gender, they met all admission requirements. The lower federal court disagreed. South Carolina, the judge ruled, had established a wide range of educational institutions at the college and university level that varied in purpose, curriculum, and location. All institutions were coeducational, with only two exceptions: Winthrop College, which restricted its students to females only, and the Citadel, which restricted its admissions to males.

The judge explained that there were historical reasons for the admission limitations of the two single-sex schools in the state. The Citadel had been designated as a military school and demanded an all-male student body. Winthrop had been designed as a "school for young ladies" and offered courses particularly helpful to female students. The Equal Protection Clause of the Fourteenth Amendment did not require identical treatment for all citizens, the judge opined. Instead, only when the discriminatory treatment is arbitrary and wanting in any rational justification can the law be declared unconstitutional. Here, the court ruled, the gender distinction was warranted. If the state operated only one college and that college denied admission to males, it would clearly be a violation of the Equal Protection Clause. But because the men in South Carolina had access to a varied range of state institutions, they could simply attend a different college.

In 1972 Congress passed Title IX of the education amendments, which made it illegal for any school that received federal funds to discriminate against students on the basis of their gender. That act also, however, allowed some previously single-gender educational facilities to remain single gender. In 1982 the Supreme Court entered the fray in *Mississippi University for Women v. Hogan* and ruled that an all-female nursing college had to admit men into its student body. In 1996 the Supreme Court reexamined the issue (in *United States v. Virginia*) and ruled that an all-

male military college had to admit women into its corps of cadets since the college was funded with federal dollars. The following month, in an attempt to prevent the forced admission of women into the Citadel, the South Carolina legislature funded the Institute of Leadership for Women at Converse College for several million dollars. The legislature argued that it would be a similar institution to the Citadel but only for women. The following year, it was closed and women were admitted to the Citadel.

See also Faulkner, Shannon; Fourteenth Amendment; *Mississippi University for Women v. Hogan; Reed v. Reed;* Title IX; *United States v. Virginia; Vorchheimer v. School District of Philadelphia.*

References and Further Reading

American Women's History Web site: http://www.mtsu.edu/~kmiddlet/history/women/wh-educ.html.

Costello, Cynthia, and Anne J. Stone, eds. 1994. *Where We Stand: Women and Health.* New York: W. W. Norton.

Cushman, Clare, ed. 2001. *Supreme Court Decisions and Women's Rights: Milestones to Equality.* Washington, DC: Congressional Quarterly Press.

Jackson, Donald W. 1992. *Even the Children of Strangers: Equality under the U.S. Constitution.* Lawrence: University Press of Kansas.

Rishe, Patrick J. 1999. "Gender Gaps and the Presence and Profitability of College Football." *Social Science Quarterly* 80: 702–717.

Singleman, Lee, and Paul J. Wahlbeck. 1999. "Gender Proportionality in Intercollegiate Athletics: The Mathematics of Title IX Compliance." *Social Science Quarterly* 80: 518–538.

FAMILY LAW

Adoption

Adoption was not legally recognized by U.S. law until the 1850s. Transfers of children to substitute parents had, of course, occurred informally since colonial times, but most states failed to legitimize informal adoptive arrangements. Part of the reason the law was delayed in recognizing adoption was that there was no formal procedure in the states for recording births or deaths; a child whose parents could or would not provide a home was simply given to a third party who wished to care for the child, and no records were kept.

In fact, until relatively recently, many adoptive arrangements were economically motivated. This was particularly true among families who were involved in agriculture and needed inexpensive labor. With the advent of the industrial revolution, however, many families had migrated to cities for work and were unable to care for large numbers of children. The people who stayed behind to run the farms tended to be the most frequent adopters, and informal transfers of the children were done family-to-family or by charitable and religious institutions.

In 1851 Massachusetts became the first state to pass a statute dealing with adoptions. The statute required judicial approval, consent of the child's parent or guardian, and a finding that the adoptive parents could sufficiently provide for the child. But many of the state statutes that followed the example of Massachusetts offered no safeguards for the children in question; further, there were no state agencies to follow up on the well-being of the child after the adoption had taken place. Although early statutes defined the relationship between adoptive parents and child, the safety of the child and the child's ties to biological parents were unclear.

During the 1930s and into the 1950s, the adoption issue focused almost exclusively on relieving children of the legal stigma of illegitimacy. Judges tended to permit the adoption of out-of-wedlock children without their father's consent as long as the mother consented. Most judges (and states) permanently sealed birth and adoption records, largely to allow the parent or parents who had given the child up for adoption to forever remain nameless and free from possible stigma. As a result, adopted children had no knowledge of their parents, their medical histories, or the circumstances regarding their births.

Until the 1970s, biological fathers who were not wed to the mothers of their children had no right to consent or veto an adoption. But by the 1980s most states had provisions requiring both parents to consent and/or veto adoption of their biological children. Some states also allowed a parent to give up his or her parental rights, for example, as long as the other parent was informed as such. Biological parents could also require that the child given up for adoption not receive any information about them, thereby restricting contact in the future. Today all states treat biological mothers and fathers similarly; that is, the mother must produce an affidavit to the court listing all potential fathers of the child who is to be adopted, and notice of the impending adoption is served on these potential fathers, who can then veto the adoption.

The most controversial debate currently tends to focus on whether adoption records of the children should be sealed. Some states allow adopted children access to their biological parents' names (whether the biological parents wish this or not) and the biological parents' access to their adopted children's new names. Other states are less intrusive and allow both biological parents and the children they give up for adoption to remain anonymous.

Most recent legal cases concerning the adoption process involve state efforts to limit parental rights and allow a third party to adopt. A third party (usually the mother's new husband) typically asks a court for adoptive rights over a child, whereas the natural parent claims his or her own parental rights. An unwed father can be stripped of his parental rights only if the court determines that termination is in a child's best interest; this is true even when he is a fit parent and has actively sought custody of the child for a long period. Similarly, an unwed father cannot escape financial support obligations on grounds that the woman deceived him by falsely claiming she was on some form of contraception. Should a man deny paternity of a child, he can be compelled to take paternity tests, which are not considered an unconstitutional invasion of privacy or improper search and seizure.

See also Child Custody; Divorce; Infertility
   Alternatives; *Lehr v. Robinson.*
Reference D'Emilio, John, and Estelle B.
   Freedman. 1988. *Intimate Matters: A
   History of Sexuality of America.* New York:
   Harper and Row.

Alderson v. Alderson (1986)

Jonne Koening and Steve Alderson met in 1966 in Reno, Nevada. The following year, she moved to Portland, Oregon, to be closer to Steve, and they began cohabiting. Although they planned eventually to marry, they instead lived together for twelve years, sharing finances in a joint bank account and even filing a joint federal income tax return, but never marrying. They purchased a house in Steve's name only, although the down payment came from the couple's joint savings account. Jonne would later testify that she understood the couple owned the property together. The couple had three children together and purchased fourteen separate properties for investment purposes, the down payments coming from the couple's joint savings account and loans from Jonne's parents. In many of the purchases, title was given to the couple as "husband and wife" or "married persons."

Similarly, the couple portrayed themselves as a married couple. Jonne assumed Steve's surname, as did their three children. When they separated in 1979, Jonne signed quitclaim deeds for the couple's property "under duress." According to her, Steve made threats and "told me that I would never get any property. He would see me dead before I got any of them." She later filed an action against him, claiming part ownership in the assets the couple acquired during their cohabitation, validation of the children's parentage, as well as damages for a broken arm she had received in a scuffle with Steve. Steve denied paternity of two of the children, claiming Jonne had sexual relations with other men during the course of their relationship. (He later admitted his paternity of the children and accepted blame for Jonne's broken arm.)

The question for the state court was how much of the couple's property should be distributed equitably even though they never formally married. The California court established that Jonne was entitled to an undivided one-half interest in the property, $15,000 in compensatory damages, and another $4,000 in punitive damages for Steve's battery. Steve appealed. He claimed that the judgment was erroneous because of a former decision, *Marvin v. Marvin* (1976), which held that a contract between two unmarried persons living together "will not be enforced if an inseparable part of the consideration for the contract is an agreement to provide sexual services." Presumably, Steve's argument was that he and Jonne had such a contract to provide sexual services to each other. The appellate court found no merit to Steve's argument.

Divorce in the United States is at an all-time high and has a disproportionate impact on women, leading to what is termed the "feminization of poverty." After divorce, women tend to become the primary caretakers of children and thus see an increase in their monthly expenditures and a decrease in family income; the glass ceiling in the workplace further limits their income (which is lower than men's even before divorce).

See also Marriage; *Marvin v. Marvin.*

Alimony

Alimony is a court-ordered financial allowance to one party in a divorce for either the life of that party or a limited period of time. Under the English doctrine of coverture, man and wife were one person, with the man responsible for his wife's financial welfare and the wife responsible for keeping the couple's home and children. Alimony simply builds on that concept. Following divorce, an award of alimony usually ceases when the spouse receiving support remarries or begins cohabiting with another partner. Critics contend that alimony decisions may also reflect and reinforce the view that once she enters into a sexual relationship, a woman becomes financially dependent on her partner. Historically, alimony was awarded to ensure a woman's financial support until her death or remarriage, when she would become the

responsibility of another man; to reward virtue and punish wrongdoing; to maintain the status or standard of living the wife attained by marriage; and to compensate the wife for her labor during the marriage. Alimony also became a means of adjusting equities, especially after property was distributed, to ensure that wives shared in the fruits of the marriage. The award of alimony changed dramatically in the last decade of the twentieth century. Although provisions vary somewhat from state to state, there is generally a much greater emphasis on demonstrated need and the spouse's potential for becoming self-supporting.

There are essentially three types of alimony: permanent, restitutional, and rehabilitative. Permanent alimony is an allowance for support and maintenance (i.e., the provision of food, clothing, housing, and other necessities) of a former spouse for life. A party who requests permanent alimony must establish not only a need for such support but also that the former spouse has sufficient means and abilities to provide for part or all of that need. Restitutional and rehabilitative alimony, in contrast, are for a specified period of time. Rehabilitative alimony is designed to provide the financial support necessary to enable a spouse to refresh or enhance job skills necessary to become self-sufficient. A party's foregone education and employment opportunities during the marriage, the length of absence from the job market, and the skills and time necessary to become self-sufficient are considered when determining the amount. Restitutional alimony, intended to punish one party for transgressions during the marriage, is no longer used.

Throughout the twentieth century, alimony was typically awarded to wives in divorce cases. In awarding any type of alimony, courts were required to evaluate the respective fault of each party in the dissolution of the marriage . But by the end of the century, awards of alimony had become less common, and the spouse seeking support has the burden of demonstrating the need. The courts consider the length of the marriage; the parties' prospective financial conditions after the property division; the parties' ages, health, and physical conditions; and the parties' educational and occupational status or social standing. Although some states still take fault into consideration, the alimony now awarded is generally temporary, transitional support to allow a period of adjustment and retraining.

Supporters for changes in alimony laws argue that divorced women are entitled to more alimony, particularly when they have put their husbands through professional school or enhanced the value of their husbands' businesses or careers through entertaining, managing the home, or other efforts. Here, too, the different ways of valuing these past contributions reflect changing views of marital relations. The husband's degree or business may be evaluated and split by the marital partners the same way business partners would divide their assets if their partnership dissolved. A second approach would simply reimburse the wife for her actual contributions (such as her husband's support and educational or business expenses) as though the two spouses were separate individuals who were involved in a business deal. Obviously, women in traditional homemaker roles without independent sources of income have foregone opportunities to develop their own earnings.

The skyrocketing divorce rate in the United States has complicated this issue as well. Divorced women suffer severe financial limitations largely because they usually retain responsibility for children born into the marriage. Although divorced women suffer economic disadvantages following divorce, divorced men tend to see an increase in their economic well-being. Critics argue that inadequate alimony and child support are the most important factors contributing to poverty among divorced women and their children. And as courts are less and less likely to award alimony in divorce cases, divorce-related poverty becomes worse. When alimony is awarded, it is often low and generally seen as a temporary measure to provide transitional support while women retrain themselves, locate a new job, or remarry.

See also Coverture; Divorce.
Reference Langley, Winston E., and Vivian C. Fox, eds. 1994. *Women's Rights in the United States.* Westport, CT: Greenwood.

Annulment of Marriage

Annulment is a judicial declaration that a marriage never existed. Divorce, in comparison, is the judicial dissolving of a legitimate marriage. Division of marital property and obligations like alimony thus occur following divorce but not in cases of annulment. The concept of annulment comes from the contractual agreement parties enter into when they marry; a contract cannot exist if one party is legally incapable of entering into contracts. For example, in a case of polygamy, no formal annulment is necessary since polygamy renders the second marriage void: one party is already legally married and so cannot enter into yet another marriage contract. Incestuous marriages are treated similarly.

States have established various other grounds for annulment, which must have existed at the time of the "marriage." A marriage can be annulled if one or both partners were under the legal age required for marriage at the time of the wedding ceremony, if one party is permanently physically incapable of normal sexual relations, if one party has venereal disease, or if violence or the threat of violence forced one party to marry another. Mental incapacity to enter into a contract is also a ground in some states.

Perhaps the most controversial reason for annulment is fraud, and some states apply a harsher punishment for the offending party if the marriage has already been consummated before the other party was aware of the fraud. If one party never intended to have children but indicated at the time of the marriage ceremony that he or she did, the marriage could be annulled on the grounds of fraud, as it could be if one party denied the other conjugal rights, particularly if that party never intended to have sexual relations after marriage. The most common form of fraud occurs when one party enters into the marriage for a limited purpose, such as obtaining a work visa through the Immigration and Naturalization Service.

One of the most interesting aspects of annulment statutes are those that allow a court to declare that the marriage never existed (because of one or more of the above grounds) even if it was relatively long standing. The goal of annulment is to put both parties in the same positions they would have been in had they never gone through a marriage ceremony. Although there are few studies on annulments, parties typically file for annulment instead of divorce for religious reasons. In such cases, courts may declare marriages invalid from the date of the court judgment, freeing both parties from any financial claims of their former partner but making children born to or adopted by annulled parents legitimate and setting up child support and custody agreements.

See also Divorce; Domestic Partners; Marriage.
Reference Michael Smith Foster. 1999. *Annulment: The Wedding That Was: How the Church Can Declare a Marriage Null.* New York: Paulist Press.

C. K. v. Shalala (1996)

C. K. v. Shalala upheld the family cap provision, a New Jersey law that eliminated the standard increase provided by Aid to Families with Dependent Children (AFDC) for any child born to someone receiving AFDC. New Jersey residents receiving AFDC filed a class-action suit against the state for implementing the Family Development Pro-

gram, of which the family cap was one provision. The court noted that New Jersey did not attempt to fetter or constrain the welfare mother's right to bear as many children as she chose but simply required her to find a way to pay for her additional progeny's care.

See also Temporary Assistance to Needy Families (TANF).

California, Secretary of Health, Education, and Welfare v. Westcott (1979)

California, Secretary of Health, Education, and Welfare v. Westcott was a class-action suit brought by two married couples against the secretary of the Department of Health, Education, and Welfare in Massachusetts. They questioned Act 407 of the Social Security Act, which gave Aid to Families with Dependent Children (AFDC) only to families in which the father was unemployed. AFDC, of course, is intended to provide aid to low-income families. The couples argued that the act was gender biased because it did not allow aid to be provided for families headed by mothers, and so was a violation of the Fifth and Fourteenth Amendments. The district court did not nullify the act but stated that benefits must be paid to families regardless of whether it was the mother or the father who was unemployed.

See also Fourteenth Amendment; Temporary Assistance to Needy Families (TANF).

Child Custody

In colonial times custody battles between parents were few because women had almost no legal rights to their children upon divorce. In the English common law (later adopted by the American colonies), children were seen as the property of the father, who had a legal obligation to protect, support, and educate them. Until the 1800s, a father had almost absolute right to his children regardless of circumstances; he even had the legal right (if not the moral one) to sell his children into forced labor as indentured servants. If a woman was widowed, the court could assign custody of her children to a male guardian. In the case of illegitimacy, the court could punish and fine both parents and decide the fate of the children.

But among the expanded rights women won after the Civil War were more rights to their children. Courts generally began granting custody on the basis of the "tender years" doctrine, which gave mothers custody of children under six years and fathers custody of older ones. By the 1920s legislation helped mothers even more, and the courts favored maternal custody regardless of the child's age. The mother was seen as the more nurturing parent and thus the better party to receive custody. Child-support laws are were also passed at this time forcing financial support from absent fathers.

But by the 1970s, as divorce rates soared, fathers pushed for custody determinations based on the "best interests of the child," that is, the child's needs and interests rather than the gender of the parent. Generally, a mother's legal claim to child custody following divorce weakened. By the 1980s and 1990s, the courts moved toward concepts such as joint custody, particularly as more women moved into the workforce. In 1979 California initiated the first joint-custody statute; by 1991 forty-eight states had similar laws. As divorce became more and more common, few households were untouched by custody matters. A child born in 1990, for example, had about a 50 percent chance of falling under the jurisdiction of a court involving where (and with whom) that child would live.

The courts use expert witnesses, usually mental health professionals, to assist them in selecting the best parent for custody in divorce cases. The courts evaluate the potential harmful effects on the moral development of the children, and can terminate parental rights involuntarily on grounds of abuse, abandonment, and neglect if there is clear and convincing proof. Neither financial inability to provide for a child nor lack of time to properly raise a child is sufficient grounds to remove a child from a parent's custody, nor is the parent's sexual orientation.

With the exploding divorce rate, as well as an increase in out-of-wedlock children, the idea of parenthood has been redefined. In 1999 one-third of mothers had never been married, and 18.6 million children in the United States were living with only one parent. Further, approximately two-thirds of all children were living with divorced or separated parents, and nearly six out of ten children living only with their mothers were near (or below) the poverty line. States have handled their increasing child-custody caseloads differently. Many routinely grant joint legal custody, which gives the nonresidential parent the right to participate in major decisions about the children's upbringing and to view certain records of the child. Less common is joint physical custody. Under this arrangement, the child lives with both parents, often on an alternating-week basis. Joint custody was nearly unheard of before 1970 because of the judicial preference for placing children with their mothers. Mothers still win custody in 85 percent of custody cases.

See also Adoption; Child Support; Divorce; *Lehr v. Robinson; Schuster v. Schuster.*
Reference Peter Jaffe, Nancy Lemon, and Samantha Poisson. 2002. *Child Custody and Domestic Violence: A Call for Safety and Accountability.* Thousand Oaks, CA: Sage.

Child Support

The issues of child support and welfare benefits for indigent children have been aligned since 1935, when Congress established Aid to Families with Dependent Children (AFDC), changed to Temporary Assistance to Needy Families in 1996. This program gives money to states to provide a minimum monthly stipend to indigent families and ensures all American children a basic standard of living. In 1984 Congress passed

Table 4.1: Child Support in the United States

All Custodial Parents	Number (millions)
Total	13,529
Awarded Child Support	7,945
Percent	58.7
Number of Those Due Child Support	6,791
Average Child Support Due	$4,755
Average Child Support Received	$2,791
Received Any Child Support	5,005
Percent	73.7
Received Full Amount of Child Support	3,006
Percent	45.1

Source: U.S. Census Bureau, Current Population Survey, 1999.

the Child Support Enforcement Amendments (CSEA), which required states to strengthen enforcement of child-support judgments of delinquent parents in an attempt to make them help carry the financial burden of caring for children. This act required employers, for example, to withhold paychecks of parents who were delinquent in paying their support obligation, allowed liens to be imposed against the property of delinquent parents, and allowed states to confiscate federal and state income tax refunds to pay support obligations. States were also required to offer such services to parents receiving child-support payments even if they were not eligible for AFDC benefits (which make up at least 50 percent of all delinquent child-support obligations).

But the most far-reaching mandate of the federal government was the Child Support Recovery Act of 1992 (CSRA), which made nonpayment of child support to a child in another state a federal criminal offense. The intent behind the law was twofold: to prevent noncustodial parents from fleeing across state lines to avoid paying their child-support obligations, and to facilitate recovery of unpaid child support. Punishment includes up to six months of federal detention and a fine with no right to a jury trial. For subsequent violations, the sentence is increased to two years' imprisonment.

But typically it is up to the state courts to get parents to pay child support. Most states impose fines and jail sentences for delinquency of payments. Courts may also order a defendant to be placed on probation for several years, with additional jail time for violating any conditions of probation. In general, as elements of probation, states have required that defendants support their dependents financially, that they maintain employment or pursue an education that will equip them for employment, or that the defendants appear at all child-support hearings. Federal charges are filed only when there are patterns of flight from state to state, seemingly to avoid payment, or patterns of deception to avoid payment (such as changing employment or concealing assets).

But neither the states nor the federal government has been particularly successful in getting support payments paid. In 1999, for example, 5.6 million custodial parents had no child-support agreements with the noncustodial parent. Of the nearly 8 million custodial parents entitled to child support, only 75 percent received the payments. The average payment was $3,800 per child.

See also Child Custody; Divorce; Temporary Assistance to Needy Families (TANF).

Civil Unions

In July 2000 Vermont passed the first civil union law in the country, allowing couples of the same sex (or opposing sexes) to enter into unions that granted similar legal rights as marriage. Lois Farnham and Holly Puterbaugh, who had lived together for almost twenty-eight years, were one of three same-sex couples who in 1997 challenged the Vermont marriage laws, which denied same-sex couples the privileges of marriage. Since passage of the civil union law, over 4,200 gay and lesbian couples have entered into civil unions in Vermont.

One complication of the new law, however, is the difficulty in dissolving the unions (or having the court grant "divorces" to partners in civil unions). Vermont requires one partner of the union to reside in that state before a dissolution can be granted. But couples from other states have traveled to Vermont to take advantage of the civil union law, and since no other state recognizes civil unions, there are many situations in which no state court has jurisdiction over a couple's wish to dissolve their union. It would take the Supreme Court to grant such a divorce in order to force states to recognize civil unions.

> *See also* Divorce; Gay and Lesbian Adoption; Marriage.
> *Reference* William N. Eskridge. 2001. *Equality Practice: Civil Unions and the Future of Gay Rights.* New York: Routledge.

Community Property

Community property is a system of property distribution during a dissolution of marriage whereby all income and property acquired during the marriage (other than gifts or inheritance) generally belongs to both spouses and is to be divided equally, even though only one spouse may have legal control over it. States that have community-property systems are Arizona, California, Idaho, Louisiana, Nevada, New Mexico, Texas, and Washington. In the contrasting system, a common-law system, income or property generally goes to the spouse who has title to it or should be accorded title based on a court's determination.

In states with a community-property system, neither spouse can, during divorce, sell, mortgage, or lease his or her undivided interest in the community property until it is partitioned by the court, since each party has a 50 percent interest in it. This distribution of property encompasses only property that was acquired during the marriage through the effort, skill, or industry of either spouse. Homemakers (or spouses that have not worked or received a salary for work outside the home) can receive an equitable distribution of marital property upon divorce, no matter which partner formally owned or earned the property. What is most controversial in a community-property system is which assets are considered part of the marital estate for the purpose of redistribution. Real estate or savings acquired during the marriage are clearly subject to community-property laws, but what about a professional degree a husband has earned while being supported by his wife? Further, it is unclear whether a spouse's business that has increased enormously in worth during the course of the marriage should be part of the redistribution (particularly if only one spouse worked at that business).

Courts have used several methods to calculate the contribution of homemakers. Some courts have sought to determine what a homemaker's services were worth in terms of their replacement cost (i.e., how much would it cost to hire someone to do x hours per day of child care or housecleaning?). Others have sought to determine the homemaker's lost opportunity costs (i.e., how much would she have earned had she not sacrificed her occupation in the interest of homemaking?).

> *See also* Divorce.
> *Reference* Friedman, Lawrence M. 1985. *A History of American Law.* 2d ed. New York: Simon and Schuster.

Divorce

Divorce was unavailable under the jurisdiction of English courts prior to the reign of King Henry VIII. Although parliamentary or legislative divorces did exist during the latter seventeenth century, they were very rare and given usually to wealthy litigants because of the expense of waging extensive legal campaigns. By the early twentieth century, however, all American states (except South Carolina, which did not permit permanent divorce until 1948) had enacted laws authorizing courts to dissolve marriages for justifiable legal grounds (or "fault" of one of the parties). These grounds usually included adultery, cruelty, desertion, incurable insanity, or voluntary separation for an extended time. Prior to the twentieth century, however, husbands had a legal right to "use such a degree of force as is necessary to make the wife behave herself and know her place," thus subverting her right to divorce on grounds of abuse.

Those with sufficient means often undermined their state's requirements by establishing temporary domicile in a more permissive jurisdiction or by staging a courtroom charade to fit one of the justifiable legal grounds for divorce. For those without such resources, informal separation was the only alternative. But after the 1960s, divorce policies in almost all Western countries were either completely revised or substantially reformed. In 1969 California became the first state to adopt a divorce code that dispensed entirely with fault-based divorce; it recognized circumstances for divorce where there was no legal need to attribute fault, responsibility, or offense to either spouse for a divorce to be granted.

There had been examples of no-fault provisions in former divorce codes (e.g., divorce by mutual agreement or reasons of incompatibility, insanity, impotence, or unavoidable absence), yet these grounds for divorce did place responsibility on one spouse, even if fault was not actually attributed. In no-fault divorce codes, spouses are not considered either innocent or guilty; the court simply recognizes the permanent and irretrievable breakdown of the marriage and both spouses agree to a divorce. Every state has now instituted no-fault procedures based on an irreparable collapse of the marriage or on some other no-fault criterion, such as separation for a relatively short interval.

As such, no-fault divorce does not rest on the precise circumstances that produced the failure of the marriage but simply on the fact of the breakdown. Most laws specify a period during which a couple must have lived separately and the marriage has ceased to have practical meaning; thus, much of the onus of defining the breakdown is given to the spouses themselves and not the courts. This is a profound change in divorce law because it overcomes the centuries-long principle that divorce must be closely regulated by the church or

---

Figure 4.1: U.S. Divorce Statistics

Total divorces granted in 1997: 1,163,000

Rate per 1,000 population (1999) (excluding CA, CO, IN and LA): 4.1

State with the highest divorce rate: Nevada. Rate per 1,000 population (1997): 9.0

Current number of divorced adults (1998): 19,400,000 (9.8%)

Median age at divorce: (1997):
    Males: 35.6
    Females: 33.2

Median duration of marriage (1997): 7.2 years

Likelihood of new marriages ending in divorce in 1997: 43%

Source: http://www.divorcemag.com/statistics/statsUS.shtml

state and, instead, allows divorce to be managed by the couple. Additionally, alimony has now been severely limited (*Orr v. Orr* [1979]) and almost always terminates when the dependent former spouse remarries. Spousal maintenance generally is avoided entirely or limited to only brief rehabilitative periods. In theory, equality between the parties can be more easily accomplished through distribution of existing assets rather than future income. In 2003 only about one-sixth of all divorcing women received maintenance, and two-thirds of the awards were for limited duration, averaging about two years.

When minor children are involved, the legal divorce must address both their physical custody and financial support. The court must also address the interests of the spouses in the distribution of their joint property, which includes, of course, assets, cash, property, and retirement benefits or pensions but can also include professional degrees gained during the course of the marriage and contributions to the marital household that a homemaker spouse has made. In common-law states, the court attempts to distribute the property equally between the parties. In community-property states, each spouse has legal title to one-half of the marital property and the court manages its distribution.

About half of all contemporary marriages in the United States currently end in divorce, and 60 percent of all children will spend time in single-parent homes. As a result, prenuptial contracts have become more common. These are agreements prospective brides and grooms enter into that identify each party's legal interest in the other's property upon divorce (or death). The courts have tended to uphold both prenuptial and postnuptial contracts providing fraud, duress, mistake, or unconscionably changed circumstances did not occur. Generally, however, these contracts are not set aside even if one party does not fully understand the terms, one party fails to make a full disclosure of assets, or the agreement is not fair to one party.

> *See also* Annulment of Marriage; Child Custody; Child Support; Community Property; Divorce; *Marvin v. Marvin; Orr v. Orr;* Prenuptial and Postnuptial Agreements; *Schuster v. Schuster.*
> *Reference* Herbert Jacob. 1998. *Silent Revolution: The Transformation of Divorce Law in the United States.* Chicago: University of Chicago Press.

Domestic Partners

By the early 1980s, the number of unwed partners living together was on the rise and some of these couples were of the same sex. In 1996 Congress passed the Defense of Marriage Act, which prohibits federal recognition of same-sex marriages and gives states the authority to deny "full faith and credit" to same-sex marriages from other states. Prior to this act, under the Full Faith and Credit Clause of the Constitution, all states had to recognize the legitimacy of marriages (and other contracts) formed in other states. Directly following passage of the 1996 law, twenty-seven states passed laws against same-sex marriages.

Although there is currently no state that recognizes domestic partners, and certainly none that recognize same-sex marriages, Vermont has come close by recognizing "civil unions." In 1999 the high court of Vermont held that same-sex couples could no longer be denied equal protections, benefits, and responsibilities under the law. The court held that "the issue before the Court . . . does not turn on the religious or moral debate over intimate same-sex relationships, but rather on the statutory and constitutional basis for the exclusion of same-sex couples from the secular benefits and protections offered married couples." The court then turned the issue over to the state legislature, which acknowledged (via statute) civil unions. Civil unions provide virtually the same state-sponsored protections, responsibilities, and benefits afforded through marriage. Any couple (whether of the same sex or of opposing sexes) can enter into a civil union, but no other state has to recognize this union outside of Vermont and grant the benefits that come with marriage. Further, since the Vermont legislature reserved marriage to heterosexual couples, same-sex couples entering into civil unions do not qualify for federal benefits such as Social Security, immigration status, and certain tax breaks.

Vermont's civil union law is the only one of its kind in the country but many critics charge that the law simply promotes a "separate but equal" system for same-sex couples (although heterosexual couples who do not wish to join into a traditional marriage contract can also use the state's civil union mandate). In 2001, opponents of the legislation proposed an amendment to the Vermont constitution that defined marriage as a union between one man and one woman. The amendment failed. A similar amendment that limits marriage to a man and a woman and bans recognition of same-sex marriages from any other state was passed in California.

In late 2002 the first real test of Vermont's law began. Glen Rosengarten died after filing suit in his home state of Connecticut to dissolve his same-sex civil union with his former partner, Peter Downes. The couple joined into a civil union in 2000 in Vermont directly after the civil union law was passed. Rosengarten first filed suit in Vermont, but that state was unable to dissolve the union because neither partner was a Vermont resident so the state courts had no jurisdiction over the couple. But when he filed suit in Connecticut, where both partners lived, that state also denied relief because it does not recognize civil (or same-sex) unions. He had argued that if a civil union was not a marriage then it was a contract like any other, and therefore the state courts did have jurisdiction. As of late 2003 there was no resolution of the issue.

The Supreme Court first entered into a debate regarding the Full Faith and Credit Clause with *Loving v. Virginia* (1967), when it ruled that Virginia's miscegenation statute (banning interracial marriage) was unconstitutional. But Rosengarten's case is the first time any state was asked to acknowledge the Vermont civil union law.

The legal nature of domestic partnership for heterosexual couples has changed as well. In 1979 a California court awarded Michelle Triola Marvin compensation for an oral contract she had entered into with her live-in partner, Lee Marvin. Although she did not receive one-half of the couple's property, as she would have if the couple had married, the case (*Marvin v. Marvin*) established the legal concept of "palimony" for couples who failed to enter into matrimony yet lived together as husband and wife.

See also Annulment of Marriage; Gay and Lesbian Adoption; Marriage; *Marvin v. Marvin*; Palimony.

Gay and Lesbian Adoption

The number of adoptions by same-sex partners has increased at the turn of the twenty-first century, mirroring the rise in the number of same-sex biological parents. In 1975 there were between 300,000 and 500,000 same-sex biological parents, but by 1990 the number of children in the United States with gay or lesbian parents rose to over 6 million. Part of the reason states are more willing to allow same-sex partners adoption privileges is the enormous number of children in foster care who are eligible for adoption. In 1999, for example, there were over 115,000 such children, but there were qualified adoptive families available for only about 20 percent of them.

According to certain estimates, approximately 10 percent of the American population (or 25 million people) are homosexual. Some children living in same-sex parental homes are adopted, others were born to donor-inseminated women in lesbian partnerships, but most are in fact children of divorce: they are the biological children of a

Lesbian couple with adopted child. (Laura Dwight)

heterosexual partnership that has dissolved, one parent taking the children into a new, same-sex partnership.

The most controversial aspect of same-sex parenting involves whether such a lifestyle is harmful to the child or promotes an unhealthy environment for the child. Conservative political and religious groups point to research indicating the negative impact such parenthood has on children, whereas those supporting equal rights to same-sex couples point to research indicating the contrary. Nevertheless, before 1973 homosexuality was listed as a mental disorder, and state courts barred gays and lesbians from adopting or having many parental rights for fear of harming the child. The Supreme Court has stepped in to attempt to address such parenting issues only once. In *Palmore v. Sidoti* (1984), a Florida father sought custody of his daughter because his white ex-

wife had married a black man; the father feared that his daughter would be exposed to the stigma of an interracial family. But the Court held that the daughter could stay with her mother: "Private biases may be outside the reach of the law, but the law cannot, directly or indirectly, give them effect." Although this case did not explicitly explore the impact of same-sex parents on their children, it does seem to indicate that a child's best interests are not necessarily violated when he or she is raised in a family that may be stigmatized by society.

States have differed in their treatment of same-sex couples who wish to adopt children. Nine states (California, Massachusetts, New Jersey, New Mexico, New York, Ohio, Vermont, Washington, and Wisconsin) as well as the District of Columbia allow gays and lesbians to adopt. Most such adoptions are granted to one person, who then applies for his or her partner to adopt as a coparent. Second-parent, or coparent, adoption is the only way for both members of a same-sex couple to become legal parents of their children, since only one state (Vermont) recognizes same-sex unions.

Vermont is also the only state court that has explicitly ruled on the issue of second-parent adoption, in the case *Adoptions of B.L.V.B. and E.L.V.B.* (1993). Jane Van Buren gave birth to two children through anonymous donor insemination. Under Vermont law at the time, she was considered the only possible parent of the children. Her partner, Deborah Lashman, had no parental rights since the couple was not legally married under state law. When the couple asked the trial court for a second-parent adoption, they were denied because Lashman was not married to the children's biological parent (Van Buren). The supreme court of that state ruled in 1993 that joint custody could be given to both parents, thus making it the first state court to recognize lesbian second-parent adoptions. Of course, in 2000, Vermont passed the country's first civil union law, recognizing the right of same-sex couples to enter into contracts similar to a marital contract.

Of all the states who have broached the same-sex adoption debate, only two states, Florida and New Hampshire, explicitly bar gays and lesbians from adopting children, whether by adoption of a new child or co-parent adoption.

See also Adoption; Domestic Partners; Marriage; Palimony.

References Hicks, Stephen, and Janet McDermott, eds. 1998. *Lesbian and Gay Fostering and Adoption: Extraordinary Yet Ordinary.* Philadelphia: Jessica Kingsley Press; Starr, Karla J. 1998. "Adoption by Homosexuals: A Look at Differing State Court Opinions." *Arizona Law Review* 40 (Winter): 1497.

Kirchberg v. Feenstra (1981)

In *Kirchberg v. Feenstra* the Supreme Court ruled that Louisiana's community-property system—which gave husbands full title over all marital property—was unconstitutional. In 1974 Joan Feenstra filed a criminal complaint against her husband, Harold, for molesting their minor daughter. While in jail, Harold hired attorney Karl Kirchberg to represent him and signed a promissory note for $3,000 to cover initial attorney fees. To pay for other attorney fees, Harold later received a second mortgage on the home he owned with his wife. But Joan was not informed of this second mortgage because of the state statute giving the husband exclusive control over a married couple's property.

The child molestation charge was later dropped, and the couple separated. But in 1976, after the Feenstras failed to pay his fees for representing Harold in the molestation charge, Kirchberg began foreclosure proceedings on the Feenstras' home for payment of the promissory note Harold had signed. Joan Feenstra challenged the constitutionality of Louisiana's community-property system. The Court ruled that a state law that classifies individuals on the basis of their gender, as the community-property

statute did here, must carry the burden of showing an "exceedingly persuasive justification" for the classification. Since Louisiana failed to do this, the statute violated the equal protection guarantee of the Fourteenth Amendment.

Louisiana changed their law and gave both spouses equal control over the disposition of community property in 1980. Currently, a lease or other encumbrance cannot be placed on a property without the consent of both parties.

See also Common Law; Community Property; Divorce; Fourteenth Amendment.

Lehr v. Robinson (1983)

Lehr v. Robinson involved an unmarried father who filed a petition to vacate the adoption of his child. At two years of age, the child had been given up for adoption by the natural mother and her husband (who was not the natural father of the child). The natural father had never supported the child and never entered his name in a father registry, which would have notified him of the adoption proceeding. He was also not included in a class created by New York statute to receive notification of adoption proceedings. The Supreme Court ruled that the biological father's due process rights were not violated because he never had any significant custodial, personal, or financial relationship with the child.

See also Adoption; Child Custody.

Marriage

Marriage has provided societies with a way to transfer property rights as well as perpetuate the species. In the early nineteenth century, the church had jurisdiction over marriage and divorce in the United States. Often couples were simply common-law spouses. A common-law marriage (in states that recognized this form of marriage) was a legally valid yet relatively informal verbal agreement between a man and a woman who considered themselves married while cohabiting; no formal ceremony preceded this agreement. Common-law marriages were most frequent before the Civil War because of the lack of clergy members to perform formal civil ceremonies before the beginning of the twentieth century.

But legally defining who was married was very important, since women gave up so many rights upon their marriage. Rooted in English common law, life in colonial America was organized around a preindustrial, family-based economy, and although women were an integral part of this arrangement, these contributions rarely allowed women to participate in the important decisions in family or community. Under the doctrine of coverture, the husband was considered lord of the manor, and a woman's legal identity ceased to exist upon marriage.

Prior to the twentieth century, the Supreme Court gave the states almost unfettered latitude in controlling the conditions of both common-law as well as religious marriages. The Court insisted only that one state recognize the legitimacy of a marriage that had transpired in another state. But in 1878 the tide began to turn. In *Reynolds v. United States* the Court refused to recognize polygamy as a legitimate form of marriage and thus began the process of creating a national standard of legal marriage. After *Griswold v. Connecticut* in 1965, when the Court declared marriage a "sacred" relationship" that the state could not intrude upon except for certain circumstances, the Court decided a series of cases that forever defined the institution of marriage in the United States. The Court overturned a Virginia law banning interracial marriages in 1967, and in 1978 voided a Wisconsin law prohibiting the remarriage of a noncustodial parent delinquent on court-ordered child-support payment to a former spouse (any person subject to child support could not marry without demonstrating financial responsibility; no similar restriction was placed on the custodial parent, usually the

mother). In other areas of marriage where the Court has yet to act, states have consistently limited the rights and benefits available for separating partners who only cohabited. Social Security and retirement benefits are not given to an unwed partner, and good moral character—a requirement for taking the Virginia state bar examination, for example—cannot be denied because one lives with a person or is cohabiting with an unmarried partner.

Currently, marriage is a completely secular institution, protected by the Fourteenth Amendment and monitored by the courts. It is a civil contract or legal agreement between a man and a woman. No state forbids religious ceremonies, however, and in fact most civil marriages are performed by religious officials. Further, many of the limitations that marriage brought for women have been removed. As such, the rights, duties, and obligations of husband and wife are controlled by laws of the relevant state and not the parties themselves. As the population has increased, marriage has also become more formalized. All states now have nearly uniform provisions for marriage licenses and civil ceremonies. Most states today have abolished the concept of the common-law marriage largely because these marriages go unrecorded, greatly complicating distribution of property upon dissolution of the union. There are restrictions in all states today on who can get married and the age of consent.

And finally, courts in all states have refused to recognize marital status and the property distribution of individuals involved in same-sex unions. This is true even in states that have an Equal Rights Amendment. One state, Vermont, has legalized "civil unions," but they are not "marriages" so do not gain all the benefits, including acknowledgment by other states of their existence, that go along with matrimony.

With the increasing divorce rate, most cases regarding marriage today focus on the issue of property rights upon dissolution of the marriage. States are either common-law property states or community-property states. In community-property states, each spouse has legal ownership of one-half of the earnings of the other spouse. Until the women's movement, since husbands exercised legal control over all property, they could manage it (or even sell it) if they so chose. But wives now have powers of management over joint property. In common-law states, each party generally owns the property for which it has legal title. All states recognize prenuptial contracts that are entered into before marriage; these contracts seek to identify each party's legal interest in the other's property upon death or divorce. Courts generally respect the terms of the contract as long as neither party was defrauded or under duress. Courts have, however, modified agreements pertaining to child support and custody.

> *See also* Annulment of Marriage; Child Custody; Community Property; Coverture; Divorce; Domestic Partners; Fourteenth Amendment; Gay and Lesbian Adoption; *Griswold v. Connecticut*; *Kirchberg v. Feenstra*; Marital Rape; Married Women's Property Acts; Palimony; Prenuptial and Postnuptial Agreements.
>
> *References* Hendrik Hartog. 2000. *Man and Wife in America: A History*. Cambridge, MA: Harvard University Press; Ellen K. Rothman. 1984. *Hands and Hearts: A History of Courtship in America*. New York: BasicBooks.

Marvin v. Marvin (1976)

Unmarried domestic partners have always existed, but before the twentieth century the law classified them as common-law spouses. After most states ended common-law marriage, however, unmarried domestic partners were treated as not only illegal but also immoral. Today, of course, it is more acceptable for people to live together outside of marriage. Many states have attempted some sort of fair compensation when faced with long-term relationships that ultimately fail.

Michelle Triola Marvin (Bettmann/Corbis)

Michelle Triola Marvin, the live-in companion of celebrity Lee Marvin, sued after the couple's relationship soured. She argued that because the couple had a contract similar to a marriage contract, she had the same rights as a spouse and she deserved compensation for her contributions to their "marital" home. Ultimately, the California court disagreed with her, but she was awarded $104,000 to allow her to learn new employable skills. This figure was estimated by taking the highest salary Michelle had ever received, $1,000 per week as a singer, and multiplying it over the years.

The parties began living together in 1964 and, according to Michelle, "entered into an oral agreement" that while "the parties lived together they would combine their efforts and earnings and would share equally any and all property accumulated as a result of their efforts whether individual or combined." The couple agreed to "hold themselves out to the general public as husband and wife," and, Michelle contended, she agreed to contribute her "services as a companion, homemaker, housekeeper and cook" to Lee. In doing so, she gave up "her lucrative career as an entertainer and singer" in order to devote herself full time to Lee. In return, Lee agreed to provide for all of Michelle's "financial support and needs for the rest of her life." During the next seven years, the couple acquired substantial real estate and personal property, including motion picture rights worth over $1 million.

After Lee moved out of the couple's home, he continued to support Michelle for over a year, but when his support stopped, Michelle sued. She asked the court to determine whether the couple's contract was valid; if it was, then she asked for one-half of the couple's property acquired during the course of the relationship. A trial court dismissed her claims largely because of Lee's contention that the alleged contract was closely related to the "immoral" character of the couple's relationship. He rested his argument on the fact that he was still legally married to another woman, Betty, while living with Michelle. Thus, enforcing the alleged contract between the couple would violate public policy. Further, Lee had argued that previous cases decided in California held that a contract between nonmarital partners was unenforceable if it involved an "illicit relationship" or was made in contemplation of one. Finally, he contended that even if there had been an agreement, a California law provided that "all contracts for marriage settlements must be in writing." So, if nothing else, this law would render any agreement the parties made unenforceable.

The trial court, however, concluded that a contract between nonmarried partners was nonenforceable only if it rested upon the immoral and illicit considerations of "sexual services." Therefore, if a man and a woman live together outside the bounds of marriage and engage in a sexual relationship,

agreements can be made (and would be legally enforceable) as to the distribution of property. These agreements are invalid only if the relationship rests on the exchange of sexual services because such a contract would be, in essence, an agreement for prostitution and unlawful. If the couple does not have a contract, courts can explore the conduct of the parties to determine whether there was an implied contract or some tacit understanding between the couple.

The court pointed out that the prevalence of nonmarital relationships in society (and societal acceptance of them) gave the relationships a sense of legitimacy. The "mores of society have indeed changed so radically in regard to cohabitation that the court [could not] impose a standard on alleged moral considerations that have apparently been so widely abandoned by so many [people]."

See also Divorce; Domestic Partners; Palimony.

O'Brien v. O'Brien (1985)

In *O'Brien v. O'Brien*, a state appellate court held that a medical license obtained during marriage is marital property subject to equitable distribution upon divorce. When the O'Briens were married in 1971, they were employed as public school teachers. But in order for her to get a permanent teaching certificate, the wife needed eighteen months of postgraduate classes. She claimed (and a lower trial court found) that she had relinquished the opportunity to try to obtain certification while her husband pursued and completed his medical education. His education allowed him, upon divorce, to make significantly more money than his wife. She claimed she had lost the opportunity to increase her potential salary during the course of the marriage so that her husband could increase his potential salary, and she believed she deserved compensation. A New York appellate court agreed, and its ruling now pertains to the state of New York.

See also Community Property; Divorce.

Orr v. Orr (1979)

In 1974 William and Lillian Orr divorced, and William was required to pay Lillian $1,240 per month in alimony. Lillian filed suit in 1976 when William was in arrears in alimony payments, and William claimed that alimony violated the Equal Protection Clause of the Fourteenth Amendment because only husbands were required to pay it. A lower court ruled against him and sustained the constitutionality of the Alabama statute, saying that the law helped serve an important government objective, namely, compensating women for discrimination in marriage; a woman was harmed financially upon dissolution of a marriage because she lost her husband's income and typically did not work during the course of her marriage. William appealed.

The Supreme Court agreed with him and ruled that giving alimony exclusively to wives in divorce actions violated men's equal protection of the law. The Court applied the rational basis standard (in use at the time) and found that the state's objective of providing financial resources for needy wives, as well as compensating wives for discrimination that occurred during marriages that left them unprepared to enter the workplace, were valid. But these objectives could also be achieved by a gender-neutral standard. As compared to a gender-neutral law that places alimony obligations on the spouse able to pay, not solely on the husband, the state statute under question here gave an advantage only to the financially secure wife whose husband is in need, the Court ruled. Although a financially secure wife might have to pay alimony under a gender-neutral statute, the present statute exempted her from that obligation. Thus, "[the wives] who benefit from the disparate treatment are those who were . . . nondependent on their husbands" (see *Califano v. Goldfarb* [1979]). The Court went on to say that those wives were not "needy spouses" and were "least likely to have been victims of . . . discrimination" by the institution of marriage.

A gender-based classification that generates additional benefits only for those it has no reason to prefer cannot survive equal protection scrutiny. Therefore, if a legislature makes a classification that distributes benefits and burdens on the basis of gender, those laws carry the inherent risk of reinforcing stereotypes about the "proper place" of women and their need for special protection. So even statutes purportedly designed to compensate for and ameliorate the effects of past discrimination must be carefully tailored. In this case, for example, the state's purpose would have been just as well served by passing a gender-neutral classification rather than one that classifies on the basis of gender and carries with it the baggage of sexual stereotypes.

See also Califano v. Goldfarb; Community Property; *Craig v. Boren;* Divorce.

Palimony

Palimony recognizes that marital obligations and responsibilities exist when a couple lives together without the benefit of marriage. It usually involves the right of one of the partners to alimony after the relationship has ended. The California Supreme Court in *Marvin v. Marvin* (1976) distinguished between married and unmarried couples but allowed for some compensation to be given in nonmarital relationships. That is, with a marriage contract, each spouse has the explicit right to receive alimony after divorce, as well as a share in the marital property. A "pal" (or a partner in a palimony contract) does not have an automatic right to the couple's property or financial support; instead, the party must show some underlying basis for a claim, such as an expressed or implied contract that was entered into by both parties for distribution of property when the relationship ended.

It is important to note that this is an individual state concept; there are no federal guidelines pertaining to palimony claims. In

1932 California first established the principle when that state's supreme court held that nonmarital partners could enter into a lawful contract to distribute their property. The Trutalli couple had lived together for eleven years and raised two children. When the couple ended their relationship, he sued to gain ownership of the couple's real estate, and she asserted an implied agreement had already been decided by the parties. The court held that living together in a relationship not recognized by law did not disqualify the couple from entering into a lawful agreement concerning their jointly owned property as long as "immoral relations" were not part of their agreement. The following decade, the state court further upheld an implied contract between nonmarried partners.

As the number of nonmarried, live-in couples have increased, other state courts have continued to uphold property interests of both parties. And in 2000 Vermont was the first state to pass a civil union law, granting couples the right to enter into a contract distributing property interests and giving each partner explicit rights such as those enjoyed by married partners. Although most couples who entered into these civil unions were same-sex partners, Vermont grants the same right to opposing-sex couples.

> *See also* Domestic Partners; Gay and Lesbian Adoption; Marriage; *Marvin v. Marvin.*

Prenuptial and Postnuptial Agreements

Pre- and postnuptial agreements regard property distribution in case of divorce and are signed by a couple either directly before they enter into a marriage contract or some time thereafter. Typically, a prenuptial will make provisions for property that is acquired during the course of the marriage and whether that property will be treated as separate (belonging to one party) or community property (belonging to both par-

ties). Additionally, these agreements can cover related marital obligations following divorce, such as spousal maintenance.

Both parties are required to fully disclose all assets and financial obligations before entering into such an agreement. Although there is no federal law pertaining to these agreements, state courts have tended to enforce the contracts to the benefit of the harmed party if one party fails to disclose significant assets. Traditionally, prenuptial agreements were used by couples marrying for the second time who had assets they wished to preserve for their children from a prior marriage. The agreements, then, protected a significant amount of money. But increasingly these agreements are used by people marrying for the first time who have been in the workforce for several years and have thus accumulated substantial assets that they wish to keep separate in case of divorce.

The validity of these agreements largely depends on the state. Generally, however, the odds of a court's not upholding an agreement is greater the closer to the wedding date the agreement was signed by both parties. Also, if one side was represented by a lawyer and the other was not, or both sides were represented by the same attorney, either party can argue that he or she did not understand what was signed, and the agreement may not be valid. Finally, courts have regularly ignored provisions in such agreements concerning child custody and support in favor of the best interests of the children in question.

> *See also* Child Custody; Divorce.
> *Reference* Vox Experientiae. 1994. *Marriage, Divorce, and Solvency: The Prenuptial Agreement.* New York: Vantage Press.

Schuster v. Schuster (1978)

In this case, the Washington Supreme Court refused to award custody of several children to their respective fathers because the mothers were living together. Two women separated from their husbands and began living together and raising their respective children. In their respective divorce cases, both mothers received custody of their children but were ordered by a lower court to live separately. One of the fathers, Schuster, later filed a petition for review of his children's custody and argued that the women violated that order because they were renting separate apartments in the same building; the women were essentially living together and he wanted custody. The high court of Washington acknowledged that the women had entered into a lesbian relationship and by living together had violated the original custody agreement, but declared that agreement null and refused to give the father custody.

See also Child Custody; Divorce.

Temporary Assistance to Needy Families (TANF)

This program provides cash grants to families and children whose incomes are not adequate to meet their basic needs. Families are eligible if they have a child who is financially needy because of the incapacity, unemployment, or absence of a parent; a child is eligible for the aid if he or she is living with a foster care provider under court order. Current law provides for an additional monthly payment (now $47 per month) to all pregnant women who are receiving TANF so as to ensure that these women have adequate resources to support nutritional and other health needs arising from the pregnancy. This program does not, however, allow increases in a family's aid because of the addition of children conceived while the family was on aid (except in cases of rape, incest, or failure of contraceptives). Adult recipients who have been on TANF for two years are required to participate in a work preparation assignment unless they are already working at least fifteen hours per week.

See also C. K. v. Shalala; California v. Westcott; Child Support.

References and Further Reading

D'Emilio, John, and Estelle B. Freedman. 1988. *Intimate Matters: A History of Sexuality of America.* New York: Harper and Row.

Starr, Karla J. 1998. "Adoption by Homosexuals: A Look at Differing State Court Opinions." *Arizona Law Review* 40 (Winter): 1497.

Temporary Assistance for Needy Families Web site: http://www.acf.dhhs.gov.

REPRODUCTIVE RIGHTS

Abortion

One of the most controversial issues of the women's rights movement has been women's efforts to control their reproductive capabilities. The major battle has been over abortion. From 1900 until 1970, the penal code in every state in the United States forbade abortion except in certain narrowly defined instances. Few officials or communities, however, showed much enthusiasm for enforcing these bans. In fact, illegal abortions remained readily available throughout the twentieth century. Women who wished to terminate their pregnancies were usually able to procure an abortion, although not necessarily a safe one, in virtually every region of the country.

Although precise figures are difficult to ascertain, most scholars estimate that one out of every five pregnancies in the United States was (illegally) aborted during the first seventy years of the twentieth century. The women who endured illegal abortions often took terrible risks; it is estimated that by the mid-twentieth century 5,000 to 10,000 women died and 350,000 women were injured each year from complications resulting from criminal abortions. In fact, abortion remained the leading cause of maternal death in this country until the U.S. Supreme Court decided *Roe v. Wade* in 1973. Aside from the dangers of the procedure, abortion also presented a financial burden to poor women, who often found it difficult to pay for either the abortion itself or the necessary travel to another state to get a legal abortion.

The years directly prior to *Roe v. Wade* saw widespread legislative and judicial action among states regarding the issue. Most states allowed abortion only to save the life of the mother, but by 1970 four states—New York, Washington, Alaska, and Hawaii—had legalized abortion statutes. By 1972, statutes prohibiting abortion had been held unconstitutional in eight states: New Jersey, Florida, Illinois, Connecticut, Wisconsin, California, Texas, and Georgia.

When courts in Texas and Georgia held their states' anti-abortion statutes unconstitutional, the Supreme Court accepted the cases for review. The first case, *Roe v. Wade,* was a challenge to the Texas law by a woman using the pseudonym Jane Roe. Roe (who later publicized her true name, Norma McCorvey) was an unmarried pregnant woman who wanted an abortion that was not medically necessary. In Texas, as in most other states, all abortions were forbidden except for the purpose of saving the life of the mother.

Roe v. Wade ultimately guaranteed a woman's right to get an abortion because of her right to privacy, originally established by the Court in *Griswold v. Connecticut* (1965), in which the Court had defined the right to privacy as "right of the individual, married or single, to be free from unwarranted governmental intrusion into matters so fundamentally affecting a person as the decision whether to bear or beget a child." This right, the Court explained in *Roe*, is "broad enough to encompass a woman's

Important Supreme Court Decisions Regarding Abortion Laws

Griswold v.Connecticut (1965)—the Supreme Court invalidated a Connecticut statute that prohibited the use of contraceptives, holding that the statute violated the constitutional right to marital privacy.

Eisenstadt v. Baird (1972)—the Court rules that unmarried people also have the right to privacy and, thus, reproductive decisions.

Roe v. Wade (1973)—the Court holds that a woman's right to privacy includes the right to obtain an abortion if she so wishes. The Court also ruled on when and how a state may regulate abortions by breaking a pregnancy into trimesters: in the first trimester, states may not regulate the abortion procedure; in the second, the states have a greater interest; and in the third, they can ban the procedure.

Doe v. Bolton (1973)—in the companion case to *Roe,* the Court ruled that a state cannot require abortions be performed only in hospitals. Additionally, a woman could not be required to secure the approval of three physicians and a hospital committee before receiving the procedure, nor did she have to be a resident of the state before receiving the procedure in that state.

Bigelow v. Virginia (1975)—Virginia could not prohibit the advertisement of abortion services.

Connecticut v. Menillo (1975)—states could prohibit nonphysicians from performing abortions.

Bellotti v. Baird (I) (1976)—the Court rules that states may require a minor woman to receive parental consent before obtaining an abortion in some circumstances.

Planned Parenthood of Central Missouri v. Danforth (1976)—the Court overturned a state law requiring married women to obtain spousal consent before obtaining an abortion, and prohibited a physician to preserve the life of a fetus at each stage of pregnancy. Additionally, for states that required parental consent for minors to obtain abortions, they also had to allow for some sort of alternative if parental consent was not possible. Also, for the first time, the Court defined "viability of a fetus"

as: "that stage of fetal development when the life of the unborn child may be continued indefinitely outside the womb by natural or artificial life supportive systems."

Maher v. Roe (1977)—the Court allows states to prohibit public funding of abortions except for those that are "medically necessary."

Carey v. Population Services (1977)—states cannot prohibit the sale or distribution of contraceptives to minors, the Court rules.

Colautti v. Franklin (1979)—the Court rules that states cannot require physicians to use the 'degree of care' most likely to preserve the life of the fetus if viability of the fetus was a possibility.

Harris v. McRae (1980)—the Hyde Amendment, which prohibited the use of federal funds for abortions not necessary to preserve the woman's life, was constitutional, the Court rules.

Akron v. Akron Center for Reproductive Health (1983)—states could not require physicians to give patients antiabortion information, require 24-hour waiting periods after receiving this information, mandate that all abortions after the first trimester be performed in a hospital, require parental consent for minors without some type of bypass provision, or require physicians to dispose of fetal remains in a "humane and sanitary manner," the Court rules.

Planned Parenthood Association of Kansas City, Mo. v. Ashcroft (1983)—the Court holds that states cannot require second-trimester abortions be performed in hospitals. But states can require a second physician be present during late-term abortions and parental consent or judicial bypass for minors.

Thornburgh v. American College of Obstetricians and Gynecologists (1986)—states cannot require women to give "informed consent" after receiving antiabortion material, nor can states make public detailed information about the women obtaining the abortion.

Webster v. Reproductive Health Services (1989)—

states can prohibit the use of public facilities or public personnel to perform abortions, as well as require physicians to perform tests on the fetus regarding its age, weight, and lung maturity. The Court also upholds the "essence" of *Roe v. Wade.*

Hodgson v. Minnesota (1990)—states cannot require both parents consent for a minor's abortion without allowing for a judicial bypass, but states can require a 48-hour waiting period for minors seeking the procedure.

Ohio v. Akron Center for Reproductive Health (1990)—states are allowed to require minors to notify one parent (with a judicial bypass option).

Rust v. Sullivan (1991)—the Court rules that health care professionals that receive federal funding can be prohibited from giving women abortion information, including informing a pregnant woman that abortion is legal.

Planned Parenthood of Southeastern Pennsylvania v. Casey (1992)—the Court upheld a state law requiring physicians to provide antiabortion information (including pictures of fetuses) to women seeking an abortion, a mandatory 24-hour waiting period following receipt of this material, and the filing of reports on abortions that could be made public. However, spousal notification requirements were unconstitutional.

Bray v. Alexandria Women's Health Clinic (1993)—protestors at abortion clinics cannot be limited by a federal civil rights law from approaching women entering the clinic.

Schenck v. Pro-Choice Network (1997)—the Court rules that states could create 36-foot buffer zones from protestors outside abortion clinics, and protestors could be prohibited from talking to people entering or leaving the clinic if the person made this wish known to the protestor. States could not, however, create 300-foot buffer zones around the clinic, ban protestor's signs and images outside the clinic, nor place 300-foot bans on picketing outside the residences of clinic employees.

Mazurek v. Armstrong (1997)—states can require that only physicians perform abortions, the Court holds.

Stenberg v. Carhart (2000)—states are prohibited from enacting "partial-birth" abortions, the Court holds. There must be exceptions that protect the woman's health.

Hill v. Colorado (2000)—states can prohibit a protestor from approaching within eight feet of a person entering an abortion clinic for the purpose of displaying a sign, engaging in oral protest, or distributing paper material. States can prohibit protestors within a 100-foot radius from abortion clinic entrances, as well.

decision whether or not to terminate her pregnancy." The word "person" specified in the Fourteenth Amendment applies only after the birth of a child and thus does not include the unborn. And in fact common law also fails to recognize "people" who die, for example, before they are born. A state, the Court ruled in *Roe,* may limit a woman from getting an abortion, but only after the fetus is viable.

First and foremost, state restrictions on abortion must be narrowly tailored to serve compelling state interests, and a state must allow abortion throughout the entire pregnancy if it will protect a woman's life or health. But the Court recognized three trimesters of a pregnancy; as a pregnancy proceeds and the fetus she is carrying becomes more viable outside the womb, a woman's right to obtain an abortion may be subjected to increasingly restrictive state regulations. Specifically, before the end of the first trimester of a pregnancy, the state cannot restrict abortion; the abortion decision must be left to the woman and the medical judgment of her physician since the mortality rate for childbirth is higher than it is for abortion. A state may require only that her choice of abortion be made in consultation with her doctor. After the first trimester,

Brandishing homemade signs, hundreds of pro-choice advocates attend a rally in 1993, when the Pope visited, in downtown Denver to show their support for a woman's right to a legal abortion. (Bettmann/Corbis)

the state has the power to restrict abortions, but only if the restrictions are reasonably related to maternal health. And for the third trimester of a pregnancy, the state may promote its interest in the potential of human life by regulating (or even proscribing) abortion as long as it does not interfere with the life or health of the mother.

To say that *Roe* was a controversial decision is to understate the issue. Probably the most common criticism of the decision was that it was based on law made by judges rather than law made by a legislature. That is, *Roe* is based on the fundamental right to privacy established in the *Griswold* decision. But because the right to privacy is not mentioned in the U.S. Constitution, it is illegitimate law. There have also been several legal challenges to abortion rights since *Roe* was decided. Overall, the Court has ruled that although *Roe* protects the right to choose abortion, it does not require the government to subsidize that choice; it means only that a

state may not place undue burdens on a woman's right to obtain an abortion. As such, a state's refusing to fund abortion procedures and a woman's inability to pay for that abortion is not considered a substantial obstacle in allowing a woman the right to choose abortion.

The Court has granted the states great latitude in restricting the procedure. For example, the Court has ruled that Congress can prohibit federal funding of organizations that are involved in providing abortions and that states may insist on a woman's "informed" consent before she can receive an abortion, requiring her to wait for twenty-four hours after receiving information provided by the state before her abortion can take place. This waiting period may be imposed even if the woman can obtain an abortion only in a distant city, sometimes requiring her to travel and obtain lodging twice, which may be a financial hardship. The Court has also upheld policies requiring informed parental consent if the woman requesting an abortion is a minor, although states must allow a minor to bypass the parental consent requirement if she can demonstrate to a judge that she is mature enough to make a decision that an abortion is in her best interest. The Court has ruled spousal consent requirements unconstitutional but upheld policies requiring abortion facilities to give regular reports to the state.

In sum, states may not prohibit or interfere with a woman's right to choose to get an abortion, in consultation with her physician, during the first trimester of pregnancy. But after this point a state may act to further its interest in potential life; it may adopt provisions that seek to make sure the woman considers the value of the potential life she is carrying. It is only when the regulations place an "undue burden" on the woman's ability to obtain an abortion that the restrictions are considered unconstitutional. And from the end of the second trimester of pregnancy until viability of a fetus (about the twenty-fourth to twenty-eighth week of pregnancy), the state can prohibit abortions. The only exception the state faces in limiting abortion in this last trimester is that they must allow abortions when they are necessary to protect the life or health of the mother. Currently, about 1.6 million abortions are performed annually in the United States. Private charitable sources now fund a majority of these abortions.

The controversy over abortion has changed course dramatically since the Court handed down the original *Roe* decision. Those who oppose the constitutionality of abortion have relatively recently turned physical and even violent. First was the blocking of access to abortion clinics, organized primarily by Operation Rescue (led by Randall Terry) and litigated in court. This was followed by the shootings of several physicians who performed abortions by radical fringe groups promoting a "pro-life" stance, then by the bombing of several clinics that performed abortions. Among the groups who oppose abortion, the strategy for protest has become increasingly divisive, as those who insist on peaceable means move to separate themselves from those who advocate violence.

State courts have waded into the controversy by defining when a pregnant woman may use deadly force to protect her fetus during an assault. In Michigan Jaclyn Kurr and the man who impregnated her, Antonio Pena, were involved in an altercation that resulted in Kurr's fatally stabbing Pena. She claimed that Pena had repeatedly punched her in the stomach; at the time she was sixteen weeks pregnant with quadruplets and later miscarried. Although the state court noted that the fetuses could not have survived outside the womb and therefore Kurr could have aborted them under *Roe v. Wade,* it also held that she could use deadly force to protect them, which could result in ending someone else's life. Essentially, causing a miscarriage could be legally construed as murder, yet a woman's aborting a first-trimester pregnancy would not be. At this writing, the case is currently under appeal. Congress is currently debating the Unborn Victims of Violence Act that would criminalize acts that cause miscarriages or stillbirths.

Another major conflict over abortion has focused on the termination of pregnancies in the third trimester, called "partial-birth abortions" by those who oppose them but in medical terms described as "intact dilation and extraction." Pro-choice advocates, who support abortion rights, maintain that such abortions are necessary to save the life or health of the mother or, in some cases, to terminate pregnancies where the fetus cannot survive birth or long after birth. Pro-life advocates, in contrast, maintain that in most such abortions, the life of the fetus is not a hopeless matter. The Supreme Court has ruled that states cannot prevent physicians from performing the procedure, particularly if the woman's life is in danger. Meanwhile, the development of RU-486, an abortion-inducing drug, approved by the Food and Drug Administration in 2000, is likely to change the terms of the debate about abortion.

Contraception

The earliest recorded attempt at contraception was in 1500 B.C.E. Methods have included magic, coitus interruptus, spermicidal douches, homemade devices to obstruct the opening of the cervix (including ground dates, tree bark, honey, elephant and crocodile dung, and wood), and even condoms (used by the Egyptians), and abortions. As societies became more agricultural, making large families an economic advantage, religious and secular law generally restricted birth control. But with industrialization, large families no longer made economic sense, and the population used whatever means were available to control pregnancy.

The first U.S. law to focus on birth control was the 1873 Comstock Act, which specified that birth control information was obscene and illegal to obtain or distribute. Information on contraception during this period was ineffective at best and most often impossible to find. The average family at the time had seven children. Abortion (usually an option available only to the wealthy) was eventually banned outright under many state laws and was certainly considered "obscene" under the Comstock Act.

After the Comstock Act was passed, however, several movements that campaigned for public access to birth control information emerged. Some secular movements promoted contraception in order to control the population; others advocated it to control hereditary diseases, to improve hereditary stock, to liberate women from reproductive drudgery, and even to allow greater sexual freedom. Some religious radicals promoted birth control as well, but for different ends. Most of these groups were committed to improving women's condition and public health generally, but they tended to reject contraception as artificial and in-

stead tried to practice birth control by changing the nature of sexual activity itself. At one extreme, for example, was the Oneida community of New York in the 1840s, which supported male continence for self-discipline and heightened sexual pleasure. Reproductive sex was practiced only by couples appointed by the leader for the purpose of breeding superior offspring. Other religious groups, of course, believed sex should be reserved exclusively for the purpose of conceiving children, so birth control was unnecessary.

By the late 1870s, members of the first feminist movement created a long-lasting political demand with the slogan "voluntary motherhood." But most of the movement's members and leaders called for abstinence in order to decrease the numbers of children women would bear, which would ultimately benefit women's health. The speakers for this movement were regularly arrested on indecency and obscenity charges and often jailed. But social mores change. By the beginning of the twentieth century, birth control leagues developed in every major city of the United States, and by World War II Planned Parenthood was operating nationwide. Although Planned Parenthood initially pushed contraception as a form of population control, it later called for medical research to improve the birth control options available. Yet the dissemination of birth control devices and information continued to be outlawed in many states. In 1965, in a landmark case involving Planned Parenthood and its medical director, the Supreme Court declared that the right to privacy afforded to all Americans was present in the pursuit of birth control information: "Would we allow the police to search the sacred precincts of marital bedrooms for telltale signs of the use of contraceptives?" Justice William O. Douglas wrote in the majority opinion in *Griswold v. Connecticut.* "The very idea is repulsive to the notions of privacy surrounding the marriage relationship." (Connecticut had forbidden the use of contraceptives as well as aiding or counseling others in their use, yet no users were charged in the case.)

But even following the *Griswold* decision, birth control devices were still not particularly reliable, nor were they available to the general public. It was not until the late 1960s, as part of an overall campaign for women's self-determination and fulfillment, that the women's movement helped to finance and promote the most widely used form of contraception in America today: the birth control pill. Few scientific inventions have had as fundamental and powerful an impact on society as what became known simply as "the Pill." The Pill was the brainchild of Margaret Sanger, who raised $150,000 in 1950 (when she was in her sixties) to get reproductive scientist Gregory Pincus started on research that would lead to a successful universal contraceptive. It had been established in the 1930s that hormones could prevent ovulation in rabbits, but it was considered unethical to conduct such experiments on humans. Pincus was leery of using the hormone estrogen because of severe cancer risks inherent in increasing hormonal dosages in humans. Instead, he first developed a progestin-only contraceptive, which he tested on poor Puerto Rican women in the 1950s. The original Pill came onto the market under the brand name Enovid and was considered a marvel. But after millions of women had taken Enovid and thousands had died or became disabled by blood clots, it was discovered that the amount of hormones in Enovid was ten times what was needed for successful contraception.

The newer birth control pills contained a much lower dose of estrogen and had very few side effects. With the advent of the Pill, public attention focused more intently on the issue of birth control. As mentioned, in 1965 the Supreme Court recognized a "zone of privacy" and allowed married couples to obtain birth control information. A few years later, in 1972, the Court extended to single people the same right to privacy enjoyed by married couples. Thus, married and single people alike would be free from unwarranted governmental intrusion preventing the use of contraceptives.

Then, in 1973, the Supreme Court upheld a woman's right to obtain an abortion in *Roe v. Wade*. Largely in response, a widespread antiabortion movement arose, directed mainly by religious groups. Unlike the nineteenth-century movement to limit abortions and contraception, recent controversy focuses on the "right to life," that is, the rights of fetuses. Planned Parenthood, which provides contraception for poor woman more frequently than it provides abortion services, has now become the target of many of the groups opposing abortion. Several clinics have been bombed and abortion doctors maimed and even killed.

Courts have also been increasingly involved in the issue of injuries resulting from flawed birth control methods. The intrauterine device (IUD) known as the Dalkon Shield was marketed to the American public in 1971 without the normal extensive testing typically done on drugs introduced onto the American market. Only when more than 190,000 women claimed damages after using this IUD, which caused several deaths, severe infections, injuries, and permanent sterility, was it removed from the market in 1974. The manufacturer eventually paid $2.5 billion to more than 100,000 claimants. And the drug diethylstilbestrol (DES), used to prevent miscarriage during the 1960s and 1970s, caused vaginal cancer and sterility in many of the female children (and later, their children) that resulted from those pregnancies. A class-action suit brought the manufacturer to near bankruptcy.

American women at the beginning of the twenty-first century have an average of fewer than three children. They and their partners have access to condoms (both male and female), diaphragms, spermicides, oral and injectable contraceptives like Norplant, contraceptive implants and sterilization, and the abortion-inducing drug RU-486, as well as the "morning-after" pill. IUDs are also being reintroduced onto the American market. Although in 2002, nineteen states had introduced bills requiring contraceptive coverage in all health insurance plans and twenty states had passed such measures, most health care plans still do not include contraceptive coverage.

> *See also* Abortion; Feminism; *Griswold v. Connecticut*; Norplant; *Roe v. Wade*; Sanger, Margaret.
>
> *References* Ellen Chesler. 1992. *Woman of Valor: Margaret Sanger and the Birth Control Movement in America.* New York: Simon and Schuster; Planned Parenthood Federation of America Web site: www.plannedparenthood.org; John M. Riddle. 1994. *Contraception and Abortion from the Ancient World to the Renaissance.* Cambridge, MA: Harvard University Press; Andrea Tone. 2002. *Devices and Desires: A History of Contraceptives in America.* New York: Hill and Wang.

Contraceptive Equity

When Viagra, used to treat male impotence, was introduced onto the American market in the early 1990s, health insurance organizations quickly covered it. But birth control pills, which cost the average American woman $35 per month, and other contraceptive devices are rarely covered.

Birth control is a fundamental part of women's health care, and most women spend approximately thirty years of their lives trying to prevent pregnancy. Several medical lobbying groups have argued that promoting birth control ultimately saves employers money by reducing the number of unwanted pregnancies. In 2000 the Equal Employment Opportunity Commission ruled that not providing insurance for contraceptives amounts to sex discrimination, and two federal courts have ruled similarly. But there is still no federal law requiring contraceptive coverage in health care plans, although several states have introduced or passed bills mandating contraceptive coverage (exempting employers who object for religious reasons).

Davis v. Davis (1992)

The parties in *Davis v. Davis* could agree on all matters of their divorce except for who was to have custody of the seven frozen embryos (or pre-embryos) the couple had earlier conceived through in vitro fertilization and stored in a Knoxville fertility clinic. Mary Davis first asked for custody intending to use the embryos to become pregnant following the divorce; she argued they were her last chance to have her own child. Junior Davis objected to becoming a parent outside the bounds of marriage and asked that the embryos be left in their frozen state until he decided whether or not he wanted to become a father. By the time a high court heard the case, both parties had remarried and their situations had changed. Mary had left the state and no longer wished to have the frozen embryos implanted in her uterus; instead, she wanted to donate them to a childless couple. Junior still did not want to become a parent with his former wife and was opposed to giving the embryos away.

The lower state trial court awarded custody of the embryos to Mary and directed that she "be permitted the opportunity to bring these children to term through implantation." The state court of appeals reversed, finding that Junior had a "constitutionally protected right not to beget a child where no pregnancy has taken place." Further, that court held "there is no compelling state interest to justify ordering implantation against the will of either party." Since the parties shared an interest in all seven fertilized embryos, the court returned the case to the lower trial court to give joint control to both parties and "an equal voice over [the embryos'] disposition."

When Mary appealed to the supreme court of Tennessee, that court agreed to hear the case not because it disagreed with the basic legal analysis of the lower court but because of the obvious importance of the case in terms of the development of new law regarding reproductive technologies. None of the judges hearing the case at either the trial level or the appellate level had any case law to guide their decision. Further, no other state had laws regarding the distribution of previously created embryos since the procedure for creating them was so new.

The Davises had tried to have a child since their marriage in 1980. Mary had suffered miscarriages and finally a tubal pregnancy, which forced her to undergo emergency surgery to remove one of her fallopian tubes. She would later have her other fallopian tube removed, leaving her unable to conceive a child naturally. The couple tried unsuccessfully to adopt a child before resorting to in vitro fertilization. After six attempts (with a cost of approximately $35,000), Mary had not become pregnant.

In 1988 a new procedure allowed for fertilized ova to be preserved through cryogenic means. The one-celled ova, called zygotes before cell division, may be removed from a woman's body after hormone stimulation forces the release of multiple eggs. These ova are then fertilized with sperm from the woman's partner (or a donor) and allowed to develop in petri dishes in a laboratory until they mature into four- to eight-celled entities. The cells are frozen, allowing them to be implanted into a woman's body later, without additional rounds of hormonal stimulation and extraction of additional ova.

At the time of the cryogenic procedure, the couple testified that they had no plans to divorce. There was no attempt by the fertility clinic to determine how the couple wished to dispose of embryos in the event they were unused. In fact, the parties testified that they had never been informed of any storage implications beyond the few months it would take to transfer any remaining frozen embryos. There was certainly no agreement concerning the disposition of the embryos in the event of divorce. When no pregnancy developed after the first round of the procedure in late 1988, Junior filed for divorce, leaving the status of the seven embryos in question.

The trial judge had reasoned that since "human life begins at the moment of conception," the pre-embryos had a legal right to be born. The appellate court rejected this reasoning. This caused considerable public sentiment; nineteen organizations filed amicus curiae ("friend of the court") briefs, requesting that the supreme court of Tennessee address the issue because of its far-reaching implications in other, similar cases. But the court instead chose to address the issue of whether the embryos should be considered persons or property. The justices were in agreement that they could not be considered persons under state law since the law did not allow a wrongful death for a viable fetus that is not first born alive. Additionally, state statute did not allow viable fetuses in the womb to be entitled the same protection as persons; instead, the law incorporated the trimester approach to a viable fetus specified in *Roe v. Wade*. As the embryos developed, they were given more legal rights because of the increasing potential for life. Yet even after the cells became viable, they could not be given the legal status of persons because they had yet to be born. This concept was reflected in state murder and assault laws, which provided that an attack or homicide of a viable fetus is a crime but abortion is not. And even under federal law, embryos do not enjoy protection as persons largely because of the lack of scientific consensus as to when life begins. The high court stated that if they were to grant pre-embryos the legal status of persons, then the effect would be to essentially outlaw in vitro fertilization programs in the state.

Yet the pre-embryos were not property either, although they occupied a category that entitled them to special respect because of "their potential for human life." So the Davises did not have a true property interest in the pre-embryos, but they did have some sort of ownership to the extent that they had decision-making authority concerning their disposition.

Had the couple signed an agreement regarding the disposition of the pre-embryos, the trial court held it would not be enforced in the case of a disagreement between the parties. A court would have to make a "best interest of the child" determination in each individual case. But the high court disagreed. Any agreement regarding the disposition of unused pre-embryos is presumed valid since the parties would be giving bodily material to create the pre-embryos and thus must retain decision-making authority in considering their disposition.

In the Davises' case, there had been no agreement between the parties or with the fertility clinic as to what would happen to any unused embryos. Essentially, Junior had been given virtual veto power over their disposition by ensuring that they would not be used, and presumably discarded, if the couple decided not to use them. Junior's argument to the court was that the value of an embryo was in the "potential to become, after implantation, growth and birth, children." He argued that the issue was not the storage of the pre-embryos but whether a party could be forced to be a parent. The court concluded that the social and political beliefs of American culture and law rest upon the idea that all people have certain inherent and inalienable rights. Among these rights are the right to protection of life, liberty, and the pursuit of happiness; the right to enjoy and possess property; and the right to establish a home and family. All these rights are protected by the law. This notion of individual liberty is so strong that it grants individuals the right to resist government oppression even to the extent of overthrowing an unjust government.

Both federal and state law gives an individual the right to procreate; in fact, it is a vital part of an individual's right to privacy. In 1942, in *Skinner v. Oklahoma*, the U.S. Supreme Court struck down a statute that authorized the sterilization of categories of criminals, describing the right to procreate

as "one of the basic civil rights of man" and declaring that "marriage and procreation are fundamental to the very existence and survival of the race." In 1972 the Court went even further and stated in *Eisenstadt v. Baird*: "If the right of privacy means anything, it is the right of the individual, married or single, to be free from unwarranted governmental intrusion into matters so fundamentally affecting a person as the decision whether to bear or beget a child." The Tennessee high court admitted that the U.S. Supreme Court had never directly addressed the issue of procreation in the context of in vitro fertilization. Thus a state court was required to attempt to discern what the law required.

The interests of the parties in *Davis v. Davis* were different than the parental interests considered in other cases that largely dealt with the childbearing and child-rearing aspects of parenthood, as well as abortion cases that dealt with gestational parenthood. In *Davis v. Davis* the justices had to define the question of genetic parenthood. As such, an interest in avoiding genetic parenthood is significant; that someone unknown to the Davises could use the pre-embryos for themselves did not alter the fact that the Davises would then become parents, at least in the genetic sense.

Second, if one party wishes to continue the in vitro fertilization process and the other does not, the interests of both parties must be balanced. Under common law, courts resolve questions of conflicting interests by considering the positions of the parties, the significance of their interests, and the relative burdens that would be imposed by differing resolutions. With the Davises, the court was required to balance Mary's right to procreate with Junior's right to avoid procreation. If the disposition of the embryos resulted in gestation, Junior would be forced with unwanted parenthood and possible financial and psychological consequences. Junior described the potential psychological effects as severe; he testified that his parents divorced and because his mother was mentally unable to care for her children, Junior and three of his siblings lived in an orphanage. He saw his parents only sporadically throughout his life and suffered emotional damage as a result. He was therefore vehemently opposed to fathering a child that would not live with both parents. Junior argued that a child's bond with a noncustodial parent would not be acceptable and instead create psychological obstacles for the child. He was also opposed to donation of the embryos because the couple could divorce, leaving the child again separated from one parent.

For her part, Mary believed that refusing her the right to donate would burden her with the knowledge that the lengthy, painful, and expensive procedures she had undergone to have a child had been useless, and the pre-embryos to which she had contributed genetic material would never become people. The court concluded that although this was a substantial emotional burden, her interests in donation were not as significant as Junior's interest in avoiding parenthood. If the pre-embryos were implanted, he would face a lifetime of either not knowing about his parental status or knowing but having no control over it. Donation would decrease his procreational autonomy and erase a relationship with his offspring.

In future cases, the court ruled, the disposition of pre-embryos should be controlled by the two people who created them. In disputes, the prior agreement of the parties concerning the pre-embryos' disposition should be used. If there is no prior agreement, the relative interests of the parties must be balanced. And the party wishing to avoid procreation should prevail if the other party has a reasonable possibility of achieving parenthood through other means. If one party cannot achieve parenthood by other means, using the pre-embryos to achieve pregnancy should be considered, but donating them to a third party would not be more important than preventing parenthood. Mary Davis did not appeal the decision of the court, and no further federal holdings on this matter have been decided.

See also Infertility Alternatives; *Jhordan C. v. Mary K; Johnson v. Calvert; Matter of Baby M.*

Ferguson v. City of Charleston (2001)

In *Ferguson v. City of Charleston*, the Supreme Court ruled that a hospital's drug testing of pregnant women to obtain evidence for law enforcement purposes was a violation of the Fourth Amendment's restriction on unreasonable searches and seizures. The Medical University of South Carolina (MUSC) had tried to address the problem of cocaine use by pregnant women, which poses health risks to fetuses and mothers, by drug testing pregnant women who were using cocaine. The hospital then turned positive drug screens over to local police. Ten women who had been immediately taken into custody or arrested following the births of their children sued. This case was the first time the Court had addressed the issue of whether drug-using pregnant women could be prosecuted for harming their unborn children.

The MUSC case, decided by the Supreme Court, dealt with many of the same issues. But here the state of South Carolina was taking a proactive stance, testing the women without their knowledge when they arrived at the hospital. In prior state cases, children who showed signs of drug withdrawal because of their mothers' drug habits were taken from their mothers only after the children's symptoms were evident.

The state argued that MUSC's intention in testing the women was to provide a threat of criminal sanction and thus a deterrent to pregnant women from using cocaine in the future. But the Court ruled that the state's interests were solely to arrest and prosecute offenders and not to benefit the women. As such, testing the women was a direct violation of the Fourth Amendment, which prevents the government from unreasonable searches and seizures. Further, the Court held that drug screening without turning over the positive results to police could have accomplished the goal of helping doctors to manage pregnancies.

The case gained widespread national attention, and many feminist interest groups filed briefs to the Court on behalf of the women plaintiffs. They argued that the Charleston policy reflected an outmoded view toward "women as mere incubators of the fetus." Further, MUSC's policy treated women who tested positive for drugs with a lack of respect; some women were removed from the hospital in handcuffs and shackles, still garbed in hospital gowns, bleeding and in pain from recent childbirth. The policy also encouraged women to be untruthful with their doctors (who typically rely heavily on voluntary disclosure of cocaine use because of testing accuracy) and even to avoid seeking prenatal care. This case helped define more clearly the common-law concept of doctor-patient privilege because doctors could not, presumably, turn over such information to outside sources without permission from their pregnant patients. Finally, the policy was both racist and classist, for the vast majority of affected patients were impoverished women of color.

See also Fetal Protection; Pregnancy.

Fetal Protection

Beginning in the mid-1980s, several states instituted policies to protect fetuses and punish pregnant mothers suspected of drug abuse. In some cases women were forced to accept medical treatment against their will. In general the medical community was against forced treatment of pregnant patients, the American Medical Association warning physicians that it was their job to respect their pregnant patients' wishes not to obtain certain medical care, even if such choices could put the unborn fetus at risk: "While the health of a few infants may be preserved by overriding a pregnant woman's decision, the health of a great many more may be sacrificed."

The first case to reach the courts was a 1987 dispute involving George Washington University Hospital. Hospital administrators asked for a judicial order forcing Angela Carder, a pregnant woman with cancer, to undergo a cesarean section, which she refused. After receiving the order, the hospital performed the cesarean section on Carder, and both she and her premature infant died shortly after surgery. Because the cesarean section was listed as a contributing cause of Carder's death, a loud public outcry followed. Carder had survived two previous bouts of cancer by the age of twenty-seven, but chemotherapy, radiation, and various surgeries had weakened her body. During one remission in her cancer, she married and immediately became pregnant. At twenty-six weeks into her pregnancy, Carder's cancer returned, and her family and doctors attempted to keep her alive for two more weeks to give the fetus as long as possible to mature in Carder's body and to give Carder an opportunity to hold her child.

When Carder's condition rapidly deteriorated, hospital administrators asked the court to intercede and force Carder's family to authorize an immediate cesarean section. Carder's family and several experts argued that the operation was "medically inadvisable both for Angela Carder and the fetus." Nonetheless, the court issued an order, the cesarean section was performed, and both Carder and her child died. Following her death, Carder's family requested the court to vacate its earlier order so that the precedent would not stand for others in similar circumstances. They argued that forcing a cesarean section on Carder violated her right to informed consent of all medical procedures performed on her body, as well as her constitutional right of privacy against unwarranted medical intrusion. The American Medical Association, the American College of Obstetricians and Gynecologists, and 1,118 other medical, religious, and civil rights groups; disability rights organizations; and leading bioethicists supported Carder's family by filing amicus curiae (or "friend of the court") briefs. The court ultimately ruled in Carder's favor (see *Matter of A. C.*) and vacated its earlier decision. In virtually all situations, the court held, the mother can make the medical decision whether or not to have a cesarean section. In contrast, court-ordered intervention in such matters "drives women at high risk of complications during pregnancy and childbirth out of the health care system to avoid coerced treatment." Carder's family later settled with the hospital for damages.

The medical establishment has been consistently critical of policies that punish women for their conduct and behavior during pregnancy. Yet as a result of increased crack cocaine use in the 1980s, several states established procedures to punish pregnant cocaine users for harming their unborn children. In some cases states passed statutes prohibiting delivery of controlled (and illegal) substances to minors, with penalties for child abuse and neglect. By the mid-1990s several cases had made their way into state courts across the country. Florida was the first to convict a women for drug trafficking to her unborn infant. When the mother volunteered that she had used cocaine while pregnant, the state removed her children from her custody and filed criminal charges against her. She was convicted of delivery of a controlled substance to a minor and sentenced to one year in a treatment program and fourteen years of probation. The court also required her to undergo court-supervised prenatal care if she were to become pregnant again and forbade her to use drugs or alcohol, go to bars, or associate with people who used drugs or alcohol. The state high court overturned her conviction because in its opinion the lower court had conceded that the legal basis for the woman's arrest would apply equally to a woman who smoked or drank alcohol dur-

ing her pregnancy: "Prosecuting women for using drugs and 'delivering' them to their newborns appears to be the least effective response to this crisis. Rather than face the possibility of prosecution, pregnant women who are substance abusers may simply avoid prenatal or medical care for fear of being detected."

There is as yet no established federal law on this issue. In 2001, however, the Supreme Court did attempt to partially define some limitations on states' fetal protection policies. *Ferguson v. City of Charleston* involved South Carolina's secret testing of pregnant women suspected of drug use. When pregnant women who had positive drug tests were admitted to the Medical University of South Carolina hospital to give birth, they were immediately turned over to the state police, who would arrest these women often while they were still in their hospital beds following childbirth. Several women sued the hospital, claiming both racial discrimination (since nearly all the women chosen for testing were minorities) and violations of their Fourth Amendment rights prohibiting unreasonable searches and seizures. The Court ruled for the women, holding that states could not drug test pregnant women without their consent.

In a different but related matter, courts have also been active in examining policies that exclude women from certain professions and jobs if these could harm their reproductive health. Most companies that instituted such policies argued that fetal protection policies were necessary and an unavoidable consequence was that all women of childbearing age were excluded from employment in such positions. The women who have challenged such laws do so under Title VII of the Civil Rights Act of 1964, which prohibits discrimination on the basis of sex. Additionally, the Pregnancy Discrimination Act of 1978 specifically bans discrimination against pregnant women. The most common defense that employers use in such fetal protection policies is disparate impact; that is, the employer had no intention of discriminating against women of childbearing age, but the policy instituted happened to affect those women more than other people. Further, in order to prevail, the employer must be able to show that the policy was the result of a legitimate business purpose. Typically, employers are able to do this by arguing either that the policy was necessary for the safety of their employees or that the policies protect employers from liability in the future because of any children born deformed as a result of the mother's employment. But in order to demonstrate the latter, the employer must prove "that there is a substantial risk of harm to the fetus or potential offspring of women employees from the women's exposure, either during pregnancy or while fertile, to toxic hazards in the workplace."

In most cases linking workplace environment to fetal deformity, courts rarely find that the harm was intentional. Part of the reason for this is the near impossibility of proving causation; few deformities can be blamed on a particular chemical at a place of employment. And in cases where courts have declared the harm was intentional, worker's compensation laws prevent damages from being assessed. These cases have not produced a consistent ruling, however. One state court, for example, held that a hospital could not fire an x-ray technician after determining she was pregnant (and instead should have granted her a leave of absence); another held that an employer could terminate a female employee of childbearing age when her job required constant exposure to harmful chemicals that "could" have harmed her unborn child; yet another court ruled that the safety of fetuses could be considered a business necessity.

The most publicized case decided on this issue, *Johnson v. Transportation Agency of Santa Clara, California,* involved a fetal protection policy put in place in 1982 that excluded women from working in positions that exposed workers to lead. In this case a federal court ruled that the policy was acceptable because a female worker could unknowingly endanger her fetus when exposed to lead during the very beginning of pregnancy, before she had determined that she was pregnant.

As a result of such confusion among state courts and the absence of pertinent federal law, the Fetal Protection Act was passed in 2001 making the killing or harming of a fetus a federal crime. Twenty-four states immediately passed similar laws, limiting the protection to viable fetuses only and requiring conviction only if the assailant was aware that the woman was pregnant. But the difficulties with Fetal Protection Act abound. For example, a woman who obtains an abortion cannot be prosecuted, whereas her abortion provider can, though both are presumably harming the fetus.

Although the War on Drugs has boosted prison populations generally, it has had a disproportionately high impact on women. More women than ever before in U.S. history have now been incarcerated because of drugs, and the impact has been devastating to the children and families left behind. Today 1.5 million children have a parent in prison. And with this comes an increase in poverty, homelessness, and substance abuse by children. Children with incarcerated mothers are more likely than children without an incarcerated parent to be sent to prison themselves at some point in their lives.

Furthermore, the War on Drugs is expensive. Approximately $49.2 billion was spent on the effort in 2002, drug offenders make up 55 percent of the prison population, and state spending on corrections increased 30 percent (at the same time that spending on higher education decreased 18 percent).

See also Civil Rights Act; Disparate Impact; *Ferguson v. City of Charleston; Matter of A. C.;* Pregnancy Discrimination Act (PDA).

Reference Kathleen Stratton, Cynthia Howe, and Frederick Battagli, eds. 1996. *Fetal Alcohol Syndrome: Diagnosis, Epidemiology, Prevention, and Treatment.* Washington, DC: National Academy Press.

C. Lee Buxton (center), the medical director of the Planned Parenthood Center, and Estelle Griswold (right), the executive director, appear here in police headquarters after their arrest. The two were held for violating an old Connecticut anti–birth-control law. (Bettmann/Corbis)

Griswold v. Connecticut (1965)

While working with the United Nations Relief and Rehabilitation Association during World War II, Estelle Griswold witnessed the effects of poverty in the slums of Rio de Janeiro, Algiers, and Puerto Rico. Her experiences there convinced her that lack of family planning was one of the primary causes of poverty and women's poor health across the globe. After beginning her tenure as executive director of the Planned Parenthood League of Connecticut, she organized volunteers to shuttle women to birth control clinics in nearby states where contraceptives were legal.

But by 1961 she realized that states like Connecticut were not going to liberalize their laws on contraception unless they were forced to do so—that is, the issue would have to be tried in court. In order to get arrested for violating state law and thus gain standing to appeal to the Supreme Court, Griswold teamed up with Dr. Lee Buxton and opened a birth control clinic to dispense contraceptives to married women. When they were convicted, the U.S. Supreme Court accepted their case for review. In 1965 the Court handed down *Griswold v. Connecticut,* which established not only that states could not deny contraceptive information to married people but that there was a right to privacy implied in the

U.S. Constitution and that this right protected the decision "whether or not to beget a child."

This case became the most important decision of the 1965 term and has fueled controversy for decades. Before *Griswold,* a state could prohibit the sale or use of contraceptives and typically would hand down criminal penalties to people who violated this ban. A few states, however, allowed people to receive birth control information from physicians. New York, for example, in 1918 decided that although Margaret Sanger was guilty of violating a state obscenity statute for selling contraceptives, a physician in that state could sell them. But *Griswold* involved a Connecticut law that forbade the use of contraceptives by married people, as well as the aiding or counseling of others in the use of contraceptives. Two officials of a Planned Parenthood clinic were arrested for dispensing information about contraceptives and each was convicted and fined $100. None of the users of these contraceptive devices was charged.

The Court overturned their convictions on the grounds that the state law violated the fundamental "right to privacy," a right not explicitly mentioned in the Constitution. The Court previously had upheld similar unwritten rights; for example, people had the right to teach their children a foreign language, to send their children to private schools, to procreate, to resist certain invasions of the body, and to travel abroad. But never before had the Court justified so thoroughly the practice of granting such implied rights actual constitutional protection. The Court justified the right to privacy by delineating the several guarantees found in the first ten amendments to the Constitution (the Bill of Rights). These rights protect individual privacy interests, which create penumbras, or zones, of privacy. The right of married people to use contraceptives, the Court said, fell within these penumbras.

The Court continued that there are three meanings of the word "liberty" (or "privacy") in the Constitution. First, "autonomous control over the development of one's intellect, interests, tastes, and personality" are "absolute" rights protected by the First Amendment. Second, freedom of choice in the basic decisions of life respecting marriage, divorce, procreation, contraception, and the education and upbringing of children are "fundamental" rights not subject to control by the state. And third, freedom to care for one's health and person, freedom from bodily restraint or compulsion, and freedom to walk, stroll, or loaf are guaranteed by the Bill of Rights.

The Court first recognized the concept of a fundamental right to procreation in 1942, when it declared unconstitutional a statute ordering the sterilization of habitual criminals (*Skinner v. Oklahoma*). To involuntarily sterilize an individual would forever deprive that person of a basic liberty, the Court ruled. But *Skinner* focused on the fundamental right to have children, whereas *Griswold* focused on the right not to have children.

Six years after it decided *Griswold,* the Court extended to single people the same right to obtain information on contraception that it had already defined for married couples: "[w]hatever the rights of the individual to access to contraceptives may be, the rights must be the same for the unmarried and the married alike. . . . If the right of privacy means anything, it is the right of the individual, married or single, to be free from unwarranted government intrusion into matters so fundamentally affecting a person as the decision whether to bear or beget a child." Directly following that decision, the right to privacy was used to guarantee a woman's right to choose an abortion in *Roe v. Wade.* The Court has not, however, applied this logic to all social relations. Not all choices regarding abortion have been protected, nor have sexual relations among homosexuals.

See also Abortion; Contraception; Fourteenth Amendment; *Roe v. Wade*; Sanger, Margaret.

Infertility Alternatives

If a couple is unable to conceive a child naturally, they may seek help from one of several medical procedures. Artificial insemination was first developed to multiply the possible offspring of a prized animal and to breed endangered species. Now human gametes (the spermatozoa) are collected (often from anonymous male donors) and introduced artificially into the female genital tract to fertilize the egg. Prepared semen can be preserved for long periods by refrigeration and shipped over great distances. Use of frozen spermatozoa leads to pregnancy about 60 percent of the time, whereas freshly collected semen has a higher success rate, about 90 percent. Neither method is known to create birth defects, but frozen semen often becomes unsuitable for fertilization after an extended length of time.

Most states have legislation providing for parental rights of children conceived through AI. A husband is generally allowed to adopt children born to his wife via insemination of sperm from a third-party donor. If an unmarried woman knows the donor of the semen with which she was inseminated, the man is entitled to visitation rights of the child and is responsible for the child's financial support.

In vitro fertilization involves mixing spermatozoa and ovum in a nutrient medium outside the woman's body, then implanting the fertilized egg into her uterus. The eggs can be obtained either from the woman who will carry the fetus or from a donor. This method is usually used when a woman's fallopian tubes are blocked, preventing the spermatozoa from reaching the ovum. Although this technique has been successfully used in animals since the 1960s, it is more expensive and invasive than AI and generally less reliable (in 1990, for example, the success rate was lower than 5 percent). The first human conceived this way was the famous English "test-tube baby" Louise Brown, born in 1978. In 1984 an embryo was frozen for two months in Australia before it

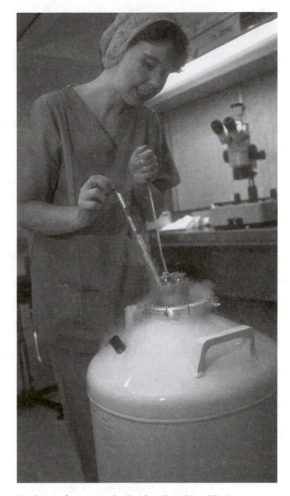

Embryos frozen at the Bridge Fertility Clinic (Matthew Polak/Corbis)

was implanted and a successful birth occurred. In 1984 an ovum was first fertilized within one woman's uterus and then transferred to another woman. Eggs can now be removed from a woman's ovaries and placed into her fallopian tubes along with her partner's sperm.

Davis v. Davis, the first in vitro fertilization case decided by the courts, involved a couple who had, through in vitro fertilization, conceived seven embryos, which they had frozen for future use. After the couple divorced, the ex-wife wanted custody of the unused embryos and planned to donate them to a childless couple. The father sued for the right to have them discarded, not wishing to have children with his former wife. The Tennessee Supreme Court in 1992 ruled all seven frozen embryos should remain undisturbed and in the joint custody of the divorced couple, who have equal voice in their disposition. No higher court reviewed the decision.

A fertilized egg may also be implanted into a woman who carries it to term for another couple, who then adopt the child. The first such surrogacy, in 1979, was pioneered by Dr. Richard Levin. States either ban surrogacy or severely restrict it, prohibiting any payments to the surrogate mother beyond medical expenses and prebirth contracts that the surrogate mother cannot revoke. If a state does not have a statute regarding surrogate parenting, courts generally strike down surrogate contracts and determine child custody on the basis of what is best for the child. For example, a California court in 1988 granted custody of a child to its biological parents, holding that the nonbiological, gestational mother was similar to a foster parent and had no parental rights (*Matter of Baby M.*).

Beginning in the 1980s, when in vitro fertilization, surrogate motherhood, and artificial insemination became more or less routine, the question became: Who may enjoy the privileges of parenthood? Because doctors have the right to refuse treatment to any patient, most fertility clinics are closed to "unmarried women," which of course includes lesbian couples. Sperm banks are relatively expensive, but in many states they are the only option for single women and lesbians. Another option is to find a male friend who will donate his sperm. But no state has yet extinguished male parental rights on this basis; thus, if a donor changes his mind about giving up the resulting child, a woman may be left with few legal options to retain sole custody of the child.

See also Adoption; *Jhordan C. v. Mary K; Johnson v. Calvert; Matter of Baby M.*
Reference Lori B. Andrews. 1985. *New Conceptions: A Consumer's Guide to the*

Newest Infertility Treatments: Including in Vitro Fertilization, Artificial Insemination, and Surrogate Motherhood. New York: Ballentine.

Jhordan C. v. Mary K. (1986)

In 1978 Mary K. wished to bear a child by artificial insemination (AI) and raise it with Victoria, her partner. She chose Jhordan C. as a semen donor. She claimed to have told Jhordan C. that he would have no role in the child's life but would be allowed to see the child occasionally. He later claimed they had agreed he could have an ongoing relationship with the child. After the child was born, he sued for visitation rights. California law allowed that if a man donated sperm to a licensed physician for use in AI of a woman other than the donor's wife, he was treated legally as if he were not the natural father of the child. But Mary K. could not use this law because she performed the AI procedure on herself with his donated sperm and without the help of a physician. Jhordan C. was thus considered the legal and biological father of the child and the court gave him visitation rights.

See also Davis v. Davis; Infertility Alternatives; *Johnson v. Calvert; Matter of Baby M.*

Johnson v. Calvert (1993)

Crispina Calvert and her husband contracted with Anna Johnson to be the surrogate mother of their biological child following Calvert's hysterectomy in 1984 that left Calvert unable to bear children but able to produce eggs. Under the terms of the surrogacy agreement, in return for carrying the child conceived through the union of the Calverts' sperm and egg, Johnson would receive $10,000 cash and relinquish all parental rights once the baby was born. But after the implantation of the Calverts' embryo, Johnson changed her mind and refused to relinquish parental rights. The court, for the first time, defined which woman in such a case was the natural mother of a child; it was also the first time a state court validated a surrogacy contract.

When the Calverts filed suit in 1990, declaring they were the legal parents of the child yet to be born, Johnson countersued, seeking a declaration from the court that she was the biological mother of the child. A trial court first ruled that the Calverts were indeed the child's "genetic, biological and natural" father and mother and that Johnson had no parental rights to the child. This decision was later affirmed by the state court of appeals. But on appeal, the California Supreme Court took the decision a step further. It stated that because each of the women presented acceptable proof of maternity, the case could not be decided without inquiring into the parties' intentions as manifested in the surrogacy agreement signed by all parties.

Specifically, the high court ruled that a surrogate mother, because she is not genetically related to the child she gave birth to, has no parental rights to the child. California law recognizes both genetics and giving birth as a means of establishing a mother-child relationship. But when these two factors do not coincide in one woman—that is, when one woman is the genetic mother and another woman actually gives birth to the child—the woman who intended to procreate the child is the natural mother. That is, she who intended to bring about the birth of a child that she would raise as her own is the natural mother. Further, the court held that surrogacy contracts as a general rule are legal; they do not violate public policy or run afoul of prohibitions on involuntary servitude. In the end, custody of the child born from the Calvert-Johnson surrogacy contract, a son, was awarded to the Calverts, and Johnson was denied all visitation rights.

The California court's ruling contradicted other state courts' rulings on the legality of surrogacy contracts. Two years before the California court ruled for the Calverts, a New Jersey court declared surrogacy contracts in that state invalid in the 1988 *Matter of Baby M.*

case. The New Jersey court granted visitation rights to the surrogate mother, who had been artificially inseminated. Because the birth mother had a genetic claim to the child, however, the case was significantly different from the Calvert case.

See also Davis v. Davis; Infertility Alternatives; *Jhordan C. v. Mary K.*; *Matter of Baby M.*

Matter of A. C. (1990)

A. C. had been diagnosed with cancer at thirteen and undergone chemotherapy and several operations. During remission of her cancer, she married and immediately became pregnant. Four months into her high-risk pregnancy, she was admitted to George Washington University Hospital so that her doctors could continually monitor A. C. and her fetus, which had only a 60 percent chance of survival. Largely because of the pregnancy, A. C.'s health quickly deteriorated and put her fetus at risk. Because she was on life support, the hospital was uncertain whether she was competent enough to agree to a cesarean birth, which it believed was necessary to ensure the life of the fetus. A. C.'s mother, husband, and physician were against the cesarean section, fearing it would endanger A. C.'s life and go against her wish to have a natural birth. The hospital petitioned the court, which ordered that a cesarean section be performed. A baby girl was delivered. The baby died immediately, however, and A. C. died two days later.

The court ultimately ruled that the life of the fetus had a greater chance of survival than the mother, and the state had a vested interest in protecting that life even when that interest conflicted with the incapacitated mother, as well as the wishes of her family and physician. A court later ruled that the first court erred in issuing the order forcing the cesarean section against A. C.'s wishes, and her family settled with the hospital for an undisclosed sum of money.

See also Fetal Protection.

Matter of Baby M. (1988)

In the *Matter of Baby M.*, a court was asked for the first time to determine the validity of a surrogacy contract. In 1985 William Stern and MaryBeth Whitehead entered into a surrogacy contract that would provide a child to Stern and his spouse. The contract specified artificial insemination of Whitehead's egg with Stern's sperm. For a fee of $10,000, Whitehead agreed to carry the fertilized egg to term, then relinquish to Stern and his wife any parental rights to the child. The contract further gave Mrs. Stern sole custody of the child if Mr. Stern died either before or after the birth of the child Whitehead was carrying.

Called Baby M. by the court, the child was born in 1986. Directly following the birth, Whitehead handed the baby over to the Sterns. But she later took the baby and left the state unexpectedly. Whitehead and the baby were not found until four months later, when the baby was returned to the Sterns.

The court awarded the baby to her biological father and his wife, who formally adopted her. Whitehead, the biological surrogate mother, was granted visitation rights only. The California court held that the surrogacy contract was invalid because it conflicted with laws prohibiting the use of payment of money for an adoption; payment can only be used for medical and related expenses. Further, the contract was invalid because parental rights cannot be terminated and an adoption granted without proof of parental unfitness or abandonment. And finally, the surrogacy contract was illegal because it made the surrender of custody of a child and consent to adoption irrevocable in a private-placement adoption. In other cases involving gestational mothers who have been implanted with fertilized eggs not their own, courts have held that nonbiological gestational mothers are similar to foster parents and have no parental rights.

See also Adoption; *Davis v. Davis;* Infertility Alternatives; *Jhordan C. v. Mary K.; Johnson v. Calvert.*

McCorvey, Norma

Norma McCorvey is the actual name of "Jane Roe," the alias she assumed as the lead plaintiff in the case that legalized abortion in the United States. In 1971 McCorvey was a twenty-one-year-old single woman pregnant with her second child. Her mother was raising McCorvey's first child, and having another child would make it impossible for McCorvey to continue to work to support herself. She had found an illegal clinic where she could get an abortion but "didn't like the looks of it." She had no money to travel to another state where abortion was legal.

McCorvey asked for information on abortion providers from a group that helped women in states where abortion was illegal; she was later contacted by one of the group's members, Sarah Weddington, a Texas lawyer who had graduated from law school only five years before. Having experienced an illegal abortion herself in the late 1960s and realizing that from 1970 to 1972, 350,000 women had left their own states to obtain abortions in states where abortion was legal, Weddington had decided to take action. She teamed up with fellow lawyer Linda Coffee in looking for a plaintiff to overturn the abortion statute in Texas and, ultimately, other states. Coffee and Weddington assured McCorvey that she would not have to answer written or oral questions from opposing lawyers, she would not have to attend any hearings, nor would she have to pay the attorneys for their work. They simply wanted a test case, and McCorvey's situation fit the bill almost perfectly: she wanted an abortion, was currently pregnant, and could not obtain one in Texas. If she had a right to privacy, as the Court had specified in *Griswold v. Connecticut* in 1965, then wasn't that right being violated?

The Supreme Court, of course, held that her rights had been violated and states could not make abortion illegal in the first trimester of pregnancy. Ironically, in 1995,

Norma McCorvey, "Jane Roe" in Roe v. Wade, *is the center of media attention following arguments in a Missouri abortion case at the Supreme Court in April 1989. (Bettmann/Corbis)*

McCorvey released her name to the press and switched sides; she is now a vocal anti-abortion activist and has organized a ministry called Roe No More. McCorvey has publicly committed her life to abolishing abortion while "serving the Lord and helping women save their babies."

Norplant

A relatively new, long-term method of birth control for women, Norplant consists of six soft capsules the size of matchsticks that are surgically inserted under a woman's skin on the inside of her upper arm. The capsules release a synthetic hormone called progestin for five years. Norplant is over 99 percent effective against pregnancy but like other chemical-based birth control devices does not provide protection against sexually transmitted diseases.

Probably the greatest benefit of Norplant is that once implanted, it can be removed at any time, yet while in place it provides an extremely effective method of birth control for such a long period of time. An additional benefit is that since it does not contain estrogen, women who cannot use birth control pills (which do contain estrogen) can use it. Further, there is some evidence that it may offer protection against endometrial cancer.

Although Norplant is relatively new to the American market, it was first developed in 1966 by Population Council's International Committee for Contraceptive Research and approved by the U.S. government in 1990. Currently, it is used by 1 million American women. The greatest debate on the use of Norplant involves poor women: several states have required that women receiving public assistance use Norplant.

See also Contraception; Right to Privacy; Sanger, Margaret.

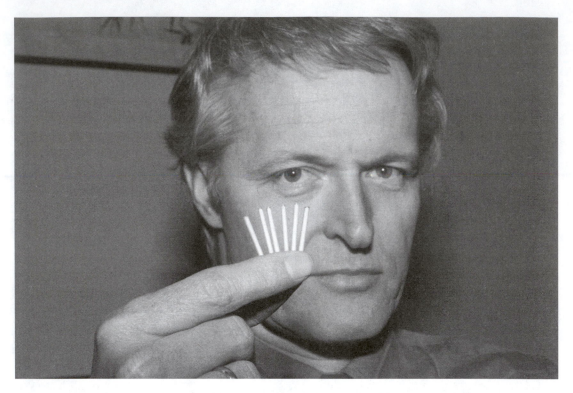

Dr. Wayne Bardin, vice-president of the Population Council, holds implants, which, when injected into a woman's arm, release levonorgestrel, probibiting conception for a period of up to five years. (Bettmann/Corbis)

Reference Andrea Tone. 2002. *Devices and Desires: A History of Contraceptives in America.* New York: Hill and Wang.

Planned Parenthood of Southeastern Pennsylvania v. Casey (1992)

In *Planned Parenthood of Southeastern Pennsylvania v. Casey,* the Supreme Court clarified several issues surrounding the abortion debate that had not been addressed in either *Roe v. Wade* or the later *Webster* decision. Because the Court had never ruled on the appropriate standards states could use in establishing restrictions on abortions, state laws were varied. In this particular case, five abortion clinics and a doctor challenged five provisions of the Pennsylvania Abortion Control Act of 1982. In sum, the Court held that states could enact provisions mandating that a woman give "informed consent" before receiving an abortion, spousal notification requirements were unlawful,

and states had to allow judicial bypasses in cases of parental consent for minors.

Largely in response to the Court's decision in *Webster v. Reproductive Health Services* (1989), Pennsylvania's Abortion Control Act was revised in 1988 and 1989, strongly restricting access to abortions in that state. The Court of Appeals (Third Circuit) upheld many of the restrictions but not the spousal notification mandate. Relying on the 1983 Supreme Court decision in *Akron v. Akron Center for Reproductive Health, Inc.*, this lower court gave strict scrutiny to any restriction that might "unduly burden" a woman's attempt to receive an abortion; abortion restrictions were permissible only if they had a rational basis in the state's interest in protecting maternal health. Under the Pennsylvania law, the physician performing an abortion had to receive a statement from the woman prior to the procedure that she had notified her spouse that she was "about to undergo an abortion." As an alternative to this notification, the woman could "provide a statement certifying that her husband was NOT the man who impregnated her; that her husband could not be located; that the pregnancy was the result of spousal sexual assault, which she had reported; or that the woman believed that notifying her husband would cause him or someone else to inflict bodily injury upon her." Physicians who performed abortions without signed statements from women regarding spousal notification would be subject to losing their licenses. And women who falsely signed such statements would be guilty of a third-degree misdemeanor. When strictly scrutinizing that provision, the appellate court concluded that it unduly burdened women by potentially exposing them to spousal abuse, violence, and economic duress by their husbands.

But the court upheld the "informed consent" provision. Women could be required to be informed of "the nature of the procedure, the health risks of the abortion and of childbirth, and the probable gestational age of the unborn child" and a woman could be required to "certify in writing" that she understood the consequences of her decision ("informed consent") and then be required to wait for twenty-four hours before the procedure was performed.

In the case of minors, parental consent had to be given before the procedure could be performed. There was a judicial bypass option, however, whereby a minor could ask the court to declare that she was sufficiently mature enough to make the decision on her own or that notifying her parents would not be in her best interest. The lower court ruled that this provision of the act did not pose an undue burden to a minor. Nor did that court find that the provision requiring a report to be made by the state on all abortions that took place in that state was unconstitutional; all facilities that performed abortions were required to file reports containing the women's ages, the number of prior pregnancies or abortions

they had had, "pre-existing medical conditions that would complicate" the pregnancies, the weights and ages of the aborted fetuses, whether or not the women were married, and, if relevant, why the women had failed to notify their spouses. This court ruled these reports did not pose an undue burden on the women even though this information would become public if the abortions were performed in facilities funded by the state.

When the lower court upheld all provisions of the act except the spousal notification requirement, five abortion clinics appealed to the Supreme Court, asking the court to issue a nonambiguous decision to either affirm or overturn *Roe v. Wade.* In 1986 the Court had been asked to decide a virtually identical case in *Thornburgh v. American College of Obstetricians and Gynecologists.* There the Court had struck down (by a bare majority) virtually all requirements. But by 1992 the Court had substantially altered its analysis of abortion law and held several restrictive laws constitutional. As a result, several lower federal courts had begun upholding restrictions on abortions, declaring they did not constitute "undue burdens" on women.

In a split decision (5–4), the Court upheld the "essence" of *Roe v. Wade.* The Court recognized a right to liberty found in the Due Process Clause, which includes bodily integrity and privacy interests as to whether or not to choose to continue a pregnancy. Requirements designed to further a woman's health, such as the informed consent provisions found in the Pennsylvania law, were not necessarily inconsistent with this right. This part of the ruling allowed states much more leeway to enact regulations regarding abortions.

But state laws must balance this constitutional right to abortion and the state's interest in potential life. A state law is unconstitutional, the Court ruled, if its purpose or effect is to "place a substantial obstacle in the path of a woman seeking an abortion before the fetus obtains viability"; any law would be found unconstitutional if it made abortion more difficult or expensive to obtain. Written by Justice Sandra Day O'Connor, the decision also rejected the rigid pregnancy trimester format of *Roe,* finding that the framework, particularly the ban on all regulations before viability, undervalued the state's interest in potential life.

The Court also ruled that spousal notifications are invalid. The Court found that the spousal notification requirement in the Pennsylvania law would be likely to prevent a significant number of women from obtaining abortions, particularly those who were victims of physical, psychological, or sexual abuse or who feared for their safety and the safety of their children. Further, the Court upheld the judicial bypass provision for minors seeking abortions.

> *See also* Contraception; Fourteenth Amendment; *Griswold v. Connecticut;* Right to Privacy; *Roe v. Wade; Webster v. Reproductive Health Services.*

Pregnancy

The first time the Supreme Court ruled on the issue of employment and motherhood was in *Muller v. Oregon* (1908). In that case the Court upheld the state's power to limit a woman's working hours for protection of her "maternal functions." But at the time, very few American women worked outside the home. As the century progressed, however, that changed dramatically. The right to be pregnant, or to choose not to be pregnant, was seemingly protected in the landmark Supreme Court decision of *Griswold v. Connecticut* (1965), which allowed women access to information on birth control. And later, in 1973, the Court legalized abortion for women in the first trimester of pregnancy. But how to manage motherhood in the workplace would prove to be more difficult for the courts.

Until 1974, when the Supreme Court ruled that mandatory maternity leaves had no rational purpose (*Cleveland Board of Edu-*

cation v. LaFleur), employers could fire pregnant workers or impose mandatory maternity leaves. In the late 1970s, the Court ruled that employee health insurance plans could exclude pregnancy. But in 1978 the Pregnancy Discrimination Act was passed, forcing employers to treat pregnancy like any other physical disability. The issue of maternity leave, however, remains unresolved. The Family and Medical Leave Act of 1993 passed by Congress under the administration of Bill Clinton allows some U.S. workers maternity leave, but since it guarantees only unpaid leave, few employees can take advantage of it.

Teenage pregnancy is the primary reason young women drop out of school. The courts have ruled that barring pregnant students from class is a violation of their personal liberty. Additionally, the Supreme Court has ruled that minors under sixteen have a constitutional right to information about and access to contraceptives, even without parental permission.

The Court has also recently ruled on the privacy rights of pregnant women suspected of drug abuse of the fetus they are carrying. A large public hospital in Charleston, South Carolina, had subjected pregnant women to drug screens of their urine without their knowledge or consent. The results of these drug tests were turned over to law enforcement authorities; of the thirty women arrested, twenty-nine were African American. Although the Fourth Amendment allows for the exception of search warrants in "special" circumstances, the Court held that this was not one of those circumstances and that pregnant women were free from unwarranted intrusion from the state absent their consent for a drug test.

> *See also* Contraception; Family and Medical Leave Act (FMLA); *Ferguson v. City of Charleston; Geduldig v. Aiello; Griswold v. Connecticut;* Pregnancy Discrimination Act; Right to Privacy; *Roe v. Wade.*

Right to Privacy

Although the right to privacy does not appear in the U.S. Constitution, the Supreme Court has recognized privacy to protect the independence necessary for people to raise families, to choose not to have a child, to be secure in their homes and possessions, and to allow them to keep certain facts to themselves if they so choose. Throughout most of U.S. history, however, states have been concerned with private sexual behavior. The colonists enacted laws that regulated, in varying degrees, private sexual conduct; homosexual activity, extramarital sex, and any marital relations other than genital intercourse were prohibited. The Supreme Court has strictly defined the sexual relations that can be left to individuals today, but states are still free to regulate many of these activities. Privacy is a rather illusive concept. One hundred years ago, Supreme Court justice Louis Brandeis called the right to privacy "the right to be left alone." This definition, however, offers no legal guidance as to how much privacy the government can violate.

Under the Supreme Court's interpretation of privacy, for example, contraception and abortion are now protected under the Constitution. Privacy is implied from the broad concept of liberty found throughout the Constitution, which encompasses certain fundamental rights not specifically listed in the Constitution. For example, the Fourth Amendment provides for protection against unreasonable searches and seizures from the government. This protection of privacy in citizens' homes, persons, and possessions, then, is implied by the protections afforded in the Fourth Amendment. Further, the Due Process Clause of the Fourteenth Amendment declares that no person shall be denied "life, liberty, or property, without due process of law." Liberty thus acts as a sort of umbrella under which all privacy rights are protected.

Early in the twentieth century, the Supreme Court began building the foundation upon which it would eventually establish a right to privacy. In the 1920s the justices held that liberty takes in a parent's right to make certain decisions about his or her child's education without state interference. These privacy rights include the right to send a child to private school and the right to have the child study a foreign language. Later, in *Griswold v. Connecticut* in 1965, the Court specifically used the term "privacy" in deciding that married couples have a right to obtain birth control information and states could not limit that right. The justices ruled that it was not possible for the government to regulate the size of a family without violating the right to liberty explicit in the Constitution. As Justice William O. Douglas wrote in his opinion, "We deal with a right to privacy older than the Bill of Rights." The Bill of Rights (the first ten amendments to the Constitution) created "zones of privacy" broad enough to protect various aspects of personal and family life. The dissenters in the case helped to define the concept as well. Justices Hugo Black and Potter Stewart dissented from the majority, arguing that unless specifically stated, the government has every right to invade the privacy of the citizens. And the right to privacy, the dissenters said, was simply not present in the Constitution.

By 1967 the Court once again used the right to privacy and further defined the concept when it struck down a Virginia miscegenation statute that forbade interracial marriages. Under the umbrella of liberty the Court included the right to marry whomever one wishes. In 1972 the Court held in *Eisenstadt v. Baird* that a ban on contraception for unmarried people was a violation of their rights under the Equal Protection Clause of the Fourteenth Amendment and thus unconstitutional. Justice William Brennan wrote in the opinion for the Court, "If the right to privacy means anything, it is the right of the individual, married or single, to be free form unwarranted governmental intrusion into matters so fundamentally affecting a person as the decision whether to bear or beget a child." With these words, the right to privacy was greatly expanded.

But in subsequent cases the Court used the right to privacy in a much more controversial manner. A short ten months after *Eisenstadt*, the Court decided *Roe v. Wade*, holding that a Texas law criminalizing all abortions except those necessary to save the life of the mother violated the constitutional right to privacy. The Court considered diverse medical, philosophical, and religious opinions on the issue of abortion. But they confined their discussion to the legal treatments of abortion and not the "difficult question of when life begins." It was the conclusion of the Court that "persons," as used in the Constitution, had never included the unborn. This finding was consistent, the justices ruled, with various state laws that restricted a fetus from inheriting property or recovering damages. To the Court, "the unborn have never been recognized in the law as persons in the whole sense."

The Court went on in *Roe* to explicitly define "privacy," which included personal rights that were "fundamental" or "implicit in the concept of ordered liberty." Specifically, then, the right to privacy included rights pertaining to marriage, procreation, contraception, family relationships, child rearing, and education. The Court added abortion to the list: "This right of privacy . . . is broad enough to encompass a woman's decision whether or not to terminate her pregnancy."

But it is important to realize that the opinion of the Court in *Roe* made clear that the right to privacy was not absolute; in the case of abortion, for example, the state had an interest in protecting both the health of the woman and that of "the potential for life" growing within her. So it is possible for the interest of the state to limit a woman's right to terminate her pregnancy. For example, the state's interest in maternal health allows the regulation of the procedures used to perform abortions. This interest of the state becomes compelling around the end of the first trimester of pregnancy, after which time the fetus becomes viable outside the mother's womb and abortion is no longer statistically safer than childbirth. In dissent, Justice William Rehnquist argued that if the justices were to use the Fourteenth Amendment, they must look to the original intent of the framers of that amendment. When the Fourteenth Amendment was written following the Civil War, at least thirty-six states or territories limited and often criminalized abortion. Because twenty of those laws were still used by states, Rehnquist contended, the right to abortion could hardly be "so rooted in the traditions and conscience of our people as to be ranked as fundamental."

Following *Roe*, the Court handed down several major abortion decisions, striking down nearly all restrictions on abortion. These restrictions ranged from requirements that a woman obtain consent from her husband before having an abortion and a mandatory twenty-four-hour waiting period between the initial consultation and the procedure, to requirements that all second-trimester abortions be performed in a hospital and that minors (under the age of eighteen) have the consent of both parents before obtaining an abortion. The only provisions the Court upheld were withdrawals of federal funding for abortions and requirements that all second-trimester abortions be performed in a licensed clinic, that a second physician be present during an abortion performed after viability of a fetus, and that parents of minors must be notified of an impending abortion "if possible." On this last provision the Court ruled that parental consent could be waived entirely if a minor could show a judge that she was sufficiently mature to make the decision on her own or that notifying her parents would not be in her best interest. This process is known as judicial bypass.

By 1989 the tide began to shift, and the

strict outlines of the right to privacy specified under *Roe* began to soften. In *Webster v. Reproductive Health Services,* the Court upheld the most severe restrictions on abortion until that time and nearly overturned *Roe.* This case dealt with a Missouri law designed to "encourage childbirth over abortion" by banning the use of public facilities or staff to perform abortions except to save the life of the mother. Also required by the law were tests to determine the viability of the fetus if a woman was more than twenty weeks pregnant. In issuing six separate opinions in this case, the justices demonstrated the tension on the Court. Justice Antonin Scalia called for the Court to overrule *Roe* outright. In a separate opinion, Justices Rehnquist, Byron White, and Anthony M. Kennedy called for doing away with the trimester framework spelled out in *Roe.* This opinion specified that abortion was not a fundamental right but could be regulated as the states saw fit, as long as it was not outlawed altogether. Providing the swing vote, Justice Sandra Day O'Connor was in favor of the restrictions but against revisiting *Roe.* She also expressed dissatisfaction with the trimester framework but concluded that *Webster* was not the proper case in which to reexamine it.

Leading the dissent, Justice Harry Blackmun, the author of *Roe,* maintained that the Constitution recognized a sphere of individual liberty that includes the right to make personal decisions of the greatest importance without government interference. He wrote: "In a Nation that cherishes liberty, the ability of a woman to control the biological operation of her body . . . must fall within that limited sphere of individual autonomy that lies beyond the will or power of any transient majority. . . . This court stands as the ultimate guarantor of that zone of privacy, regardless of the bitter disputes to which our decisions may give rise."

When the justices decided *Planned Parenthood v. Casey* in 1992, they were faced with an area of law that had become confusing and often conflicting. *Casey* would update the definition of "privacy" first given in *Roe* nearly twenty years prior. Justice O'Connor wrote the joint opinion reaffirming what the Court considered the "essential holdings" of *Roe*: a woman has a right to choose abortion before viability and to obtain it without undue interference from the state; the state has the power to restrict abortion after viability (with exceptions for cases in which the woman's health is endangered); and the state has legitimate interests from the outset of pregnancy in protecting the health of the woman and the life of the fetus. Further, O'Connor dealt with the argument that the Fourteenth Amendment should be interpreted on the basis of the framers' intent. The Court, she argued, was not limited by the practices of framers. Instead, it is the Court's responsibility to balance individual liberty against the demands of organized society through an exercise of reasoned judgment. "It is a promise of the Constitution that there is a realm of personal liberty which the government may not enter. . . . At the heart of liberty is the right to define one's own concept of existence, of meaning, of the universe, and of the mystery of human life. Beliefs about these matters could not define the attributes of personhood were they formed under compulsion of the State."

In dissent, Rehnquist, Scalia, White, and Clarence Thomas gave their definition of "privacy." Although acknowledging that the Court had long protected liberties such as the right to procreate, marry, and use contraceptives, these rights were simply separate protected liberties and did not create a more general constitutionally protected right to privacy. Certainly, they argued, abortion was different from these other protected rights because it "involves the purposeful termination of potential life." Justice Scalia exhorted his colleagues to "get out of this area, where we have no right to be, and where we do neither ourselves nor the country any good by remaining."

The controversy over the right to privacy has not been limited to the question of abortion. Although the Court has given heterosexuals wide latitude in exercising their privacy against governmental intrusion, they have not given homosexuals the same protections. In 1986 the Court held, for example, that privacy did not apply to homosexuals practicing sodomy and upheld a Georgia statute outlawing that practice in *Bowers v. Hardwick*. But in June of 2003 the Supreme Court changed course.

In *Lawrence v. Texas* (2003), the Court considered whether two adult males could engage in private, consensual sex without violating a Texas law that forbid two persons of the same sex engaging in intimate sexual conduct. The Court held that the Texas law violated the liberty protections of the Due Process Clause. As the majority opinion specified, the *Bowers* decision had failed to

appreciate the extent of liberty at stake. To say that the issue in *Bowers* was simply the right to engage in certain sexual conduct demeans the claim the individual put forward, just as it would demean a married couple were it said that marriage is just about the right to have sexual intercourse. Although the laws involved in *Bowers* and here purport to do no more than prohibit a particular sexual act, their penalties and purposes have more far-reaching consequences, touching upon the most private human conduct, sexual behavior, and in the most private of places, the home. They seek to control a personal relationship that, whether or not entitled to formal recognition in the law, is within the liberty of persons to choose without being punished as criminals. The liberty protected by the Constitution allows homosexual persons the right to choose to enter upon relationships in the confines of their homes and their own private lives and still retain their dignity as free persons.

See also Contraception; Fourteenth Amendment; Ginsburg, Ruth Bader; *Griswold v. Connecticut; Planned Parenthood of Southeastern Pennsylvania v. Casey; Roe v. Wade;* Sanger, Margaret; *Webster v. Reproductive Health Services.*

References Alderman, Ellen, and Caroline Kennedy. 1997. *The Right to Privacy.* New York: Vintage; Garrow, David J. 1998. *Liberty and Sexuality: The Right to Privacy and the Making of* Roe v. Wade. Berkeley: University of California Press; Paul, Ellen F., Fred D. Miller, and Jeffery Paul. 2000. *The Right to Privacy.* New York: Cambridge University Press.

Roe v. Wade (1973)

Roe v. Wade established the right to privacy and gave a woman a right to obtain an abortion at least in the first trimester of pregnancy. Norma McCorvey, a single, pregnant woman in Dallas, Texas, was recruited by two attorneys, Sarah Weddington and Linda Coffee, to challenge the constitutionality of the state law forbidding all abortions not necessary "for the purpose of saving the life of the mother." Although they aimed to establish a woman's constitutional right to "control her own body," they later became part of a larger historical movement and political struggle.

McCorvey's name was hidden from the public by filing the case under the pseudonym of Jane Roe. "Roe" argued that she wanted an abortion performed by a licensed and competent physician under safe conditions. But since her life was not threatened, she could not get a legal abortion in Texas and could not afford to travel to another jurisdiction where abortion was legal. Thus, she claimed, the Texas statute abridged her personal right to privacy.

By the late 1960s, fourteen states had liberalized laws to permit abortions when the woman's health was in danger, when there was a likelihood of a fetal abnormality, and when the woman had been a victim of rape or incest. The argument against the Texas law (and presumably others like it) was that in considering whether a woman's health was in danger, doctors were not free to consider the effects of pregnancy on the woman's mental health. Further, although some states had relatively liberal abortion laws, women like Roe who were poor and could not claim an abortion was necessary to save their lives, were unable to simply travel to another state to obtain an abortion. They faced either unwanted children or medically unsafe illegal abortions that could be fatal.

The Court ruled that a woman's right to end her pregnancy is absolute based on the considerable psychological, physical, and economic impact that it has on her if she is forced to bear an unwanted child. This absolute right bars any state imposition of criminal penalties for that choice.

But the Court also acknowledged the state had an interest in recognizing and protecting prenatal life. So until the first trimester of a pregnancy was over, the decision must be left to the woman and the medical judgment of her doctor. During the second trimester, the state may regulate abortions in ways that are reasonably related to her maternal health. But during the third trimester, the state's interest in the potential life becomes compelling, since it is significantly riskier for a woman to have an abortion than for her to go through childbirth. The compelling point, then, is the viability of the fetus, or when the fetus becomes capable of meaningful life outside the mother's womb. The Court never resolved when life begins or when the fetus becomes viable.

Using these standards, the Court ruled that state laws (like the one in Texas) completely outlawing abortions were too broad and thus unconstitutionally invaded a woman's right to privacy, a right guaranteed previously in *Griswold v. Connecticut*. For the next few decades, there were several challenges to abortion rights. Probably the most important ruling following *Roe* was *Harris v. McRae* (1980), which allowed Congress to

prohibit the use of Medicaid funds to pay for nontherapeutic abortions; in an earlier ruling the Court did not require states to fund abortions for indigent women. In separate rulings the Court did strike down spousal consent provisions and upheld laws requiring the notification of parents of minors seeking abortions but allowing for judicial bypass of parental consent.

> *See also* Contraception; *Griswold v. Connecticut; Planned Parenthood of Southeastern Pennsylvania v. Casey;* Right to Privacy; Sanger, Margaret; Weddington, Sarah.
>
> *References* Jelen, Ted G., and Marthe A. Chandler. 1994. *Abortion Politics in the United States and Canada.* London: Praeger; Luker, Kristin. 1984. *Abortion and the Politics of Motherhood.* Berkeley: University of California Press; Weddington, Sarah. 1992. *A Question of Choice: The Lawyer Who Won* Roe v. Wade. New York: Grosset/Putnam.

RU-486 (Mifepristone)

The Food and Drug Administration approved the use of RU-486 in 2000 and made available the abortion pill that had been available in Europe for decades. RU-486 consists of two drugs, the first of which blocks progesterone, a hormone necessary to sustain a pregnancy, and the second of which (misoprostol) forces the uterus to contract, making surgical abortion unnecessary. The combination of drugs is over 92 percent effective in ending pregnancy.

One of the biggest benefits of RU-486 is that it can be used much earlier than surgical abortions can be performed; surgical abortion cannot be performed until the seventh week of pregnancy, whereas this drug can be used anytime up to seven weeks of pregnancy. The drug also makes abortion more easily available to women living in communities without abortion providers; they need only a prescription and a pharmacy to begin the process. Further, several studies of physicians indicate that many gynecologists who refused to perform surgical

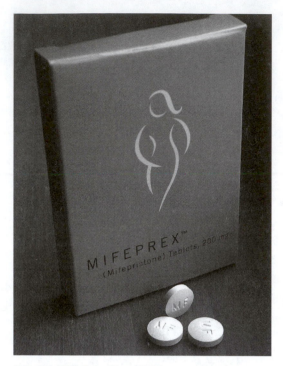

RU-486 (Bill Greenblatt/ UPI)

abortions are willing to prescribe this non-surgical option. Part of the reason for this is that the entrance of the drug onto the American market makes it more difficult for protestors to focus on abortion providers, so physicians are allowed more freedom in prescribing the drug.

But three years after its introduction onto the American market, fewer women were using the drug than was expected. Part of the reason for this was the cost; RU-486 is approximately $100 more expensive than a surgical abortion (which ranges from $300 to $400). Additionally, a woman who takes the drug must make a follow-up visit to her doctor's office, and the doctor must remain on call for several days while the woman experiences bleeding and cramping, posing an even greater deterrent to low-income women. In contrast, a surgical abortion is completed with one office procedure and does not require medical monitoring. Finally, many states refuse to pay for medical abortions under Medicaid.

Reference Andrea Tone. 2002. *Devices and Desires: A History of Contraceptives in America.* New York: Hill and Wang.

Sanger, Margaret (1883–1966)

Margaret was born in New York to devout Irish Catholic parents. Her mother died young from tuberculosis, and Margaret pointed to her mother's frequent pregnancies as the underlying cause: Margaret had been the sixth of eleven children, and her mother had had seven miscarriages. After attending two small colleges (with the help of her older siblings), she entered a nursing program at White Plains Hospital in 1900. Directly before graduation, she married architect William Sanger and in quick succession had three children.

The Sangers moved to New York City in 1910. Margaret returned to nursing to support the family when her husband could no longer work as a draftsman. The Sangers were involved in the bohemian culture that flourished before World War I and joined other intellectuals and activists that included Upton Sinclair and Emma Goldman. Margaret joined the Women's Committee of the New York Socialist Party and led labor protests with the Industrial Workers of the World.

But it was her job as a visiting nurse that gave Margaret her life's work, sex education and women's health. She wrote a column for the New York *Call* in 1912 on sex education entitled "What Every Girl Should Know." However, censors often banned her work, such as her column on venereal disease, calling it "obscene." But the longer she nursed indigent women suffering from too-frequent childbirth, miscarriage, abortion, and their aftermath, the more adamant she became in her belief that women needed access to birth control information. She argued for birth limitation—she coined the term "birth control"—as the tool by which lower-class women could gain independence and improve their health. "No woman can call herself free unless she can

Margaret Sanger (Library of Congress)

choose consciously whether she will or will not be a mother," said Sanger.

In 1914 Sanger published the first issue of *The Woman Rebel*, which promoted the right to practice birth control (considered a radical feminist idea at the time). Several issues were banned, and Sanger was indicted for violating postal obscenity laws for mailing the pamphlet. Before spending any time in jail, however, Sanger fled to England. From there, her supporters released several thousand copies of *Family Limitation*, which provided explicit instructions on how to obtain and use contraceptives. While in England, Sanger educated herself on new theories that expanded her understanding of contraceptives. One theory in vogue at the time was Malthusianism, which argued that poor health among the indigent was simply a way of clearing out society's undesirables. Another was the work of psychologist Havelock Ellis, who advocated the importance of sexuality among women (a concept completely unheard of at the time). Sanger realized that the need for contraceptives

was even greater than she had originally believed. If women were allowed to limit the number of children they had, their health would improve, the health of their children would improve because parents would be able to better care for the children they had, and women would be allowed to explore their own individuality. As it was, women were constantly struggling to care for enormous families. Birth control would also allow women to be happier because it would enable women to explore their own sexuality without constantly fearing pregnancy.

By 1915 she returned to New York to face the obscenity charges from the previous year. Sanger's five-year-old daughter died a month after she returned, bringing her widespread public support and forcing the prosecution to drop charges. This seemed to spur Sanger on; she immediately embarked on a nationwide speaking tour and was arrested for violating obscenity laws in several cities.

In 1916 she opened the first birth control clinic in the United States. Before seeing such clinics in England and the Netherlands, she had advocated suppositories or douches as reliable contraceptives. But European clinics were using the more flexible diaphragm, which snuggly fitted over a woman's cervical opening and was much more reliable. Sanger was able to smuggle several hundred diaphragms out of Europe and give them to women upon her return. Sanger and her entire staff were arrested nine days after her clinic opened, and she was sentenced to thirty days in jail. She later appealed her conviction and was denied. The New York court did, however, allow physicians to disseminate contraceptive information to women, which provided Sanger with a small victory. But physicians could prescribe birth control only for medical reasons.

Following her time in jail, Margaret and William Sanger separated. Margaret had several affairs with high-profile men, including Havelock Ellis and H. G. Wells, which guaranteed her even more publicity—most of it negative. But Sanger was able to use her increasing notoriety to her advantage. If newspapers made fun of her in cartoons, her speaking engagements attracted enormous crowds, and wealthy supporters began sending in contributions to allow her to continue her work and organize other protest organizations around the United States.

She established a monthly newspaper called the *Birth Control Review* in 1917 and the American Birth Control League (later renamed Planned Parenthood) in 1921. Her goal, she said, was to educate Americans on the need for birth control and eventually win political support. She believed in teaching doctors about contraceptive measures (at the time, this was not part of the medical school curriculum). She argued for the need for birth control as a means of reducing genetically transmitted mental and physical birth defects. She even advocated for the involuntary sterilization of people with mental disabilities as an inroad to birth control support for all. She refused, however, to support birth control as a means of limiting population growth solely on the basis of class, ethnicity, or race.

In 1929, largely as a result of her enormous efforts, the National Committee on Federal Legislation for Birth Control was formed to lobby for legislation allowing physicians to distribute contraceptives. The most difficult audience Sanger had was the Catholic Church, which believed that birth control invalidated God's plan for the universe. Sanger was unsuccessful in her push for a federal law to legalize birth control.

By 1928 Sanger was out of touch with her audience and advocated values that were out of line with American values at the time. She resigned as president of the American Birth Control League, and a younger, more conservative set took the reins. By World War II she was seen as the instigator of changing mores but had very little power and public image. She retired to Arizona in 1942.

Following the war, the population growth of the Third World propelled Sanger into the spotlight again, this time as an activist for an international birth control movement. She helped found the International Planned Parenthood Federation in 1952, serving as its first president until 1959.

Although she had learned about expanding birth control options in her earlier travels abroad, she continued searching for inexpensive but effective method. She helped arrange for a U.S. company to manufacture the Dutch diaphragms and raised funds to develop spermicidal jellies and foams and, finally, hormonal contraceptives. In the 1950s the birth control pill was developed and showed great promise. The Pill was released on the Canadian market late that decade and entered the American market in 1960.

By 1965, in *Griswold v. Connecticut*, the U.S. Supreme Court finally established the legal right to obtain birth control information, declaring that the decision "whether or not to beget a child" was a fundamental constitutional right. Sanger, the woman who had done the most to make the ruling possible, died a few months after it was handed down.

See also Abortion; Contraception; Feminism; *Griswold v. Connecticut*; Norplant; *Roe v. Wade*.

Reference Chesler, Ellen. 1992. *Woman of Valor: Margaret Sanger and the Birth Control Movement in America*. New York: Simon and Schuster.

Skinner v. Oklahoma (1942)

In *Skinner v. Oklahoma* the Supreme Court examined a state law that allowed the sterilization of any person convicted three times of "felonies involving moral turpitude" for fear that criminal tendencies were handed down to their children. These felonies excluded any white-collar crimes and seemed to allow different rights for different classes of people. The Court declared the statute unconstitutional because the right to have children was a fundamental right, and forced sterilization deprived people of a basic liberty. It was not until 1965, however, in the case of *Griswold v. Connecticut,* that the Court addressed the issue of whether people had the right to choose not to have children.

Convicted in 1926 for stealing chickens, Skinner was sentenced to Oklahoma's State Reformatory. By 1934 he had been convicted of two more crimes, including robbery with a firearm. Because of the number of his felony convictions, Skinner faced a state-mandated vasectomy under Oklahoma's Habitual Criminal Sterilization Act. This act required sterilization for offenses of "moral turpitude" but did not require the same procedure for felonies such as embezzlement or other white-collar crimes.

At trial, the jury was instructed to decide only whether a vasectomy would endanger Skinner's "general health." The jury ruled that the procedure would not do so, and the Oklahoma Supreme Court later upheld their decision. Skinner then appealed to the U.S. Supreme Court, arguing that the sterilization was unconstitutional under the Fourteenth Amendment's Equal Protection Clause.

The Court granted the petition for certiorari because the case touched on a basic civil right (the right to "perpetuation of a race"). Skinner attempted to persuade the Court that the Oklahoma act was unconstitutional because, first, sterilization was not a legitimate exercise of police power since scientific evidence at the time questioned whether criminal traits were hereditary. Second, due process was not granted since the act narrowly limited defendants from providing evidence that they would procreate; it was just as likely, Skinner argued, that defendants would choose not to have children. Third, Skinner argued that the act violated the prohibition against cruel and unusual punishment in the Eighth Amendment, as well as the Equal Protection Clause of the Fourteenth Amendment.

The Court did not deliver a ruling on any

of Skinner's arguments. Rather, the justices unanimously held that the right to reproduce is a basic civil right and, specifically, that the act failed to meet the Equal Protection Clause of the Fourteenth Amendment because it restricted the procedure only to those who had committed certain felonies. As an example, the majority opinion explained that a person could steal chickens three times, be convicted, and face sterilization. But if the person "embezzled" the chickens (that is, if he worked for the farmer, so the crime would be considered embezzlement and not stealing), he could be convicted of the offense numerous times and never face sterilization.

Justice Harlan Stone concurred with the Court's decision but disagreed with the majority's ruling that the Equal Protection Clause had been violated. Citing the Court's previous case of *Buck v. Bell* (1927), which upheld sterilization for mentally ill people, he argued that states do have the right to determine how best to deal with societal ills; it was possible for a state to decide that sterilization to prevent the further transmission of socially undesirable traits was appropriate. But Stone was concerned with the lack of due process rights provided by the Oklahoma act; that is, the act did not allow the defendant a hearing to determine whether or not "his criminal tendencies were of an inheritable type." Justice Robert Jackson also delivered a concurring opinion. He argued simply that genetic science was too new to be used as a criterion for permanent actions such as sterilization. Thus, legislators should not have the power to "conduct biological experiments" at the expense of a segment of the population, even if they are guilty of felonies.

Skinner was a landmark case because the Court declared that marriage and procreation are basic human rights, even if they are not specifically listed in the Constitution. Because of this, *Skinner* was cited in cases involving the right of married and single people to obtain information on birth control, the right of women to obtain abortions, the legality of homosexual marriages, and artificial insemination and in vitro fertilization.

> *See also* Fourteenth Amendment; *Griswold v. Connecticut*; Right to Privacy.

Thalidomide and Abortion

In 1962 the new drug Thalidomide was given to pregnant women in West Germany and England to relieve headaches and morning sickness. But there were significant side effects, including serious birth defects to the child; Thalidomide babies had small fingers from their shoulders and toes at their hips. Sherri Finkbine, a Phoenix mother of four, took Thalidomide before evidence of such side effects had been made public. Because of the likelihood that her child would be severely deformed, she decided to have an abortion. But Arizona law allowed abortions only to save the pregnant woman's life. Finkbine's doctor then convinced the hospital administration that continuing her pregnancy would endanger her life. When the media was alerted, Finkbine's story ended up on the front page of most newspapers in the country and in *Life* magazine, which ran a headline that read, "Abortion: With the Future Grim, Should the Unborn Die?" next to pictures of Finkbine's healthy children. In light of the enormous publicity, the county attorney feared the hospital would be sued and demanded that it not perform Finkbine's abortion.

The Finkbines defied state law in traveling to Sweden, where Sherri Finkbine was able to receive an abortion; Swedish doctors confirmed that the fetus had been severely deformed by Thalidomide. Vatican radio called her abortion a "homicide," and the controversy followed the Finkbines back to the United States, though a Gallop Poll reported 52 percent of those polled supported the Finkbines' decision to abort the pregnancy.

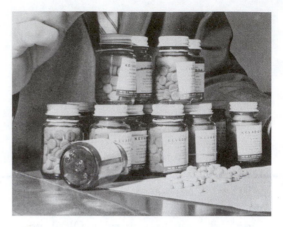

Some of more than 2,000 thalidomide tablets collected by the health department (Bettmann/Corbis)

Wattleton, Faye (1943–)

Born in St. Louis, Faye Wattleton earned a nursing degree at Ohio State University in 1964 and an M.A. at Columbia University in 1966. In her work as a nurse, she saw that birth control and abortion were often necessary for maternal and infant health. She became the executive director of an Ohio chapter of Planned Parenthood in 1971 and president of Planned Parenthood of America in 1978, becoming the youngest person and first woman to head the organization. She was extremely visible in that role and credited with making Planned Parenthood the nation's seventh largest charity (with 170 affiliates across the country) as well as improving women's health across the globe with its Family Planning International Assistance program. In 1995 she became president of the Center for Gender Equality, a research, policy, and educational institution that promotes strategies to help women obtain full equality.

She is active on the lecture circuit and was named by NOW as a "Woman of Courage" in 1994.

Webster v. Reproductive Health Services (1989)

In *Webster v. Reproductive Health Services*, the Supreme Court examined a Missouri law

Faye Wattleton, right, president of Planned Parenthood of America Federation, testifies with Kate Michelman, president of National Abortion and Reproductive Rights Action League (NARAL), before the Senate Judiciary Committee. (Bettmann/Corbis)

that comprehensively regulated abortion services in that state. The law not only defined life as beginning at conception but also required that abortions after sixteen weeks of pregnancy had to be performed in hospitals, that "informed consent" was required of all women who wished to have an abortion, that there would be fetal viability tests proceeding all abortions to determine fetal weight and lung capacity, and that public funds could not be used for abortion counseling or procedures. The case was controversial, to say the least; nearly 100 amicus curiae ("friends of the court") briefs were filed by supporters and opponents of abortion rights.

In delivering the Court's decision, Chief Justice William Rehnquist held that defining life as beginning at conception did not violate *Roe v. Wade;* only if Missouri's law had prohibited abortion would *Roe* be violated. The statute's proscription against use of fed-

eral funds for abortion was allowed since the constitutional principle of due process did not confer "affirmative right to governmental aid, even where such aid may be necessary to secure life, liberty, or property interests of which the government may not deprive the individual."

Justices Byron White and Anthony M. Kennedy joined Rehnquist in upholding the determination of viability of the fetus after twenty weeks of pregnancy. They held that the law was valid since it did not actually require a viability test for all pregnancies and instead left some discretion to the physician in charge of the woman's health. Their opinion went on to point out that this test demonstrated the weakness of the "rigid trimester analysis" of *Roe.* Although their opinion did not explicitly overturn *Roe,* it pointed out that medical technology had improved enough to make the trimester approach to pregnancy somewhat uncertain.

They also rejected Justice Harry Blackmun's call for the Court to determine whether a right to privacy is granted in the Constitution. Justice Sandra Day O'Connor, the only female justice, joined the Court in holding that Missouri's test of fetus viability was neither unconstitutional nor in conflict with *Roe*. But she also said that states had the authority to protect life, and Missouri's test allowed the state to determine when to intercede in abortion decisions on a case-by-case basis.

Justice Antonin Scalia, probably the most conservative justice on the Court at the time, dissented from the majority opinion and in fact called for a review and potential reversal of *Roe v. Wade*. His argument was that *Roe* forced the Court to rule on grounds that were too narrow and by doing so simply continued the Court's involvement in a political issue, not a judicial issue.

See also Right to Privacy; *Roe v. Wade.*

Sarah Weddington (Bettmann/Corbis)

Weddington, Sarah (1945–)

Born in Texas to a Navy chaplain and his wife, Sarah Weddington finished high school at sixteen and graduated from college and then the University of Texas School of Law by twenty-one. While a law student at the University of Texas, she was active in a group that gathered information about abortion providers in states where abortion was illegal and disseminated that information to women seeking abortions. At the time, of course, groups in states that did not allow abortion could not publish such information for fear of being charged as accomplices in abortion. While researching women's options for abortions across the United States, Weddington found several cases challenging anti-abortion statutes and decided to file suit herself.

One of the young women seeking information on abortion was Norma McCorvey. Under the name "Jane Roe," she became the plaintiff in the suit that Weddington (along with her co-counsel, Linda Coffee) filed on behalf of all women who wanted to obtain an abortion. In 1971 Weddington argued the case before the Supreme Court at the age of twenty-six, returned to Texas, and successfully ran for the state legislature. The Supreme Court in 1973 ruled that there was a constitutional right of privacy that allowed individuals to decide whether to continue or terminate an unwanted pregnancy. Weddington became the youngest person ever to win a case before the Court.

After three terms in the state legislature, she became general counsel of the U.S. Department of Agriculture, then served as an assistant to President Jimmy Carter on issues pertaining to women. Weddington is now a distinguished lecturer at Texas Woman's University and an adjunct professor at the Department of History and Government at the University of Texas at Austin. She was active in creating the Women's Museum in Dallas and is a prolific author.

References and Further Reading

American Civil Liberties Union Web site: www.aclu.org.

Costello, Cynthia, and Anne J. Stone, eds. 1994. *Where We Stand: Women and Health.* New York: W. W. Norton.

D'Emilio, John, and Estelle B. Freedman. 1988. *Intimate Matters: A History of Sexuality of America.* New York: Harper and Row.

Irving, Howard H. 1981. *Family Law: An Interdisciplinary Perspective.* Toronto, ON: Carswell.

Langley, Winston E., and Vivian C. Fox, eds. 1994. *Women's Rights in the United States.* Westport, CT: Greenwood Press.

McGlen, Nancy E., and Karen O'Connor. 1998. *Women, Politics and American Society.* Upper Saddle River, NJ: Prentice-Hall.

National Abortion Rights Action League Web site: www.naral.org.

National Right to Life Committee Web site: www.nrlc.org.

O'Brien, David M. 1997. *Constitutional Law and Politics: Civil Rights and Liberties.* 3rd ed. New York: W.W. Norton.

Operation Rescue Web site: www.operationrescue.org.

Weddington, Sarah. 1992. *A Question of Choice: The Lawyer Who Won* Roe v. Wade. New York: Grosset/Putnam.

Violence against Women

American Booksellers Association v. Hudnut (1986)

In *American Booksellers Association v. Hudnut,* a federal court declared unconstitutional an Indianapolis ordinance that prohibited pornography in that city. The city of Indianapolis treated pornography as a practice of discrimination against women and equated it with other forms of discrimination. It defined pornography as "graphic sexually explicit subordination of women" and included any descriptions of women as sexual objects who enjoy pain and humiliation or who experience sexual pleasure in being raped. It also outlawed depictions of women penetrated by objects or animals and women as objects of sexual domination or conquest.

The court of appeals struck down the ordinance because it was "not content neutral" and verged on "mind control." The ordinance outlawed any speech that portrayed women in a pornographic light because pornography affects society's views on women and leads to discrimination. The court agreed that pornography could be harmful to women but stated that pornography was essentially speech and could not be abridged. Just as racist views may lead to discrimination, they are still protected under the Constitution's guarantee of free speech. The Supreme Court later upheld the federal court's decision.

See also Dworkin, Andrea; MacKinnon, Catharine.

Battered Woman Syndrome (BWS)

Often considered a subcategory of post-traumatic stress disorder, battered woman syndrome (BWS) is a psychological reaction by women who have been subjected to continuous physical, sexual, and/or psychological abuse by their partners. Most experts agree that it does not actually occur until the victim experiences at least two complete battering cycles. These cycles involve three distinct phases. First is a tension-building phase, then the explosion or acute battering incident, culminating in a calm, loving respite often referred to as the honeymoon phase.

Domestic violence is learned behavior used to obtain and maintain power and control over a partner (usually a woman). Although racial and cultural issues might influence the availability of resources for victims, they do not determine incidence or prevalence of domestic violence. Exposure to violence in the childhood home is the highest indicator that a person will become involved in a violent relationship; poverty, immigration status, and prior abuse also determine the risk of being battered. Factors that best predict who will become a batterer are a history of violent behavior (e.g., witnessing, receiving, and committing violent acts in childhood); violent acts toward pets, inanimate objects, or other people; previous criminal records; and a lengthy military service.

The victim of prolonged domestic violence typically goes through three phases in preparing to defend against threats. In the "fight" mode, the body and mind prepare to deal with danger by becoming hypervigilant to cues of potential violence, resulting in an exaggerated startle response. A person becomes focused on the single task of self-defense, impairing concentration and causing physiological responses usually associated with high anxiety. In serious cases fearfulness, panic disorders, phobic disorders, irritability, and constant crying result. The "flight" response is the next stage of the process. If physical escape is impossible, then individuals will escape mentally by emotionally numbing themselves with denial, minimization, rationalization, and dissociation. The third stage is psychological amnesia: victims are often unable to remember details or events of the abuse. In this stage of disassociation, nightmares may be the only coherent memories of what occurred.

Experts explain that women are positively reinforced to stay in violent relationships because of the honeymoon stage that occurs following each episode of abuse. The adverse economic consequences of divorce, the potential for increased abuse if a woman leaves a batterer, and threats from the batterer that he will kill himself are other reasons women tend to remain in such abusive relationships.

First introduced into the courts in 1979, BWS is used increasingly as a legal defense, particularly in cases involving battered women who have killed or wounded their attackers. Domestic violence is also frequently raised as an issue in divorce and child-custody cases. In an Oregon case in 1985, a judge turned his opinion in part into a lengthy discussion on the prevalence of BWS in U.S. society and its use as an argument for self-defense. He wrote that "numerous psychiatrists, psychologists and social workers now consider the battered spouse syndrome an accepted basis for identification, counseling and treatment . . . . If a witness qualifies as an expert and a sufficient

foundation is laid, evidence of the battered spouse syndrome should be admissible."

Many courts have used BWS extensively because of numerous studies suggesting that prolonged domestic violence harms children in the family; children who witness parental violence (but are not abused themselves) exhibit aggressive behavior and emotional problems similar to those experienced by physically abused children. In fact, witnessing violence between parents is a more consistent predictor of future violence than being a victim of child abuse. These children learn that coercive power can be used to influence loved ones and indeed that such behavior is acceptable and approved of by their most important role models. In such abusive situations, evidence suggests that the battered women are likely to be better custodians of the children than their partners. Most courts have ruled simply that placing a child with a batterer perpetuates the cycle of violence by exposing the child to an environment in which violence is acceptable behavior.

With numerous state courts allowing BWS as a defense, Congress passed the Violence Against Women Act in 1994, which permitted victims of rape, domestic violence, and other crimes "motivated by gender" to sue their attackers in federal court in civil actions (following, presumably, a criminal conviction in state court). But in 2000 the Supreme Court invalidated part of the law, concluding that Congress could not give federal courts this jurisdiction under its power to regulate interstate commerce.

See also Kansas v. Stewart; North Carolina v. Norman; United States v. Morrison; Violence Against Women Act (VAWA).

References Donald Alexander Downs. 1996. *More Than Victims: Battered Women Syndrome, Society, and the Law* (Morality and Society Series). Chicago: University of Chicago Press; Lenore E. A. Walker. 2001. *The Battered Woman Syndrome.* New York: Springer Press.

Date and Acquaintance Rape

Date rape and acquaintance rape are forms of sexual assault involving coercive sexual activities perpetrated by someone who is emotionally involved in a relationship with the victim or otherwise knows the victim. These forms of rape are gaining recognition as a growing societal problem associated with domestic violence. Several celebrity cases of date rape (specifically, those of Mike Tyson and William Kennedy Smith) brought wide media coverage to the issue, as did the Academy Award–winning movie *The Accused*.

Along with the increased awareness of the problem have come important legal decisions and changes in the legal definitions of rape. The traditional common-law definition of rape is "unlawful carnal knowledge of a woman by force and against her will." Under this definition, in order for a sexual assault to be "rape" there had to be "forcible penetration of the vagina by the penis, however slight." Rape thus included only an assault by a male perpetrator on a female victim, and a husband could not, by definition, rape his wife. Because rape was traditionally seen as a crime of theft of a man's property (either a husband's or a father's), the sentences for men convicted of rape were severe, typically the death penalty or life imprisonment. Until the 1970s, jurors in rape cases were read the warning from Sir Matthew Hale, a former chief justice of the English Court, that although rape is a horrific crime "it is an accusation easy to be made, hard to be proved, but harder to be defended by the party accused, though innocent."

In 1990 California amended its definition of rape to mean sexual intercourse "where it is accomplished against a person's will by means of force, violence, duress, menace, or fear of immediate and unlawful bodily injury." Additionally, the definition of consent was expanded to mean "positive cooperation in act or attitude pursuant to an exercise of free will. A person must act freely and voluntarily and have knowledge of the nature of the act or transaction involved." Consent was not necessarily implied because the victim and the accused had been or were currently involved in a relationship. Most states followed California's provision and refined the definition of consent to exclude compliance by victims debilitated by drugs or alcohol.

But in 2002, the California Supreme Court changed course and redefined rape, particularly date rape. In *In re John Z.*, the court held that a woman who initially consents to sexual intercourse does not give up her right to end the encounter at whatever point she chooses. Essentially, if a woman tells her partner to stop, and he forces her to continue, he is guilty of rape. In other words, as long as she is clear in conveying her desire to end a sexual interaction, a man's disregard to her decision is classified as rape. John Z. had argued that "[b]y essence of the act of sexual intercourse, a male's primal urge to reproduce is aroused. It is therefore unreasonable for a female and the law to expect a male to cease having sexual intercourse immediately upon her withdrawal of consent." The court obviously disagreed. But before this case, most states declared that once consent to penetration was given, it could not be withdrawn. This view was based on outdated notions about the biological imperatives of men who are engaged in sexual intercourse and removed male accountability for sexual assault. Instead, the responsibility was placed upon the woman to take all possible steps to avoid awakening the man's "primal urge."

Like opinions on pornography, views on acquaintance rape are divided. On one side are those who believe that many date-rape victims are actually willing, consenting participants; on the other side are those who believe that almost all the victims were raped. Psychologist Mary Koss is the best-known researcher in the area and has served on many investigations concerning acquaintance rape. Her research argues that the peak ages for acquaintance rape are from the late teens to the early twenties. Today approximately one in four women will be the victim of a rape or attempted rape, and 84 percent of these women will know their attacker. An additional one in four women has been touched sexually against her will or has been the victim of sexual coercion, 57 percent of the time during a date. And only 27 percent of the women whose sexual assault met the legal definition of rape thought of themselves as rape victims. As a result, only about 5 percent of rape victims report the crime to the police, and 30 percent of women identified as rape victims contemplate suicide after the rape. But men and women have different perspectives on date rape. One in twelve male students surveyed had committed acts that met the legal definitions of rape or attempted rape, yet 84 percent of those men said that "what they did was definitely not rape." What is clear, however, is that women who subscribe to a "traditional" view that men occupy a position of dominance and authority relative to women have an increased risk of acquaintance rape in their lifetimes.

One explanation for the alarmingly high numbers of date rape is that because young people have been constrained for most of their lives by their parents, they are unprepared to act responsibly in a "free" environment. This freedom can lead to unrestrained drug and alcohol use, which then leads to sexually irresponsible acts that can include rape.

As for why survivors of rape tend not to report it, guilt may play a role. Research indicates that family and friends often reinforce this feeling either intentionally or unintentionally by questioning the victim's decision to drink or to invite the perpetrator to the rape environment, the use of provocative behavior, or previous sexual relations. An additional factor that inhibits reporting is the anticipated response of authorities. The victim's fear that she will be blamed contributes greatly to her apprehension about interrogation. Also entering into a victim's decision not to report the attack is the duress of reexperiencing the attack and testifying at trial and the low conviction rate for the accused.

Levels of depression, anxiety, complication in subsequent relationships, and difficulty attaining prerape levels of sexual satisfaction appear to be similar between survivors of acquaintance rape and survivors of stranger rape. The failure of others to recognize the emotional impact of acquaintance rape is what makes coping more difficult for the victims. Those survivors who tend to deal the most effectively with their experience take an active role in acknowledging the rape, disclosing the incident to appropriate others, finding the right help, and educating themselves about acquaintance rape and prevention strategies.

Perhaps the most serious disorder that can develop as a result of acquaintance rape is post-traumatic stress disorder (PTSD). As it relates to acquaintance rape, PTSD is defined as "the development of characteristic symptoms following exposure to an extreme traumatic stressor involving direct personal experience of an event that involves actual or threatened death or serious injury, or another threat to one's physical integrity" (*Diagnostic and Statistical Manual of Medical Disorders*, fourth edition). Symptoms include persistent reliving of the event, avoidance of stimuli associated with the event, and symptoms of increased anxiety.

See also Marital Rape; *Michigan v. Lucas*; Rape Shield Law.
Reference Francis, Leslie, ed. 1996. *Date Rape: Feminism, Philosophy, and the Law.* University Park: Pennsylvania State University Press.

Dworkin, Andrea (1946–)

A controversial author, lecturer, and law professor, Andrea Dworkin is an outspoken feminist who argues in her writings that rape and sexual abuse of women are direct consequences of society's definitions of men and women. Men, she argues, are defined

Andrea Dworkin (McPerson Colin/Corbis)

by society as aggressive, dominant, and powerful, whereas women are defined as passive, submissive, and powerless. Rape and sexual abuse, then, are not committed by sexual deviants but rather by "perfect" male examples of our society's norms. In order to stop such violence against women, we must destroy the "very definitions of masculinity and femininity." Furthermore, as a result of societal definitions of male and female behavior, she has argued, women will never be able to function equally in sexual relations with men.

In collaboration with law professor Catharine MacKinnon, Dworkin has worked to abolish or restrict pornography. She argues that pornography perpetuates stereotypical notions of men as aggressors and women as passive recipients of their aggression. In 1983 Dworkin and MacKinnon succeeded in convincing the Minneapolis City Council to consider restricting pornography

because it subordinates women and interferes with their civil rights. They persuaded the council to add pornography-based claims to the city's civil rights ordinance, essentially making the city pornography free. Although the city council approved the measure in 1984, the mayor immediately vetoed it on free speech grounds. Dworkin has been relatively successful in getting other cities to banish pornography, but the courts have voted her down in every case.

Dworkin was one of the most radical feminists of the second feminist wave. For example, in her 1981 book *Pornography: Men Possessing Women,* she writes: "Men are rapists, batterers, plunderers, killers; these same men are religious prophets, poets, heroes, figures of romance, adventure, accomplishment, figures ennobled by tragedy and defeat. Men have claimed the earth, called it Her. Men ruin Her. Men have airplanes, guns, bombs, poisonous gases, weapons so perverse and deadly that they defy any authentically human imagination." And in her 1987 book *Ice and Fire,* she asserts: "I want to see a man beaten to a bloody pulp with a high-heel shoved in his mouth, like an apple in the mouth of a pig."

See also MacKinnon, Catharine; Sexual Harassment.
References Andrea Dworkin. 1997. *Intercourse.* New York: Touchstone Books; Andrea Dworkin. 2002. *Heartbreak: The Political Memoir of a Feminist Militant.* New York: BasicBooks.

Kansas v. Stewart (1988)

Peggy Stewart fatally shot her husband, Mike, while he was sleeping. Charged with murder in the first degree, she pleaded not guilty and argued that she shot her husband in self-defense. After an expert witness testified that Peggy suffered from battered woman syndrome (BWS), the judge instructed the jury to regard her actions as self-defense. The jury found her not guilty. The state then appealed, arguing that the statutory justification for the use of deadly force in a claim of self-defense did not excuse a homicide committed by a battered woman where there was no evidence of a deadly threat. In essence, because Peggy was not in imminent danger, she could not claim self-defense. The state conceded that she had "suffered considerable abuse at the hands of her husband" but said the jury should not have been given self-defense instructions since her husband was sleeping when she shot him.

The higher court agreed that the jury should not have been given self-defense instructions, as this indicated that the defendant's belief that she was in imminent danger was reasonable. Yet her belief that she was exposed to an imminent threat was a subjective viewpoint, which was not the viewpoint a reasonable person would have had in the same circumstances.

The trial record was clear that immediately following the Stewarts marriage in 1974, Peggy and her two daughters from a prior marriage suffered extreme abuse from her husband. In 1977 two social workers received reports that Mike had taken "indecent liberties" with Peggy's two daughters. Because Peggy was afraid of leaving Mike alone with the girls, she stopped working so she could monitor his whereabouts. By 1978 Mike was taunting Peggy that her twelve-year-old daughter was "more of a wife" to him than Peggy. Mike had a Jekyll-and-Hyde personality: although he was usually gregarious and ingratiating around friends, he was belligerent and domineering in private and to family members. In fact, he seemed almost to take pride in hurting them, which resulted in Peggy's severe emotional problems with symptoms of paranoid schizophrenia. Mike would take advantage of the situation by overdosing Peggy on her medication and then withholding it from her after she became dependent on it, making her progressively more passive and helpless. Mike abused drugs and alcohol. At one point he held a shotgun to Peggy's head and threatened to

"blow it off"; another time he woke her from a sound sleep by beating her with a baseball bat. It was not until several years later that she filed for divorce. At the murder trial, Peggy's divorce lawyer testified that Peggy was afraid for both herself and her children's lives.

She had attempted to leave him before the murder, in 1986, by moving out of state. But shortly after arriving in Oklahoma, Peggy's daughter had Peggy admitted to a hospital after she overdosed on medications. The hospital released Peggy into Mike's care, and he drove her back to Kansas. Immediately upon their return home, Mike forced Peggy to perform oral sex on him several times. The following day she discovered a loaded gun and hid it under the mattress of the couple's bed. She testified that she was terrified that Mike was going to kill her for leaving him. After the couple went to bed that evening, Peggy claimed to have thought of suicide and heard voices telling her to "kill or be killed." Two hours after Mike fell asleep, she removed the gun from under the mattress and shot Mike. She then ran to a neighbor's house and called the police, telling them that she had shot him to "get this over with, this misery and this torment."

Two of the expert witnesses at Peggy's murder trial testified that Mike was preparing to escalate the violence in retaliation for Peggy's running away, as the loaded gun, veiled threats, and increased sexual demands suggested. The cycle of violence in BWS begins with an initial building of tension; after an explosion comes a honeymoon period. Women become conditioned to try to make it through one more violent eruption with its attendant battering in order to receive the reward of the honeymoon phase with its expressions of love and remorse. They become helpless when they begin to believe that their batterers are omnipotent and all-powerful, which Peggy obviously did. But the state's expert discredited the concept of BWS, calling it a theory of learned helplessness to explain why women such as Peggy do not leave an abusive relationship. Abuse such as repeated forced oral sex, this expert believed, would not be sufficient to trigger post-traumatic stress disorder or BWS. According to this witness, Peggy was unable to escape the abusive relationship because she suffered from schizophrenia.

The state also disagreed that there had been enough of a threat to Peggy that she needed to defend herself. There was no evidence of any argument or altercation between Peggy and her husband prior to the killing. Further, Peggy had received divorces from former husbands and had filed for divorce from Mike proving that Peggy was well aware of nonlethal methods by which she could extricate herself from an abusive relationship. Under state law, "[a] person is justified in the use of force against an aggressor when and to the extent it appears to him and he reasonably believes that such conduct is necessary to defend himself or another against such aggressor's imminent use of unlawful force."

Peggy's defense, however, argued that the concept of self-defense had changed dramatically. Statutes assumed that conflicts were between persons of relatively equal size and strength—not the situation for a battered spouse. If there is a history of prior abuse and a difference in strength and size between the abused and the abuser, the accused may choose to defend herself during a momentary lull in the abuse rather than during a conflict.

Nonetheless, the highest court in Kansas held that self-defense had not occurred, saying that a battered woman cannot reasonably fear imminent, life-threatening danger from her sleeping spouse. A dissenting justice fumed that this was "a clearly fallacious conclusion."

See also Battered Woman Syndrome (BWS); *North Carolina v. Norman.*

MacKinnon, Catharine A. (1946–)

Catharine MacKinnon is a lawyer, teacher, writer, activist, and expert on sexual equality. She graduated from Smith College (B.A. 1968) and Yale Law School (1977) and received a Ph.D. in political science from Yale University (1987). Her theories are extremely controversial, particularly her claim that all heterosexual sex is inherently exploitative of women. In the late 1970s MacKinnon pioneered claims for sexual harassment as a form of sexual discrimination. After passage of the Civil Rights Act of 1964, courts resisted the notion that sexual harassment in the workplace was a form of sex discrimination that should be prohibited. MacKinnon is generally credited with distinguishing between the two types of harassment that the Court finally acknowledged. By her definition, "quid pro quo" harassment occurs when a supervisor links job rewards or threats to an employee's acceptance or refusal of sexual advances. In a "hostile environment" the conduct or sexual advances are so pervasive or severe that they compromise the victim's working conditions.

In 1983, with Andrea Dworkin, MacKinnon conceived and wrote several city ordinances recognizing pornography as a violation of civil rights. The state courts immediately struck down those ordinances as a violation of freedom of speech. MacKinnon has responded that banning all forms of pornography is justified because the First Amendment's protection of speech ignores hate speech, which includes pornography. MacKinnon believes pornography is neither a legitimate vehicle for the expression of ideas nor deserving of constitutional protection under the First Amendment because it constitutes acts of violence against women. The harm of pornography comes both directly from the pornographic industry, which exploits poor and previously sexually abused women, as well as from the impact that pornography has on society, perpetuating the oppression of women. If society bans this form of speech in the name of fighting subordination, MacKinnon contends, it is in effect advancing the constitutional ideal of equality.

MacKinnon is also known for her commentaries on rape law reform. She argues that the incremental reform of rape laws on a state-by-state basis cannot work because the laws are predicated on a social structure with a power differential between men and women. So, for example, the very definition of rape (intercourse with force or coercion and without consent) is problematic because it implies that some forced or coerced intercourse is consensual. Probably her most controversial argument has concerned the distinction between rape and sex; she argues it is too difficult to distinguish rape from sex and determine the difference between normal "acceptable" force and "too much" force in a society where men are taught to be sexual aggressors, to expect women to resist, and to dismiss their objections. According to MacKinnon, until the power differential is eradicated or until the law reflects the "fundamental social powerlessness" of women, the laws will not be effective or reflect the reality of rape.

> See also Dworkin, Andrea; Oncale v. Sundowner Offshore Services; Rape Shield Law; Sexual Harassment.
> Reference Catharine A. MacKinnon. 1997. Toward a Feminist Theory of the State. Cambridge, MA: Harvard University Press.

Marital Rape

Generally, marital rape is defined as intercourse or penetration (vaginal, anal, or oral) that a husband obtains from his wife by force or threat of force or when she is unable to consent. It is most prevalent in physically abusive relationships, typically when the female partner is pregnant. Most experts agree that marital-rape survivors seem to suffer longer-term psychological consequences as a result of the rape than typical rape victims do. They commonly experience anxiety, shock, intense depression, thoughts of suicide, and other aspects of post-traumatic stress disorder. (The more severe reactions may be a result of prolonged physical and emotional abuse rather than the rape itself, but the research is not clear.)

Traditional common law viewed rape as a crime of property against a man (either a husband or father), and the punishment—life imprisonment or death—reflected this. Most rape statutes enacted before 1970 define rape as forced sexual intercourse with a woman other than one's wife. Since the 1980s, several states have drastically reformed laws pertaining to the definition and prosecution of rape. All states, for example, have now enacted rape shield statutes, which prevent a victim's past sexual history (with the defendant or with a third party) from being used at trial. In seventeen states and the District of Columbia, marital rape is a crime for which husbands can be prosecuted. In thirty-three states, however, husbands retain at least some exemptions, allowing spousal prosecution only if, for example, the offense is accompanied by extra factors, such as force, injury, or threats, and particularly if the couple has a legal agreement for separation. Some of these states explicitly exempt spouses from prosecution for all sex crimes. Critics call these exemptions throwbacks to Blackstone's coverture laws, which made women the property of their husbands.

The concept of the marital rape exemption came from Sir Matthew Hale, an eighteenth-century British chief justice who wrote that "the husband cannot be guilty of a rape committed by himself upon his lawful wife, for by their mutual matrimonial consent and contract the wife hath given up herself in this kind unto her husband, which she cannot retract." Even in the twentieth century, some states argued that the marital rape exemption should be extended to cohabitants and not just married partners. Rape exemptions to married men, the argument went, was unfair to unmarried men who were in committed, monogamous relationships that entitled them to the same sexual access to their partners as married men. Connecticut, Kentucky, and Pennsylvania enacted laws granting such exemptions to unmarried cohabiting partners. In these states, once a woman had assented to penetration, she had no right to change her mind, as it would be "unfair" to demand that a man stop once his biological urges had taken over. The man, in other words, had no obligation to exercise self-control after he had first received his partner's consent.

See also Coverture; Date and Acquaintance Rape; Marriage; Rape Shield Law; Statutory Rape.

Reference Connerton, Kelly C. 1997. "The Resurgence of the Marital Rape Exemption: The Victimization of Teens by Their Statutory Rapist." Albany Law Review 61: 237.

Michigan v. Lucas (1991)

Under the common law, rape is defined as unlawful carnal knowledge of a woman without her consent. The law requires victims to present evidence of three elements of the crime in order to prove that a rape did indeed take place: force or lack of consent, penetration, and identity of the assailant. Because the crime usually takes place without witnesses, however, it is often difficult to corroborate a victim's claims. During the early 1990s, several states, including Michigan, reformed rape laws to allow for a relaxation of the corroboration requirement. A provision of Michigan's rape shield law permitted a rape defendant to introduce evidence of his own past sexual conduct with the victim within ten days of being charged with the crime of rape in that state. The evidence had to be shown to a judge who would allow the information into the defendant's defense, assuming that evidence was material and not prejudicial against the victim.

In Michigan v. Lucas, the defendant was charged with raping a former girlfriend. She said that Lucas forced her at knifepoint to have sex with him two weeks after she broke off their relationship. He claimed she consented to have sex with him and noted that she did not leave his home until late in the evening of the following day. The lower court judge refused to allow evidence of a past relationship between the couple, and the defendant was convicted of rape.

The Supreme Court ruled that state rape shield laws, like the one in Michigan, could bar evidence of past consensual sexual relations between the alleged attacker and victim. But the only reason Michigan had excluded such evidence in his case, Lucas argued, was because he had failed to notify prosecutors within ten days of his arraignment that he would seek to introduce such evidence. Lucas claimed his Sixth Amendment rights allowing defendants to confront their accusers had been violated. The state argued that the ten-day rule was designed to give prosecutors enough time to investigate a defendant's claim, allowing them to question other witnesses before the trial began to assess the truth or falsity of the claim. The Court decided that the state's ten-day rule served a legitimate state interest in protecting victims from surprise, harassment, and undue delay of their trial. In some cases, according to the opinion written by Justice Sandra O'Connor, failure to comply with the ten-day requirement may "justify even the severe sanction of barring the evidence of the previous relationship."

See also Date and Acquaintance Rape; Rape Shield Law.

North Carolina v. Norman (1988)

North Carolina v. Norman marked one of the first times that battered woman syndrome (BWS) was used as a defense for killing an abusive spouse. Judy Norman was indicted for the first-degree murder of her husband; a jury found her guilty of voluntary manslaughter and sentenced her to six years in prison. On appeal Norman was awarded a new trial because the original court had refused to submit to the jury a possible verdict of acquittal by reason of self-defense. Norman claimed that she had exhibited BWS and the homicide was an act of self-defense.

Evidence was presented at trial that demonstrated a long history of physical and mental abuse by Norman's alcoholic husband. At the time Norman shot her husband three times in the back of the head, she was thirty-nine years old, had been married to him for twenty-five years, and had several children with him. Her husband had begun drinking heavily and abusing her five years into the marriage. Norman described how her husband burned her with cigarettes, threw hot coffee and food at her, broke glasses against her face, deprived her of food, and threatened numerous times to kill her. Finally, her husband had forced her to prostitute herself, beating her if he was unsatisfied with the amount of money she earned.

The day before the murder, Norman had called the sheriff's office to the couple's home. She complained to officers that her husband had been beating her all day and she "couldn't take it anymore." The officers encouraged her to file a complaint against him, but she declined, fearing her husband "would kill her" if she had him arrested. Deputies left and were called back to the residence that night after Norman ingested a bottle of pills; her husband cursed her while she was attended by paramedics, who transported her to the local hospital. She was released that night. A therapist who saw her while she was in the hospital later testified at trial that the defendant had seemed depressed and hopeless and expressed considerable rage toward her husband, threatening to kill him "because of the things he had done to her." The day of the murder, Norman talked about filing charges against her husband and confronted him about having him committed to a hospital. He said he would cut her throat first. She also sought welfare benefits that day at a social service office, claiming neither she nor

her children had been allowed to eat for some time. But her husband had shown up, demanding she go home with him and making further threats.

The evening of the shooting, Norman's husband became intoxicated and assaulted her. He had been taken into custody for driving while impaired that night and a later autopsy revealed a 0.12 percent blood alcohol level in his body. Norman's mother bailed him out of jail that night and he resumed his drinking and abuse of Norman when he arrived home. After he fell asleep, Norman came into the bedroom with a pistol and shot her husband in the head three times. When asked why she killed him, Norman replied: "Because I was scared of him and I knowed [sic] when he woke up, it was going to be the same thing, and I was scared when he took me to the truck stop that night it was going to be worse than he had ever been. I just couldn't take it no more. There ain't no way, even if it means going to prison. It's better than living in that. That's worse hell than anything."

Expert forensic psychiatric witnesses testified that in their examination of Norman directly after the shooting, she fit the profile of a woman who suffered from BWS. BWS is characterized by such abuse and degradation that the battered woman comes to believe she is unable to help herself and cannot expect help from anyone else. She believes that she cannot escape the complete control of her partner and that he is invulnerable to law enforcement and other sources of help. After her conviction in the lower trial court, the appellate court ruled that a jury should be allowed to consider whether Norman's killing of her husband was justified as an act of self-defense even if he was asleep when she killed him.

But the law in North Carolina mandated that a defendant could claim self-defense only when the evidence showed that at the time of the killing the defendant believed it was necessary to kill the decedent to save his or her own life or prevent great bodily harm. In such cases a killing is completely justified and constitutes no legal wrong. But Norman was not entitled to a claim of self-defense because there was no evidence that at the time of the killing she reasonably believed that she had to kill her husband to save herself from imminent death or serious physical injury. In fact, the evidence showed that no harm was "imminent" before she shot her husband; she was not faced with a choice between killing her husband or having him kill her. Instead, the evidence demonstrated that Norman had ample time and opportunity to turn to other means of preventing further abuse by her husband. The higher court, therefore, was not persuaded to reevaluate the law even if BWS occurred. And in Norman's case, no new trial should be granted in order to change the jury instructions to allow for a claim of self-defense. Further, her six-year term of imprisonment was acceptable punishment.

Part of the reason for the high court's reluctance to expand a claim of self-defense was that it would expand the law "beyond the limits of immediacy and necessity." Four elements had to exist at the time of a killing for a claim of self-defense to be realistic. First, the defendant had to believe it was necessary to kill in order to save her- or himself from death or great bodily harm. Second, this belief had to be reasonable. Third, the defendant could not be the aggressor, entering into a fight without provocation. And finally, the defendant could not use excessive force in killing the aggressor. Although the court ruled that Norman's case did not meet these requirements, one dissenting judge believed it did, citing the twenty-year history of beatings and other dehumanizing and degrading treatment Norman suffered at the hands of her husband. Further, this judge wrote, her intense fear that her husband intended to kill her could have led jurors to conclude that Norman perceived a threat to her life as "imminent" even if her husband was sleeping.

Within five years of Norman's case, state courts became more likely to accept BWS as a defense, and in 1994 Congress passed the federal Violence Against Women Act, allowing for greater leeway in prosecuting such cases.

See also Battered Woman Syndrome (BWS); *Kansas v. Stewart; United States v. Morrison;* Violence Against Women Act (VAWA).

Prostitution

Prostitution is the practice of indiscriminate sexual intercourse for hire. In legal terms it refers to those of either sex who engage in overtly sexual acts for a specified sum of money. But in practice it is quite different. All states in the United States (except for Nevada) have criminalized prostitution, but most statutes (either expressly or as enforced) select only women for prosecution, and male customers are seldom subjected to criminal penalty. There have been several legal challenges to prostitution statutes, but courts have continued to rule that these statutes do not offend equal protection or the due process rights of women, even though most statutes do not make the customer criminally liable for seeking out or purchasing a prostitute. Nevertheless, most states' prostitution laws are now written in gender-neutral language to prevent challenges, particularly since men are increasingly identified as prostitutes who serve other men and sometimes impersonate women.

Prostitution has been prevalent in all human cultures. In the United States it began in the southern colonies. Indentured servants were given transportation across the Atlantic in exchange for their servitude. Since men were the preferred servants (they could better manage the backbreaking labor necessary in the colonies), women were outnumbered. In times of economic turmoil, women were then able to barter their sexual favors for goods and materials; as such, prostitution in early America was not so much an occupation as an economic barter mechanism. Later, separate spheres doctrine contributed to the prostitution trade. Since woman was the nurturer of the home, her pious nature was valued; if she lost her virginity, she was worthy of public contempt and unlikely to be marriageable. She had few ways to earn her keep as a part of hearth and home. Prostitution afforded significantly more money than the scant other professions open to women.

There have been various attempts since the 1700s to combat prostitution in the United States A late-nineteenth-century feminist campaign against regulation of prostitution evolved into a broader social purity movement directed toward abolishing prostitution, pornography, and homosexuality and culminated with the anti-vice Comstock Act of 1873. In 1910 Congress passed the Mann Act, which made it a federal crime to transport women over state lines for immoral purposes. It was also called the "white slave act" because it defined a white slave as "only those women or girls who were literally slaves—those women who were held as property and chattels . . . those women who given a fair chance, would, in all human probability, have been good wives and mothers."

In the past, antiprostitution crusaders campaigned on the grounds of morality; today the debate is much different. Antiprostitution proponents claim prostitution is linked to organized crime, that it tends to attract young runaways or impoverished women from former iron curtain countries, that it is responsible for much ancillary crime (e.g., drugs), and that it is a public health hazard because it spreads sexually transmitted diseases. Many of these arguments against prostitution appear to be warranted.

Surveys in the 1990s indicated that one of the largest problems with prostitution is that it harms the youngest and most vulnerable in society; 90 percent of prostitutes are survivors of incest or sexual abuse, and the average age of entry into prostitution is thirteen to fourteen. Most studies suggest that prostitution is one of the most dangerous professions for women; prostituted women are raped approximately once a week, and female prostitutes have a mortality rate forty times higher than the national average. Male prostitutes have slightly higher rates of being subjected to violence than do female and transgendered prostitutes.

Reference Gilfoyle, Timothy J. 1994. *City of Eros: New York City, Prostitution, and the Commercialization of Sex, 1790–1920.* New York: W.W. Norton.

Rape Shield Law

In the 1970s many states passed rape shield laws to protect victims of rape from being subjected to irrelevant questions concerning their past sexual behavior. Specifically, rape shield laws prohibit defendants from introducing at trial evidence of a rape victim's past sexual conduct, thus preventing the jury from weighing the victim's sexual history when deciding the guilt of a man accused of rape.

The passage of such laws revolutionized the prosecution of rape. Common law defined rape as sexual intercourse without consent; it required the victim to prove that her resistance was overcome and that the rape occurred "against her will." In fact, in most states a victim had to demonstrate that she "resisted to the utmost" before she was raped, and during the trial her previous sexual history and encounters with the accused and third parties were used to determine whether she had a "tendency to consent." If a woman had had several sexual partners in the past, then a man accused of raping her was less likely to be prosecuted.

Generally, every state has some type of rape shield statute, which allows a victim's past sexual history (whether with the defendant or with a third party) into trial only after inspection by a judge. A defendant may be permitted to introduce evidence of his own sexual conduct with the victim, provided that he follows certain procedures, such as written notice offered within ten days after his arraignment. Only the judge will initially investigate this sexual history (in camera inspection) and determine if the victim's past sexual history with the defendant is relevant to the immediate case; if it is, the evidence can be presented to a jury via either direct or cross-examination of a witness. Although rape shield laws are subject to criticism (for the most part by those who say they are discriminatory toward men), public opinion polls show that most Americans agree that a woman's past sexual life should not be at issue in rape cases.

In recent years the most sensational case involving a rape shield law was the 1996 rape trial of Oliver Jovanovic, a thirty-two-year-old doctoral student at Columbia University. Jovanovic met Jamie Rzucek in an online chat room, and they kept in close e-mail contact for six months before meeting for a date. During the date, Rzucek alleged, Jovanovic removed her clothing and tied her to a futon bed, holding her forcibly for twenty hours, sexually torturing her with hot wax, and repeatedly sodomizing her with a baton. Jovanovic attempted to have e-mail transcripts submitted as evidence that Rzucek had wanted bondage activities to take place, but the judge denied his request because the rape shield law in that state limited introduction of evidence of Rzucek's past sexual relationships. Jovanovic was convicted of kidnapping and rape. His conviction was later dismissed, however, largely because Rzucek was reluctant to testify a second time on appeal.

See also Marital Rape; *Michigan v. Lucas.*

Reno, Janet (1938–)

Janet Reno was born in Florida; both of her parents worked as reporters for Miami newspapers. In 1956 she graduated from Cornell University with a degree in chemistry after working her way through school as a waitress. She entered Harvard Law School as one of sixteen women in a class of 500. Following her graduation, she became

Janet Reno (Chris Corder/UPI)

staff director for the Judiciary Committee of the Florida House in 1971 and worked on restructuring the state's court system. She later worked in the state attorney's office and in 1976 became a partner in a private law firm in Dade County, a firm that had previously denied her a position because she was a woman.

Appointed attorney general for that county in 1978, she was the first woman to head a county prosecutor's office in Florida. She was also the first Florida prosecutor to assign lawyers to collect child-support payments from deadbeat fathers. She was elected state attorney general and won re-election bids four additional times. During her tenure as attorney general for Florida, she reformed the juvenile court system, aggressively pursued parents owing child support, and established the Miami Drug Court.

Reno gained national prominence in 1993 when President Bill Clinton appointed her as the first female U.S. attorney general. For most of her seven years in that position, she focused on enforcing civil rights legislation and incarcerating habitual offenders as a way of reducing crime. She was known as a staunch defender of principles. Her tenure as U.S. attorney general coincided with two important laws regarding violence against women, which she was charged with enforcing. The first was the 1994 Freedom of Access to Clinic Entrances Act (FACE), which made it illegal to harass and commit violence against women entering abortion clinics. The second was the 1994 Violence Against Women Act (VAWA), which provided funds for training police departments and court officials in the unique aspects of cases involving domestic violence and sexual assault. Reno made enforcement of laws pertaining to women a priority for her administration in a way no other U.S. attorney general had done.

Reno was the longest-serving attorney general in the twentieth century. In 2000 the National Women's Hall of Fame inducted her into membership as a role model to young women. Shortly thereafter, she ran for governor of Florida but failed to beat the incumbent, Jeb Bush.

Reference National Women's Hall of Fame Web site: http://www.greatwomen.org

Statutory Rape

Statutory rape is sexual activity between two people when at least one party is below a certain age. The ages for such rape laws vary from state to state, as do the punishments for offenders. Many states, in fact, do not use the term "statutory rape," referring to it simply as "rape" or "unlawful sexual penetration." Rarely are these laws applied solely to intercourse but rather are targeted to any type of sexual contact. In general there are no laws prohibiting dating an underaged person if no sexual activity is taking place. Holding hands and kissing may be permitted as long as there is no intention of engaging in more overtly sexual activity, in which case the date itself could be considered "enticing a minor."

Statutory rape charges are most often brought by the parents of the minor victim, although in most states charges can also be raised by the state. California, for example, has taken the lead in filing charges against perpetrators, over the protests of both the minor females and the parents of the involved parties.

All states have an "age of consent" at which a person can legally agree to sexual activity; it ranges from fifteen to eighteen years old. Some states also have laws that look at the age difference between the two people as well as their individual ages and whether there was a large difference in authority between the parties; for example, a minor or young adult and a teacher, coach, or tutor. Many states further restrict the type of sexual activity (i.e., anal or oral sex and sodomy); these restrictions typically run until the age of eighteen, although some states still have laws against oral sex or sodomy at any age. There are virtually no federal laws regarding such issues.

The punishment for statutory rape varies among the states as well. For some states, punishment involves a minimum of a week's incarceration and extensive community service; for others (like Georgia), punishment is a minimum of ten years.

These laws have historically rested on the fiction that young women are incapable of consent; presumably males are capable of consent, since most states' statutory rape statutes set limits for female age only. The Supreme Court clarified the issue in 1981 in the case of *Michael M. v. Superior Court of Sonoma County*. Michael M., a seventeen-year-old male, was found guilty of violating California's statutory rape law. Under the California penal code, unlawful sexual intercourse was defined as "an act of sexual intercourse accomplished with a female not the wife of the perpetrator, where the female is under the age of 18 years." The statute thus made men alone criminally liable for such conduct. Michael M. challenged the constitutionality of the law, arguing it violated the Equal Protection Clause because it punished only men for the offense and not women. The Court ruled against him. "Young men and young women are not similarly situated with respect to the problems and the risks of sexual intercourse," said the Court, and the states were free to enact such laws in the interest of preventing "illegitimate pregnancy." The Court noted that "[i]t is hardly unreasonable for a legislature acting to protect minor females to exclude them from punishment. Moreover, the risk of pregnancy itself constitutes a substantial deterrence to young females. No similar natural sanctions deter males." Statutory rape is one of the few areas in which states are permitted to enact sex-based laws as long as the objective is legitimate and the law reflects a physical difference between the sexes.

> See also Date and Acquaintance Rape;
> Marital Rape; Michael M. v. Superior Court
> of Sonoma County; Rape Shield Law.

United States v. Morrison (2000)

In *United States v. Morrison*, the Supreme Court held that part of the Violence Against Women Act (VAWA) was unconstitutional in allowing women to sue their alleged rapists for monetary damages in federal court. While a student at Virginia Polytechnic Institute, Christy Brzonkala was raped by two men on the school's football team. Directly following the rape, Brzonkala filed a claim against the men under the school's sexual assault policy. The school investigated and found only one of the men guilty and gave him a two-semester suspension from the school. It later deferred the suspension, allowing him to resume attendance under a full athletic scholarship; the young man later graduated. Brzonkala withdrew from school permanently.

Brzonkala then filed suit under a provision of the VAWA that allowed for victims of "crimes of violence motivated by gender" to sue for compensatory and punitive damages in federal court for violations of their civil rights. The lower federal court dis-

missed the case, concluding that Congress did not have the authority to grant rape victims the right to sue their alleged rapists for monetary damages in federal court. In an appeal, the higher federal court affirmed the lower court's decision, and Brzonkala took her case to the U.S. Supreme Court. She argued that violence against women was a national problem, not just a state problem, and that Congress was responding to it in passing the VAWA. In fact, she said, violence might deter women from interstate travel, and any interstate commerce, economic or noneconomic, is within the domain of Congress. The accused argued instead that Congress can enact regulations only for activity that is economically related to interstate commerce. The VAWA, then, was simply an attempt by Congress to exercise general policy power across the nation, which is clearly unconstitutional.

In the majority opinion, the Court ruled that the men were correct: only when interstate commerce is "substantially affected" can Congress interfere. In this case the VAWA sought to regulate noneconomic, criminal conduct, which is purely the domain of states. Congress cannot regulate violence affecting the national economy, for if it could, it would be regulating any activity in states that may lead to violent crimes. In the dissenting opinion, Justices David Souter, John Paul Stevens, Ruth Bader Ginsburg, and Stephen Breyer argued that the VAWA was a valid exercise of congressional power since evidence demonstrated that such violence cost the national economy between $5 billion and $10 billion each year in health care costs, judicial expenses, and social costs. Finally, they held, it is the duty of Congress, and not the Court, to decide whether an activity "substantially affects interstate activity." It is the Court's job to examine federal laws that had been passed "not for soundness, but simply for rationality."

> See also Battered Woman Syndrome (BWS);
> North Carolina v. Norman; Violence Against
> Women Act (VAWA).

Violence Against Women Act (VAWA)

Enacted as part of the Violent Crime Control and Law Enforcement Act of 1994, the Violence Against Women Act (VAWA) is administered by the Department of Health and Human Services (HHS) and the Department of Justice (DOJ). In part, the act provides funding for more prosecutors in domestic violence cases and improves domestic violence training among prosecutors, police officers, and health and social services professionals; funds more domestic violence shelters, counseling, and research into the causes of domestic violence; and provides grants to states for victim services programs. But just as important, the act set new federal penalties for those who cross state lines to continue abuse of a spouse or partner, thus making domestic abuse and harassment an interstate crime and thus a federal offense. It also requires states to honor protective orders issued in other states and gives victims the right to mandatory restitution and the right to address the court at the time of sentencing of a perpetrator.

Congress considered passing the VAWA for four years, during which time it heard testimony by experts on the need for federal intervention in the increasing problem of domestic violence and the difficulty states faced in prosecuting such cases. The Bureau of National Affairs provided estimates showing that domestic violence costs U.S. employers $3 billion to $5 billion annually in increased absenteeism and lost productivity due to physical and psychological injuries. For victims, the National Institute of Justice indicated that costs attributable to rape amounted to $7.5 billion in economic harm annually and $119 billion per year in emotional costs. It also affects victims in limiting their employment possibilities; one-third of battered women reported that their batterers kept them form working, one-fourth said that they had lost a job due to domestic violence, and almost one-half of rape victims lose their jobs in the aftermath of the assault.

In a victory hailed by women's groups, the first case prosecuted under the VAWA resulted in the conviction of a West Virginia man who put his wife in a coma. After beating her unconscious, Christopher Bailey locked his wife in the truck of his car and drove between West Virginia and Kentucky for six days, never seeking medical attention for her. If Bailey had been tried under state law, he would have received a maximum of ten years in prison. But prosecution under the act, and therefore federal law, ensured that Bailey would receive a sentence of twenty years to life.

Probably the most controversial part of the act allowed rape victims to bring civil suit against their attackers in federal court, allowing them to seek monetary damages after the criminal trial had taken place. In 1998 a female student at Virginia Polytechnic Institute sued two football players at the school for repeatedly raping her (see *United States v. Morrison* [2000]). The school originally suspended one of the men but then reinstated him and allowed both men to graduate. The woman filed suit against the school for not punishing the young men for the rape and for the damages she suffered as a result of the rape. The Supreme Court ruled that Congress did not have the authority to allow women to sue their attackers in federal court for damages they experienced as a result of the rape.

See also Battered Woman Syndrome (BWS); *North Carolina v. Norman*; *United States v. Morrison*.

References and Further Reading

Gelb, Joyce, and Marian Lief Palley. 1982. *Women and Public Policies*. Princeton, NJ: Princeton University Press.
Lunardini, Christine. 1994. *What Every American Should Know about Women's History*. Holbrook: Bob Adams.
National Institute of Crime Prevention Web site: http://www.nicp.net.
National Violence Against Women Prevention Center Web site: www.vawprevention.org.
U.S. Department of Justice, Office on Violence Against Women Web site: http://www.ojp.usdoj.gov/ vawo.

Workplace Rights

Affirmative Action

Affirmative action refers to public policies aimed at increasing the number of people from certain underrepresented groups in particular sectors of employment, education, business, and government. In the United States, these groups include women and ethnic minorities such as African Americans, Asian Americans, Hispanic Americans, American Indians, disabled people, and Vietnam veterans. In general, affirmative action is intended to benefit groups that are thought to have suffered from discrimination in the past. Institutions with affirmative action policies usually set timetables for greater diversity and use recruitment and racial preference as ways of achieving these goals.

The United States has a long history of attempting to curb discrimination in government agencies. In 1941 President Franklin Roosevelt signed an executive order prohibiting government contractors from engaging in employment discrimination. This order, however, was primarily intended to prevent strikes or demonstrations that might hamper the war effort rather than encourage diversity in government jobs. In 1948 President Harry Truman signed another executive order to desegregate the military, which allowed for greater troop buildup in the Korean conflict. But it was not until 1961, two months after assuming office, that President John F. Kennedy established the President's Committee on Equal Employment Opportunity to end job discrimination by the government and diversify the government workforce. Later renamed the Equal Employment Opportunity Commission (EEOC), this committee had the authority to impose sanctions for violations of the executive order.

By executive order, Kennedy required every federal contract to include a pledge that government contractors would not discriminate against any employee or applicant for employment because of race, creed, color, or national origin. Further, his policy ensured that the government would take affirmative acts to ensure that government contracts did not discriminate against these groups. The Civil Rights Act of 1964 broadened the application of the executive order to gender and called for the government to step up affirmative actions to prevent discrimination. When Lyndon B. Johnson entered the White House, he immediately supported the act, saying: "You do not take a person who for years has been hobbled by chains and liberate him, bring him up to the starting line of a race and then say, 'you're free to compete with all the others,' and still justly believe that you have been completely fair." Although it was controversial when Johnson signed the bill into law, President Richard Nixon later required all government contractors to develop affirmative action programs.

Critics argue that some groups benefit from affirmative action as a result of their political influence. That is, the groups under question are no longer underprivileged or underrepresented but because of their

Road dispatcher Diane Joyce, plaintiff in the land-mark Johnson *case (Bettmann/Corbis)*

to ensure that women or minorities are included in preset proportions. The Supreme Court overruled the direct use of quotas in university admissions in 1978 (*Regents of the University of California v. Bakke*) and held that in order to achieve racial diversity within a student body, a school can apply several criteria besides grade point averages in their admission process but may not resort to quotas. And in 1995 the Supreme Court ruled again on affirmative action programs. A federal program requiring preference based on a person's race, it held, is unconstitutional unless the preference is designed to make up for specific instances of past discrimination. That meant that affirmative actions must be aimed at eliminating specific problems and not trying to right social shortcomings as a whole (see *Johnson v. Transportation*).

Several states have attempted (by referendums) to severely limit the use of affirmative action policies, particularly in universities. California, Texas, and Florida have been at the forefront in establishing policies that abolish so-called reverse discrimination in university admissions and state hiring decisions. Many groups, though supportive in general of affirmative action policies, have become restrained in their public support of such policies, fearing that the benefits of affirmative action are not worth the perception that women's and minorities' successes are unwarranted.

The Supreme Court recently clarified whether affirmative action policies in university admission procedures are allowed under the Civil Rights Act and the *Bakke* decision. In two sharply divided opinions in June 2003 involving admission policies at the University of Michigan, the Court upheld the policy in place in law school admissions but rejected an undergraduate policy that awarded points to potential students based on race. In *Gratz v. Bollinger* the Court ruled that the use of race in deciding the university's freshman admission was not narrowly tailored to achieve a com-

political power are granted benefits they should no longer receive. Women are cited as an example; because they make up over 50 percent of the American population, they cannot clearly be considered a "minority." An additional criticism of affirmative action concerns whether it can in fact become reverse discrimination. Several cases take issue with university policies that attempt to diversify student bodies, for example, by admitting students of color who are no longer economically disadvantaged even though their GPAs and test scores are lower than those of white applicants.

There are various types of affirmative action programs. Some seek only to remove barriers so that all people may compete equally. Others use numerical goals (quotas) pelling interest of achieving diversity; here, the university was using race as the deciding factor for virtually every minimally qualified minority applicant. But the Court upheld the university's law school policy (in *Grutter v. Bollinger*), designed to achieve diversity within the student body, which considered the applicant's race as well as other factors. Since the law school did not seek to admit any particular number or percentage of underrepresented minority students, and instead viewed race as a "potential plus factor," the policy survived the Court's scrutiny. The opinion held that the law school policy aimed to achieve a "critical mass" of blacks, Hispanics, and Native Americans, "who without this commitment might not be represented in [the] student body in meaningful numbers." This opinion seemed to contradict public opinion at the time; a month before the opinion was released, a Gallup Poll showed that 69 percent of Americans believed that college applicants "should be admitted solely on the basis of merit, even if that results in few minority students being admitted."

See also Civil Rights Act; Equal Employment Opportunity Commission (EEOC).

AFSCME v. Washington (1985)

In *AFSCME v. Washington*, the Supreme Court ruled that the state of Washington violated Title VII of the Civil Rights Act by compensating female employees at a lower rate than male employees in comparable positions. The case was initiated in a class-action suit filed by 15,500 members of the American Federation of State, County, and Municipal Employees (AFSCME) who worked for the state. The Court ordered the state to provide raises and compensatory back pay to female state employees who were found to be earning 20 percent less than their male coworkers. The case brought to political prominence the issue of comparable worth, the notion that men and women should be compensated equally for work re-

quiring comparable skills, responsibilities, and effort. As a result a number of states and municipalities in the late 1980s enacted pay equity laws, which have been opposed by conservative groups and businesses.

See also Civil Rights Act; Comparable Worth.

Alexander v. Yale University (1980)

In *Alexander v. Yale University,* one of the first sexual harassment cases to reach the Supreme Court, five women filed suit against Yale University, arguing that the university had failed to appropriately deal with their allegations. The Supreme Court upheld the lower courts' decisions.

The first plaintiff, Ronni Alexander, was a 1977 graduate of Yale University. Alexander said that she quit playing the flute and thereafter "abandoned" her pursuit of a professional music career because of sexual advances by her instructor that included "coerced sexual intercourse." Furthermore, when she attempted to report the harassment and sexual attack to university officials, they ignored her allegations outright and "discouraged" her from making any further accusations. The Connecticut court initially dismissed her case on the grounds that her graduation from the school made her case moot; if she was able to graduate, the harm she had suffered was obviously minimal. The second plaintiff, Margery Reifler, was a 1980 graduate who claimed that the hockey team coach sexually harassed her when she was the team's manager. The continued harassment caused her "humiliation" and "distress" and denied her "recognition due her as a team member." Reifler stated that she "wanted to complain" to the appropriate administrators but was "intimidated" and unsure of how to go about reporting the matter. The Connecticut court dismissed Reifler's claim as well because she did not report the alleged harassment to anyone. The third plaintiff, Lisa Stone, was a 1978 graduate who alleged emotional distress when she witnessed the university's failure to recognize another female student's claim of harassment. Stone said she was deprived of "the tranquil atmosphere necessary to her pursuit of a liberal education," resulting in a "fear of her own associations with men in positions of authority at Yale." The fourth plaintiff, Ann Olivarius, was a 1977 graduate who claimed that she was "forced" to find avenues of reporting such abuse herself because none were provided by the university. She was "subjected to threats and intimidation from individuals involved in her investigations" and was not protected by officials at the university. Her case was also dismissed by the lower court.

The final plaintiff was Pamela Price, a 1979 graduate who accused one of her instructors of offering her a grade of A in exchange for sexual favors in what is now considered a charge of quid pro quo sexual harassment. She refused his advances and was given a C in the course, which she claimed was not a "fair evaluation" of her work but was a direct reflection of her denying her instructor sexual favors. When Price complained to officials, she was told nothing could be done. The lower court did not dismiss her case, instead holding that "academic advancement conditioned upon submission to sexual demands constitutes sex discrimination in education." But the court found for the university in the matter of sexual harassment, the judge ruling that "the alleged incident of sexual proposition did not occur and the grade of 'C' that Miss Price received on the paper submitted and the resulting grade of 'C' that she received in the course did not reflect consideration of any factor other than academic achievement."

The Connecticut court held that the plaintiffs could not be considered in a class-action suit against the university. The U.S. Supreme Court affirmed the state court's decision to dismiss the cases of Olivarius, Stone, Alexander, and Reifler, holding that their cases did not rise to the required "justiciable case or controversy" as required. The Court also affirmed the Connecticut court's decision regarding Price's request to enter all the plaintiffs into a class-action suit. "As Price failed to prove her case," the Court said, "she failed to prove any perceptible harm and therefore she lacks standing to attack Yale's failure to establish a complaint procedure, and she is not a proper representative of the purported class."

Six years later, in *Meritor Savings Bank v. Vinson* (1986), the Supreme Court reversed its primary stance on sexual harassment suits and ruled that a hostile work environment, similar to the environment claimed by the plaintiffs in the *Alexander* case, violated the Civil Rights Act.

> *See also Meritor Savings Bank v. Vinson; Sexual Harassment.*

Allred, Gloria (1941–)

Born in Philadelphia, Gloria Allred graduated from the University of Pennsylvania with a degree in English and received her M.A. from New York University and her law degree from Loyola University in Los Angeles. She worked as a secondary-school teacher before practicing law. She is known as one of the pioneers in protecting the rights

Gloria Allred (Reuters NewMedia, Inc./Corbis)

of those discriminated against on the basis of sex, race, age, and sexual orientation.

As one of the most public feminist speakers, Allred is currently president of the Women's Equal Rights Legal Defense and Education Fund (WERLDEF), has a radio talk show, and is a regular commentator for feminist issues in the media. She is best known, however, for her work in high-profile cases that take on sexist traditions in the consumer world; for example, she filed suit against a dry cleaner for charging more to clean women's clothing than for men's, she sued a hair salon for charging more for haircuts for girls than for boys, and she sued a store for charging women but not men for alterations of clothing.

Backus v. Baptist Medical Center (1982)

In *Backus v. Baptist Medical Center*, a court ruled that sex was a bona fide occupational qualification (BFOQ) for a position as a nurse in a hospital's labor and delivery section; in other words, a hospital could limit this job to women. In 1978 Gregory Backus was employed by the Baptist Medical Center in Little Rock, Arkansas, as a registered nurse. He requested assignment in the gynecology department and was denied because the hospital was concerned about female patients' privacy. He appealed to the administrator of the hospital, who offered him an assignment in the intensive care nursery at the same pay, which he accepted. In 1979 he again asked to be moved to the gynecology department and was refused. He filed complaints with the Equal Employment Opportunity Commission (EEOC), claiming the hospital discriminated against him because he was male. But later that same year after receiving performance evaluations that, he claimed, reflected harassment for filing his discrimination charge and hurt his chances for advancement within the hospital, he left his job there. The following year he finally brought suit against the hospital. Although his suit was unsuccessful, the case defined BFOQ for the first time.

> *See also* Bona Fide Occupational Qualification (BFOQ); *Cheatwood v. South Central Bell Telephone and Telegraph Company*; Civil Rights Act; *Diaz v. Pan American World Airways*; Equal Employment Opportunity Commission (EEOC); *Phillips v. Martin Marietta Corporation*.

Bona Fide Occupational Qualification (BFOQ)

Employers can engage in overt discrimination of their employees only if they can prove the policy in question is necessary for a legitimate, nondiscriminatory reason, or is a bona fide occupational qualification (BFOQ). This concept was largely defined in the Supreme Court case of *Backus v. Baptist Medical Center* (1982), which involved a male nurse who sued the hospital in which he was employed because of its refusal to move him to the labor and delivery section. The Court ruled that sex in this case was a BFOQ.

Title VII of the Civil Rights Act of 1964 provides that an employer may legitimately make job distinctions based on an employee's gender as long as the distinction is necessary to the normal operation of the particular business. But the defense is limited to hiring and assignments, and courts have not allowed practices grounded in sexual stereotypes. Today employees cannot be excluded from specific jobs by statute because of their sex; in fact, the ability to lift a certain weight and other physical requirements have been rejected as BFOQs. Title VII protects an employee's right to demonstrate individual capability to do the required tasks of any job.

> *See also* *Backus v. Baptist Medical Center*; *Chambers v. Omaha Girls Club et al.*; *Cheatwood v. South Central Bell Telephone and Telegraph Company*; Civil Rights Act; *Diaz v. Pan American World Airways*; Equal Employment Opportunity Commission (EEOC); *Phillips v. Martin Marietta*

Corporation; United Auto Workers v. Johnson Controls.

Reference Andrew J. Maikovich and Michele D. Brown. 1989. *Employment Discrimination.* Charlotte, NC: McFarland.

Burlington Industries v. Ellerth (1998)

Burlington Industries v. Ellerth was one of four landmark rulings the Supreme Court handed down in 1998 that defined the issue of sexual harassment in the workplace. The Court had ruled in previous cases that there were two distinct types of sexual harassment; quid pro quo and hostile work environment. Quid pro quo involves an employer or supervisor who insists that an employee submit to a sexual relationship or lose her (or his) job; hostile work environment involves a work environment so hostile to an employee because of sexual innuendo that the employee cannot continue to perform her (or his) job.

In *Burlington Industries v. Ellerth,* the Court specified the conditions of quid pro quo harassment. Kim Ellerth's supervisor repeatedly implied that her job would be jeopardized unless she succumbed to his advances. Although he never carried out the threats and she never registered a formal complaint, she ultimately left her job because of the situation. Her employer, Burlington Industries, argued that since she had suffered no job consequence and, further, had failed to use the company's sexual harassment complaint procedure, the company should not be held liable for any sexual harassment. The Court disagreed. It held that employers are liable for supervisors' conduct if the company failed to institute an anti–sexual harassment policy for employees.

> **See also** Civil Rights Act; Equal Employment Opportunity Commission (EEOC); *Faragher v. City of Boca Raton; Gebser v. Lago Vista Independent School District; Meritor Savings Bank v. Vinson; Oncale v. Sundowner Offshore Services;* Sexual Harassment.

California Federal Savings and Loan Association v. Guerra (1987)

California Federal Savings and Loan Association v. Guerra was similar to many other gender discrimination cases in which males claimed discrimination under Title VII of the Civil Rights Act and the Pregnancy Discrimination Act (PDA). The PDA requires employers to reinstate to their original jobs women who return from a childbearing leave, but workers returning from other forms of disability leave are not afforded this opportunity. California was one of four states that had laws requiring employers to provide reasonable maternity leaves and benefits for pregnant employees. California law required employers covered by Title VII to grant unpaid pregnancy disability leave of up to four months and allow employees who took the leave to return to work. Title VII prohibited employers from discriminating on the basis of sex, which would include discrimination on the basis of pregnancy.

Lillian Garland, a receptionist employed by a California savings and loan association, took a pregnancy disability leave starting in January 1982. When she attempted to return to work four months later, in April, she was told her job had been filled by someone else and that there were no similar positions available. After she filed a complaint with the California Department of Fair Employment and Housing, her employer was charged with violating state law. The only time an employer was not required to grant returning employees their jobs back following leave was if those positions were no longer available because of business necessity.

The savings and loan association argued that employers who complied with the state law were subject to reverse discrimination suits under Title VII. That is, temporarily disabled males who did not receive the same treatment as female employees (who were disabled by pregnancy) could claim discrimination. Essentially, Title VII prohibits discrimination on the basis of sex, and the state law under question here promoted may not rise. Further, the history of the PDA indicates that the act was to be construed as forbidding an employer to extend any benefit to pregnant women that they do not already provide to other disabled employees.

This case divided the feminist community. One side argued that in order to make women substantively equal to men, society should focus on the commonalities between male and female workers; all workers who were temporarily disabled should receive equal and extended disability benefits. The other side argued that explicitly recognizing women's potential for pregnancy and the disabilities occurring from childbirth was essential to finding equality between the sexes. Special provisions for pregnancy in the workplace, even when there were no provisions for disabilities of other workers, were essential since women already carried a heavier burden than men with regard to pregnancy. Only when pregnant workers received benefits, this side believed, would benefits for other disabilities follow.

> *See also* Civil Rights Act; Family and Medical Leave Act (FMLA); *Geduldig v. Aiello; General Electric v. Gilbert*; Maternity Leave; Pregnancy Discrimination Act (PDA).

Chambers v. Omaha Girls Club et al. (1986)

The stated purpose of the Girls Club organization is to provide behavioral guidance and promote the health, education, and vocational and character development of girls, regardless of race, creed, or national origin. Specifically, its mission is to offer "a safe alternative from the streets and to help girls take care of themselves." The Girls Clubs maintain their difference from school programs and other youth programs because they serve females only and have a high staff-to-member ratio, with each staff member expected to act as a role model for the girls and to be committed to the Girls Club philosophy, including the belief that teenage pregnancy limits opportunities for young women.

Lillian Garland, a California woman who went on maternity leave and lost her job, stands on the steps of the Supreme Court building with her lawyer, Patricia Shiu (left) and feminist Betty Friedan. (Bettmann/Corbis)

sex discrimination by giving preferential treatment to female employees disabled by pregnancy or childbirth, disabilities men could not have.

A key question in the case was, Which ruled—Title VII (which banned all sex discrimination) or the state law (which gave women special benefits)? The Court held that Title VII (and the PDA) did not preempt the California statute, since both the federal and the state provisions share the goal of promoting equal employment opportunities for women. Further, Congress intended the federal provision to be a floor beneath which pregnancy disability benefits could not drop, not a ceiling above which they

Following the pregnancies of two unmarried staff members in 1981, the executive director of a Girls Club in Nebraska established a rule that single staff members who became pregnant or caused a pregnancy would no longer be permitted to continue their employment with the club. Three months after the new rule was set, Crystal Chambers, a twenty-two-year-old unmarried black female who had been employed with Girls Club since 1980, notified her supervisor that she was pregnant; she immediately received notice of her termination. Chambers filed charges of discrimination on the basis of her sex and marital status with the Nebraska Employment Opportunities Commission (NEOC) and the federal Equal Employment Opportunity Commission (EEOC). The NEOC found that there was no "reasonable cause" to believe that the plaintiff had been discriminated against because of her sex, even though she was told she was fired because of her pregnancy.

The Girls Club, however, prevailed at trial. In order to establish a case under the Civil Rights Act, the plaintiff must be able to show purposeful or intentional discrimination. But Chambers produced evidence of the general impact of the policy upon black women and single black women. It was true that many members of the Girls Club were from households headed by a single black woman, that the neighborhood in which the club was situated was mainly black, and that white employees of the club had been allowed maternity leave. But, the court held, Chambers had failed to show that she had been treated differently because of her race or that race was a factor in the decision to end her employment. Further, her claim of discrimination was dramatically discredited by two things: first, the club was located specifically to better serve a primarily black population and, second, Chambers's position was filled by a black staff person who in turn was replaced by a new employee who was also black.

Chambers argued that a conspiracy existed with the club attempting to cover up the discriminatory motive of their policies. The court held that Chambers had failed to "produce even a shred of evidence" to this claim. Chambers also alleged that she suffered from disparate treatment because of the club's policy. Disparate impact occurs when a facially neutral rule falls more harshly on one group than another. Disparate treatment, though, occurs when an employer treats employees differently because of race, color, religion, sex, or national origin. Proof of discriminatory motive is critical, although in some situations it can be inferred. Chambers had to demonstrate that the defendant intentionally discriminated against her, and the Girls Club would have to explain a nondiscriminatory reason for its action. The court held that the club's policy was simply to provide positive role models for the girls in an attempt to discourage teenagers from becoming pregnant. Further, this goal was a legitimate and nondiscriminatory reason for the policy. The policy of the club was a business necessity; the club's only purpose is to serve girls between the ages of eight and eighteen and to make them aware of the opportunities available to them. To permit single pregnant staff members to work with the girls of the club would convey the impression that the Girls Club condoned pregnancy for the girls in the age group it served. The testimony of board members made clear that the policy was not based upon a morality standard but rather on a belief that teenage pregnancy severely limits opportunities for teenage girls. Further, the policy was just one part of a comprehensive attack on the problem on teenage pregnancy.

The court warned, however, that its decision was based upon the unique mission of the Girls Club, the age group of young women it served, the geographic location of the club's facilities, and the comprehensive methods it employed to address the problem of teenage pregnancy. Thus, its decision would not be applicable in many other, similar situations.

AFL-CIO vice-president Linda Chavez-Thompson, the highest-ranking woman in the labor movement, cele-brated election results with Richard L. Trumka (right) and President John Sweeney (left), 1995. (Associated Press/AP)

See also Bona Fide Occupational Qualification (BFOQ); Disparate Impact; Equal Employment Opportunity Commission (EEOC); *Phillips v. Martin Marietta Corporation.*

Chavez-Thompson, Linda (1944–)

Born as one of eight children to cotton sharecroppers in West Texas, Linda Chavez began working in the fields by age ten, earning thirty cents an hour (adults earned fifty cents). She dropped out of school in the ninth grade and cleaned houses for a living. But by 1967, while she was the secretary for the Laborers' International Union and the union representative for the Hispanic American members, she came to understand the need for the labor movement in the United States. During the 1970s she worked for the American Federation of State, County, and Municipal Employees (AFSCME) and began her political activism.

She became executive vice-president of the AFL-CIO in 1995 and made history as the first woman and the first person of color elected to the top offices of the organization. In that capacity she attempted to align the labor movement with women and other minority groups. Her standing not only as a Hispanic American but also as a blue-collar worker gave her legitimacy because she had suffered discrimination on both fronts. As a result, she was appointed by President Bill Clinton to serve on the President's Initiative on Race and as vice-chair of the President's Committee on Employment of People with Disabilities.

References AFL-CIO Web site: http://www. aflcio.org/yourjobeconomy; National

Women's History Project Web site: http://www.nwhp.org/tlp/biographies/chavez-thompson/chavez-thompson-bio.html.

Cheatwood v. South Central Bell Telephone and Telegraph Company (1969)

Claudine Cheatwood filed suit against her employer, South Central Bell Telephone and Telegraph Company, alleging discrimination on the basis of sex. When the company announced a vacant position, Cheatwood and two other female employees submitted their applications immediately. But the employer awarded the job to a male applicant solely, Cheatwood argued, because he was male.

The Equal Employment Opportunity Commission (EEOC) first received her allegations of discrimination and declared that reasonable cause existed to believe that the company had committed a violation of Title VII. The employer later admitted a prima facie violation of one section of Title VII—namely, that it had refused to hire an individual because of her sex and that it had limited employees in a way that deprived them of employment opportunities solely because of their sex. But the company contended that their practice fit within an exception to the general prohibition of discrimination against women. That is, an employer can hire employees on the basis of their sex if sex is a bona fide occupational qualification (BFOQ) that is reasonably necessary to the normal operation of the particular business or enterprise. When Cheatwood later filed her lawsuit, the only question for the court was whether all women would be unable to perform their duties at the company safely and efficiently.

The job description Cheatwood applied for was as a commercial representative, who would handle "commercial matters primarily outside the company's office, such as visits to customers' premises in connection with criticisms, facilities, securing signed application where required, credit information, deposits, advance payments, coin telephone inspections and visits in connection with live and final account treatment work." The representative could also be "assigned to work inside the office pertaining to service and collections." The company argued that it would be inappropriate for women to be required to visit customers because tires might need to be changed and rest-room facilities would occasionally be inaccessible. Because these duties of the job would subject women to harassment and danger, in addition to the strenuous physical demands made on representatives, which included collecting coins from pay boxes around their route, the company said, it acted appropriately.

The court held that there was no proof that all or nearly all women would be unable to cope with these challenges. It is up to an individual woman to determine whether or not to take on such tasks, and not to the employer to decide that she is not able. As for the physical danger, the court held that there was nothing in the record of other representatives that indicated the danger was functionally related to sex. And with the physical demands, the court pointed to evidence indicating that the coin boxes representatives would be required to handle weighed between 45 and 80 pounds apiece. Although medical experts agreed that there were certain genetic and musculoskeletal differences between the sexes, it was not enough to convince the court that being male was a BFOQ in this situation.

The court ruled that the company would have to change its hiring practices so as not to exclude women from the positions of commercial representatives and that the company would be responsible for Cheatwood's court and attorney fees incurred in the action.

See also Backus v. Baptist Medical Center; Bona Fide Occupational Qualification (BFOQ); Civil Rights Act; Diaz v. Pan American World Airways; Equal Employment Opportunity Commission (EEOC); Phillips v. Martin Marietta Corporation.

City of L.A. Department of Water and Power v. Manhart (1978)

Since women live longer than men, the city of Los Angeles required females to contribute nearly 15 percent more than males to the city pension fund. Like insurance premiums that are computed from tables that factor in life expectancy and lifestyle, pension plans regularly figure employee contributions on the basis of their longevity. One result of the disparity in this case was that females took home less money than males who made the same salary. One female plaintiff in the suit had contributed over $18,000; had she been a male, she would have been required to contribute only $13,000. Several women brought suit against Los Angeles in 1973, arguing that the city's policy violated Title VII of the Civil Rights Act by treating women differently than their male counterparts. But while the suit was pending, the California legislature enacted legislation prohibiting municipal agencies from taking more money from females for pension plans. The Supreme Court ordered a refund of excess contributions made before the legislation was passed but did not require retroactive pay.

Over the next decade, the Court made various rulings regarding gender-based actuarial tables used by state agencies to calculate life insurance policies and pension plans. No case has yet addressed gender-based practices in fire, auto, and disability insurance policies purchased outside of state employment.

See also Civil Rights Act.

Civil Rights Act (1964)

The Civil Rights Act bans job discrimination because of a person's color, race, national origin, religion, or gender; it also forbids the segregation of public accommodations. The act protects primarily the rights of ethnic minorities and women and is by far one of the nation's strongest civil rights laws. The rights protected under the act include freedom to seek employment; vote; and use hotels, parks, restaurants, and other public places. The Equal Employment Opportunity Commission (EEOC) was created to enforce the act in an effort to protect fair employment practices. Any individual who suspects he or she has been discriminated against by an employer can file a complaint with the EEOC, which will then pursue the complaint in court on behalf of that employee. The act also forbids discrimination by any program that receives money from the federal government; the government may cut off financing for a program that does not end discriminatory policies or practices. This includes school desegregation programs.

John F. Kennedy proposed the Civil Rights Act; Lyndon B. Johnson later pushed its passage as part of his Great Society program. The act was finally passed after a seventy-five-day filibuster in the Senate—one of the longest filibusters in U.S. history. Unlike the New Deal, which was a response to a severe economic crisis, the Great Society programs largely instituted by the Johnson administration following Kennedy's death emerged in a period of great prosperity in America. Many of these programs—the Medicare program (which provided medical care for the elderly), the Medicaid program (providing care for the poor), Corporation for Public Broadcasting, and the Food Stamps program—were efforts to retain the level of economic prosperity for generations to come. Other programs came about because of pressure from the intermittently violent black struggle for equality; the social disorder would not exist, black leaders explained, if black urban poverty were wiped out and blacks were allowed to work without discrimination and vote without the required poll taxes and literacy tests in place among southern states. One of the great successes of the Johnson administration was the passage of several pieces of legislation and key initiatives that attempted to deal with these social problems. There were actually three Civil Rights Acts passed: the 1964 act, which forbade job discrimination; a 1965 law guaranteeing black voting rights; and a 1968 act banning housing discrimination.

The most important legislation ever passed by the federal government to eliminate gender-based discrimination in employment is Title VII of the 1964 act. Efforts to add sex as a category to the original act were vigorously opposed. Representative Howard Smith of Virginia, hoping to sabotage passage of the entire act, proposed an amendment to add sex as a protected category. Much to his surprise, however, the act passed even with the addition of gender.

Title VII reads:

It shall be an unlawful employment practice for an employer—(1) to fail or refuse to hire or to discharge any individual, or otherwise to discriminate against any individual with respect to his compensation, terms, conditions, or privileges of employment, because of such individual's race, color, religion, sex, or national origin; or (2) to limit, segregate, or classify his employees or applicants for employment in any way which would deprive or tend to deprive any individual of employment opportunities or otherwise adversely affect his status as an employee, because of such individual's race, color, religion, sex, or national origin.

Additionally, employers are forbidden to classify their employees in any way that tends to deprive them of employment opportunities because of their gender. This includes prehiring advertisements, postemployment references, interviewing, placement, promotions, wages, benefits, working conditions, working atmosphere, seniority, transfers, reassignments, layoffs, and discharges. Title VII has been used in most of the precedent-setting cases in gender discrimination issues in the workplace. Title VII applies to employers who have fifteen or more employees (including part and full time) at least twenty weeks during any calendar year who work in an industry affecting commerce. Although the federal government was originally excluded from the Title VII definition of employer, today federal government employees are included. Violations of Title VII are investigated (and potentially litigated by the EEOC) and civil penalties are possible, including punitive damages. Employers who intentionally violate the law or exhibit malice toward female employees can be penalized.

Even though Title VII does not explicitly mention sexual harassment, such behavior is considered a form of sex discrimination, is illegal, and is investigated by the EEOC. In filing sexual harassment charges, an employee must show that he or she is a member of a protected class and has been subjected to unwelcome sexual harassment severe or pervasive enough to affect their work, and that the employer either knew or should have known of the harassment. In essence, the employee must show that one gender was exposed to general hostility because of their sex.

Some limitations for litigating violations of Title VII, however, do exist. For example, an employer who requires English language as a basic skill for employment is not practicing discrimination and violating the act. But employers who discriminate against employees because their English is accented are not protected. Preferring employees because of their sexual attractiveness or morality would not legally be discrimination, but having rules that hinder one sex only (e.g., no children for female employees or limiting jobs available to married women but not unmarried women) would be considered discrimination.

See also Affirmative Action; *AFSCME v. Washington; Alexander v. Yale University;* American Civil Liberties Union— Women's Rights Project (ACLU—WRP); *Backus v. Baptist Medical Center;* Bona Fide Occupational Qualification (BFOQ);

Cheatwood v. South Central Bell Telephone and Telegraph Company; City of L.A. Department of Water and Power v. Manhart; Comparable Worth; *Diaz v. Pan American World Airways;* Equal Employment Opportunity Commission (EEOC); Feminism; Glass Ceiling; *Glenn, Johns and Nugent v. General Motors Corporation; Meritor Savings Bank v. Vinson; Phillips v. Martin Marietta Corporation;* Sexual Harassment; Title IX; *Vorchheimer v. School District of Philadelphia.*

References Bernard Grofman, ed. 2001. *Legacies of the 1964 Civil Rights Act.* Arlington: University Press of Virginia; Bruno Leone, Bonnie Szumski, Carol Wekesser, Karin L. Swisher, and Christina Pierce, eds. 2001. *Sexual Harassment.* San Diego: Greenhaven Press; Karen J. Maschke, ed. 1997. *The Employment Context.* New York: Garland; Anne E. Morris and Susan M. Nott. 1993. *Working Women and the Law: Equality and Discrimination in Theory and Practice.* New York: Routledge.

Comparable Worth

Comparable worth is the principle that men and women should be compensated equally for work requiring comparable skills, responsibilities, and effort. It is obviously difficult to uphold in the United States, where women earn 25 percent less than what men earn. Also referred to as sex equity or pay equity, comparable worth was introduced in the 1970s by reformers seeking to correct inequities in pay between occupations traditionally held by men versus those held by women. Following congressional passage of the Equal Pay Act of 1963, which required that men and women receive "equal pay for equal work," wages for occupations in which most working women were concentrated continued to lag behind comparably skilled but predominately male occupations. Efforts to correct such discrepancies through legislation have been met with skepticism from those who object that comparable worth principles interfere with the operation of a free market and that the worth of an occupation is not absolute and so cannot be compared.

The Supreme Court originally opened the door to the concept of comparable worth in the case of *Washington v. Gunther* (1981). There the Court held that plaintiffs could successfully use Title VII of the Civil Rights Act to claim sex discrimination in pay between two different jobs without actually meeting the equal work standard of the Equal Pay Act.

Currently, the public debate centers on women's tendency to work in professions and occupations that simply pay less. The main question is whether it is a coincidence that women are simply in lower-paying jobs by choice (because, for example, they need the flexibility to care for their children) or whether the economic system pays these professions less because there are more women occupying such positions. Comparable worth claims must be based on a point system that determines the value of a particular job. Under this system a certain number of points is awarded for job criteria (such as skill, effort, and responsibility requirements) as well as working conditions. Those jobs with the same number of points are determined to be of equal worth.

The largest logistical problem with implementing a comparable worth doctrine for the United States is that market-based wages are needed to retain workers. For example, when Minnesota implemented a comparable worth doctrine, the unemployment rate for women rose 5 percent, four times the rate for men. Another problem is that there is now a higher percentage of women with children under the age of five than at any other time in history (from 1969 to 1996 the rate has increased 129 percent), and these women are demanding flexible work hours to care for their children.

See also Civil Rights Act; Equal Pay Act; Glass Ceiling; *Glenn, Johns and Nugent v. General Motors Corporation; Washington v. Gunther.*

References Kelly, Rita Mae, and Jane Bayes. 1988. *Comparable Worth, Pay Equity, and Public Policy.* Westport, CT: Greenwood; Remick, Helen, ed. 1985. *Comparable Worth*

and *Wage Discrimination: Technical
Possibilities and Political Realities.*
Philadelphia: Temple University Press.

Diaz v. Pan American World Airways (1971)

Celio Diaz applied for work as a flight attendant with Pan American in 1967 and was rejected because of the airline's policy to place only women in such positions. Diaz filed charges with the Equal Employment Opportunity Commission (EEOC), arguing that the airlines had unlawfully discriminated against him on the sole basis of his sex. The EEOC found probable cause for his claim but was unable to resolve the matter with the airlines. Diaz was then forced to file suit in federal court alleging that Pan Am violated his rights under the 1964 Civil Rights Act and specifically Title VII of that act. The question for the court was whether being a female was a bona fide occupational qualification (BFOQ) for the job of flight attendant—that is, that it was reasonably necessary to the normal operation of the airline's business to have women as flight attendants. A BFOQ is the one exception to Title VII's prohibition of sex discrimination.

The court examined the history of Pan Am's flight attendants, passenger preference for women attendants, as well as the basic psychological reasons for this preference. In expert testimony, a psychiatrist explained to the judge that an airplane cabin represented a unique environment in which an air carrier was required to take account of the special psychological needs of its passengers. This position was better suited for female attendants, who were superior in such nonmechanical aspects of the job as "providing reassurance to anxious passengers, giving courteous personalized service, and in general, making flights as pleasurable as possible within the limitations imposed by aircraft operations." If the airline were forced to hire males for this position, these males would be unable to attain satisfactory evaluations and thus promotion. If

the airline did not use female sex qualification in selecting their flight attendants, it would lose the best tool for eliminating "nonacceptable" employees for these positions. The court concluded that the airline's hiring policy was the result of a pragmatic decision and thus did not violate Title VII.

Diaz appealed to the federal appellate court. That court disagreed with the lower court judge's decision. Under Title VII a BFOQ is allowed only if a sex qualification is "reasonably necessary to the normal operation of business." But "necessary" indicates a business necessity and not a business convenience. That is, discrimination on the basis of sex is valid only when the essence of the business operation would be undermined by not hiring exclusively one sex over another. If the primary function of an airline is to transport passengers safely from one point to another and a pleasant environment is attained by the cosmetic effect of female attendants, this is tangential to the essence of the business involved. Female attendants are performing only nonmechanical functions, and the safe transportation of passengers (the actual business the airline is involved in) is not influenced by their presence. "Before sex discrimination can be practiced, it must not only be shown that it is impracticable to find men that possess the abilities that most women possess, but that the abilities are necessary to the business, not merely tangential." Although the public may initially expect female attendants, such prejudices cannot determine whether sex discrimination is valid; customer preference may be taken into account only when it is based on the company's inability to perform the primary function or service it offers.

See also Backus v. Baptist Medical Center; Bona Fide Occupational Qualification (BFOQ); *Cheatwood v. South Central Bell Telephone and Telegraph Company;* Civil Rights Act; Equal Employment Opportunity Commission (EEOC); *Phillips v. Martin Marietta Corporation; United Auto Workers v. Johnson Controls.*

Disparate Impact

Assuming an employer classification is gender neutral, yet the plaintiff still believes discrimination has occurred, the Court has recognized two distinct ways that discrimination can be proven under Title VII of the Civil Rights Act of 1964. One is disparate treatment (discussed below). A second is disparate impact. This type of discrimination involves "employment practices that are facially neutral in their treatment of different groups, but that, in fact, fall more harshly on one group than another and cannot be justified by business necessity." In other words, disparate impact occurs if the practice has a disproportionate effect on one gender.

Disparate impact relies upon a statistical concept of bias. That is, it is not the employer's motive behind the gender classification but the selection procedure that is biased. The plaintiff does not have to prove intentional discrimination. Instead, the plaintiff has only to demonstrate that the policy of an employer, which is nondiscriminatory on its face, has an adverse impact on members of a group protected by the Civil Rights Act (e.g., women or racial minorities). In order to prevail against these charges, the employer must prove the policy is job relevant and necessary to the business, that is, that the gender-based classification is a bona fide occupational qualification, allowed under federal law.

The principal case for disparate impact theory arose in a race discrimination setting in 1971 (*Griggs v. Duke Power Co.*). Before Title VII was passed, Duke Power Company openly discriminated on the basis of race in job assignments. But after passage of the act, a neutral rule was adopted requiring all applicants for certain jobs to have a high school diploma and to pass two written tests. A higher percentage of blacks than whites did not possess high school diplomas and also failed to pass the test; so although the demand for education and successful completion of the exam was neutral on its face, it had a disparate impact on applicants depending on their race. Title VI' unlawful employment practice ployer to limit, segregate, or class ployees to deprive them of employment portunities or adversely affect their status because of race, color, religion, sex, or national origin. But the act also authorizes the use of any professionally developed ability test as long as it is not designed or intended to discriminate. Duke Power argued that its test was not intended to discriminate and so the company was not violating Title VII.

The Supreme Court ruled that discriminatory impact from such a neutral rule was sufficient to establish a Title VII case. Therefore, plaintiffs do not need to prove discriminatory motive (e.g., that the employer has intentionally engaged in a prohibited behavior), only that the behavior was not accidental in having a disparate impact on a class of people.

Besides disparate impact, disparate treatment can be used to prove discrimination under Title VII of the Civil Rights Act of 1964. The ultimate factor at issue in disparate treatment cases is intent to discriminate, and proof of discriminatory intent or motive is required for the employee to prevail. The evidence does not need to be direct but may be inferred from differences in treatment between, for example, men and women.

> *See also* Backus v. Baptist Medical Center; Bona Fide Occupational Qualification (BFOQ); Chambers v. Omaha Girls Club et al.; Civil Rights Act; Dothard v. Rawlinson.
> *Reference* Acker, Joan. 1989. *Doing Comparable Worth: Gender, Class, and Pay Equity.* Philadelphia: Temple University Press.

Dothard v. Rawlinson (1977)

Employers can engage in overt discrimination of their employees only if they can prove the policy is a bona fide occupational qualification (BFOQ), a necessary component of a job. In *Dothard v. Rawlinson*, the Supreme Court ruled unconstitutional an Alabama statute specifying minimum height (5'2") and weight requirements (120 pounds) for positions as state prison guards. By establishing height and weight requirements for jobs that involved continual close proximity to inmates, particularly potentially violent inmates, the state excluded 41 percent of the female population but less than 1 percent of males. The Supreme Court ruled that the statute violated Title VII of the Civil Rights Act and unlawful sex discrimination had occurred.

> **See also** Backus v. Baptist Medical Center; Bona Fide Occupational Qualification (BFOQ); Civil Rights Act; Disparate Impact; Torres v. Wisconsin Department of Health and Social Services.

Equal Employment Opportunity Commission (EEOC)

Established in 1964 by Title VII of the Civil Rights Act, the Equal Employment Opportunity Commission enforces all statutes prohibiting employment discrimination (on the basis of race, color, religion, sex, or national origin) and sexual harassment. This includes enforcement of the Equal Pay Act of 1963, Age Discrimination in Employment Act of 1967 (which prohibits employment discrimination against anyone forty years or older), Titles I and V of the Americans with Disabilities Act of 1990, and the Civil Rights Act of 1991 (which provides monetary damages in cases of intentional discrimination). The EEOC has field offices throughout the United States with three goals: to prevent discrimination through education and outreach; to mediate complaints between parties in potential discrimination cases and attempt to resolve or settle the disputes; and when that fails, to enforce antidiscrimination laws.

The EEOC is run by a five-member bipartisan committee. This committee cannot, by law, have more than three members from the same party; each member is nominated to five-year terms by the current president and confirmed by the Senate. Individual commissioners investigate charges by individuals who believe that they have been unlawfully discriminated against by an employer. If the EEOC determines that there is "reasonable cause" to believe that discrimination has occurred, it attempts to mediate between the parties in order to resolve or settle the complaint. If settlement is impossible, the EEOC brings suit in federal court.

Upon its establishment in 1964, the EEOC was immediately deluged with complaints of employment discrimination; in fact, within one year of its organization, the EEOC received 400 percent more cases than it had expected. In the next three years, charges escalated, suggesting that the problem of employment discrimination was higher than originally anticipated. The EEOC now handles approximately 75,000 to 80,000 charges of discrimination annually.

Probably the most efficient use of the EEOC's time has been its issuance of guidelines on how companies should handle discrimination charges. The EEOC has begun outreach programs that provide education and assistance for companies voluntarily complying with potential discrimination investigations. Additionally, the commission has been involved in collecting data used to analyze the discrimination in the workplace.

In 1972 the Equal Employment Opportunity Act was passed, giving the EEOC litigation authority and expanding Title VII coverage. The Supreme Court thereafter showed the EEOC great deference in legal cases involving workplace discrimination. During the administration of Jimmy Carter, the EEOC was tasked with coordinating all federal equal employment opportunity programs and enforcing the Age Discrimination in Employment Act of 1967 and the Equal Pay Act of 1963. In addition, the Civil Service Reform Act of 1978 abolished the Civil Service Commission and transferred to the EEOC the responsibility for enforcing discrimination laws applicable to the federal civilian workforce.

In its early days the EEOC dealt mainly with charges related to race discrimination and segregation policies. By the 1980s the EEOC began to see sexual harassment charges proliferate. In response it created its first "Guidelines on Sexual Harassment," and courts began using the guidelines regularly. The commission was also instrumental in writing the Americans with Disabilities Act of 1990, which prohibits discrimination on the basis of disabilities. In the 1990s the EEOC began focusing on enforcement strategies instead of litigation and experienced dramatic increases in discrimination claims. The Civil Rights Act of 1991, which authorized compensatory and punitive damages in cases of intentional discrimination and provided for the possibility of attorney's fees and jury trials, also directed the EEOC to expand its technical assistance and outreach activities.

Today the EEOC has programs that categorize charges based on the likelihood that discrimination occurred. It has also created a nationwide mediation program for employees charging discrimination of their employers. The EEOC averages approximately 40,000 pending cases per year, and mediation alone resolved nearly 5,000 cases in 2002. It has also received nearly $60 million in benefits for employees charging discrimination and resolved nearly 300 lawsuits without going to trial.

See also Affirmative Action; *Chambers v. Omaha Girls Club et al.; Cheatwood v. South Central Bell Telephone and Telegraph Company;* Civil Rights Act; *Diaz v. Pan American World Airways; Equal Employment Opportunity Commission v. Brown and Root, Inc;* Equal Pay Act; Feminism; Hill, Anita; *Lindahl v. Air France; Phillips v. Martin Marietta Corporation.*

Reference U.S. Equal Employment Opportunity Commission Web site: http://www.eeoc.gov.

Equal Employment Opportunity Commission v. Brown and Root, Inc. (1982)

Sarah Joan Boyes was employed as an electrician's helper by Brown and Root, a construction company. While working on an overhead steel beam in Mississippi, she be-

came paralyzed by fear and was unable to move. Brown and Root fired her, saying she "was not capable of performing assigned work," and hired another woman to replace her. Boyes filed a complaint with the Equal Employment Opportunity Commission (EEOC). After an investigation, the EEOC verified that men who manifested the same paralyzing fear were not discharged from their jobs; four male employees supplied affidavits as such. If Boyes had been a man, would she have suffered dismissal from her job as a result of her phobia?

Employment discrimination claims must show that a person was fired because of sex, race, or age. In order to demonstrate discrimination, an employee must show, (1) that he or she was a member of a protected minority; (2) that he or she was qualified for the job; (3) that he or she was discharged; (4) that following the dismissal the employer filled the position with a nonminority. Boyes was able to demonstrate all but the last, since her job was filled with another woman. But if Boyes could show that she was let go under circumstances in which an employee of another sex would not have been fired, discrimination had occurred irrespective of the employee's replacement. Since Boyes could show that men who had the same paralyzing fear were not discharged, she met the last requirement for a claim of discrimination, and the appellate court ruled in her favor.

In an earlier case (*Brown v. A. J. Gerrard Manufacturing* [1983]), the appellate court had defined with more specificity a four-part test for demonstrating discriminatory discharge of employment. The plaintiff had to be a member of a protected group and had to show that there was a company policy or practice concerning the activity for which he or she was discharged; that nonminority employees either were given the benefit of a lenient company practice or were not held to compliance with a strict company policy; and that the minority employee was disciplined either without the application of a lenient policy or in conformity with the strict one.

See also Equal Employment Opportunity
    Commission (EEOC).

Equal Pay Act (1963)

Passed in 1963, the Equal Pay Act prohibits employers from paying unequal wages to men and women who are doing substantially equal work in the same establishment and who are performing under similar working conditions. An amendment to the Fair Labor Standards Act of 1938, the Equal Pay Act is administered and enforced by the Equal Employment Opportunity Commission (EEOC). During World War II, large numbers of women took over jobs that were originally held by men; the National War Labor Board urged employers to equalize pay rates once it became evident that women were being paid much less than the male employees they replaced. During the 1960s the disparity in pay between men and women was so evident that newspapers published separate job listings for men and women. Newspapers would also run separate pay scales, based on sex, for the same jobs.

The Equal Pay Act had been proposed for a number of years but originally focused on equal pay for "comparable work." The final bill that passed called for equal pay for "equal work"; this requires that two jobs that entail equal skill, effort, and responsibility and are performed under similar conditions must pay the same wage regardless if the employee is male or female. But defining "equal work" has been left to the courts. Courts have ruled that work need not be identical but merely "substantially equal." That is, two distinct job titles (e.g., maid and janitor) involving the same tasks 95 percent of the time (e.g., cleaning) are usually found by the courts to be substantially equal jobs thus requiring equal pay. In such an example, the maid would have to prove that she was being paid less than a janitor even though the work they were performing was

substantively the same. Once she had successfully established a pay disparity, the burden of proof would shift to the employer to justify its actions. The employer would have to defend its pay disparity in one of four ways: by showing that the disparity was based on a seniority system, a merit system, a system that determined wages based on the quantity or quality of work produced, or some "factor other than sex."

The Equal Pay Act bars employers from reducing the wages of either sex to comply with the act; rather, the employer must raise the lower salary. It makes no provision as to wage discrimination based on race or ethnicity; it addresses only the issue of sex-based wage discrimination and covers only situations involving substantially equal work.

As the act was gradually expanded through the courts, women were eventually paid $26 million in back wages by 1971. But the act has not been completely successful in decreasing the wage gap between male and female workers. For example, when the act was passed in 1963, women made 64 cents for every dollar earned by a man; by 1999, women were making only 72 cents for every dollar earned by men. One explanation for the continued pay disparity between men and women is that older women still work in lower-paying jobs that are subject to discriminatory attitudes and conditions of the past, and the pay disparity is therefore simply a product of a free market economy. This explanation, however, does not entirely account for the disparity in salary, since women under twenty-five still earn just 92 cents for every dollar made by a man.

See also Disparate Impact; Equal
    Employment Opportunity Commission
    (EEOC); Feminism; Glass Ceiling; Glenn,
    Johns and Nugent v. General Motors
    Corporation.
Reference Walter A. Fogel. 1984. The Equal
    Pay Act. New York: Praeger.

President Kennedy hands out pens during a ceremony at the White House in which he signed into law a bill aimed at assuring women of paychecks equal to those of men doing the same work. (Bettmann/Corbis)

Table 7.1: Median weekly earnings of full-time wage and salary workers 25 years and older by sex and educational attainment, annual averages, selected years, 1995–2000

Characteristics	1995	1996	1997	1998	1999	2000
Total						
Total, 25 years and over	$510	$520	$540	$572	$592	$611
Less than a high school diploma	309	317	321	337	346	360
High school graduates, no college	432	443	461	479	490	506
Some college or associate degree	508	518	535	558	580	598
College graduates, total	747	758	779	821	860	896
Men						
Total, 25 years and over	588	599	615	639	668	700
Less than a high school diploma	347	357	365	383	395	409
High school graduates, no college	507	516	535	559	580	594
Some college or associate degree	596	604	621	643	665	699
College graduates, total	845	874	896	939	977	1022
Women						
Total, 25 years and over	428	444	462	485	497	515
Less than a high school diploma	262	268	275	283	290	303
High school graduates, no college	356	365	378	396	405	421
Some college or associate degree	427	442	459	476	488	504
College graduates, total	644	657	672	707	740	760

Family and Medical Leave Act (FMLA)

In 1993 President Bill Clinton signed the Family and Medical Leave Act (FMLA) entitling eligible employees to take up to twelve weeks of unpaid, job-protected leave in a twelve-month period for specified family and medical reasons. The issue of family leave had been pushed by women's groups since World War II, as more women entered the workforce. By the start of the twenty-first century, women constituted more than two-fifths of all workers and an estimated nine out of ten women were employed outside the home at some point in their lives. As a result, the issue of family leave took on greater importance, especially after Clinton won the race for president in 1992 in part because he garnered more support from professional women than did any previous presidential candidate in U.S. history. Their continued support, of course, was necessary for his reelection.

But the issue of maternity leave from employment certainly did not originate with the Clinton administration. Beginning in the 1970s, the Court had ruled that employment disability insurance programs could not exclude pregnancy benefits, an employer could not refuse to hire a pregnant woman, nor could a woman be fired because of her pregnancy or be compelled to take maternity leave. Yet until the FMLA, because there was no federal law allowing for maternity and/or family leave, many employees did not have the option of leave for pregnancy or family matters.

The FMLA provides certain employees not only the leave but also group health care benefits to be maintained during the leave as if the employee continued to work instead of taking leave. It was intended to minimize the potential for employment discrimination on the basis of gender and promote equal employment opportunity for men and women. It applies to employees of all public agencies, including state, local, and federal employers; employees of local education agencies (schools); and those who work in the private sector at companies that have fifty or more employees. To be eligible to take this leave, an employee must have worked for a covered employer for at least twelve months and at a location where at least fifty employees work. The family leave is allowed for the birth of a child, the adoption or foster care of a child, the care of an immediate family member (e.g., spouse, child, or parent but not a parent-in-law) with a serious health condition, or the employee's own serious health condition. Spouses who are employed by the same employer can be restricted from taking leave at the same time.

The FMLA was an addition to the Fair Labor Standards Act of 1938 and is administered and enforced by the Equal Employment Opportunity Commission (EEOC), the federal agency charged with investigating allegations of discrimination in employment. Its passage was extremely controversial and soundly opposed predominately by small-business leaders who criticized the costs of administering it. Many supporters have also criticized the act because it fails to provide paid leave. Although employees may choose to use accrued sick or vacation time to cover some or all of the leave taken (as well as some of their loss of salary), once that paid time has been used, the employee goes without pay during a family leave. As a result, critics charge, the act has not been useful and many women and their families have been unable to take advantage of it. And although the act demands that employees who takes the leave must be restored to their original jobs upon their return to work, in circumstances where restoration to employment will cause "substantial and grievous economic injury" to the business' operations, an employer can refuse to reinstate certain highly salaried "key" employees, which may also make employees reluctant to use the leave.

Passage of the FMLA generated enormous publicity, with many members of

Congress pointing out how "family friendly" the act was. But it is useful to put U.S. maternity leave policy into perspective. The United States is still the only industrialized country in the world that does not offer paid maternity leave and fails to make maternity leave a mandatory policy of all employers (it is restricted only to companies who employ over fifty employees). Further, every European country grants longer maternity leave than outlined in the FMLA, with many allowing several months (usually up to six) of extensions; the average maternity leave across industrialized countries in the world is sixteen weeks compared to the twelve in the FMLA. Finally, these countries always provide leave at least one month before the birth of a child.

In the fall of 2002, California became the first state to offer paid family leave to care for either a new child or an ailing relative. It is the most expansive family benefit program in the nation. Any worker can take up to six weeks of paid leave to cope with a "family emergency." The benefit is paid solely out of employee contributions, and the payout is capped at just under $800 per week.

In 2003, the Supreme Court held in *Nevada Department of Human Resources v. Hibbs* that states are not immune from lawsuits for violations of federal laws. In this case, Hibbs was an employee of Nevada's Human Resource Department and was fired after seeking leave in order to care for his sick spouse. He alleged that his firing violated the FMLA; previous decisions gave states immunity from lawsuits for violating congressional statutes like the Americans with Disabilities Act (ADA) and the FMLA. But in a surprise move, the Court allowed a higher level of scrutiny in claims regarding violations of FMLA; if a state allegedly violates the ADA the laws enjoy little scrutiny, but for violations of the FMLA, the courts are now forced to apply an intermediate level of scrutiny to the gender discrimination claim.

See also Equal Employment Opportunity Commission (EEOC); *Geduldig v. Aiello; General Electric v. Gilbert;* Intermediate Scrutiny Standard; Pregnancy; Pregnancy Discrimination Act (PDA).

Reference Schwarts, Robert M. 2001. *The FMLA Handbook: A Union Guide to the Family and Medical Leave Act.* Cambridge, MA: Work Rights Press.

Faragher v. City of Boca Raton (1998)

In *Faragher v. City of Boca Raton,* the Court examined again the employer liability issue in sexual harassment claims. This decision was handed down the same year as three other cases involving sexual harassment (see *Burlington Industries v. Ellerth; Gebser v. Lago Vista Independent School District; Oncale v. Sundowner Offshore Services, Inc.*).

Faragher was employed as a lifeguard by the city of Boca Raton, Florida, and claimed she had been subjected to a hostile environment at a remote location. The city asserted that it could not be held responsible because the alleged harassment was not reported to supervisors at city hall. The Court held that the dichotomy of quid pro quo and hostile work environment sexual harassment was of little use in assessing employer liability. Instead, it focused on whether supervisory power was used to carry out the harassment. The Court then articulated a new test: generally, an employer is liable to a victimized employee for sexual harassment if that harassment was carried out by any supervisor with authority over the employee. An employer is free from liability only if it can prove that (1) it exercised reasonable care to prevent and correct promptly any sexually harassing behavior and (2) the employee failed to take advantage of any preventive or corrective opportunities provided by the employer to avoid the harassment. So an employer is not held responsible for sexual harassment claims if it has an antiharassment policy and the employee had no reason for failing to utilize it. If the employee reasonably feared retaliation for coming forward, however, the employer would not be able to use this defense. In *Faragher* the city had failed to provide employees with preventative or corrective opportunities to prevent sexual harassment.

Both critics and defenders of sexual harassment policies were supportive of this decision. Employers could now institute sexual harassment policies and be free from liability for employees making claims of harassment. Employees were satisfied that the burden of proof for sexual harassment claims rested on the employers and not the employees themselves. Additionally, supporters of the case (and the other cases decided the same year) claimed that the Court's new framework for resolving sexual harassment complaints would have the unintended benefit not only of encouraging employers to adopt sexual harassment policies but also of deterring would-be harassers in the workplace.

> *See also* Burlington Industries v. Ellerth; Civil Rights Act; Equal Employment Opportunity Commission (EEOC); *Gebser v. Lago Vista Independent School District; Meritor Savings Bank v. Vinson; Oncale v. Sundowner Offshore Services;* Sexual Harassment.

Frank v. Ivy Club (1990)

Sally Frank filed a complain against Princeton University and three male-only eating clubs associated with the university, alleging they had discriminated against her on the basis of gender by not granting her membership while she was a student in 1979. She asserted that these clubs were "public accommodations" because they functioned as "arms of Princeton" and were thus prevented from discriminating against her under both state and federal discrimination laws (specifically the Civil Rights Act). The clubs argued that they were "bona fide private clubs" and therefore exempt from federal law that prohibited discrimination. Princeton denied that the clubs were part of the university.

An appellate court ruled that the eating clubs' special relationship with Princeton deprived those clubs of exempt status and that the clubs' bylaws and policies against admission of women violated state antidiscrimination law. There was no appeal of this ruling.

Fullilove v. Klutznick (1980)

In *Fullilove v. Klutznick,* the Court treated with deference a federal set-aside program (a program granting preferential treatment to racial minorities in the award of public funds or licenses for public works) and helped define the outlines of government affirmative action programs. The case involved a federal program for local public works projects in New York State under which 10 percent of funds had to be spent on businesses owned or controlled by members of specified minority groups. Nonminority construction contractors and heating, ventilation, and air conditioning workers brought suit against the administrator of the project.

In passing laws such as this one, the Court said, Congress may decide that the "prospective elimination of barriers to minority firms" (e.g., giving a percentage of grants to minority-controlled businesses) allows minorities access to public contracting opportunities and ensures the elimination of any further barriers to participation in federal grant monies.

> *See also* Affirmative Action; Civil Rights Act; Equal Employment Opportunity Commission (EEOC).

Gebser v. Lago Vista Independent School District (1998)

In *Gebser v. Lago Vista Independent School District,* in one of four sexual harassment cases decided by the Court in the same year, the Court examined the harm of sexual harassment to students. Star Gebser was a junior high school student when her favorite teacher began a campaign of sexual innuendo and provocation, culminating in a yearlong "affair" that was later prosecuted as statutory rape. When the relationship between Gebser and her teacher was discovered by a local law enforcement authority, the teacher was immediately fired. But Gebser sued under Title IX, claiming she did not feel that she could tell anyone, not even her parents, and did not know to whom at the school she could report the incidents.

Although Title IX is best known for its challenges to school sports programs that provide more benefits to male athletes than female athletes, it also requires educational institutions that receive federal financial assistance to provide education that is free from sex discrimination. Until 1992, if an institution engaged in discriminatory practices, federal financial aid could be withdrawn. But the Court ruled in *Franklin v. Gwinnett County Public Schools* that year that Title IX allowed monetary damages as well for victims of sex discrimination in schools. Franklin was assaulted by her teacher and school officials failed to intervene. She was able to use the Title VII liability standard (that the employer—the school—knew or should have known that the discrimination was occurring) in her Title IX case.

The most important distinction between Title VII and Title IX claims rests on the definition of an employer's agent. In Title VII cases, for example, an employer is "any agent" but in Title IX cases a student who has been harassed would have to inform an official who has the authority to address alleged discrimination and institute corrective measures of the harassment, and that official would have to exhibit deliberate indifference in failing to respond to the discrimination. Thus, the burden is much higher for a plaintiff in Title IX cases than it is in Title VII cases. In this case, in a 5–4 decision written by Justice O'Connor, the Court held that absent a clear directive from Congress, this school district could not be held liable for sexual harassment since there was no official with knowledge of the alleged harassment who exhibited "deliberate indifference" to the claim.

The practical impact of the decision was significant. In many school districts, even school principals do not have authority to take corrective action for alleged harassment of a student, and harassed students may be required to report harassment to the local school board. Further, the decision creates a disincentive for school districts to take steps to discover harassment, since they can avoid liability through an "ostrich defense," or by claiming they were not aware of the harassment. The dissenting justices argued that the Court's approach "thwarts the purposes of Title IX." Other critics called later for congressional response that would make it easier for students to pursue harassment claims from the individual school and not the school district.

See also *Burlington Industries v. Ellerth*; Civil Rights Act; Equal Employment Opportunity Commission (EEOC); *Faragher v. City of Boca Raton*; *Oncale v. Sundowner Offshore Services*; Sexual Harassment; Title IX.

General Electric v. Gilbert (1976)

General Electric v. Gilbert addressed the question of whether pregnancy constituted a sex-based classification of women that is prohibited under Title VII of the Civil Rights Act. In *Geduldig v. Aiello* (1974), the Court had allowed pregnancy benefits to be excluded in employment disability insurance programs. In *General Electric v. Gilbert* the Court ruled that pregnancy could also be excluded from disability benefit plans because the exclusion, again, was "not a gender-based discrimination" strategy. This case was essentially overturned upon passage of the Pregnancy Discrimination Act in 1978.

See also Civil Rights Act; Family and Medical Leave Act (FMLA); *Geduldig v. Aiello*; Maternity Leave; Pregnancy Discrimination Act (PDA); *United Auto Workers v. Johnson Controls*.

Glass Ceiling

The glass ceiling is a set of "artificial barriers based upon attitudinal or organizational bias that prevents qualified minorities and women from advancing into mid- and senior-management positions." The term does not refer to the failure to hire minorities or women but rather the failure to promote them to senior positions and pay them accordingly.

In 1991 the U.S. Department of Labor issued the "Glass Ceiling Report," which found that there was truly a level beyond which few minorities and women had advanced. It also found that the ceiling varied according to function and salary level; that is, although the barrier existed at lower levels of employment, the higher the position, the stronger the barrier. For example, only 3 to 5 percent of senior management positions are currently held by women, and less than 7 percent of the seats on corporate boards of directors were held by women in 1994.

Minorities tend to plateau at a level lower even than women. Although 23 percent of the female workforce is made up of women of color, only 15 percent of female managers are members of minority groups. And of the female senior managers in Fortune 1000 and Fortune 500 companies in 1992, 10 percent were white women, 2 percent were African American women, less than 2 percent were Asian American women, and less than 1 percent were Latinas.

Business leaders claim that women and minorities do not face a glass ceiling because of discriminatory practices by employers but because these groups congregate in jobs that do not provide pipelines to upper management. They tend to take positions related to human resources, research, or administration rather than sales and production, the positions considered the path to the executive suite. But it has been difficult to assess the accuracy of this argument, since there have been no centralized means to track developmental opportunities and credential-building experiences for employ-ees. Training programs, developmental job rotations, and committee assignments help to ensure that all qualified employees are given equal consideration for promotion, but it is unclear whether women and minorities are actually excluded from these opportunities. Since 1994, however, many companies began not only to use affirmative action programs but also to keep more adequate records concerning recruitment or development for promotion. Further, many companies began to hold higher-level managers responsible for eradicating the glass ceiling.

As a result, there are signs of improvement. For example, the percentage of women architects rose from 3 percent in 1972 to nearly 17 percent in 1996, and the percentage of women physicians rose from 10 percent to 26 percent during the same period. Affirmative action programs have certainly helped this increase, particularly with regard to set-aside programs for women small-business owners. In 1972, before most affirmative action programs were in place, there were 402,000 women business owners in the United States; by 1996 that number had jumped to 7.95 million. But even with the growth in numbers of women in professional positions, the wage gap persists. The General Accounting Office points to a continuing wage gap between full-time women and men wage earners of 76 percent. As mentioned, one reason may be that male and female managers tend to work in different occupations and industries. Personnel or human relations managers are more likely to be men, as are managers in marketing, advertising, and public relations. Women tend to be administrators in education and related fields that traditionally pay less.

Those who deny the existence of a glass ceiling say that women tend to take time off from their full-time jobs to have children, whereas men are less likely to do so. The gap between male and female workers is indeed widest between those who are parents and those who are not. But women managers tend to have fewer children than their male counterparts; nearly 60 percent of male managers have children in the home, compared to little more than 40 percent of female managers.

> *See also* Affirmative Action; Comparable Worth; Equal Employment Opportunity Commission (EEOC); Equal Pay Act; Feminism; *Glenn, Johns and Nugent v. General Motors Corporation; Washington v. Gunther.*
> *References* Linda Wirth. 2001. *Breaking through the Glass Ceiling: Women in Management.* Washington, DC: The Brookings Institution; C. J. Wyckoff. 1995. *Glass Ceiling.* Mercer Island, WA: Goodfellow Press.

Glenn, Johns and Nugent v. General Motors Corporation, Saginaw Steering Gear Division (1988)

Sheila Glenn, Patricia Johns, and Robbie Nugent filed suit against General Motors Corporation (GM) and its Saginaw Steering Gear Division, alleging violation of the Equal Pay Act. The federal district court in Alabama found that gender discrimination had occurred because there was a practice of pay disparity. That court found that the three plaintiffs were hired for less pay than all their male coworkers in the same section of the company hired near the same time.

GM argued that the women were paid less simply because the positions they held after their initial hire were not the same as those held by their male counterparts, which required different skills. The court rejected this distinction. For cases such as this, once a prima facie case of pay discrimination has been established, it is up to the employer to prove that the difference in pay was justified by one of the four exceptions in the Equal Pay Act—that is, that the pay disparity was necessary because of either a seniority system, a merit system, a system that measured earnings by quantity or quality of production, or a differential based on any factor other than sex. GM sought to jus-

tify that the disparity was grounded in a factor other than sex by presenting evidence that Nugent had been hired "off the street" and Glenn and Johns had transferred from their salaried secretarial positions. In contrast, their male counterparts had transferred from hourly wage jobs. In an attempt to encourage employees to move out of hourly wage jobs and into salaried jobs, GM had maintained a long-standing, unwritten, corporate-wide policy against requiring an employee to take a cut in pay in order to make such a transfer. Thus, GM argued, its policy constituted a factor other than sex that legitimated the pay disparity.

The district court did not agree. GM's salary "policy" was, in fact, not a policy at all but merely one aspect of a practice. The company simply paid these employees what was necessary to entice them to accept the employment. And historically, companies like GM hire women at lower starting salaries. Thus, the three female employees were paid less money than their male counterparts "for equal work without justification."

GM appealed the decision, and the appellate court affirmed the lower court's holding. The company argued that prior salary of an employee can be a factor other than sex to justify pay disparity. But the appellate court held that this exception applies when the disparity results from unique characteristics of the same job, including an individual's experience, training, or ability or from "special exigent" circumstances connected with the business. GM failed to demonstrate that the pay disparity here resulted from any of these reasons. GM additionally argued that the statute of limitations had been exceeded so the plaintiffs should not have been allowed to file their action in the first place. But the appellate court held that causes of action can be barred if not filed in a timely manner except in cases where willful violations of the law occurred. In this case, GM's actions were willful, so the suit was allowed. Further, GM showed reckless disregard for employees in seeking to rely on the market force theory, a theory long discredited by the Supreme Court.

Damages under the Equal Pay Act may be recovered if an employer is found to have violated the act. The lower court initially held that GM had violated the act, and although individual GM officials may have believed in good faith that GM had adopted a transfer pay policy, the company lacked reasonable grounds to support a belief that its acts were in conformity with the law. The appellate court also affirmed this holding.

> See also Civil Rights Act; Comparable Worth; Equal Pay Act; Glass Ceiling; Washington v. Gunther.

Harris v. Forklift Systems, Inc. (1993)

In *Harris v. Forklift Systems, Inc.*, the Supreme Court strongly endorsed the rights of sexual harassment victims to bring claims against their employers by reaffirming and clarifying the standard necessary to prevail in such cases. Brought under Title VII of the Civil Rights Act (which prohibits discrimination with respect to the conditions of employment), this case asked the Court to decide the following fundamental question pertaining to sexual harassment suits: Is a plaintiff in a sexual harassment case also required to prove that she suffered severe psychological injury because she was offended by harassing conduct? The Court held that in order to show violation of Title VII claims, the work environment must be hostile; it is not necessary for the environment to be psychologically injurious. This case further defined sexual harassment law established in the 1986 case of *Meritor Savings Bank v. Vinson,* in which the Court ruled that to demonstrate hostile environment the victim need not show direct economic injury but only that the employer had actual knowledge of the harassment and failed to take reasonable action to correct the situation.

As a manager at the Tennessee-based Forklift Systems, Inc., Teresa Harris was often insulted by the company president,

Charles Hardy, because of her gender and was made the target of unwanted sexual innuendo. At one time Hardy announced in the presence of other employees that it was time for the two of them to go to the local Holiday Inn to negotiate her raise. In 1987 Harris complained to Hardy, and he promised to stop the offensive behavior. Shortly thereafter, however, he again made lewd comments in front of other employees and customers. Harris resigned from her job and filed a discrimination suit against the company, alleging that she had been treated differently than the male managers in terms of salary and benefits and by being subjected to discriminatory and sexist conduct. She claimed that she suffered from extreme anxiety, cried frequently, and began drinking heavily when not working.

In the lower Tennessee court, the company demonstrated that Harris and her husband had socialized with Hardy and his wife. The company also offered testimony by other female employees that they were not offended by Hardy's sexual comments and that they were not aware that Harris was offended. But Harris was able to show that Hardy sought to manufacture documentation to justify terminating Harris after she had left the company and filed charges. This court found that Hardy was "a vulgar man and demean[ed] the female employees at his workplace" and that Harris was "the object of a continuing pattern of sex-based derogatory conduct from Hardy." The court, however, concluded that Harris "was not able to prove that Hardy's conduct was so severe as to create a hostile work environment for that plaintiff ... nor was able to show that she was treated disparately as to other terms or conditions of employment." The court dismissed Harris's Title VII claim because she had not suffered injury.

The U.S. District Court dismissed Harris's claim and the court of appeals affirmed the dismissal. In her appeal to the Supreme Court, Harris argued that the dismissal of her case was based on a subjective, psychological harm test rather than the more objective "reasonable person" test. Harris contended that based on the Court's prior decision in *Meritor Savings Bank v. Vinson*, psychological harm is irrelevant in determining if offensive sexual conduct is actionable. The company argued that Hardy's conduct toward Harris would not have affected the performance of a reasonable person and that therefore the test used by the lower courts was objective.

The Court in *Meritor* had established that a plaintiff in a hostile work environment case had to show only that the alleged sexual conduct was "sufficiently severe or pervasive to alter the conditions of [the victim's] employment and create an abusive working environment." The Court had not specified the elements that constituted hostile work environment sexual harassment. As a result, lower courts had struggled with delineating the specific requirements for proving hostile work environment; particularly difficult was determining whether to apply a subjective or objective test or both. Some courts had adopted the subjective approach, focusing on the impact of the allegedly offensive conduct on the plaintiff. Other courts took a more objective approach and focused on whether a reasonable person would find the environment to be abusive.

The Court in *Harris* applied both the objective and subjective tests, thereby resolving the debate on the issue. Harris's contention was that by applying a subjective standard, she could prevail without proof of either impact on work performance or psychological injury caused by harassment. She argued that proof of offensive conduct should be sufficient to establish a harassment claim. The Court rejected her argument and refused to make actionable "any conduct that is merely offensive." But the Court also refused to require proof that the conduct caused "tangible psychological injury" or had an impact on work performance, noting that "Title VII comes into

play before the harassing conduct leads to a nervous breakdown." Further, the Court ruled that whether a hostile or abusive work environment exists and violates Title VII could be determined by looking at numerous factors, including the impact the conduct has on an employee's psychological well-being, the frequency and severity of the conduct, whether the conduct was physically threatening, whether it was merely an offensive utterance, and whether it unreasonably interfered with the employee's work performance.

The Court's approach raises two problems. First, the test articulated by the Court lacks clarity. The list of circumstances to be considered is not exhaustive, and the range of conduct that would be unlawful is not defined by example or guidelines. In his concurring opinion, Justice Antonin Scalia raised this point, saying that the decision "lets virtually unguided juries decide whether sex-related conduct . . . is egregious enough to warrant an award of damages." Second, the Court adopted the "reasonable person" standard as opposed to a "reasonable victim" or "reasonable woman" standard; that is, the standard to be used in hostile work environment cases highlights the conduct of the alleged harasser and requires an evaluation of whether a reasonable person would find the conduct had created an intimidating, hostile, or offensive working environment. But several scholars argue that the reasonable person standard may not be adequate in achieving effective enforcement of Title VII in sexual harassment cases. When societal norms in a certain locality tolerate discriminatory conduct it does not necessarily make the conduct acceptable. As such, the application of a reasonable person standard could lead to the sanctioning of unlawful conduct. Some lower courts have explicitly rejected a standard based solely on societal norms, adopting a "reasonable woman" standard in determining whether a hostile work environment exists.

The facts of the case, as presented by Harris, demonstrate the difficulty in using a reasonable person test versus using a reasonable woman or victim test. The reasonable person test usually relies on some tangible detriment experienced by the victim because of the harasser's conduct. Harris was offended by Hardy's conduct, but his conduct did not interfere with her performance at work, and she voluntarily left her job. As a result, while the Harris decision resolved some of the legal issues pertaining to hostile work environment, it did not provide detailed guidelines concerning workplace conduct. Its impact will most likely not be significant in guiding employees in their behavior or assisting employers in judging what sort of behavior is acceptable and what is unlawful.

> *See also* Civil Rights Act; Equal Employment Opportunity Commission (EEOC); *Meritor Savings Bank v. Vinson; Oncale v. Sundowner Offshore Services;* Sexual Harassment.

Hill, Anita (1956–)

Born in Lone Tree, Oklahoma, in 1956, Anita Hill received her law degree from Yale, worked at the Equal Employment Opportunity Commission (EEOC), and later taught law at the University of Oklahoma. She came to national attention in 1991 during the Senate confirmation hearings of Clarence Thomas's nomination to the Supreme Court. Although Judge Thomas was confirmed, the controversy surrounding his appointment brought sexual harassment to the spotlight.

Thomas was nominated by President George Bush to replace Justice Thurgood Marshall, the first African American to sit on the Court. Thomas had been a commissioner at the EEOC and was known as a prominent black conservative. Anita Hill was an attorney working directly for Thomas for several years. But during the background investigation prior to the Senate confirmation vote, the media reported that Hill had accused Thomas of sexual ha-

Anita Hill (Center for the American Woman and Politics)

rassment to friends. She had made no claim of the harassment, however.

The Senate Judiciary Committee called Thomas, Hill, and several other witnesses to testify on the harassment allegations. Hill claimed before the Senate that during her tenure under Thomas, he had made vulgar remarks and described to her hard-core pornographic films he had seen. Although his conduct made her uncomfortable, she did not come forward to file an official claim of sexual harassment, an assertion many found implausible considering that her job with the EEOC included enforcement of sexual harassment law. Her testimony was broadcast live around the world, and reactions to Hill and her story were highly polarized. Men were more likely to believe she was a liar and mentally unstable, whereas women tended to view her as a martyr and found her testimony before the contentious, all-male Senate committee disturbing largely because the members grilled her not only about the graphic details of the alleged harassment but also about her personal life. Thomas denied Hill's allegations and called the hearings a "high-tech lynching for uppity blacks."

Thomas's confirmation vote was 52–48, the smallest margin of approval for a Supreme Court justice in more than 100 years. Following the confirmation battle, in the 1992 elections, women voted more women into state and federal office than at any other time in American history. Eleven women won Senate seats and twenty-four won House seats. Further, the EEOC reported a 50 percent increase in complaints filed for sexual harassment in the year following Hill's testimony, and awards for victims of harassment went from $2 million to $28 million.

Hill left her law professorship in 1996, saying the publicity had become too onerous. She began speaking around the country and in 1998 published *Speaking Truth to Power,* her memoir about the Thomas hearings.

> *See also* Equal Employment Opportunity
>   Commission (EEOC); Sexual Harassment.
> *References* Anita Hill. 1998. *Speaking Truth to*
>   *Power.* New York: Anchor Books; Jane
>   Mayer and Jill Abramson. 1994. *Strange*
>   *Justice: The Selling of Clarence Thomas.* New
>   York: Houghton-Mifflin.

Hodgson v. Robert Hall Clothes (1973)

The U.S. secretary of labor brought action against Robert Hall Clothes in 1966, claiming that company discriminated against saleswomen on the basis of sex because it compensated them less than male employees for equal work. Only women were permitted to work in the women's sections and only men were permitted to work in men's sections, yet the men were receiving higher salaries. The company claimed that it was an economic benefit for it to have only men working in the men's section, which was why employees in that section were paid more. Largely because the company demonstrated that for every year of the store's operation, the men's department was substantially more profitable than the women's department, the courts found its method of determining salaries was not discriminatory.

Dolores Huerta, cofounder of the United Farmworkers of America, with raspberry worker Valentin Leon. (Associated Press/AP)

> *See also* Equal Pay Act; Fourteenth
>   Amendment.

Huerta, Dolores (1930–)

Born in New Mexico to a miner and union activist, Dolores Huerta worked in her family's restaurant and hotel before receiving a teaching degree and having eleven children. She became a lobbyist for farmworkers in California, helping to remove citizenship requirements from public assistance programs, allow people to vote as well as take driver's license examinations in Spanish, and secure disability insurance for farmworkers.

Huerta met Cesar Chavez in 1962, and together they organized farmworkers into the National Farm Workers Association (NFWA), which later became the United Farm Workers of America, AFL-CIO (UFW). She and Chavez lobbied for higher wages for grape growers in California; partly as a result, 5,000 grape workers walked off their jobs in the great Delano grape strike in 1965 and stayed on strike for five years until wages were raised. As a well-known spokesperson for the UFW, she campaigned for Robert F. Kennedy in the 1968 presidential primary. The UFW turned its energy to consumer boycotts of lettuce and Gallo wines; it was so successful that California passed the Agricultural Labor Relations Act, granting farmworkers the right to collectively organize for better wages. Huerta continues as the first vice-president emerita of the UFW.

Johnson v. Transportation (1987)

With *Johnson v. Transportation* the first affirmative action program directly involving women reached the Supreme Court. The Court upheld the promotion of a woman over a marginally more qualified male. In the earlier case of *United Steelworkers v. Weber* (1979), the Court had held that Title VII does not prohibit voluntary race-conscious affirmative action where it is necessary "to eliminate conspicuous racial imbalance in traditionally segregated job categories." In *Johnson* the Court expanded the concept to include voluntary affirmative action where it is necessary to eliminate a "manifest imbalance that reflect[s] underrepresentation of women in 'traditionally segregated job categories.'" The transportation agency of a California county adopted a temporary affirmative action plan that considered gender as a factor in promoting (within traditionally segregated job categories) women and members of racial minority groups who had previously been underrepresented. At the time the plan was adopted, women constituted 76 percent of the office and clerical employees but zero percent of its skilled workers. The program did not set aside quotas for hiring women and minority workers; rather, it established annual goals to promote "statistically measurable yearly improvement" in diversifying their workforce.

When a dispatcher job came open, a female with a score of 73 on the entrance exam was hired over two men who scored a 75. The men sued, but the Court held the agency had acted in compliance with Title VII. The dissenters (William Rehnquist, Antonin Scalia, and Byron White) argued that affirmative actions programs violated the Equal Protection Clause of the Fourteenth Amendment and put males at a disadvantage. But the majority held that the county was free to undertake affirmative action programs "to remedy the effects of past practices and to permit attainment of an equitable representation of minorities, women and handicapped persons." The county was merely trying to correct the imbalance of women in skilled jobs and so had established flexible promotional goals recognizing gender as one of several factors to be considered in promotions. Further, the Court concluded that the plan was temporary and intended simply to attain rather than maintain a diversified workforce; as such, it did not impose a complete ban on male employees' opportunities for advancement.

> *See also* Affirmative Action.
> *References* Rubio, Philip F. 2001. *A History of Affirmative Action, 1619–2000.* Jackson: University of Mississippi Press; Skrentny, John David. 2001. *The Ironies of Affirmative Action: Politics, Culture, and Justice in America.* Chicago: University of Chicago Press; Smith, James P., and Finis Welch. 1984. "Affirmative Action and Labor Markets." *Journal of Labor Economics* (April): 2.

Lindahl v. Air France (1991)

In *Lindahl v. Air France,* a courts of appeals ruled that a company could not make promotion decisions on the basis of stereotypical images of men and women. Michelle Lindahl had worked as a customer promotion agent in an agency of Air France that largely provided assistance to the sales representatives who did fieldwork. When Lindahl was denied a promotion to senior customer promotion agent, she sued, arguing that she did not receive the job because of her gender.

The appeals court held that decisions regarding Lindahl's promotion were not based on leadership abilities but rather on sexist stereotypes—specifically, the myth that women do not make good leaders because they are too "emotional." The manager in charge of making promotions testified that he believed that female candidates get "nervous" and "easily upset [and lose] control." Ironically, this manager also said Lindahl tended "not to back away from a situation, to take hold immediately of the situation, to attack the situation right away, to stay cool throughout the whole process," suggesting that he found her aggressive.

See also Equal Employment Opportunity Commission (EEOC).

Maternity Leave

In 1908, in *Muller v. Oregon*, the Court emphasized a woman's "maternal functions" and held that a state could severely restrict pregnant women's work hours in the interest of protecting women and their families. Of course, protective legislation like this also limited the money that women could bring home to their families, and feminist groups largely opposed such laws. But at this time few women worked outside the home. By the 1990s more than one-half of mothers of preschool children worked outside the home. The 1970s saw the greatest growth in mothers working outside the home, and it was during this decade that several cases defining the parameters in which employers could organize pregnant workers were decided. The Court ruled in 1974 in *Cleveland Board of Education v. La-Fleur* that employers could not fire pregnant workers or impose mandatory maternity leaves. Later that year (in *Geduldig v. Aiello*) and in 1976 (in *General Electric v. Gilbert*), the Court ruled that employee health insurance plans that excluded pregnancy coverage did not violate the Constitution. By distinguishing between pregnant employees (who were women) and nonpregnant employees, employers were simply distinguishing between employees who voluntarily changed their status and those who did not; pregnancy, unlike other disabilities, was a matter of choice.

In 1978 Congress passed the Pregnancy Discrimination Act, which prevented em-

Murphy Brown (Candice Bergen) sparked a national controversy when she chose to combine single motherhood with her career as a reporter. (Bettmann/Corbis)

ployers from refusing to hire a pregnant woman, terminating her employment upon pregnancy, or compelling her to take maternity leave. In essence, this act required employers to treat pregnancy in the same manner as any other temporary disability and allowed pregnant workers to sue for violations under Title VII of the Civil Rights Act. The Pregnancy Discrimination Act was passed largely in response to the Court's decisions in *Geduldig* and *Gilbert* and essentially negated both decisions. It was controversial, however, as critics contended that pregnancy should not be treated as any other physical condition; although it may be similar to other conditions that temporarily disable workers, breast-feeding, bonding, and care after the birth of a child are not like other temporary ailments or disabilities protected under federal law.

In 1987, the Court ruled on the issue of maternity leave in *California Federal Savings and Loan Association v. Guerra.* California had passed the Fair Employment and Housing Act, which required employers to grant at least four months' unpaid "pregnancy disability leave"; the California Federal Savings and Loan Association refused to comply with the state law because, it argued, the law violated the Title VII prohibition against sex discrimination by treating men and women differently. The California law was extremely divisive, and feminists could not agree whether it would help or hurt pregnant workers. Critics feared the law would deter employers from hiring all women of childbearing age, whereas supporters claimed it would protect female workers from discrimination. The Court found the state law did not conflict with the Civil Rights Act; both laws simply "guarantee[d] women the basic right to participate fully and equally in the workforce, without denying them the fundamental right to full participation in family life."

The Court has never validated arguments that physical capacity is diminished during pregnancy. Employment disability insurance programs that exclude pregnancy benefits are valid, for example. Yet the Court has overturned a state's denial of unemployment compensation to women in the last months before birth and the first six weeks after birth of a child. Any claims against policies regarding maternity leave are examined under the rational basis test (and not the intermediate scrutiny standard).

The United States is quite different from other industrialized countries in allowing for maternity leave. The federal Family and Medical Leave Act (FMLA) allows only for unpaid maternity leave for both parents for twelve weeks. Other industrialized countries provide paid leave—from eight weeks (in Switzerland) to twenty weeks (in Italy) following the birth of a child. These countries also offer maternity leave to all new mothers, whether they are employed in the private or the public sphere. The FMLA has strict guidelines limiting the number of employers who are subject to federal mandates on maternity leave.

> *See also* California Federal Savings and Loan Association v. Guerra; Civil Rights Act; Family and Medical Leave Act (FMLA); Geduldig v. Aiello; General Electric v. Gilbert.

Meritor Savings Bank v. Vinson (1986)

With *Meritor Savings Bank v. Vinson,* the Supreme Court established the hostile or abusive work environment standard in sexual harassment suits and allowed such suits to be filed as such under Title VII of the Civil Rights Act. Michelle Vinson had worked at Meritor Savings Bank for four years. She had requested sick leave in September 1978, and in November of that year the bank discharged her for excessive use of that leave. She filed suit claiming she had been terminated because of her gender, a violation of Title VII of the Civil Rights Act.

Vinson claimed she was subjected to a hostile work environment under her supervisor, Taylor. She received various promotions over the years and said that although Taylor had not terminated her employment, he had fondled her publicly and made sexual demands upon her, forcing her to acquiesce for fear she would lose her job. Vinson admitted that she had had intercourse with Taylor approximately forty or fifty times while she was employed at the bank. A lower court ruled that her participation in any sexual conduct over such a long time frame was voluntary and had nothing to do with her continued employment at the bank; thus, Vinson was not subject to sexual harassment. But Vinson further argued that Taylor's sexual advances were "unwelcome" because she feared that her refusal would result in her losing her job. Taylor denied that he had had any sexual relationship with Vinson during her employment at the bank.

The Supreme Court upheld Vinson's claim, ruling that she had been subjected to a hostile and abusive work environment. Further, proof of a hostile work environment does not demand a tangible financial detriment to a party; Vinson did not have to be fired from her job and suffer the economic penalties that went along with her termination. It was enough that during the course of her work, she was subjected to a hostile environment. Additionally, the fact that any sexual relations between the parties was "voluntary," in that Vinson was not forced to participate against her will, is not a defense to a sexual harassment suit under Title VII. In this case it was clear that Vinson feared she would be fired if she refused, which made her part in the relationship involuntary. And finally, a written sexual harassment policy does not prevent employers from being liable for hostile work environment claims; an employer may, however, use evidence of an employee's "provocative clothing or language" in determining whether or not sexual advances were welcome.

See also *Alexander v. Yale University;* Civil
Rights Act; Sexual Harassment.

Moody et al. v. Albermarle Paper Company, Halifax Local No. 425, United Papermakers and Paperworkers, AFL-CIO (1975)

Several black employees in North Carolina brought suit against their employer for violating Title VII of the Civil Rights Act of 1964. The employees argued that the plant's seniority system and the company's program of employment testing had "locked" black employees in lower-paying job classifications, and they demanded back pay. A lower trial court ordered the company to change the seniority system but refused to order back pay for the employees because the company's violation of Title VII was not done in "bad faith," and the employees had failed to ask for back pay until five years after their complaint was filed. Finally, the company's testing program may have had a disproportionate adverse impact on blacks but had undergone validation studies so was valid.

The employees appealed the back pay issue, as well as the employment test issue. The court of appeals reversed the trial court's decision, finding that when unlawful discrimination occurs, back pay should not be denied if it is reasonable to attain the purposes Congress intended in enacting Title VII, that is, as a way of eliminating discrimination. "Good intent or absence of discriminatory intent" was not needed for employees to get back pay. Further, the employees' tardiness in making back pay demands had no relevance. According to a former decision by the Supreme Court, the appellate court held, the guidelines by the Equal Employment Opportunity Commission (EEOC) for employers using validation studies states that the studies must be "predictive of or significantly correlated with important elements of work behavior which comprise or are relevant to the job or jobs for which candidates are being evaluated." Using this standard, the court held, the company's studies were invalid because they compared test scores with subjective supervisory rankings, affording no means of knowing what job performance criteria the supervisors were considering. Further, the fact that the employees working at the top of the company scored well on a test does not necessarily mean that the test accurately measures the qualifications of new workers entering lower-level jobs. Finally, the studies dealt only with experienced white workers, but the tests themselves were given to new job applicants, who were younger, largely inexperienced, and in many instances nonwhite.

The Supreme Court accepted the case for review and in an opinion by Justice Potter Stewart (signed by William O. Douglas, William Brennan, Byron White, Thurgood Marshall, and William Rehnquist) held that the case raised two distinct issues of Title VII. First, if an employee loses the opportunity to earn wages because an employer has engaged in an unlawful discriminatory employment practice, what standards should the courts follow in deciding whether to award or deny back pay? And second, what must an employer show to establish that pre-employment tests were racially discriminatory in effect, though not in intent?

One element the Court took into account was that the employees brought suit with the EEOC in 1966 and at that time assured the court that their suit involved no claim for any monetary award. It was not until 1970 that the employees asked for back pay. Congress gave courts the power to award back pay in discrimination cases. If an employer favors one race over another and is punished only with the threat of an injunctive order (demanding the practice of racism cease), there is little incentive for the employer to end discrimination. It is only the reasonably certain prospect of paying back wages that "provides the spur or catalyst which causes employers and unions to self-examine and to self-evaluate their employment practices and to endeavor to eliminate, so far as possible, the last vestiges of an unfortunate and ignominious page in this country's history."

One of the main purposes of Title VII is to make persons whole for injuries suffered on account of unlawful employment discrimination. Where racial discrimination is concerned, "the [district] court has not merely the power but the duty to render a decree which will so far as possible eliminate the discriminatory effects of the past as well as bar like discrimination in the future." Although the lower trial court denied back pay because the company's breach of Title VII had not been in "bad faith," this was insufficient reasoning. If back pay were awarded only upon a showing of bad faith—that an employer has maintained a practice that is known to be illegal or of highly questionable legality—the remedy would become a punishment for moral turpitude rather than a compensation for worker's injuries. To condition the awarding of back pay on a showing of bad faith would be to open an enormous chasm between injunctive and back

pay relief under Title VII. The Court went on to hold that there was nothing on the face of the statute or in its legislative history that justifies the creation of drastic and categorical distinction between those two remedies.

In *Griggs v. Duke Power Company* (1971), the Court had unanimously held that Title VII forbids the use of employment tests that are discriminatory in effect unless the employer meets "the burden of showing that any given requirement [has] . . . a manifest relationship to the employment in question." If the employer can show that the tests are job related, it is then up to the employee to show that other tests, without a similarly undesirable racial effect, would also serve the employer's legitimate interest in "efficient and trustworthy workmanship." Such a showing would be evidence that the employer was using its tests merely as a "pretext" for discrimination. The Supreme Court sent the case back to the trial court to determine how tests should be administered in the future.

See also Disparate Impact; Equal Employment Opportunity Commission (EEOC).

9to5, National Association of Working Women

Ellen Bravo directs 9to5, National Association of Working Women, dedicated to improving conditions for women in the workplace. The organization works predominantly with nonmanagement employees in adopting policies for the workplace that will help end poverty and allow female workers to spend more time with their families. The organization also offers women information on sexual harassment, pay discrimination, family leave, pregnancy discrimination, and workplace violations of civil rights laws. Since its passage in 1993, 9to5 has been increasingly active in lobbying to expand the Family and Medical Leave Act (FMLA). Although the FMLA does allow workers to take leave to care for sick family members or new children, it is not paid leave, and lower-income workers can rarely take advantage of it. The organization was extremely successful in California in 2003 in establishing the first state paid family leave bill. Additionally, the group has been responsible for focusing attention on establishing a new minimum labor standard that requires employers to offer at least seven days annual paid sick leave that workers may use for any reason.

According to 9to5, there is an increasing need to focus on women workers not only because of the difficulties they face in the workplace but because of their numbers: currently they make up 46 percent of the labor force, and by 2005 that percentage is projected to rise to over 60 percent. And the pay for female workers continues to be problematic; since the Equal Pay Act was signed into law in 1963, the closing of the wage gap has been at a rate of less than half a penny a year. Many of the lowest-paying jobs are held by women; nearly 70 percent of Americans who hold two or more part-time jobs, for example, are women, with part-time jobs paying approximately 40 percent less than full-time jobs. Yet even with more women receiving less pay than men, day care costs continue to skyrocket. In all but one state, the annual cost of child care exceeds the annual cost of public college tuition. As a result, child care consumes nearly 20 percent of the income of low-income single mothers.

See also Betty Friedan; National
   Organization for Women (NOW).
Reference 9to5, National Association of
   Working Women Web site:
   http://www.9to5.org

Oncale v. Sundowner Offshore Services, Inc. (1998)

The Court ruled in *Oncale v. Sundowner Offshore Services, Inc.*, that sexual harassment can occur between two people of the same sex. Oncale worked on an eight-man platform oil rig at sea and alleged that he was forcibly subjected to humiliating sex-related actions by coworkers in front of other members of the crew. Further, he claimed that his complaints to supervisors were ignored. Ultimately, he quit his job out of fear of being raped or assaulted.

In a unanimous decision, the Court upheld Oncale's claim. Relying on the statutory requirement that discrimination actionable under Title VII must be "because of . . . sex," the Court concluded that "nothing in Title VII necessarily bars a claim of discrimination . . . merely because the plaintiff and the defendants . . . are of the same sex." If, in contrast, a harasser targets men and women equally, no one has technically been discriminated against, and Title VII has not been violated. To hold otherwise would turn Title VII into a "general civility code for the American workplace" that makes employers liable when supervisors or coworkers are discourteous to employees. This decision made Title VII available to a range of employees previously excluded from the statute's scope, yet it was not clear from the decision what proof was required to establish that same-sex harassment had occurred "because of" sex.

Following the *Oncale* decision, several lower federal trial courts attempted to discern the difference between harassment based on sexual orientation and harassment based on sex. Essentially, only if the harassment is motivated by discrimination on the basis of sex, in which sexual stereotyping would be included, is the behavior illegal. The difficulty, of course, is for the plaintiff to provide evidence of such stereotyping inherent in same-gender discrimination suits.

Generally, before *Oncale*, courts held that there were three situations in which same-sex harassment could be seen as discrimination because of sex rather than sexual orientation: (1) where there was evidence that the harasser sexually desired the victim, as when a gay or lesbian supervisor treated a same-sex subordinate in a way that was sexually charged; (2) where there was no sexual attraction but where the harasser displayed hostility toward the presence of a particular sex in the workplace, as when a doctor at a hospital who believes that men should not be employed as nurses makes harassing statements to a male nurse; and (3) when a harasser's conduct was motivated by a belief that the victim did not conform to stereotypes of his or her gender. In these situations, the harassment was typically deemed to be caused by a general hostility of one sex in the workplace or in a particular work function, and it amounted to discrimination because of sex.

The *Oncale* decision changed these interpretations. The Court here held that virtually any conduct that was sufficiently severe and pervasive, regardless of content or sexual desire, could support a claim of hostile environment harassment provided that the person making the claim was targeted because of his or her gender. In later cases lower courts have even upheld hostile environment harassment claims when the alleged misconduct was nonsexual in nature (e.g., verbal altercations). Critics claim that the ruling in *Oncale* made illegal rude or boorish behavior in the U.S. workplace.

> *See also Burlington Industries v. Ellerth; Civil Rights Act; Equal Employment Opportunity Commission (EEOC); Faragher v. City of Boca Raton; Gebser v. Lago Vista Independent School District; Harris v. Forklift Systems, Inc.; Meritor Savings Bank v. Vinson; Sexual Harassment.*

Phillips v. Martin Marietta Corporation (1971)

In 1966 Martin Marietta informed a job applicant, Ida Phillips, that it would no longer accept applications from women with preschool-age children; the company continued to employ men with small children. Phillips sued, and the lower federal district court ruled against her, holding that 75 to 80 percent of those hired for positions at Martin Marietta were women and thus there was no violation of Title VII of the Civil Rights Act of 1964. Phillips appealed, and

the appellate court affirmed the lower court's decision. The Supreme Court agreed to hear the case.

Under Title VII, applicants with similar qualifications must be given employment regardless of their gender. Thus, the Court held that one hiring policy for women and another for men violated the law, particularly since both male and female applicants had preschool-age children. "The existence of such conflicting family obligations, if demonstrably more relevant to job performance for a woman than for a man, could arguably be a basis for distinction. But that is a matter of evidence tending to show that the condition in question 'is a BFOQ reasonably necessary to the normal operation of that particular business or enterprise.'" That is, a company could have different hiring policies for men and women if these involved a bona fide occupational qualification (BFOQ) necessary for the company to thrive.

Justice Thurgood Marshall concurred with the Court's majority decision that the company's different hiring policies violated Title VII. But he disagreed that Martin Marietta could ever demonstrate a BFOQ; both men and women with preschool-age children have family responsibilities that interfere with job performance. Thus, employers could require that both male and female employees perform at a set level. There was no exception and no way that an employer could find a BFOQ to discriminate against women with such children. In essence, he argued, the majority opinion assumed a proper role for women could well be the basis for discrimination. Such exceptions should be allowed only when they are neutral to the sex of the applicant.

Of course, the impetus behind passage of Title VII was to prevent employers from refusing to hire employees based on stereotypical assumptions about the role of the sexes. BFOQ exceptions were not intended, the Court held, to allow employers the power to make assumptions and justify discrimination. The EEOC applied BFOQ exceptions only to those situations requiring specific physical characteristics that one gender possesses. Such exceptions would be allowed, for example, for "the purpose of authenticity or genuineness" in the employment of actors or actresses and fashion models.

> *See also* Backus v. Baptist Medical Center; Bona Fide Occupational Qualification (BFOQ); *Chambers v. Omaha Girls Club et al.; Cheatwood v. South Central Bell Telephone and Telegraph Company;* Civil Rights Act; *Diaz v. Pan American World Airways;* Equal Employment Opportunity Commission (EEOC); *United Auto Workers v. Johnson Controls.*

Pregnancy Discrimination Act (PDA)

The Pregnancy Discrimination Act is an amendment to Title VII of the Civil Rights Act of 1964 that bans discrimination on the basis of pregnancy, childbirth, or related medical conditions. Women affected by pregnancy or related conditions must be treated in the same manner as other applicants or employees with similar abilities or even physical limitations.

Furthermore, no employer can refuse to hire a pregnant woman as long as she can perform the major functions of her job. This extends to prejudices by coworkers, clients, or customers regarding pregnant women in the workplace. What is most controversial about this act is that an employer can apply the same screening devices used on other employees in determining a pregnant woman's ability to work before she can be granted extended leave. That is, if a non-pregnant employee is required to present a doctor's analysis of that employee's ability to work, the employer can require a pregnant employee to do so as well.

But if she is unable to perform her job due to pregnancy, the employer must treat her the same as any other worker temporarily disabled by illness. So a pregnant employee must be permitted to work as long as she is able to perform her job functions; when she is no longer able to carry out the tasks of her job, an employer must provide modified tasks, alternative assignments, disability leave, or leave without pay. Furthermore, employers cannot prohibit employees from returning to work for a predetermined length of time after childbirth. Following a pregnancy-related absence, employers must offer the same or similar job back that would be offered to another employee returning from sick or disability leave.

Pregnancy-related conditions must be covered by health insurance policies that are provided to all employees at the same cost. Any expenses related to pregnancy must be reimbursed to the same extent as are other health concerns, and this is true for both married and unmarried employees. Deductibles cannot be higher (or lower) for pregnancy-related illnesses compared to other illnesses. It is not necessary for an employer to provide health insurance for expenses arising from abortion unless the life of the mother is endangered as a result of the impending pregnancy. Finally, with regard to insurance coverage for pregnancy, health plans can exclude benefits for preexisting pregnancy.

> *See also* Family and Medical Leave Act (FMLA); *Geduldig v. Aiello; General Electric v. Gilbert;* Pregnancy.
> *Reference* Spalter-Roth, Roberta. 1990. *Improving Employment Opportunities for Women Workers: An Assessment of the 10 Year Economic and Legal Impact of the Pregnancy Discrimination Act of 1978.* Washington, DC: Women's Research Policy Institute.

Price Waterhouse v. Hopkins (1989)

In *Price Waterhouse v. Hopkins,* the Supreme Court held that employers are not to consider gender in making employment decisions. Hopkins worked as a senior manager in an accounting firm and was considered for partnership in 1982. Instead of being promoted, however, her candidacy for partnership was held for reconsideration for the following year. When Price Waterhouse subsequently refused to repropose her for partnership, Hopkins sued under Title VII, alleging that the firm had discriminated against her on the basis of sex in making its partnership decision. She claimed that in evaluations by her colleagues, most of whom were men, she was praised for her ability to secure contracts but criticized for being abrasive. Some evaluations implied that she was considered abrasive because she acted in a masculine way, and other evaluations explicitly suggested that she could improve her evaluations in the future by acting and dressing in a more feminine manner. She resigned from the firm when she filed suit.

A lower federal court ruled in Hopkins's favor that the firm had at least partially decided against her partnership on the basis of sex stereotyping. A higher federal court agreed. Any employer who has allowed a discriminatory motive to play a part in an employment decision, that court ruled, must prove that it would have made the same decision in the absence of the discrimination. Price Waterhouse had failed to demonstrate this. The Supreme Court agreed that if an illegitimate factor such as gender played a role in an employment decision, the employer would be required to prove that it would have made the same decision without consideration of the illegitimate factor. But it also held that in Title VII suits for sex discrimination, an employee must first demonstrate that an unfavorable employment decision was influenced by sexual bias. Then the employer must show that its decision was not influenced by sexual stereotypes. The Court forced the employer to promote Hopkins to partner and pay approximately $371,000 in back pay.

See also Civil Rights Act; Disparate Impact.

Richmond v. J. A. Croson Company (1989)

Richmond, Virginia, enacted a minority business utilization plan that required construction contracts funded by the city to subcontract at least 30 percent of the job to one or more minority business enterprises (MBEs). To be an MBE, a business had to be at least 51 percent owned by a minority group member. Waivers would be given to contractors only if they could prove that there were no qualified MBEs available and willing to participate. The program had been enacted because of statistics showing that although the city was 50 percent black, less than 1 percent of construction contracts were given to minorities, and local contractor associations had no minority representation in their membership.

Croson was a white contractor seeking a contract to install toilets in the city jail who claimed there were no MBEs available to participate in the contract. He filed suit stating that the set-aside violated his right to equal protection under the law. Under precedent set by the Supreme Court, Croson argued, "any government action that is explicitly race-based must be necessary to achieve a compelling government interest" because race-based affirmative programs are subject to strict scrutiny (unlike gender-based programs, which are subject to intermediate scrutiny). Further, Croson said that there was no evidence of discrimination by anyone in Richmond, there was no evidence that there would be more minority contracting firms had there not been past societal discrimination, and there was no showing of how many MBEs in the local labor market could have done the work.

The Court agreed with him, largely because the city had been unable to show clear past race discrimination. Although Congress had concluded that there was race discrimination in the United States, this was irrelevant because the degree of discrimination varied so much from market to market.

See also Intermediate Scrutiny Standard.

Sexual Harassment

Sexual harassment is unwelcome and inappropriate sexual advances or conduct in the workplace. It can include verbal harassment (i.e., derogatory comments or dirty jokes), visual harassment (i.e., derogatory or embarrassing posters, cartoons, drawings, etc.), physical harassment, and demands for sexual favors (i.e., sexual advances and confrontation with sexual demands). The most controversial part of the legal definition of sexual harassment is that it includes gender-based animosity that makes the workplace an unreasonably hostile, sexually charged environment. The courts have recently recognized that men as well as women can be sexually harassed.

Because sexual harassment constitutes an artificial barrier to promotion in employment, it is a form of sex discrimination and therefore violates Title VII of the Civil Rights Act of 1964. Title VII strictly prohibits sexual harassment and applies to any company with more than fifteen employees that is in an industry affecting interstate commerce. As such, claims of sexual harassment are initially investigated by the Equal Employment Opportunity Commission (EEOC). The agency itself was established in part because a federal government survey of its own employees found that 42 percent of women and 15 percent of men had experienced some form of work-related harassment. The legal concept was developed in the mid-1970s, when the EEOC created guidelines defining when harassment transpires.

If a supervisor makes sexual favors a condition of employment or promotion (known as quid pro quo harassment), the action is clearly a violation of Title VII. But harassment can also include an intimidating, hostile, or offensive work environment even if there is simply verbal abuse alone. To prove quid pro quo harassment, the victim must show a tangible economic loss. It is not necessary to show that the harasser explicitly conditioned promotion or continued employment on submission to the sexual request. Rather, it is enough that the words or conduct of the alleged harasser implied such an outcome. Further, the company who employed the supervisor can be held liable for the harassment even if officials in that company had no direct knowledge of the conduct. A lower court developed the reasoning behind a company's liability of an employee's (e.g., supervisor's) harassment: "Because the supervisor is acting within at least the apparent scope of his authority entrusted to him by the employer when he makes employment decisions, his conduct can fairly be imputed to the source of his authority."

Potentially more troublesome is sexual favoritism as quid pro quo harassment. These claims involve allegations by an employee denied a promotion or other job benefit that the employee who received that benefit did so because he or she performed sexual favors for a supervisor. Courts allow such claims because by allowing sexual favoritism, the employer implies to others that if an employee does not submit to such sexual advances, the employee will not receive a job benefit. The practical effect for employers is that they can potentially be sued by two or more employees for a single act or course of conduct by a supervisor. There is thus extra incentive for an employer to prevent this type of quid pro quo sexual harassment.

The most typical type of sexual harassment claim, however, is hostile work environment. These claims involve allegations that a company (or its employees) either created or condoned an intimidating, hostile, or offensive work environment. Making unwelcome sexual advances, requesting sexual favors, or engaging in other verbal or physical conduct of a sexual nature can create such an environment. Courts have been somewhat sympathetic to claims of hostile work environment because employees subject to it are faced with a dilemma: either endure the hostility, attempt to oppose it and likely make the situation worse, or leave the place of employment.

In 1986 the Supreme Court endorsed the notion of a hostile work environment for the first time in *Meritor Savings Bank v. Vinson*. The Court held that a hostile work environ-

Sexual Harassment is not wrong because it is illegal. It is illegal because it is wrong.
-Berniece Sandler

Experience has demonstrated that many complaints of sexual harassment can be effectively resolved through informal intervention. For information about informal and formal resolution options available contact:

The Women's Center 893-3778 Human Resources 893-4119 Sexual Harassment Complaint Office 893-2546

The names of other contact people can be accessed though our web page: http://www.sa.ucsb.edu/women'scenter/harass

MUTUAL RESPECT What friendships and relationships are built upon.

What is Sexual Harassment?

Sexual harassment occurs when unwanted or uninvited attention of a sexual nature interferes with a person's ability to obtain an education, work, or participate in recreational or social activities at UCSB. Sexual harassment is an abuse of informal or formal power or authority.

Sexual Harassment may include:
- Derogatory remarks about one's clothing, body or sexual activities based on gender
- Disparaging comments, jokes and teasing based on gender
- Verbal harassment or abuse
- Subtle pressure for sexual activity
- Unnecessary and unwanted touching, patting, or pinching
- Demanding sexual favors accompanied by overt threats concerning such things as one's job, grades, letters of recommendation or promotion
- Physical assault

For Sexual Harassment Prevention Education Training call (805) 893-3778

Printed for your assistance by the Sexual Harassment Prevention Education Program and the Office of the Executive Vice Chancellor.   (4/00)

A brochure from the Women's Center at the University of California at Santa Barbvara defining sexual harassment. (UCSB)

ment could exist even if there is no apparent economic detriment. Further, the Court defined hostile work environment as "such conduct [that] has the purpose or effect of unreasonably interfering with an individual's work performance or creating an intimidating, hostile, or offensive working environment." In making a hostile environment claim, an employee is required to show that he or she was subjected to a work environment in which there were sexual advances, requests for sexual favors, or other verbal or physical conduct of a sexual nature; that the conduct was unwelcome; and that the conduct was sufficiently severe or pervasive to alter the conditions of the victim's employment and create an abusive working environment.

Although the Court set the stage for such claims in *Vinson,* it was in 1992 that the issue of sexual harassment gained public attention. When George Bush nominated Clarence Thomas to fill a seat on the Supreme Court, allegations surfaced that Thomas may have created a hostile work environment while a commissioner for the EEOC, the agency tasked with investigating discrimination and harassment claims in the workforce. During his confirmation hearings before an all-male Senate Judiciary Committee, EEOC lawyer Anita Hill argued that Thomas had repeatedly made comments to her that were laced with sexual innuendo. These comments generally made her feel threatened for refusing to date him while he was her supervisor. The media interest was explosive, and working women were enraged to watch Hill facing down a hostile all-male committee that believed she was merely a "scorned woman." Some men were enraged that Hill had waited for ten years before making her allegations against Thomas and in fact had continued in his employment for years following her alleged harassment. Thomas was confirmed to the Supreme Court by one of the narrowest margins in history. A year after the Hill-Thomas hearings, the number of sexual harassment cases filed with the EEOC jumped 50 percent.

Following the Thomas-Hill fiasco, several cases worked their way up to the Supreme Court, and in the 1990s the Court handed down several decisions further defining the nature of harassment in the workplace. First, if an employee initially participated willingly in sexual conduct but then ceased to participate willingly, that employee must have clearly notified the alleged harasser that his or her conduct was no longer welcome. Also, to determine whether the conduct of a supervisor altered the conditions of the work environment, a court must evaluate the totality of the circumstances. This can include the frequency of the conduct, whether the behavior was patently offensive, whether others in the place of employment eventually joined in perpetuating the harassment, and whether the harassment was directed at more than one person. Additionally, the conduct does not have to cause psychological injury; if a workplace is permeated with unwelcome discriminatory intimidation and insult that is severe and pervasive enough to alter the conditions of the victim's employment, then a hostile environment is evident. As the Court said, "So long as the environment would reasonably be perceived, and is perceived, as hostile or abusive . . . there is no need for it to be psychologically injurious." Finally, both men and women can be sexually harassed or subject to a hostile work environment.

Courts have also been relatively sympathetic to students claiming harassment. Title IX prohibits sexual discrimination in any educational institution, program, or activity receiving financial assistance from the federal government. To state a Title IX claim for hostile educational environment sexual harassment, a plaintiff must prove that the harassment occurred because of the plaintiff's gender, the harassment altered learning conditions, and the employer knew or should have known of the harassment and failed to take prompt action to correct the situation. In such cases teachers can obviously target a student, but students can also target other students.

By the start of the twenty-first century, courts granted relief for sexual harassment far more often than they did a decade earlier, and the damage awards granted to plaintiffs created an incentive for employers to take sexual harassment claims much more seriously than in years past. In 1999 a Detroit jury granted Linda Gilbert a $21 million verdict for sexual harassment, $20 million of it for pain and suffering. A jury found that Gilbert's work environment at the Daimler Chrysler plant was hostile because male colleagues had left her pornographic messages and addressed her with vulgar talk and insults. She had reported several separate incidents of harassment to her managers, including a time she found a picture of male genitalia taped to her toolbox, a copy of *Penthouse* magazine top of it, and a ribald poem on top of that. The jury was sympathetic to her claims of hostile environment largely because the managers did nothing to stop her coworkers' behavior.

> **See also** *Alexander v. Yale University;*
> *Burlington Industries v. Ellerth;* Civil Rights
> Act; Equal Employment Opportunity
> Commission (EEOC); *Faragher v. City of*
> *Boca Raton; Gebser v. Lago Vista Independent*
> *School District;* Hill, Anita; *Meritor Savings*
> *Bank v. Vinson; Oncale v. Sundowner*
> *Offshore Services.*
>
> **References** Nicole A. Forkenbrock-
> Lindemyer. 2000. "Sexual Harassment on
> the Second Shift: The Misfit Application
> of Title VII Employment Standards to
> Title VIII Housing Cases." *Law and*
> *Inequality* 18: 351–392; Gwendolyn Mink.
> 2001. *Hostile Environment: The Political*
> *Betrayal of Sexually Harassed Women.*
> Ithaca, NY: Cornell University Press.

Tomkins v. Public Service Electric and Gas Company (1977)

Adrienne Tomkins was hired by Public Service Electric and Gas Company (PSE&G) in 1971 and was promoted to positions of increasing responsibility until 1973, when she began working in a secretarial position. Her supervisor asked to eat lunch with her outside of the office to discuss his upcoming evaluation of her work and a possible promotion. He then made several sexually implicit advances toward her and indicated that sexual relations between them would be necessary if she wanted a positive evaluation. When she attempted to leave, he threatened her with recrimination, physical force, and ultimately physically restrained her. He told her that no one at the plant would help her if she filed a complaint against him.

Tomkins filed a sexual harassment complaint against the company, alleging the company knew or should have known such incidents would occur yet placed her in a position where she would be subject to this type of behavior. The company had also failed to take adequate measures to keep her supervisor's behavior from occurring. In fact, she was offered another job after she threatened to leave the company, one that was inferior to one she had previously held. She was subjected to false and adverse employment evaluations, a disciplinary layoff, and threats of demotion by various employees at the company. Tomkins argued that as a result of her superior's conduct and continued harassment, she suffered enormous emotional stress, which resulted in absenteeism and loss of income. The district court that handled her case held that she had the burden of proof but did not adequately prove her case and that there would be an unmanageable number of sexual harassment suits under Title VII if cases like hers were allowed to continue.

The court then ruled that the supervisor's acts were abuses "of authority . . . for personal purposes" and questioned whether the company, "either knowingly or constructively, made acquiescence to her supervisor's sexual demands a necessary prerequisite to the continuation of, or advancement in, her job." The court examined whether the supervisor's conditioning her continued employment on compliance with his sexual demands was motivated by the fact that she was female (a direct violation of Title VII). The court distinguished between complaints alleging sexual advances of an individual or personal nature and those alleging direct employment consequences flowing from the advances; only complaints in the latter category violate Title VII of the Civil Rights Act. As such, it was necessary (at the time) for a plaintiff to show, first, that the term or condition of employment had been imposed because she was female and, second, that it was imposed by the employer, either directly or vicariously, in a sexually discriminatory fashion.

Further, the court stated that judicial economy is not the job of the federal courts; congressional mandate to the courts forces the judiciary to differentiate between spurious and meritorious claims. The Supreme Court would further define the issues involved in sexual harassment in the 1986 case of *Meritor Savings Bank v. Vinson*.

See also Civil Rights Act; *Meritor Savings Bank v. Vinson*; Sexual Harassment.

Torres v. Wisconsin Department of Health and Social Services (1989)

Several male correctional officers at Taycheedah Correctional Institution, the only women's maximum-security prison in Wisconsin, challenged the prison administrator's policy of hiring only female correctional officers in the living units. The prison administrator, Switala, determined that the rehabilitation of inmates at the prison would be enhanced by having only female correctional officers and that being a woman was a bona fide occupational qualification (BFOQ) because of security issues. A lower federal court ruled for the prison administrator, and the Supreme Court refused to review the case.

Switala gave three separate reasons for demanding all-female correctional officers at the prison: inmate rehabilitation, inmate

privacy, and prison security. Because at least 60 percent of the female prisoners had been sexually assaulted as children, the absence of male authority figures was necessary to foster rehabilitation and security. With the support of her superiors, Switala instituted a BFOQ to go into effect in 1980 that would ensure only female officers would be on duty in the prison. Torres and other male offices were reassigned to other positions after the BFOQ went into effect; they did not suffer a loss in pay or demotion as a result of the plan. Nevertheless, they challenged their reassignment, alleging sex discrimination in violation of Title VII of the Civil Rights Act of 1964.

The court of appeals held that a BFOQ plan cannot be justified because of concerns for prison security or basic privacy rights. But it is allowable if it is to further the goal of inmate rehabilitation. The court warned, however, that this was not a license for employers to elude Title VII's requirements against sex discrimination; rarely, if ever, can employers argue that gender-based distinctions are a "reasonably necessary" approach to the functioning of a business.

See also *Backus v. Baptist Medical Center*; Bona Fide Occupational Qualification (BFOQ); Civil Rights Act; Disparate Impact; *Dothard v. Rawlinson*.

United Auto Workers v. Johnson Controls (1991)

In 1984, petitioners filed a class-action suit charging that the fetal-protection policy of Johnson Controls, a manufacturer of batteries made primarily of lead, was sex discrimination in violation of Title VII. Of the various petitioners, Mary Craig had chosen to be sterilized to keep her job, Elsie Nason suffered loss of compensation when she was transferred out of a job where lead was exposed, and Donald Penney was denied a request for a leave of absence for the purpose of lowering his lead level because he intended to become a father. The courts on all lower appeals, ruled that the fetal-protection policies in place at Johnson Controls were BFOQ and constitutional.

Prior to passage of the Civil Rights Act of 1964, of which Title VII prohibited the discrimination of employees on the basis of gender, Johnson Controls did not hire women for fear of lead exposure to any fetus. But opponents of such policies argued that "protective regulations" such as this one only served to limit women's job opportunities partially since most regulations considered women of childbearing age to be anywhere up to sixty-three years old. In *United Auto Workers v. Johnson Controls*, the Supreme Court decided the issue in a unanimous case. It held that rules such as the one by Johnson Controls were illegal: "Decisions about the welfare of future children must be left to the parents who conceive, bear, support and raise them," wrote Justice Harry Blackmun.

> *See also* American Civil Liberties Union—Women's Rights Project (ACLU—WRP); Bona Fide Occupational Qualification (BFOQ); Civil Rights Act; *Geduldig v. Aiello; General Electric v. Gilbert; Phillips v. Martin Marietta Corporation*.

Washington v. Gunther (1981)

The case of *Washington v. Gunther* was brought by female jail guards who claimed they were paid $200 per month less than their male counterparts. Although they admitted that the work done by male and female guards was not equal, the women claimed that part of the discrepancy in pay resulted from intentional sex discrimination. In order to prove pay disparity motivated by sex discrimination, the Supreme Court held, the women must prove (with direct evidence) that their wages were depressed because of "intentional sex discrimination" by the employer in setting the wage scale for female guards. This holding was the first time the Supreme Court had sought to clarify the Bennett amendment to Title VII. That amendment provides that pay differentials between men and women are not unlawful under Title VII as long as the employer can meet at least one of the four exceptions to the Equal Pay Act. That is, pay disparity can occur if the pay is based on a merit or seniority system, quantity or quality of production, or a factor other than sex. Further, in such claims the defendant (the employer) has the burden of proof in demonstrating that the disparity results from one of the four exceptions.

> *See also* Civil Rights Act; Comparable Worth; Equal Pay Act; Glass Ceiling; *Glenn, Johns and Nugent v. General Motors, Inc.*

References and Further Reading

Judith A. Baer. 1996. *Women in American Law: The Struggle toward Equality from the New Deal to the Present.* 2nd 3d. New York: Holmes and Meier.

National Organization for Women Web site: www.now.org.

Documents

Declaration of Sentiments and Resolutions, 1848

When, in the course of human events, it becomes necessary for one portion of the family of man to assume among the people of the earth a position different from that which they have hitherto occupied, but one to which the laws of nature and of nature's God entitle them, a decent respect to the opinions of mankind requires that they should declare the causes that impel them to such a course.

We hold these truths to be self-evident: that all men and women are created equal; that they are endowed by their Creator with certain inalienable rights; that among these are life, liberty, and the pursuit of happiness; that to secure these rights governments are instituted, deriving their just powers from the consent of the governed. Whenever any form of government becomes destructive of these ends, it is the right of those who suffer from it to refuse allegiance to it, and to insist upon the institution of a new government, laying its foundation on such principles, and organizing its powers in such form, as to them shall seem most likely to effect their safety and happiness. Prudence, indeed, will dictate that governments long established should not be changed for light and transient causes; and accordingly all experience hath shown that mankind are more disposed to suffer, while evils are sufferable, than to right themselves by abolishing the forms to which they were accustomed. But when a long train of abuses and usurpations, pursuing invariably the same object evinces a design to reduce them under absolute despotism, it is their duty to throw off such government, and to provide new guards for their future security. Such has been the patient sufferance of the women under this government, and such is now the necessity which constrains them to demand the equal station to which they are entitled.

The history of mankind is a history of repeated injuries and usurpations on the part of man toward woman, having in direct object the establishment of an absolute tyranny over her. To prove this, let facts be submitted to a candid world.

He has never permitted her to exercise her inalienable right to the elective franchise.

He has compelled her to submit to laws, in the formation of which she had no voice.

He has withheld from her rights which are given to the most ignorant and degraded men—both natives and foreigners.

Having deprived her of this first right of a citizen, the elective franchise, thereby leaving her without representation in the halls of legislation, he has oppressed her on all sides.

He has made her, if married, in the eye of the law, civilly dead.

He has taken from her all right in property, even to the wages she earns.

He has made her, morally, an irresponsible being, as she can commit many crimes with impunity, provided they be done in the presence of her husband. In the covenant of marriage, she is compelled to promise obedience to her husband, he becoming, to all intents and purposes, her master—the law giving him power to deprive her of her liberty, and to administer chastisement.

He has so framed the laws of divorce, as to what shall be the proper causes, and in case of separation, to whom the guardianship of the children shall be given, as to be wholly regardless of the happiness of women—the law, in all cases, going upon a false supposition of the supremacy of man, and giving all power into his hands.

After depriving her of all rights as a married woman, if single, and the owner of property, he has taxed her to support a government which recognizes her only when her property can be made profitable to it.

He has monopolized nearly all the profitable employments, and from those she is permitted to follow, she receives but a scanty remuneration. He closes against her all the avenues to wealth and distinction which he considers most honorable to himself. As a teacher of theology, medicine, or law, she is not known.

He has denied her the facilities for obtaining a thorough education, all colleges being closed against her.

He allows her in Church, as well as State, but a subordinate position, claiming Apostolic authority for her exclusion from the ministry, and with some exceptions, from any public participation in the affairs of the Church.

He has created a false public sentiment by giving to the world a different code of morals for men and women, by which moral delinquencies which exclude women from society, are not only tolerated, but demand of little account in man.

He has usurped the prerogative of Jehovah himself, claiming it as his right to assign for her a sphere of action, when that belongs to her conscience and her God.

He has endeavored, in every way that he could, to destroy her confidence in her own powers, to lessen her self-respect, and to make her willing to lead a dependent and abject life.

Now, in view of this entire disfranchisement of one-half the people of this country, their social and religious degradation—in view of the unjust laws above mentioned, and because women do feel themselves aggrieved, oppressed, and fraudulently deprived of their most sacred rights, we insist that they have immediate admission to all the rights and privileges which belong to them as citizens of the United States.

In entering upon the great work before us, we anticipate no small amount of misconception, misrepresentation, and ridicule; but we shall use every instrumentality within our power to effect our object. We shall employ agents, circulate tracts, petition the State and National legislatures, and endeavor to enlist the pulpit and the press in our behalf. We hope this Convention will be followed by a series of Conventions in every part of the country.

WHEREAS, The great precept of nature is conceded to be, that "man shall pursue his own true and substantial happiness." Blackstone in his Commentaries remarks, that his law of Nature being coeval with mankind, and dictated by God himself, is of course superior in obligation to any other. It is binding over all the globe, in all countries and at all times; no human laws are of any validity if contrary to this, and such of them as are valid, derive all their force, and all their validity, and all their authority, mediately and immediately, from this original; therefore,

RESOLVED, That such laws as conflict, in any way, with the true and substantial happiness of women, are contrary to the great precept of nature and of no validity, for this is "superior in obligation to any other."

RESOLVED, That all laws which prevent woman from occupying such a station in society as her conscience shall dictate, or which places her in a position inferior to that of man, are contrary to the great precept of nature, and therefore of no force or authority.

RESOLVED, That woman is man's equal—was intended to be so by the Creator, and the highest good of the race demands that she should be recognized as such.

RESOLVED, That the women of this country ought to be enlightened in regard to the laws under which they live, that they may no longer publish their degradation by declaring themselves satisfied with their present position, nor their ignorance, by asserting that they have all the rights they want.

RESOLVED, That inasmuch as man, while claiming for himself intellectual superiority, does accord to woman moral superiority, it is pre-eminently his duty to encourage her to speak and teach, as she has an opportunity, in all religious assemblies.

RESOLVED, That the same amount of virtue, delicacy, and refinement of behavior that is required of woman in the social state, should also be required of man, and the same transgressions should be visited with equal severity on both man and woman.

RESOLVED, That the objection of indelicacy and impropriety, which is so often brought against woman when she addresses a public audience, comes with a very ill-grace from those who encourage, by their attendance, her appearance on the stage, in the concert, or in feats of the circus.

RESOLVED, That woman has too long rested satisfied in the circumscribed limits which corrupt customs and a perverted application of the Scriptures have marked out for her, and that it is time she should move in the enlarged sphere which her great Creator has assigned her.

RESOLVED, That it is the duty of the women of this country to secure to themselves their sacred right to the elective franchise.

RESOLVED, That the equality of human rights results necessarily from the fact of the identity of the race in capabilities and responsibilities.

RESOLVED, That the speedy success of our cause depends upon the zealous and untiring efforts of both men and women, for the overthrow of the monopoly of the pulpit, and for the securing to woman an equal participation with men in the various trades, professions, and commerce.

RESOLVED, THEREFORE, That being invested by the Creator with the same capabilities, and the same consciousness of responsibility for their exercise, it is demonstrably the right and duty of woman, equally with man, to promote every righteous cause by every righteous means; and especially in regard to the great subjects of morals and religion, it is self-evidently her right to participate with her brother in teaching them, both in private and in public, by writing and by speaking, by instrumentalities proper to be used, and in any assemblies proper to be held; and being a self-evident truth growing out of the divinely implanted principles of human nature, any custom or authority adverse to it, whether modern or wearing the hoary sanction of antiquity, is to be regarded as a self-evident falsehood, and at war with mankind.

I Announce Myself as a Candidate for the Presidency, Victoria Woodhull, 1870

As I happen to be the most prominent representative of the only unrepresented class in the republic, and perhaps the most practical exponent of the principles of equality, I request the favor of being permitted to address the public through the Herald. While others of my sex devoted themselves to a crusade against the laws that shackle the women of the country, I asserted my individual independence; while others prayed for the good time coming, I worked for it; while others argued the equality of woman with man, I proved it by successfully engaging in business; while others sought to show that there was no valid reason why women should be treated, socially and politically, as being inferior to man, I boldly entered the arena of politics and business and exercised the rights I already possessed. I therefore claim the right to speak for the unenfranchised women of the country, and believing as I do that the prejudices which still exist in the popular mind against women in public life will soon disappear, I now announce myself as a candidate for the Presidency.

. . . The present position of political parties is anomalous. They are not inspired by any great principles of policy or economy; there is no live issue up for discussion. A great national question is wanted. . . . That question exists in the issue, whether woman shall . . . be elevated to all the political rights enjoyed by man. The simple issue whether woman should not have this complete political equality . . . is the only one to be tried, and none more important is likely to arise before the Presidential election.

Printed in the New York Herald, April 2, 1870.

Speech after Being Convicted of Voting in the 1872 Presidential Election, Susan B. Anthony, 1873

Friends and fellow citizens: I stand before you tonight under indictment for the alleged crime of having voted at the last presidential election, without having a lawful right to vote. It shall be my work this evening to prove to you that in thus voting, I not only committed no crime, but, instead, simply exercised my citizen's rights, guaranteed to me and all United States citizens by the National Constitution, beyond the power of any state to deny.

The preamble of the Federal Constitution says: "We, the people of the United States, in order to form a more perfect union, establish justice, insure domestic tranquility, provide for the common defense, promote the general welfare, and secure the blessings of liberty to ourselves and our posterity, do ordain and establish this Constitution for the United States of America."

It was we, the people; not we, the white male citizens; nor yet we, the male citizens; but we, the whole people, who formed the Union. And we formed it, not to give the blessings of liberty, but to secure them; not to the half of ourselves and the half of our posterity, but to the whole people—women as well as men. And it is a downright mockery to talk to women of their enjoyment of the blessings of liberty while they are denied the use of the only means of securing them provided by this democratic-republican government—the ballot.

For any state to make sex a qualification that must ever result in the disfranchisement of one entire half of the people, is to pass a bill of attainder, or, an ex post facto law, and is therefore a violation of the supreme law of the land. By it the blessings of liberty are forever withheld from women and their female posterity.

To them this government has no just powers derived from the consent of the governed. To them this government is not a democracy. It is not a republic. It is an odious aristocracy; a hateful oligarchy of sex; the most hateful aristocracy ever established on the face of the globe; an oligarchy of wealth, where the rich govern the poor. An oligarchy of learning, where the educated govern the ignorant, or even an oligarchy of race, where the Saxon rules the African, might be endured; but this oligarchy of sex, which makes father, brothers, husband, sons, the oligarchs over the mother and sisters, the wife and daughters, of every household—which ordains all men sovereigns, all women subjects, carries dissension, discord, and rebellion into every home of the nation.

Webster, Worcester, and Bouvier all define a citizen to be a person in the United States, entitled to vote and hold office.

The only question left to be settled now is: Are women persons? And I hardly believe any of our opponents will have the hardihood to say they are not. Being persons, then, women are citizens; and no state has a right to make any law, or to enforce any old law, that shall abridge their privileges or immunities. Hence, every discrimination against women in the constitutions and laws of the several states is today null and void, precisely as is every one against Negroes.

A Black Woman Describes Prejudice in the Nation's Capital, Mary Church Terrell, 1900

For fifteen years I have resided in Washington, and while it was far from being a paradise for colored people when I first touched these shores it has been doing its level best ever since to make conditions for us intolerable. As a colored woman I might enter Washington any night, a stranger in a strange land, and walk miles without finding a place to lay my head. Unless I happened to know colored people who live here or ran across a chance acquaintance who could recommend a colored boarding-house to me, I should be obliged to spend the entire night wandering about . . .

As a colored woman I may walk from the Capitol to the White House, ravenously hungry and abundantly supplied with money with which to purchase a meal, without finding a single restaurant in which I would be permitted to take a morsel of food, if it was patronized by white people, unless I were willing to sit behind a screen. As a colored woman I cannot visit the tomb of the Father of this country which owes its very existence to the love of freedom in the human heart and which stands for equal opportunity to all, without being forced to sit in the Jim Crow section of an electric car which starts from the very heart of the city—midway between the Capitol and the White House. If I refuse thus to be humiliated, I am cast into jail and forced to pay a fine for violating the Virginia laws. Every hour in the day Jim Crow cars filled with colored people, many of whom are intelligent and well to do, enter and leave the national capital . . .

Unless I am willing to engage in a few menial occupations, in which the pay for my services would be very poor, there is no way for me to earn an honest living, if I am not a trained nurse or a dressmaker or can secure a position as teacher in the public schools, which is exceedingly difficult to do. It matters not what my intellectual attainments may be or how great is the need of the services of a competent person, if I try to enter many of the numerous vocations in which my white sisters are allowed to engage, the door is shut in my face . . .

Some time ago a young woman who had already attracted some attention in the literary world by her volume of short stories answered an advertisement which appeared in a Washington newspaper, which called for the services of a skilled stenographer and expert typewriter. It is unnecessary to state the reasons why a young woman whose literary ability was so great as that possessed by the one referred to should decide to earn money in this way. The applicants were requested to send specimens of their work and answer certain questions concerning their experience and their speed before they called in person. In reply to her application the young colored woman, who, by the way, is very fair and attractive indeed, received a letter from the firm stating that her references and experience were the most satisfactory that had been sent and requesting her to call. When she presented herself there was some doubt in the mind of the man to whom she was directed concerning her [race], so he asked her point-blank whether she was colored or white. When she confessed the truth the merchant expressed great sorrow and deep regret that he could not avail himself of the services of so competent a person, but frankly admitted that employing a colored woman in his establishment in any except a menial position was simply out of the question . . .

And so I might go on citing instance after instance to show the variety of ways in which our people are sacrificed on the altar of prejudice in the Capital of the United

States and how almost insurmountable are the obstacles which block his path to success. Early in life many a colored youth is so appalled by the helplessness and the hopelessness of his situation in this country that in a sort of stoical despair he resigns himself to his fate. "What is the good of our trying to acquire an education? We can't all be preachers, teachers, doctors, and lawyers. Besides those professions there is almost nothing for colored people to do but engage in the most menial occupations, and we do not need an education for that." More than once such remarks, uttered by young men and women in our public schools who possess brilliant intellects, have wrung my heart.

Reprinted from "What It Means to Be Colored in the Capital of the United States," The Independent, LXII (Jan. 24, 1907), pp. 181–182, 185.

Child Labor and Woman Suffrage, Florence Kelley, 1905

We have, in this country, two million children under the age of sixteen years who are earning their bread. They vary in age from six and seven years (in the cotton mills of Georgia) and eight, nine and ten years (in the coal-breakers of Pennsylvania), to fourteen, fifteen and sixteen years in more enlightened States.

No other portion of the wage earning class increased so rapidly from decade to decade as the young girls from fourteen to twenty years. Men increase, women increase, youth increase, boys increase in the ranks of the breadwinners; but no contingent so doubles from census period to census period (both by percent and by count of heads), as does the contingent of girls between twelve and twenty years of age. They are in commerce, in offices, in manufacture.

To-night while we sleep, several thousand little girls will be working in textile mills, all the night through, in the deafening noise of the spindles and the looms spinning and weaving cotton and woolen, silks

and ribbons for us to buy.

In Alabama the law provides that a child under sixteen years of age shall not work in a cotton mill at night longer than eight hours, and Alabama does better in this respect than any other Southern State. North and South Carolina and Georgia place no restriction upon the work of children at night; and while we sleep little white girls will be working to-night in the mills in those States, working eleven hours at night.

In Georgia there is no restriction whatever! A girl of six or seven years, just tall enough to reach the bobbins, may work eleven hours by day or by night. And they will do so to-night, while we sleep.

Nor is it only in the South that these things occur. Alabama does better than New Jersey. For Alabama limits the children's work at night to eight hours, while New Jersey permits it all night long. Last year New Jersey took a long backward step. A good law was repealed which had required women and [children] to stop work at six in the evening and at noon on Friday. Now, therefore, in New Jersey, boys and girls, after the 14th birthday, enjoy the pitiful privilege of working all night long.

In Pennsylvania, until last May it was lawful for children, 13 years of age, to work twelve hours at night. A little girl, on her thirteenth birthday, could start away from her home at half past five in the afternoon, carrying her pail of midnight luncheon as happier people carry their midday luncheon, and could work in the mill from six at night until six in the morning, without violating any law of the Commonwealth.

If the mothers and the teachers in Georgia could vote, would the Georgia Legislature have refused at every session for the last three years to stop the work in the mills of children under twelve years of age?

Would the New Jersey Legislature have passed that shameful repeal bill enabling girls of fourteen years to work all night, if the mothers in New Jersey were enfranchised? Until the mothers in the great industrial States are enfranchised, we shall none of us be able to free our consciences from participation in this great evil. No one in this room to-night can feel free from such participation. The children make our shoes in the shoe factories; they knit our stockings, our knitted underwear in the knitting factories. They spin and weave our cotton underwear in the cotton mills. Children braid straw for our hats, they spin and weave the silk and velvet wherewith we trim our hats. They stamp buckles and metal ornaments of all kinds, as well as pins and hat-pins. Under the sweating system, tiny children make artificial flowers and neckwear for us to buy. They carry bundles of garments from the factories to the tenements, little beasts of burden, robbed of school life that they may work for us.

We do not wish this. We prefer to have our work done by men and women. But we are almost powerless. Not wholly powerless, however, are citizens who enjoy the right of petition. For myself, I shall use this power in every possible way until the right to the ballot is granted, and then I shall continue to use both.

What can we do to free our consciences? There is one line of action by which we can do much. We can enlist the workingmen on behalf of our enfranchisement just in proportion as we strive with them to free the children. No labor organization in this country ever fails to respond to an appeal for help in the freeing of the children.

For the sake of the children, for the Republic in which these children will vote after we are dead, and for the sake of our cause, we should enlist the workingmen voters, with us, in this task of freeing the children from toil.

The Winning Plan, Carrie Chapman Catt, 1915

. . . National Boards must be selected hereafter for one chief qualification—the ability to lead the national fight. There should be a mobilization of at least thirty-six state armies [after congressional approval an amendment needed the approval of three quarters of the states—or thirty-six states], and these armies should move under the direction of the national officers. They should be disciplined and obedient to the national officers in all matters concerning the national campaign. This great army with its thirty-six, and let us hope, forty-eight divisions, should move on Congress with precision, and a will. . . . More, those who enter on this task, should go prepared to give their lives and fortunes for success, and any pusillanimous coward among us who dares to call retreat, should be courtmartialled.

Any other policy than this is weak, inefficient, illogical, silly, inane, and ridiculous! Any other policy would fail of success. . . .

When a general is about to make an attack upon the enemy at a fortified point, he often begins to feint elsewhere in order to draw off attention and forces. If we decide to train up some states into preparedness for campaign, the best help which can be given them is to keep so much "suffrage noise" going all over the country that neither the enemy nor friends will discover where the real battle is. . . .

We should win, if it is possible to do so, a few more states before the Federal Amendment gets up to the legislatures.

. . . A southern state should be selected and made ready for a campaign, and the solid front of the "anti" south broken as soon as possible.

Some break in the solid "anti" East should be made too. If New York wins in 1917 the backbone of the opposition will be largely bent if not broken. . . .

By 1920, when the next national party platforms will be adopted, we should have won Iowa, South Dakota, North Dakota, Nebraska, New York, Maine and a southern state. We should have secured the Illinois law in a number of other states.

With these victories to our credit and the tremendous increase of momentum given the whole movement, we should be able to secure planks in all platforms favoring the Federal Amendment (if it has not passed before that time) and to secure its passage in the December term of the 1920 Congress.

It should then go to the legislatures of thirty-nine states which meet in 1921, and the remaining states would have the opportunity to ratify the amendment in 1922. If thirty-six states had ratified in these two years, the end of our struggle would come by April 1, 1922, six years hence. . . .

The Nineteenth Amendment to the U.S. Constitution, 1920

The right of citizens of the United States to vote shall not be denied or abridged by the United States or by any state on account of sex.

Congress shall have power to enforce this article by appropriate legislation.

Birth Control—A Parents' Problem or Woman's? Margaret Sanger, 1920

The problem of birth control has arisen directly from the effort of the feminine spirit to free itself from bondage. Woman herself has wrought that bondage through her reproductive powers and while enslaving herself has enslaved the world. The physical suffering to be relieved is chiefly woman's. Hers, too, is the love life that dies first under the blight of too prolific breeding. Within her is wrapped up the future of the race—it is hers to make or mar. All of these considerations point unmistakably to one fact—it is woman's duty as well as her privilege to lay hold of the means of freedom. Whatever men may do, she cannot escape the responsibility. For ages she has been deprived of the opportunity to meet this obligation. She is now emerging from her helplessness. Even as no one can share the suffering of the overburdened mother, so no one can do this work for her. Others may help, but she and she alone can free herself.

The basic freedom of the world is woman's freedom. A free race cannot be born of slave mothers. A woman enchained cannot choose but give a measure of that bondage to her sons and daughters. No woman can call herself free who does not own and control her body. No woman can call herself free until she can choose consciously whether she will or will not be a mother.

It does not greatly alter the case that some women call themselves free because they earn their own livings, while others profess freedom because they defy the conventions of sex relationship. She who earns her own living gains a sort of freedom that is not to be undervalued, but in quality and in quantity it is of little account beside the untrammeled choice of mating or not mating, of being a mother or not being a mother. She gains food and clothing and shelter, at least, without submitting to the charity of her companion, but the earning of her own living does not give her the development of her inner sex urge, far deeper and more powerful in its outworkings than any of these externals. In order to have that development, she must still meet and solve the problem of motherhood.

With the so-called "free" woman, who chooses a mate in defiance of convention, freedom is largely a question of character and audacity. If she does attain to an unrestricted choice of a mate, she is still in a position to be enslaved through her reproductive powers. Indeed, the pressure of law and custom upon the woman not legally married is likely to make her more of a slave than the woman fortunate enough to marry the man of her choice.

Look at it from any standpoint you will, suggest any solution you will, conventional or unconventional, sanctioned by law or in defiance of law, woman is in the same position, fundamentally, until she is able to determine for herself whether she will be a mother and to fix the number of her offspring. This unavoidable situation is alone enough to make birth control, first of all, a woman's problem. On the very face of the matter, voluntary motherhood is chiefly the concern of the woman.

It is persistently urged, however, that since sex expression is the act of two, the responsibility of controlling the results should not be placed upon woman alone. Is it fair, it is asked, to give her, instead of the man, the task of protecting herself when she is, perhaps, less rugged in physique than her mate, and has, at all events, the normal, periodic inconveniences of her sex?

We must examine this phase of her problem in two lights—that of the ideal, and of the conditions working toward the ideal. In an ideal society, no doubt, birth control would become the concern of the man as well as the woman. The hard, inescapable fact which we encounter to-day is that man has not only refused any such responsibility, but has individually and collectively sought to prevent woman from obtaining knowledge by which she could assume this responsibility for herself. She is still in the position of a dependent to-day because her mate has refused to consider her as an individual apart from his needs. She is still bound because she has in the past left the solution of the problem to him. Having left it to him, she finds that instead of rights, she has only such privileges as she has gained by petitioning, coaxing and cozening. Having left it to him, she is exploited, driven and enslaved to his desires.

While it is true that he suffers many evils as the consequence of this situation, she suffers vastly more. While it is true that he should be awakened to the cause of these evils, we know that they come home to her with crushing force every day. It is she who has the long burden of carrying, bearing and rearing the unwanted children. . . . It is her heart that the sight of the deformed, the subnormal, the undernourished, the overworked child smites first and oftenest and hardest. It is her love life that dies first in the fear of undesired pregnancy. It is her opportunity for self expression that perishes first and most hopelessly because of it.

Conditions, rather than theories, facts, rather than dreams, govern the problem. They place it squarely upon the shoulders of woman. She has learned that whatever the moral responsibility of the man in this direction may be, he does not discharge it. She has learned that, lovable and considerate as the individual husband may be, she has nothing to expect from men in the mass, when they make laws and decree customs. She knows that regardless of what ought to be, the brutal, unavoidable fact is that she will never receive her freedom until she takes it for herself.

Having learned this much, she has yet something more to learn. Women are too much inclined to follow in the footsteps of men, to try to think as men think, to try to solve the general problems of life as men solve them. If after attaining their freedom, women accept conditions in the spheres of government, industry, art, morals and religion as they find them, they will be but taking a leaf out of man's book. The woman is not needed to do man's work. She is not needed to think man's thoughts. She need not fear that the masculine mind, almost universally dominant, will fail to take care of its own. Her mission is not to enhance the masculine spirit, but to express the feminine; hers is not to preserve a man-made world, but to create a human world by the infusion of the feminine element into all of its activities.

Woman must not accept; she must challenge. She must not be awed by that which has been built up around her; she must reverence that within her which struggles for expression. Her eyes must be less upon what is and more clearly upon what should be. She must listen only with a frankly questioning attitude to the dogmatized opinions of man-made society. When she chooses her new, free course of action, it must be in the light of her own opinion—of her own intuition. Only so can she give play to the feminine spirit. Only thus can she free her mate from the bondage which he wrought for himself when he wrought hers. Only thus can she restore to him that of which he robbed himself in restricting her. Only thus can she remake the world. . . .

Woman must have her freedom—the fundamental freedom of choosing whether or not she shall be a mother and how many children she will have. Regardless of what man's attitude may be, that problem is hers—and before it can be his, it is hers alone.

She goes through the vale of death alone, each time a babe is born. As it is the right neither of man nor the state to coerce her into this ordeal, so it is her right to decide whether she will endure it. That right to decide imposes upon her the duty of clearing the way to knowledge by which she may make and carry out the decision.

Birth control is woman's problem. The quicker she accepts it as hers and hers alone, the quicker will society respect motherhood. The quicker, too, will the world be made a fit place for her children to live.

From Margaret Sanger, Woman and the New Race (New York: Brentano, 1920), pp. 93–100.

Proposed Equal Rights Amendment, 1923

Section 1. Equality of Rights under the law shall not be denied or abridged by the United States or any state on account of sex.

Section 2. The Congress shall have the power to enforce, by appropriate legislation, the provisions of this article.

Section 3. This amendment shall take effect two years after the date of ratification.

Convention on the Political Rights of Women, 1953

The Contracting Parties,

Desiring to implement the principle of equality of rights for men and women contained in the Charter of the United Nations,

Recognizing that everyone has the right to take part in the government of his country, directly or indirectly through freely chosen representatives, and has the right to

equal access to public service in his country, and desiring to equalize the status of men and women in the enjoyment and exercise of political rights, in accordance with the provisions of the Charter of the United Nations and the Universal Declaration of Human Rights,

Having resolved to conclude a Convention for this purpose,

Hereby agree as hereinafter provided:

Article I

Women shall be entitled to vote in all elections on equal terms with men without any discrimination.

Article II

Women shall be eligible for election to all publicly elected bodies, established by national law, on equal terms with men, without any discrimination.

Article III

Women shall be entitled to hold public office and to exercise all public functions, established by national law, on equal terms with men, without any discrimination.

Article IV

1. This Convention shall be open for signature on behalf of any Member of the United Nations and also on behalf of any other State to which an invitation has been addressed by the General Assembly.

2. This Convention shall be ratified and the instruments of ratification shall be deposited with the Secretary-General of the United Nations.

Article V

1. This Convention shall be open for accession to all States referred to in paragraph 1 of article IV.

2. Accession shall be effected by the deposit of an instrument of accession with the Secretary-General of the United Nations.

Article VI

1. This Convention shall come into force on the ninetieth day following the date of deposit of the sixth instrument of ratification or accession.

2. For each State ratifying or acceding to the Convention after the deposit of the sixth

instrument of ratification or accession the Convention shall enter into force on the ninetieth day after deposit by such State of its instrument of ratification or accession.

Article VII

In the event that any State submits a reservation to any of the articles of this Convention at the time of signature, ratification or accession, the Secretary-General shall communicate the text of the reservation to all States which are or may become parties to this Convention. Any State which objects to the reservation may, within a period of ninety days from the date of the said communication (or upon the date of its becoming a party to the Convention), notify the Secretary-General that it does not accept it. In such case, the Convention shall not enter into force as between such State and the State making the reservation.

Article VIII

1. Any State may denounce this Convention by written notification to the Secretary-General of the United Nations. Denunciation shall take effect one year after the date of receipt of the notification by the Secretary-General.

2. This Convention shall cease to be in force as from the date when the denunciation which reduces the number of parties to less than six becomes effective.

Article IX

Any dispute which may arise between any two or more Contracting States concerning the interpretation or application of this Convention which is not settled by negotiation, shall at the request of any one of the parties to the dispute be referred to the International Court of Justice for decision, unless they agree to another mode of settlement.

Article X

The Secretary-General of the United Nations shall notify all Members of the United Nations and the non-member States contemplated in paragraph 1 of article IV of this Convention of the following:

(a) Signatures and instruments of ratifica-

tions received in accordance with article IV;

(b) Instruments of accession received in accordance with article V;

(c) The date upon which this Convention enters into force in accordance with article VI;

(d) Communications and notifications received in accordance with article VII;

(e) Notifications of denunciation received in accordance with paragraph 1 of article VIII;

(f) Abrogation in accordance with paragraph 2 of article VIII.

Article XI

1. This Convention, of which the Chinese, English, French, Russian and Spanish texts shall be equally authentic, shall be deposited in the archives of the United Nations.

2. The Secretary-General of the United Nations shall transmit a certified copy to all Members of the United Nations and to the non-member States contemplated in paragraph 1 of article IV.

IN FAITH WHEREOF the undersigned, being duly authorized thereto by their respective Governments, have signed the present Convention, opened for signature at New York, on the thirty-first day of March, one thousand nine hundred and fifty-three.

Equal Pay Act (1963)

SEC. 206.

(d) (1) No employer having employees subject to any provisions of this section shall discriminate, within any establishment in which such employees are employed, between employees on the basis of sex by paying wages to employees in such establishment at a rate less than the rate at which he pays wages to employees of the opposite sex in such establishment for equal work on jobs the performance of which requires equal skill, effort, and responsibility, and which are performed under similar working conditions, except where such payment is made pursuant to (i) a seniority system; (ii) a merit system; (iii) a system which measures earnings by quantity or quality of production; or (iv) a differential based on any other factor other than sex: Provided, that an employer who is paying a wage rate differential in violation of this subsection shall not, in order to comply with the provisions of this subsection, reduce the wage rate of any employee.

(2) No labor organization, or its agents, representing employees of an employer having employees subject to any provisions of this section shall cause or attempt to cause such an employer to discriminate against an employee in violation of paragraph (1) of this subsection.

(3) For purposes of administration and enforcement, any amounts owing to any employee which have been withheld in violation of this subsection shall be deemed to be unpaid minimum wages or unpaid overtime compensation under this chapter.

(4) As used in this subsection, the term "labor organization" means any organization of any kind, or any agency or employee representation committee or plan, in which employees participate and which exists for the purpose, in whole or in part, of dealing with employers concerning grievances, labor disputes, wages, rates of pay, hours of employment, or conditions of work.

The Civil Rights Act (1964)

Title VII. "To enforce the constitutional right to vote, to confer jurisdiction upon the district courts of the United States to provide injunctive relief against discrimination in public accommodations, to authorize the attorney General to institute suits to protect constitutional rights in public facilities and public education, to extend the Commission on Civil Rights, to prevent discrimination in federally assisted programs, to establish a Commission on Equal Employment Opportunity, and for other purposes. Be it enacted by the Senate and House of Representatives of the United States of America in Congress assembled, that this Act may be cited as the Civil Rights Act of 1964."

The National Organization for Women's Bill of Rights for Women, 1967

WE DEMAND:

I. That the U.S. Congress immediately pass the Equal Rights Amendment to the Constitution . . . and that such then be immediately ratified by the several States.

II. That equal employment opportunity be guaranteed to all women, as well as men . . .

III. That women be protected by law to ensure their rights to return to their jobs within a reasonable time after childbirth without loss of seniority or other accrued benefits, and be paid maternity leave as a form of social security and/or employee benefit.

IV. Immediate revision of tax laws to permit the deduction of home and child-care expenses for working parents.

V. That child-care facilities be established by law on the same basis as parks, libraries, and public schools, adequate to the needs of children from the pre-school years through adolescence, as a community resource to be used by all citizens from all income levels.

VI. That the right of women to be educated to their full potential equally with men be secured by Federal and State legislation.

VII. The right of women in poverty to secure job training, housing, and family allowances on equal terms with men, but without prejudice to a parent's right to remain at home to care for his or her children; revision of welfare legislation and poverty programs which deny women dignity, privacy, and self-respect.

VIII. The right of women to control their own reproductive lives by removing from the penal codes laws limiting access to contraceptive information and devices, and by repealing penal laws governing abortion.

Reprinted by permission of the National Organization for Women.

Equal Rights for Women, Rep. Shirley Chisholm, 1969

Mr. Speaker, when a young woman graduates from college and starts looking for a job, she is likely to have a frustrating and even demeaning experience ahead of her. If she walks into an office for an interview, the first question she will be asked is, "Do you type?"

There is a calculated system of prejudice that lies unspoken behind that question. Why is it acceptable for women to be secretaries, librarians, and teachers, but totally unacceptable for them to be managers, administrators, doctors, lawyers, and Members of Congress?

The unspoken assumption is that women are different. They do not have executive ability, orderly minds, stability, leadership skills, and they are too emotional.

It has been observed before, that society for a long time discriminated against another minority, the blacks, on the same basis—that they were different and inferior. The happy little homemaker and the contented "old darkey" on the plantation were both produced by prejudice.

As a black person, I am no stranger to race prejudice. But the truth is that in the political world I have been far oftener discriminated against because I am a woman than because I am black.

Prejudice against blacks is becoming unacceptable although it will take years to eliminate it. But it is doomed because, slowly, white America is beginning to admit that it exists. Prejudice against women is still acceptable. There is very little understanding yet of the immorality involved in double pay scales and the classification of most of the better jobs as "for men only."

More than half of the population of the United States is female. But women occupy only 2 percent of the managerial positions. They have not even reached the level of tokenism yet. No women sit on the AFL-CIO council or Supreme Court. There have been only two women who have held Cabinet rank, and at present there are none. Only two women now hold ambassadorial rank in the diplomatic corps. In Congress, we are down to one senator and ten representatives.

Considering that there are about $3\frac{1}{2}$ million more women in the United States than men, this situation is outrageous.

It is true that part of the problem has been that women have not been aggressive in demanding their rights. This was also true of the black population for many years. They submitted to oppression and even cooperated with it. Women have done the same thing. But now there is an awareness of this situation particularly among the younger segment of the population.

As in the field of equal rights for blacks, Spanish-Americans, the Indians, and other groups, laws will not change such deep-seated problems overnight. But they can be used to provide protection for those who are most abused, and to begin the process of evolutionary change by compelling the insensitive majority to reexamine its unconscious attitudes.

It is for this reason that I wish to introduce today a proposal that has been before every Congress for the last 40 years and that sooner or later must become part of the basic law of the land—the equal rights amendment.

Let me note and try to refute two of the commonest arguments that are offered against this amendment. One is that women are already protected under the law and do not need legislation. Existing laws are not adequate to secure equal rights for women. Sufficient proof of this is the concentration of women in lower paying, menial, unrewarding jobs and their incredible scarcity in the upper level jobs. If women are already equal, why is it such an event whenever one happens to be elected to Congress?

It is obvious that discrimination exists. Women do not have the opportunities that men do. And women that do not conform to the system, who try to break with the accepted patterns, are stigmatized as "odd" and "unfeminine." The fact is that a woman who aspires to be chairman of the board, or a member of the House, does so for exactly the same reasons as any man. Basically, these are that she thinks she can do the job and she wants to try.

A second argument often heard against the equal rights amendment is that it would eliminate legislation that many states and the federal government have enacted giving special protection to women and that it would throw the marriage and divorce laws into chaos.

As for the marriage laws, they are due for a sweeping reform, and an excellent beginning would be to wipe the existing ones off the books. Regarding special protection for working women, I cannot understand why it should be needed. Women need no protection that men do not need. What we need are laws to protect working people, to guarantee them fair pay, safe working conditions, protection against sickness and lay-offs, and provision for dignified, comfortable retirement. Men and women need these things equally. That one sex needs protection more than the other is a male supremacist myth as ridiculous and unworthy of respect as the white supremacist myths that society is trying to cure itself of at this time.

Title IX of the Education Amendments of 1972

No person in the United States shall, on the basis of sex, be excluded from participation in, be denied the benefits of, or be subjected to discrimination under any education program or activity receiving Federal financial assistance.

The National Women's Conference Plan of Action, 1977

Fifty-six state and territorial conventions forwarded recommendations summarized below for ratification by 2000 delegates gathered in Houston in 1977. Apart from gender, it was the most diverse elected body ever assembled.

1. Arts and Humanities: Equitable representation in management, governance, and decision-making structures in libraries, museums, media and higher education; blind-judging when possible.

2. Battered Women: Elimination of violence in the home through emergency shelters; training and intervention; strengthening and enforcement of laws; legal services for victims.

3. Business: Support for women entrepreneurs through government-related activities and contracts; inclusion of women-owned business in Small Business Administration targeting.

4. Child Abuse: Support for prevention and treatment of abused children including training for public awareness, parent counseling, service and justice agencies.

5. Child Care: Federally supported efforts and legislation at all levels to promote quality child care programs; labor and business support; education for parenthood.

6. Credit: Education and enforcement of the 1974 Federal Equal Credit Opportunity Act.

7. Disabled Women: Enforcement and expansion of legislation on education, employment, housing, and support services recognizing the special needs of disabled women.

8. Education: Enforcement of laws prohibiting discrimination in education; special consideration for physical education, leadership positions, vocation training, elimination of sex and race stereotyping.

9. Elective/Appointive Office: Joint effort by federal and state governments, political parties, and other organizations to increase women in office, policy making positions and judgeships.

10. Employment: A federal full employment policy; enforcement and extension of anti-discrimination laws; efforts by governments, institutions, business, industry and unions to reduce occupational segregation

and promote upward mobility; special attention to minority women; amendment of the Veteran's Preference Act; extensions of the labor standards and the right to unionize; support for flextime jobs.

11. Equal Rights Amendment: Ratification of the ERA.

12. Health: Establishment of a national health security program acknowledging the special needs of women; improve community facilities, contraceptive research, reproductive services, substance abuse efforts, representation in professions and on policy boards; increase review of drugs, custodial care, surgical procedures.

13. Homemakers: Revise marital property, social security, and pension laws; in divorce provide for children's needs and sharing of economic burden; support displaced homemaker programs.

14. Insurance: Adoption of Model Regulations to Eliminate Unfair Sex Discrimination amended to cover pregnancy, newborns, policy conversions.

15. International Affairs: Increased participation by women in foreign policy-making roles; enforcement of anti-discrimination laws; improvement of the image of women in the mass media.

16. Media: Increased opportunity for women in professional and policy-making roles; enforcement of anti-discrimination laws; improvement of the image of women in the mass media.

17. Minority Women: Recognition that every Plan recommendation applies to all minority women with recognition of additional burdens through institutionalized bias and inadequate data; enforcement of anti-discrimination laws as they affect education, housing, health, employment; recognition of special needs of American Indian/ Alaskan Native women, Asian Pacific women, Hispanic women, Puerto Rican women, Black women.

18. Offenders: Review of sentencing laws and practices with discriminatory effects on women in penal facilities; address legal,

counseling, health, educational needs of women, especially mothers and juveniles.

19. Older Women: Support by governments, public and private institutions of services promoting dignity and security in housing, health services, transportation, education, social security, recognition of the changing image of older women and their capacity to contribute to policy making.

20. Rape: Revise criminal codes to correct inequities against rape victims; rape crisis centers and prevention and self-protection programs; support for the National Center for the Prevention/ Control of Rape; victim compensation.

21. Reproductive Freedom: Support for U.S. Supreme Court decision guaranteeing reproductive freedom; make certain all methods of family planning are available to all women under privately or publicly funded medical services; oppose involuntary sterilization; full access to family planning and education on responsible sexuality for teens, full education programs with child care for teen parents.

22. Rural Women: Rural education policy to meet isolation, poverty and underemployment affecting women; improved data; full ownership rights for farm wives, review conditions affecting plantation/ migratory workers.

23. Sexual Preference: Legislation eliminating discrimination based on sexual preference in employment, housing, public accommodations, credit, public facilities, funding, military, repeal of laws restricting private behavior between consenting adults; evaluation of child custody suits based solely on parenting capacity.

24. Statistics: An analysis of all data collected by the government on the basis of sex and race to assess the impact of programs on women.

25. Welfare and Poverty: Focus on welfare and poverty by federal and state governments as major women's issues compounding inequality of opportunity; support for welfare reform program considering social

security, child care, minimum wage, education, job opportunities, health insurance, and legal services; federal floor to ensure an adequate standard of living.

26. Continuing Committee of National Women's Conference: Establishment of a body to consider steps to achieve the Plan and convene a second conference.

Getting Beyond Racism, Sen. Carol Moseley-Braun, 1993

Madam President, I really had not wanted to have to do this because in my remarks I believe that I was restrained and tempered. I talked about the committee procedure. I talked about the lack of germaneness of this amendment. I talked about how it was not necessary for this organization to receive the design patent extension, which was an extraordinary extension of an extraordinary act to begin with.

What I did not talk about and what I am constrained now to talk about with no small degree of emotion is the symbolism of what this vote. . . . That is what this vote really means.

I started off—maybe—I do not know—it is just my day to get to talk about race. Maybe I am just lucky about that today.

I have to tell you this vote is about race. It is about racial symbolism. It is about racial symbols, the racial past, and the single most painful episode in American history.

I have just gone through—in fact in committee yesterday I leaned over to my colleague Dianne Feinstein and I said, "You know, Dianne, I am stunned about how often and how much race comes up in conversation and debate in this general assembly." Did not I say that? . . .

So I turned to my colleague, Dianne Feinstein. You know, I am really stunned by how often and how much the issue of race, the subject of racism, comes up in this U.S. Senate, comes up in this body and how I have to, on many occasions, as the only African-American here, constrain myself to be calm, to be laid back, to talk about these issues in

very intellectual, nonemotional terms, and that is what I do on a regular basis, Madam President. That is part and parcel of my daily existence.

But at the same time, when the issue of the design patent extension for the United Daughters of the Confederacy first came up, I looked at it. I did not make a big deal of it. It came as part of the work of the Judiciary Committee. I looked at it, and I said, well, I am not going to vote for that.

When I announced I was not going to vote for it, the chairman, as is his due, began to poll the members. We talked about it, and I found myself getting drawn into a debate that I frankly never expected.

Who would have expected a design patent for the Confederate flag? And there are those in this body who say this really is not the Confederate flag. The other thing we did know was a Confederate flag.

I did my research, and I looked it up as I am wont to do, and guess what? That is the real Confederate flag. The thing we see all the time and are accustomed to is the battle flag. In fact, there is some history on this issue. I would like to read the following quote from the Flag Book of the United States.

The real flower in the southern flag began in November 1860, when the election of Lincoln to the Presidency caused widespread fear the federal government will try to make changes in the institution of slavery. The winter of 1860 to 1861, rallies and speeches were held throughout the South and, frankly, the United States flag was replaced by a local banner.

This flag is the real flag of the Confederacy. If there is anybody in this chamber, anybody, indeed anybody in this world, that has a doubt that the Confederate effort was around preserving the institution of slavery, I am prepared and I believe history is prepared to dispute them to the nth. There is no question but that battle was fought to try to preserve our nation, to keep the states from separating themselves over the issue of whether or not my ancestors could be held as property, as chattel, as objects of commerce and trade in this country.

And people died. More Americans died in the Civil War than any war they have ever gone through since. People died over the proposition that indeed these United States stood for the proposition that every person was created equal without regard to race, that we are all American citizens.

I am sorry, Madam President. I will lower my voice. I am getting excited, because, quite frankly, that is the very issue. The issue is whether or not Americans, such as myself, who believe in the promise of this country, who feel strongly and who are patriots in this country, will have to suffer the indignity of being reminded time and time again, that at one point in this country's history we were human chattel. We were property. We could be traded, bought, and sold.

Now, to suggest as a matter of revisionist history that this flag is not about slavery flies in the face of history, Madam President.

I was not going to get inflammatory. In fact, my staff brought me this little thing earlier, and it has been sitting here. I do not know if you noticed it sitting here during the earlier debate in which I was dispassionate and tried my level best not to be emotional and lawyering about and not get into calling names and talking about race and racism. I did not use it to begin with. I do want to share it now. It is a speech by the Vice President of the Confederate States of America, March 21, 1861, in Savannah, GA.

"Slavery, the Cornerstone of the Confederacy." And this man goes on to say:

"The new Confederate constitution has put to rest forever all agitating questions relating to our peculiar 'institution,' which is what they called it, African slavery as it exists among us, the proper status of a negro in our form of civilization. This was the immediate cause of the late rupture and present revolution.

The prevailing ideas entertained by Thomas Jefferson and most of the leading statesmen at the time of the formation of the old Constitution were that the enslavement of the African was in violation of the laws of nature, that it was wrong in principle, socially; morally; and politically."

And then he goes on to say:

"Our new government is founded upon exactly the opposite idea. Its foundations are laid, its cornerstone rests upon the great truth that the negro is not equal to the white man, that slavery, subordination to the superior race is his natural and moral condition."

This was a statement by the Vice President of the Confederate States of America.

Madam President, across the room on the other side is the flag. I say to you it is outrageous. It is an absolute outrage that this body would adopt as an amendment to this legislation a symbol of this point of view and, Madam President, I say to you that it is an important issue. It is a symbolic issue up there. There is no way you can get around it.

The reason for my emotion—I have been here almost 7 months now, and my colleagues will tell you there is not a more congenial, laid back, even person in this entire body who makes it a point to try to get along with everybody. I make it a point to try to talk to my colleagues and get beyond controversy and conflict, to try to find consensus on issues.

But I say to you, Madam President, on this issue there can be no consensus. It is an outrage. It is an insult. It is absolutely unacceptable to me and to millions of Americans, black or white, that we would put the imprimatur of the United States Senate on a symbol of this kind of idea. And that is what is at stake with this amendment, Madam President.

I am going to continue—I am going to continue because I am going to call it like I see it, as I always do. I was appalled, appalled at a segment of my own Democratic Party that would go take a walk and vote for something like this.

I am going to talk for a minute first about my brethren, my close-in brethren and then talk about the other side of the aisle and the responsibility of the Republican Party.

The reason the Republican Party got run out on a rail the last time is the American people sensed intolerance in that party. The American people, African-Americans sensed there was not room for them in that party. Folks took a look at the convention and said, "My God, what are these people standing for? This is not America." And they turned around and voted for change. They elected Bill Clinton president and the rest of us to this chamber. The changes they were speaking out for was a change that said we have to get past racism, we have to get past sexism, the many issues that divide us as Americans, and come together as Americans so we can make this country be what it can be in the 21st century.

That is the real reason, Madam President, that I am here today. My state has less than 12 percent African-Americans in it, but the people of Illinois had no problem voting for a candidate that was African-American because they thought they were doing the same thing.

Similarly, the state of California sent two women, two women to the U.S. Senate, breaking a gender barrier, as did the state of Washington. Why? Because they felt that it was time to get past the barriers that said that women had no place in the conduct of our business.

And so, just as our country is moving forward, Madam President, to have this kind of symbol shoved in your face, shoved in my face, shoved in the faces of all the Americans who want to see a change for us to get beyond racism, is singularly inappropriate.

I say to you, Madam President, that this is no small matter. This is not a matter of little old ladies walking around doing good deeds. There is no reason why these little old ladies cannot do good deeds anyway. If they choose to wave the Confederate flag, that certainly is their right. Because I care about the fact that this is a free country. Free speech is the cornerstone of democracy.

People are supposed to be able to say what they want to say. They are supposed to be able to join associations and organizations that express their views.

But I daresay, Madam President, that following the Civil War, and following the victory of the United States and the coming together of our country, that that peculiar institution was put to rest for once and for all; that the division in our nation, the North versus the South, was put to rest once and for all. And the people of this country do not want to see a day in which flags like that are underwritten, underscored, adopted, approved by this U.S. Senate.

That is what this vote is about. That is what this vote is about.

I say to you, Madam President, I do not know—I do not want to yield the floor right now because I do not know what will happen next.

I will yield momentarily to my colleague from California, Madam President, because I think that this is an issue that I am not going—if I have to stand here until this room freezes over, I am not going to see this amendment put on this legislation which has to do with national service. . . . If I have to stand here until this room freezes over, Madam President, I am going to do so. Because I will tell you, this is something that has no place in our modern times. It has no place in this body. It has no place in the Senate. It has no place in our society.

And the fact is, Madam President, that I would encourage my colleagues on both sides of the aisle—Republican and Democrat; those who thought, "Well, we are just going to do this, you know, because it is no big deal"—to understand what a very big deal indeed it is—that the imprimatur that is being sought here today sends a sign out to the rest of this country that that peculiar institution has not been put to bed for once and for all; that, indeed, like Dracula, it has come back to haunt us time and time and time again; and that, in spite of the fact that we have made strides forward, the fact of the matter is that there are those who would keep us slipping back into the darkness of division, into the snake pit of racial hatred, of racial antagonism and of support for symbols—symbols of the struggle to keep African-Americans, Americans of African descent, in bondage.

Statement before the Joint Hearing of the House Resources Committee and Senate Committee on Indian Affairs, Ada Deer, 1997

Good morning Chairman Campbell, Chairman Young, and Members of the Committees. I am pleased to be here to present the Department of the Interior's views on proposed amendments to the Indian Child Welfare Act (ICWA) of 1978. The Department of the Interior supports, without reservation, H.R. 1082 and its companion bill, S. 569, which have incorporated the consensus-based tribal amendments developed last year by tribal governments and the National Congress of American Indians (NCAI) and the adoption community to improve the Indian Child Welfare Act.

Background Information

Congress passed the Indian Child Welfare Act in 1978 (ICWA), after ten years of study on Indian child custody and placements revealed an alarming high rate of out of home placements and adoptions. The strongest attribute of the ICWA is the premise that an Indian child's tribe is in a better position than a State or Federal court to make decisions or judgments on matters involving the relationship of an Indian child to his or her tribe. The clear intent of Congress was to defer to Indian tribes issues of cultural and social values as such relate to child rearing.

In addition to protecting the best interests of Indian children, the ICWA has also preserved the cultural integrity of Indian tribes because it affirmed tribal authority over Indian child custody matters. As a result the long term benefit is, and will be, the continued existence of Indian tribes.

Implementation of the ICWA

The Indian Child Welfare Act of 1978 is the essence of child welfare in Indian Country and provides the needed protections for Indian children who are neglected. On the whole, the ICWA has fulfilled the objective of giving Indian tribes the opportunity to intervene on behalf of Indian children eligible for tribal membership in a particular tribe.

There have been concerns over certain aspects of the ICWA and the ICWA should be revised to address problem areas and to ensure that the best interests of Indian children are ultimately considered in all voluntary child custody proceedings. Although several high-profile cases were cited to support the introduction last year of ICWA amendments, which would have been detrimental to Indian tribes and families, those cases do not warrant a unilateral and unfettered intrusion on tribal government authority.

Implications of Proposed Amendments to the ICWA

The provisions contained in H.R. 1082 and S. 569 reflect carefully crafted consensus amendments between Indian tribes seeking to protect their children, culture and heritage and the interests of the adoption community seeking greater clarity and certainty in the implementation of the ICWA. First and foremost, the amendments will clarify the applicability of the ICWA to voluntary child custody matters so that there are no ambiguities or uncertainties in the handling of these cases. We know from experience that State courts have not always applied the ICWA to voluntary child custody proceedings.

The amendments will ensure that Indian tribes receive notice of voluntary ICWA proceedings and also clarify what should be included in the notices. Timely and adequate notice to tribes will ensure more appropriate and permanent placement decisions for Indian children. Indian parents will be informed of their rights and their children's rights under the Act, ensuring that they make informed decisions on the adoptive or foster care placement of their children. When tribes and extended family members are allowed to participate in placement decisions, the risk for disruption will be greatly reduced. While the amendments place limitations on when Indian tribes and families may intervene and when birth parents may withdraw their consent to an adoption, they protect the fundamental rights of tribal sovereignty. Furthermore, the amendments will permit open adoptions, when it is in the best interest of an Indian child, even if State law does not so provide. Under an open adoption, Indian children will have access to their natural family and cultural heritage when it is deemed appropriate.

An important consideration is that upon a tribe's decision to intervene in a voluntary child custody proceeding, the tribe must certify the tribal membership status of an Indian child or their eligibility for membership according to tribal law or custom. Thus, there would be no question that a child is Indian under the ICWA and ensures that tribal membership determinations are not made arbitrarily. Lastly, the amendments will provide for criminal sanctions to discourage fraudulent practices by individuals or agencies which knowingly misrepresent or fail to disclose whether a child or the birth parent(s) are Indian to circumvent the application of the ICWA.

In summary, the tribally developed amendments contained in H.R. 1082 and S. 569 clearly address the concerns which led to the introduction of Title III of H.R. 3286 (104th Congress), including time frames for ICWA notifications, timely interventions, and sanctions, definitive schemes for intervention, limitations on the time for biological parents to withdraw consent to adoptive placements, and finality in voluntary proceedings.

Effect of "Existing Indian Family" Concept

Chairman Campbell and Chairman Young, we want to express our grave concern that the objectives of the ICWA continue to be frustrated by State court created judicial exceptions to the ICWA. We are concerned that State court judges who have created the "existing Indian family exception" are delving into the sensitive and complicated areas of Indian cultural values, customs and practices which under existing law have been left exclusively to the judgment of Indian tribes. Legislation introduced last year, including H.R. 3286, sought to ratify the "existing Indian family exception" by amending the ICWA to codify this State-created concept. The Senate Committee on Indian Affairs, in striking Title III from H.R. 3286, made clear its views that the concept of the "existing Indian family exception" is in direct contradiction to existing law. In rejecting the "existing Indian family exception" concept, the Committee stated that "the ICWA recognizes that the Federal trust responsibility and the role of Indian tribes as parens patriae extend to all Indian children involved in all child custody proceedings." [Report 104–335 accompanying S. 1962, 104th Cong., 2nd Session].

Position of the Department of the Interior

The Department of the Interior's position on the emerging "existing Indian family exception" concept is the same as previously stated in the Administration's statement of policy issued on May 9, 1996. We oppose any legislative recognition of the concept.

The Department's position is that the ICWA must continue to provide Federal protections for Indian families, tribes and Indian children involved in any child custody proceeding, regardless of their individual circumstances. Thus, the Department fully concurs with the Senate Committee on Indian Affairs' assessment and rejection of the "existing Indian family exception" concept and all of its manifestations. We share the expressed concerns of tribal leaders and a majority of your Committee members about continuing efforts to amend the ICWA, particularly those bills which would seriously limit and weaken the existing

ICWA protections available to Indian tribes and children in voluntary foster care and adoption proceedings.

The United States has a government-to-government relationship with Indian tribal governments. Protection of their sovereign status, including preservation of tribal identity and the determination of Indian tribal membership, is fundamental to this relationship. The Congress, after ten years of study, passed the Indian Child Welfare Act of 1978 (Pub. L. 95–608) as a means to remedy the many years of widespread separation of Indian children from their families. The ICWA established a successful dual system that establishes exclusive tribal jurisdiction over Indian Child Welfare cases arising in Indian Country, and presumes tribal jurisdiction in the cases involving Indian children, yet allows concurrent State jurisdiction in Indian child adoption and child custody proceedings where good cause exists. This system, which authorizes tribal involvement and referral to tribal courts, has been successful in protecting the interests of Indian tribal governments, Indian children and Indian families for the past eighteen years.

Because the proposed amendments contained in H.R. 1082 and S. 569 will strengthen the Act and continue to protect the lives and future of Indian children, the Department fully embraces the provisions of H.R. 1082 and S. 569.

In closing, we appreciate the good faith efforts of tribal governments in addressing the ICWA-specific concerns raised by certain members of the Congress and in developing tribally acceptable legislative amendments toward resolving these issues within the past year. I would like to thank Chairman Campbell, Chairman Young, and the Committee members for all their hard work and heartfelt assistance to tribes in shepherding the tribal amendments through the legislative process. This Administration will endeavor to ensure that tribal sovereignty will not be compromised, specifically, the right of tribal governments to determine tribal membership and the right of tribal courts to determine internal tribal relations.

This concludes my prepared statement. I will be pleased to answer any questions the Committees may have.

Declaration of Sentiments of the National Organization for Women, 1998

On this twelfth day of July, 1998, the delegates of the National Organization for Women gather in convention on the one hundred and fiftieth year of the women's rights movement.

We bring passion, anger, hope, love and perseverance to create this vision for the future:

We envision a world where women's equality and women's empowerment to determine our own destinies is a reality;

We envision a world where women have equal representation in all decision-making structures of our societies;

We envision a world where social and economic justice exist, where all people have the food, housing, clothing, health care and education they need;

We envision a world where there is recognition and respect for each person's intrinsic worth as well as the rich diversity of the various groups among us;

We envision a world where non-violence is the established order;

We envision a world where patriarchal culture and male dominance no longer oppress us or our earth;

We envision a world where women and girls are heard, valued and respected.

Our movement, encompassing many issues and many strategies, directs our love for humanity into action that spans the world and unites women.

But our future requires us to know our past.

One hundred fifty years ago the women's rights movement grew out of the fight to abolish slavery. Angered by their exclusion from leadership and public speaking at abolitionist conventions and inspired by the power of the Iroquois women, a small dedicated group of women and men built a movement. After its inception, the movement was fractured by race. Our history is full of struggle against common bonds of oppression and a painful reality of separation. Nevertheless, these activists created a political force that achieved revolutionary change. They won property rights for married women; opened the doors of higher education for women; and garnered suffrage in 1920.

In 1923, on the seventy-fifth anniversary of the historic Seneca Falls convention, feminists led the demand for constitutional equality for women to win full justice under the law in order to end economic, educational, and political inequality.

Our foremothers—the first wave of feminists—ran underground railroads, lobbied, marched, and picketed. They were jailed and force fed, lynched and raped. But they prevailed. They started with a handful of activists, and today, the feminist movement involves millions of people every day.

Standing on their shoulders, we launched the National Organization for Women in 1966, the largest and strongest organization of feminists in the world today. A devoutly grassroots, action-oriented organization, we have sued, boycotted, picketed, lobbied, demonstrated, marched, and engaged in non-violent civil disobedience. We have won in the courts and in the legislatures; and we have negotiated with the largest corporations in the world, winning unparalleled rights for women.

The National Organization for Women and our modern day movement have profoundly changed the lives of women, men and children. We have raised public consciousness about the plight of women to such an extent that today the majority of people support equality for women.

In the past 32 years, women have advanced farther than in any previous generation. Yet still we do not have full equality.

We have moved more feminists than ever before into positions of power in all of the institutions that shape our society. We have achieved some measure of power to effect change in these institutions from within; yet still we are far from full equality in decision-making. We demand an equal share of power in our families and religions, in law, science and technology, the arts and humanities, sports, education, the trades and professions, labor and management, the media, corporations and small businesses as well as government. In no sphere of life should women be silenced, underrepresented, or devalued.

Today, we reaffirm our demand for Constitutional equality for women and girls. Simultaneously, we are working with sister organizations to develop and pass a national women's equality act for the twenty-first century. And we participate in and advance a global movement for women and demand that the United States join the overwhelming majority of nations of the world in ratifying the United Nations Convention on the Elimination of All Forms of Discrimination Against Women without reservations, declarations, or understandings that would weaken this commitment.

We reaffirm our commitment to the power of grassroots activism, to a multi-issue, multi-tactical strategy.

We are committed to a feminist ideology and reaffirm our historic commitment to gaining equality for women, assuring safe, legal and accessible abortion and full reproductive freedom, combating racism, stopping violence against women, ending bigotry and discrimination based on sexual orientation and on color, ethnicity, national origin, women's status, age, disability, size, childbearing capacity or choices, or parental or marital status.

We will not trade off the rights of one woman for the advancement of another. We will not be divided. We will unite with all women who seek freedom and join hands with all of the great movements of our time and all time, seeking equality, empowerment and justice.

We commit to continue the mentoring, training, and leadership development of young and new activists of all ages who will continue our struggle. We will work to invoke enthusiasm for our goals and to expand ownership in this movement for current and future generations.

We commit to continue building a mass movement where we are leaders, not followers, of public opinion. We will continue to move feminist ideals into the mainstream thought, and we will build our media and new technology capabilities to control our own image and message.

How long and hard a struggle it was to win the right for women to vote. Today, we fight the same reactionary forces: the perversion of religion to subjugate women; corporate greed that seeks to exploit women and children as a cheap labor force; and their apologists in public office who seek to do through law what terrorists seek to accomplish through bullets and bombs. We will not submit, nor will we be intimidated. But we will keep moving forward.

Those who carried the struggle for women's suffrage through to its end were not there at the start; those who started the struggle did not live to see the victory. Like those strong feminist activists, we will not let ourselves be dispirited or discouraged. Even when progress seems most elusive, we will maintain our conviction that the work itself is important. For it is the work that enriches our lives; it is the work that unites us; it is the work that will propel us into the next century. We know that our struggle has made a difference, and we reaffirm our faith that it will continue to make a difference for women's lives.

Today, we dedicate ourselves to the sheer joy of moving forward and fighting back.

Reprinted by permission of the National Organization for Women.

Statement on Equal Pay Day, Linda Chavez-Thompson, 1998

Last September, the AFL-CIO—which with 5 1/2 million women members is the largest organization of working women in the country—asked working women in every kind of job—in every part of the country—to tell us about the biggest problem they face at work.

Ninety-nine percent said a top concern is equal pay.

And most women told us that despite the economic good times, it is just as hard now as it was five years ago to make ends meet . . . or it's become even harder.

The truth is that working women need and deserve equal pay.

The wage gap between women and men is huge.

If it is not changed, the average 25-year-old working woman can expect to lose $523,000 over the course of her work life.

That's enough to make a world of difference for most working families.

It can mean decent health care . . . a college education for the kids . . . a secure retirement . . . and simply being able to pay the monthly bills on time.

That is what the wage gap now takes from working women.

It's the price of unequal pay.

Patricia Hoersten knows what that's about.

Pat served lunch and dinner at a diner in Lima, Ohio. She got paid half of what the male servers got paid—because her supervisor thought she only needed extra money, not money to live on.

The tragedy is that there are millions of women who are experiencing the very same injustice.

Is this a women's issue?

It is—but it's also a family issue, because women's wages are essential to their families.

Most working women contribute half or more of their household's income.

So when working women lose out, working families lose out.

The good news is that working women are joining together to fight for equal pay.

I've been able to hear from many of them.

One is Maria Olivas. She's a clerical worker at Columbia University.

Maria worked with her union to make sure that her employer disclosed how much it paid men and women for the same job. They found out that men were paid $1,500 more than women for the same job. After a long struggle, they were able to win equal pay.

There are lots more like her.

Grocery store clerks at Publix Supermarkets won $80 million in back pay because they were not getting equal pay and promotions.

But no woman should have to fight by herself for equal pay.

That's why the AFL-CIO has launched a nationwide grassroots campaign to fight for women's wages.

That's why the union movement is making equal pay one of the main goals of our 1998 Agenda for Working Families.

And that's why the AFL-CIO applauds, supports, and will work to enact the legislation being introduced by Senator Tom Daschle and Representative Rosa DeLauro.

This legislation will give women an important weapon to battle wage discrimination and to help close the wage gap. It's about time.

Reprinted by permission of the AFL-CIO.

The Violence Against Women Act of 2000 (VAWA 2000):

The following information highlights many of the most important aspects of the VAWA 2000.

• Defines "dating violence" as violence committed by a person who is or has been in a social relationship of a romantic or intimate nature with the victim. The existence of such a relationship is determined by the following factors: 1) length of the relationship; 2) type of relationship; and 3) frequency of interaction between the persons involved.

• Grants to Encourage Arrest Policies and Enforcement of Protection Orders Program, the STOP (Services*Training*Officers* Pros-

ecutors) Violence Against Women Formula Grant Program, the Rural Domestic Violence and Child Victimization Enforcement Grant Program, and the Grants to Reduce Violent Crimes Against Women on Campus Program.

• Grants to Indian Tribal Governments to encourage Arrest Policies and Enforcement of Protection Orders Program, the Rural Domestic Violence and Child Victimization Enforcement Grant Program, the Legal Assistance for Victims Program and the Safe Havens for Children (supervised visitation) Program.

• Grants to Encourage Arrest Policies Program facilitates widespread enforcement of protection orders as a purpose of the program and requires that priority be given to applicants that demonstrate a commitment to strong enforcement of protection orders from other states and jurisdictions, including tribal jurisdictions.

• Allows funds to be used to develop and strengthen policies and training for police, prosecutors, and the judiciary on domestic violence and sexual assault against older individuals and individuals with disabilities.

• Clarifies that strengthening legal advocacy services for victims of domestic violence under the program includes assistance to victims of domestic violence in immigration matters.

• Requires grantees under the program (and under the STOP Violence Against Women Formula Grant Program) to certify that their laws, practices, and policies do not require victims to pay filing or service costs related to criminal domestic violence cases or protection orders.

• Full Faith and Credit prohibits states and tribes from requiring notification (to the perpetrator) of the registration of an out of state or tribal protection order, unless the victim requests the notification.

• Grants to Combat Violent Crimes Against Women (which include the STOP Violence Against Women Formula Grant Program) to: 1) to support statewide, coordinated community responses; 2) to train sexual assault forensic medical personnel examiners; 3) to develop, enlarge, and strengthen programs to assist law enforcement, prosecutors, courts and others to address and recognize the needs and circumstances of older and disabled individuals who are victims of domestic violence and sexual assault; and 4) to provide assistance to victims of domestic violence and sexual assault in immigration matters.

• Rural Domestic Violence and Child Victimization Enforcement Grants assists victims of domestic violence and child abuse in immigration matters to the purpose area on counseling for victims.

• National Stalker and Domestic Violence Reduction authorizes grants to improve processes for entering data regarding stalking and domestic violence into local, state, and national crime information databases

• Domestic Violence and Stalking Offenses includes interstate cyberstalking and adds entering or leaving Indian country to the interstate stalking offense.

• Create victim services organizations at public universities.

• Civil legal assistance for victims of domestic violence, stalking, and sexual assault. Defines legal assistance to include family, immigration, administrative agency, housing, protection orders, and "other similar matters." Any person providing legal assistance has completed or will complete training that was developed with a domestic violence or sexual assault coalition or program.

• Shelter Services for Battered Women and Children

• Transitional Housing Assistance for Victims of Domestic Violence

• National Domestic Violence Hotline

• Studies Related to Violence Against Women

• Provides training for law enforcement, prosecutors and courts on elder abuse, neglect, and exploitation, including domestic violence and sexual assault against older or disabled individuals

• A pilot program to make grants to states, units of local government, and Indian tribal governments to work with non-profit entities to provide supervised visitation and safe visitation exchange of children in domestic violence, child abuse, sexual assault, or stalking cases.

• Creates court appointed special advocates for victims of child abuse.

• Child abuse training programs for judicial personnel and practitioners.

• Study the effects of parental kidnapping laws in domestic violence cases.

• Requires a study and report to Congress on federal and state laws relating to child custody, including recommendations to reduce violence against women and sexual assault of children.

• Programs on rape prevention and education.

• Education and training to end violence against and abuse of women with disabilities

• Requires the attorney general to evaluate existing standards, practice and training for sexual assault forensic examinations

• Education and training for judges and court personnel to include dating violence, domestic violence and child sexual assault issues in custody and visitation cases.

• Domestic Violence Task Force to coordinate federal research on domestic violence.

• Creates a new nonimmigrant visa for victims of certain serious crimes, including domestic violence, sexual assault, stalking, and trafficking crimes if the victim has suffered substantial physical or mental abuse as a result of the crime, the victim has information about the crime, and a law enforcement official or a judge certifies that the victim is or is likely to be helpful in investigating or prosecuting the crime.

Programs to combat trafficking of persons, especially into the sex trade, slavery, and slavery-like conditions, through prevention, prosecution and enforcement against traffickers, and protection and assistance for victims.

CHRONOLOGY

1776—Abigail Adams writes to her husband, John, one of the original founders and signers of the Declaration of Independence. She cautions him and his contemporaries in Philadelphia that summer to "remember the ladies" while writing their document to free the colonists from the tyranny of King George. They do not heed her call, and the declaration specifies that "all men are created equal."

1821—The first school for girls is founded: the Troy Female Seminary in New York.

1833—Oberlin College in Ohio becomes the first coeducational college in the United States. It awards its first academic degrees to women in 1841. Several well-known suffragists, including Lucy Stone, are alumnae.

1837—Mount Holyoke College in Massachusetts, the first four-year college exclusively for women, is established. The founding of Vassar follows in 1861 and Wellesley and Smith Colleges in 1875.

1839—Mississippi becomes the first state to pass a Married Women's Property Act. Other states follow suit.

1848—The first women's rights convention in the United States is held in Seneca Falls, New York. Many women who attend are abolitionists who were denied seating at the World Anti-Slavery Conference in London; they draw parallels between their legal rights as women and the rights of the bonded slaves they are attempting to free. They agree upon a "Declaration of Sentiments," a list of demands that become the goals for the first feminist movement.

1865 to 1880—Reconstruction begins following the Civil War (1861–1865). Congress eventually passes three amendments to the U.S. Constitution guaranteeing rights to the freed slaves: the Thirteenth, outlawing bonded servitude; the Fourteenth, guaranteeing equal rights to freed slaves; and the Fifteenth, granting suffrage to the freed slaves. Feminists are outraged that former slaves have won specific constitutional protections that women are denied.

1869—As a result of their failure to attain the same rights granted to freed slaves, women organize for suffrage. Almost immediately, however, the movement splits into two factions as a result of disagreements over whether women should demand the right to vote. Elizabeth Cady Stanton and Susan B. Anthony form the more radical, New York–based National Woman Suffrage Association (NWSA). They argue that instead of increased rights for freed slaves, women should immediately push for suffrage. As a result of this stance, they lose the support of abolitionist leaders like Frederick Douglass. Lucy Stone and others organize the more conservative American Woman Suffrage Association (AWSA), centered in Boston. In this same year, the Wyoming Territory is organized and gives women suffrage. (Wyoming will be admitted to the Union in 1890.)

1870 to 1875—Seeing that the U.S. Congress is not going to pass any amendments granting women suffrage (or equal rights), women try a different tactic: they take several cases to the U.S. Supreme Court, asking that Court to include women in the vague protections given to slaves in the Civil War amendments. Virginia Minor and Victoria Woodhull ask the Court whether "equal protection of the law" in the Fourteenth Amendment guarantees women the vote, and Myra Bradwell asks whether she is a "citizen" who is guaranteed certain privileges (such as the right to practice a profession of her choice) under the Fourteenth Amendment. The Court rules no on all cases.

1868—The Woman Suffrage Amendment is introduced in Congress. It will not be passed until 1920, when it becomes the Nineteenth Amendment.

1872—Susan B. Anthony is arrested for voting in the presidential election.

1873—The federal Comstock Act is passed, specifically calling birth control information obscene and illegal to obtain.

1895—After publishing *The Woman's Bible*, Elizabeth Cady Stanton is seen by women's groups (predominately the NAWSA) as too radical and thus damaging to the suffrage movement.

1912—Theodore Roosevelt's Progressive Party becomes the first national political party to adopt a woman suffrage plank.

1916—The National Woman's Party is founded. By using radical tactics such as hunger strikes and other forms of civil disobedience, its members hope to publicize the need for a women's suffrage amend-

ment. President Woodrow Wilson gives them support.

1916—In Montana Jeannette Rankin is the first woman elected to the House of Representatives.

1920—The Nineteenth Amendment is ratified and women are granted suffrage. Opponents argue it will simply give married men two votes and take away "women's gentle nature." Feminist leader Jane Addams says that the vote is a natural extension of the role of women in the home; giving women the right to vote allows for a more democratic, nurturing element in the political system.

1923—The Equal Rights Amendment, to protect women from discrimination, is proposed but fails passage.

1931—Jane Addams receives the Nobel Peace Prize.

1941—President Franklin Roosevelt signs the first executive order prohibiting government contractors from engaging in employment discrimination.

1948—South Carolina becomes the last state to lift its ban on divorce.

1948—In *Goesaert v. Cleary*, the Supreme Court upholds a Michigan law denying any woman from working in a bar unless she is "the wife or daughter of the owner."

1950—Margaret Sanger raises $150,000 for a reproductive scientist, Gregory Pincus, to develop a universal contraceptive. The Pill will be released on the American market in 1960.

1961—President John Kennedy establishes the President's Committee on Equal Employment Opportunity, which becomes the Equal Employment Opportunity Commission.

1963— Betty Friedan publishes *The Feminine Mystique* to critical acclaim and helps usher in the second feminist movement.

1963—The Equal Pay Act, requiring "equal pay for equal work," is passed. Women continue to make approximately 25 percent less than their male counterparts.

1964—Congress passes the Civil Rights Act, banning discrimination by employers on the basis of color, race, national origin, religion, or gender. It is probably the most far-reaching statute protecting employees from discrimination in the workplace; it also protects the right to vote and use hotels, parks, restaurants, and other public places.

1965—The Court hands down *Griswold v. Connecticut*, establishing the right to privacy. The ruling also allows married couples to obtain birth control information. The Court will not grant single people the same right until 1972.

1972—The Equal Rights Amendment is approved by the required two-thirds vote of the House and Senate but fails ratification by the states by the 1982 deadline.

1972—Congress passes Title IX of the education amendments, prohibiting sex discrimination in any educational program that receives federal funds.

1973—The Supreme Court rules in *Roe v. Wade*, establishing that the right to privacy is "broad enough to encompass a woman's decision whether or not to terminate a pregnancy."

1975—The Supreme Court decides *Weinberger v. Wiesenfeld*, which holds that men do not necessarily have primary responsibility to provide for a family—women, too, can be the primary breadwinners.

1976—*Craig v. Boren* establishes a "height-ened scrutiny" standard for measuring the constitutionality of sex-based classification. The Court rules that an Oklahoma statute allowing women to purchase beer at eighteen years old but limiting men until they are twenty-one violates the male's constitutional rights.

1978—The first "test-tube baby," Louise Brown, is born.

1978—Congress passes the Pregnancy Discrimination Act, prohibiting employment discrimination against pregnant women.

1981—Sandra Day O'Connor becomes the first woman justice on the U.S. Supreme Court.

1981—In *Rostker v. Goldberg* the Court upholds the male-only registration for the draft.

1981—The Court rules in *Michael M. v. Superior Court of Sonoma County* that only men can be criminally liable for statutory rape.

1982—The Court rules in *Mississippi University for Women v. Hogan* that the purpose of a policy restricting men from admission to a nursing program is to "exclude members of one gender because they are presumed to suffer from an inherent handicap or to be innately inferior."

1986—The Court decides *Meritor Savings Bank v. Vinson*, which defines sexual harassment law and establishes two distinct categories of harassment: quid pro quo and hostile work environment.

1988—In *North Carolina v. Norman*, battered woman syndrome is first used as a defense for killing an abusive spouse.

1991—The Court in *United Auto Workers v. Johnson Controls* gives women the right to equal employment opportunities without regard to childbearing capacity.

1991—During the confirmation hearing for the nomination of Clarence Thomas to the Supreme Court, allegations surface that he has harassed one of his employees, Anita Hill. During the televised hearing, Anita Hill is asked to testify in front of fourteen white male senators on the Senate Judiciary Committee, who attack her credibility. Thomas is confirmed by one of the narrowist margins in history. The event galvanizes U.S. women and in the 1992 election, eleven women win election to the U.S. Senate and 107 women to the U.S. House. This increases the number of women in Congress by 54 percent over the 1990 elections.

1993—Congress passes the Family and Medical Leave Act, allowing employees to take up to twelve weeks of unpaid leave within a twelve-month period for family or medical reasons.

1993—Ruth Bader Ginsburg becomes the second woman appointed to the Supreme Court.

1994—The Violence Against Women Act is passed, allowing victims of rape, domestic abuse, and other crimes "motivated by gender" to sue their attackers in federal court for civil damages and providing money to states for domestic violence resources.

1998—*Burlington Industries v. Ellerth* makes employers liable for sexual harassment if they fail to institute a policy to prevent harassment.

1998—The Court also rules in *Faragher v. City of Boca Raton* that employers are liable for sexual harassment of a supervisor unless they can show reasonable care was used to correct the harassing behavior.

1998—In *Gebser v. Lago Vista Independent School District*, the Court holds that a school is liable for harassment of a student when anyone with authority to take corrective action has received notice of the harassment yet exhibits "deliberate indifference."

1998—The Court unanimously rules in *Oncale v. Sundowner Offshore Services* that sexual harassment does not preclude same-sex harassment.

1998—In *Miller v. Albright*, the Court upholds a federal law automatically granting U.S. citizenship to a child born of an American mother but denying citizenship to a child born of an American father unless the father proves paternity.

2000—The Food and Drug Administration approves RU-486, the so-called abortion pill that renders surgical abortion unnecessary.

2000—The Supreme Court rules that the section of the Violence Against Women Act (1994) that permits victims of rape, domestic violence, and other crimes "motivated by gender" to sue their attackers in federal court in civil actions (following, presumably, a criminal conviction in state court), is unconstitutional: Congress could not give federal courts this jurisdiction under their power to regulate interstate commerce.

2001—The Fetal Protection Act makes the killing or harming of a fetus a federal crime. Twenty-four states immediately pass laws following the federal law.

2002—California becomes the first state to offer paid family leave to care for either a new child or an ailing relative.

2003—The University of Michigan's undergraduate and law school admissions come under fire after several white students sue (in two separate actions), claiming the admissions policies amounted to quotas of minority students. The university contends that race was merely a factor in the admission process and in line with the + decision of 1978 that rendered quotas unconstitutional. The Court allows the law school policy that considered applicant race as well as other factors, but rejected the undergraduate policy that used a point system for evaluating applicants on the basis of race.

TABLE OF CASES

Gebser v. Lago Vista Independent School District, 524 U.S. 274 (1998)

Geduldig v. Aiello, 417 U.S. 484 (1974)

General Electric v. Gilbert, 429 U.S. 125 (1976)

Glenn, Johns and Nugent v. General Motors, 841 F.2d 1567 (1988)

Goesaert v. Cleary, 335 U.S. 469 (1948)

Gratz v. Bollinger, 123 S.Ct. 1505 (2003)

Griggs v. Duke Power Company, 401 U.S. 424 (1971)

Griswold v. Connecticut, 381 U.S. 479 (1965)

Grove City College v. Bell, 465 U.S. 555 (1984)

Grutter v. Bollinger, 123 S.Ct. 617 (2003)

Harper v. Virginia State Board of Elections, 383 U.S. 663 (1966)

Harris v. Forklift Systems, Inc., 510 U.S. 17 (1993)

Harris v. McRae, 448 U.S. 297 (1980)

Hodgson v. Robert Hall Clothes, 473 F.2d 589 (1973)

Hoyt v. Florida, 368 U.S. 57 (1961)

In re John Z., 94 Cal. App. 4th 33 (2002)

Jhordan C. v. Mary K., Cal. Ap. Div. 179 Cal. App.3d (1986)

Johnson v. Calvert, 851 P.2d 776 (1993)

Johnson v. Transportation Agency of Santa Clara County, California, 480 U.S. 616 (1987)

Kahn v. Shevin, 416 U.S. 351 (1974)

Kansas v. Stewart, 763 P.2d 572 (1988)

Kirchberg v. Feenstra, 450 U.S. 455 (1981)

Lake v. Reno, 226 F.3d 141 (2000)

Lawrence v. Texas, 123 S. Ct. 2472 (2003)

Lehr v. Robinson, 463 U.S. 248 (1983)

Lindahl v. Air France, 930 F.2d 1434 (1991)

Lochner v. New York, 198 U.S. 45 (1905)

Loving v. Virginia, 388 U.S. 1 (1967)

Marvin v. Marvin, 557 P.2d 106 (1976)

Matter of A. C., 573 A.2d 1235 (1990)

Matter of Baby M., 537 A.2d 1227 (1988)

Meritor Savings Bank v. Vinson, 477 U.S. 57 (1986)

Michael M. v. Superior Court of Sonoma County, 450 U.S. 464 (1981)

Michigan v. Lucas, 513 U.S. 1023 (1991)

Miller v. Albright, 523 U.S. 420 (1998)

Minor v. Happersett, 88 U.S. 162 (1875)

Mississippi University for Women v. Hogan, 458 U.S. 718 (1982)

Moody et al. v Albermarle Paper Company, Halifax Local No. 425, United Papermakers and Paperworkers, AFL-CIO, 422 U.S. 405 (1975)

Morgan v. City of Atlanta, 131 F.3d 156 (1997)

Muller v. Oregon, 208 U.S. 412 (1908)

Nevada Department of Human Resources v. Hibbs, 123 S. Ct. 1972 (2003)

New York v. Santorelli and Schloss, 600 N.E.2d 232 (1992)

North Carolina v. Norman, 378 S.E.2d 8 (1988)

NOW v. Scheidler, 510 U.S. 249 (2003)

O'Brien v. O'Brien, 489 N.E.2d 712 (1985)

Oncale v. Sundower Offshore Services, Inc., 523 U.S. 75 (1998)

Orr v. Orr, 440 U.S. 268 (1979)

Padula v. Webster, 822 F.2d 97 (1987)

Palmore v. Sidoti, 466 U.S. 429 (1984)

Parham v. Hughes, 441 U.S. 347 (1979)

Pennsylvania v. Berkowitz, 641 A.2d 1161 (1994)

Pennsylvania v. Pennsylvania Interscholastic Athletic Association, 334 A.2d 839 (1975)

Personnel Administration of Massachusetts v. Feeny, 442 U.S. 256 (1979)

Phillips v. Martin Marietta Corporation, 400 U.S. 542 (1971)

Planned Parenthood of Southeastern Pennsylvania v. Casey, 505 U.S. 833 (1992)

Plessy v. Ferguson, 163 U.S. 537 (1896)

Price Waterhouse v. Hopkins, 490 U.S. 228 (1989)

Reed v. Reed, 404 U.S. 71 (1971)

Regents of the University of California v. Bakke, 438 U.S. 265 (1978)

Reynolds v. Sims, 377 U.S. 533 (1964)

Reynolds v. United States, 98 U.S. 145 (1878)

Richmond v. J. A. Croson Company, 454 U.S. 370 (1989)

Robinson v. Jacksonville Shipyard, 760 F. Supp. 1486

Roe v. Wade, 410 U.S. 113 (1973)

Rostker v. Goldberg, 453 U.S. 57 (1981)

Schlesinger v. Ballard, 419 U.S. 498 (1975)

INDEX